Life in Medieval Landscapes
People and Places in the Middle Ages

Papers in Memory of H. S. A. Fox

edited by

Sam Turner and Bob Silvester

WINDgather PRESS

Windgather Press
is an imprint of
Oxbow Books, Oxford

ISBN 978-1-905119-40-0

A CIP record for this book is available from the British Library

This book is available direct from

Oxbow Books, Oxford, UK
(Phone: 01865-241249; Fax: 01865-794449)

and

The David Brown Book Company
PO Box 511, Oakville, CT 06779, USA
(Phone: 860-945-9329; Fax: 860-945-9468)

or from our website

www.oxbowbooks.com

Printed in Great Britain by
Information Press, Eynsham, Oxfordshire

Contents

Labour and Lordship

Preface

Harold Fox died in August 2007 at the age of 62, less than a month after retiring from the University of Leicester. He had worked there for more than thirty years, the last four holding a personal chair in the Centre for English Local History. The obituaries that subsequently appeared – by Charles Pythian-Adams (*The Times*), Alan Baker (*Journal of Historical Geography*) and Christopher Dyer (*Rural History Today*, the newsletter of the British Agricultural History Society) – and the long appreciation published by Graham Jones in the journal *Landscape History* each paid tribute to a man who was greatly admired for his inspiring teaching, scholarly expertise and deeply original research.

Harold grew up by the sea in south Devon. He studied geography as an undergraduate at University College London and a postgraduate at Cambridge, both under the guidance of H. C. Darby. After tutoring in Cambridge he took up a lecturing post at Queen's University, Belfast in 1975, but within eighteen months went to Leicester on a short-term research fellowship. He was to remain there in the internationally renowned Department (latterly Centre) for English Local History for the rest of his career.

His research spanned historical geography, agrarian history, place-name studies, landscape history, local history and topography. He was never as prolific as many of his colleagues, and showed little interest in sending his publications to the journals that they would have considered the most prestigious. He preferred instead to polish his articles into sparkling gems and leave them in places where genuinely interested readers would find them.

From his earliest work, Harold made scholarly contributions of lasting value that were based on long hours in the archives. His 1971 PhD thesis revolutionised our understanding of the processes that shaped the landscape of south-west England by showing that many settlements were surrounded by small, communally worked field systems that were enclosed from about 1250 onwards. Harold's work on aspects of the medieval community – including labourers and others in the most lowly positions – became one of the most enduring parts of his scholarly legacy. In *The Evolution of the Fishing Village. Landscape and Society along the South Devon Coast, 1086–1550* he concealed research of the greatest significance behind a typically modest title. The book greatly enriched our view of fishing and people who were marginalised in the Middle Ages, in this case squeezed between the land and the sea. His second monograph, which was very near to completion at the time of his death, also explores practices that might be considered 'marginal', this time focusing on practices of transhumance (*Alluring Uplands: transhumance and pastoral management on Dartmoor, 950–1550*). Harold's fondness for Dartmoor was reflected by his frequent visits with students to Houndtor and other sites. His discoveries have their roots as early as his PhD research, but again they have allowed us to see social and economic arrangements with new eyes from the Anglo-Saxon period onwards. It is our happy fortune that his colleagues at Leicester including Matt Tompkins and Christopher Dyer have worked to finalise the book, soon to be published by the University of Exeter Press.

It is perhaps a measure of Harold Fox's influence that his unexpected death resulted in the organisation of at least five conferences in his memory in 2008. The sheer number of events provides eloquent testimony to the deep respect and fondness in which he was held. Collectively, these meetings must have been attended by over 400 scholars, students and local historians, many of whom had known Harold personally as a teacher or colleague.

Given the profound effect of his work for our understanding of the history of Devon and Cornwall, it was perhaps unsurprising that his colleagues and friends in the South West organised three meetings in his memory in summer 2008. Many groups were involved in arranging these meetings which also testifies to Harold's enthusiastic engagement with scholarly societies and local organisations, including the Devonshire Association, Devon County Council, Devon and Cornwall Notes and Queries, Devon and Cornwall Record Society, Devon Archaeological Society, Devon Buildings Group and Friends of Devon's Archives (whose conference took place on 21 June 2008); the Devon History Society (5 July 2008) and the Dartmoor Society (6 September 2008).

As many of the contributions to the present volume testify, Harold's research and scholarly influence extended far beyond the South West. In Leicester, where he worked for over thirty years, two more conferences were held in his memory. The first was hosted by the Friends of the Centre for English Local History (19 July 2008) and the second jointly organised by the Medieval Settlement Research Group and the Society for Landscape Studies (6 December 2008). Harold was a past President of the MSRG (1998–2001) and at the time of his death was Chairman of the SLS (2005–2007).

The papers presented at all the conferences reflected Harold's wide-ranging interests in historical geography, landscape and history. Some were given by his former colleagues in Belfast and Leicester, some by students he had mentored and supervised, and others by colleagues in the wider academic world who shared similar interests. It would not have been feasible or indeed possible to reproduce all of the papers given in Harold's memory in 2008. The chapters in this book have been offered in his memory by some of his colleagues, friends and former research students. They present new data, analysis and interpretations that relate to important themes in landscape history including labour and lordship, regionality and marginality (both physical and social).

We would like to thank the numerous contributors who wrote chapters for the volume, and who in many cases converted their references to the Harvard system in the name of consistency. (This despite our suspicion that Harold would have been quick to express his disapproval!). We are grateful to the many peer-reviewers who refereed papers and offered useful and constructive comments. We would particularly like to thank Professors Bruce Campbell and Christopher Dyer for their tributes to Harold, and Dr Graham Jones for allowing us to reproduce his comprehensive list of Harold's publications which first appeared in *Landscape History*. We must also thank Oxbow Books and particularly their editors, Clare Litt and Julie Gardiner, who tolerated our delays in seeing this project through to its conclusion.

The editors are grateful to the Medieval Settlement Research Group and the Society for Landscape Studies for providing grants to support the publication of this volume.

Sam Turner and Bob Silvester,
Medieval Settlement Research Group and Society for Landscape Studies

CHAPTER ONE

Harold Fox as Historical Geographer: a Personal Appreciation

Bruce M. S. Campbell

Harold Fox (HSAF) was a scholarly and deeply private man. One evening in 1973, after dining with me at Darwin College, he rose and excused himself early, saying 'I am sorry, I have to go now, I have a footnote to write'. The remark reveals both his omnipresent desire to retreat into the security of his own solitariness and the importance that he attached to footnoting (which he had elevated to an art-form). His now largely forgotten 1979 essay 'Local farmers' associations and the circulation of agricultural information in nineteenth-century England' comprises fourteen pages of closely argued text supported by seven pages of notes. After allowance for abbreviations and differences in font size, this is the equivalent of three-quarters of a page of notes to every page of text. And the notes, of course, are a goldmine of erudite information and perceptive asides. Characteristically, he adds an acknowledgement in which he thanks Miss Sue Blake (from 1970 to 1973 a postgraduate in the Department of Geography at Cambridge) 'for giving initial encouragement when he was beginning the work' and Hugh Prince (his former Geography tutor at University College London) for commenting upon an earlier draft. Such courtesy and scholarly generosity, untarnished by personal ambition, were characteristic of the man and meant that Harold was easy to like. Nevertheless, he was hard to know and cloaked almost everything he did with an air of mystery.

How many of those whom he impressed with his deep historical knowledge across a whole range of periods and subjects, awed with his command of palaeography and expertise at extracting meaning from often intractable historical sources, and inspired with his passion for the past, realised that Harold was trained not as an historian but as a geographer? In fact, he obtained a first-class honours degree in Geography from University College London (UCL), and studied for his doctorate at the Department of Geography at Cambridge. He then spent the first seven years of his academic career as a lecturer in geography, from 1969 to 1974 at Cambridge (where, as a postgraduate, I first encountered him), and then from 1975 to 1976 – following a year between posts working freelance as a college tutor – at The Queen's University of Belfast (where I worked alongside him) (Appendix 1). HSAF never denied his geographical pedigree but nor did he parade it; as his reputation and standing as a landscape and agrarian historian grew, people simply ceased to think of him as a geographer. Indeed, what defines his work is that it is intrinsically inter-disciplinary.

Even Harold's publications provide few clues to his geographical origins. Apart from various notes and comments of a mostly ephemeral nature in the geographical house journal *Area*, his only three publications in explicitly geographical journals are his 1970 essay 'Going to town in thirteenth-century England' in the *Geographical Magazine*; in the same journal, a 1973 anniversary essay co-authored with fellow Cambridge geographer David Stoddart, 'The original *Geographical Magazines*, 1790 and 1874'; and, last and by no means least, his 1988 essay in *Geografiska Annaler*, series B, 'Social relations and ecological relationships in agrarian change'. Although secretary of the Historical Geography Research Group of the Institute of British Geographers (IBG) from 1972 to 1976, his sole IBG publication was his contribution (the afore-mentioned essay on local farmers' associations) to Special Publication, 10: *Change in the Countryside: Essays on Rural England, 1500–1900* (1979), which he co-edited with fellow historical geographer, Robin Butlin. He had already made the move from a department of geography to one of local history and this, in fact, proved to be his valedictory publication as a geographer. Perversely, notwithstanding that he was the founding book-review editor of the *Journal of Historical Geography* and for over 20 years (1975–97) a member of the editorial board, with the exception of book reviews, he never published an article in that journal (unlike historian Chris Dyer, his sometime head of department at Leicester). Harold, in fact, has practically no publication profile within geography. Almost all his finest and most enduring publications were written following his move to the Department of English Local History at Leicester and were intended for a predominantly historical readership.

Nevertheless, HSAF undoubtedly owed his profile and impact as an historian to the grounding he received in the geography and historical geography practised and taught in the 1960s and early 1970s. That era's 'quantitative revolution' may have passed him by, but not the emphasis then placed upon gathering, measuring and playing with data. Other intrinsically geographical qualities exemplified by his work include an appreciation and understanding of maps; a concern with spatial patterns and geographical differentiation; an understanding of how humans interacted with, and impacted upon, their environment; an appreciation of how processes of change operate both over space and through time and often in the very long term; an awareness of the importance of scale, both temporal and spatial; and a sensitivity to the essence of 'place'. Like many another geographer, he was also an expert and dedicated fieldworker and would not have considered writing about anywhere that he did not know intimately on the ground. It is this geographical skill of marrying field and documentary evidence that sets so much of his work in a class of its own. Moreover, as those he taught will testify, he was invariably more effective and at ease teaching *al fresco* in the field than delivering a lecture in the formal setting of a class-room.

Historical geographers, when Harold became one, took an interest in the *longue durée* and their undergraduate courses typically spanned centuries and sometimes millennia. True to this tradition, Harold's teaching and research ranged from the Anglo-Saxons to the nineteenth century and embraced fishing, farming, landlessness, rural settlements and towns. His respect for and sensitivity to historical sources marks him out as belonging to the H. C. Darby 'school' of historical geography and Darby's great enterprise to reconstruct the Domesday geography of England was already at an advanced stage when Harold became Darby's student. At University College London it was, however, Hugh Prince, then working on the nineteenth-century tithe surveys, who probably exercised the greater influence, forming and nurturing Harold's interests in agricultural improvement, field systems and enclosure, and the rural landscape.

Significantly, Harold was interested in enclosure acts for the documentation they generated and their impact upon field systems, the landscape, and the productivity of agriculture rather than as the outcome of an often-contested political process. Had Harold been trained in history he would have displayed at least some concern with power, politics, pedigree, and persons *per se*, whereas he was conspicuously indifferent to such matters. Instead, what fascinated him were places, localities, and regions, and how people collectively, through their daily interaction with their immediate environments, shaped both the landscapes in which they lived, worked, and played and their individual social and economic destinies. Unlike his UCL mentors, Darby and Prince, he never championed a single source nor pitched his studies at a national scale, for the relationships that he sought to illuminate were better explored at a more local scale using a multiplicity of sources, including direct field observation. As an undergraduate he had learnt about the French *Annales* school, which so sympathetically blended history with geography, and it is this approach that he espoused and made his own. His 1989 essay, 'Peasant farmers, patterns of settlement and *pays*: transformations in the landscapes of Devon and Cornwall during the later Middle Ages', with its explicit reference to the French concept of *pays*, is a conscious tribute to, and one of the finest English exemplars of, that tradition.

Examination of Harold's modest list of publications before 1980 (he was personally unambitious, slow in building up a portfolio of publications, and was not remotely strategic about placing his papers in the most influential journals) reveals that the research themes and modes of publication with which he became so closely associated in his academic maturity derived, in fact, from the formative geographical first phase of his career (Appendix 2). Already as a historical geographer he displayed a predilection for publishing in journals that were historical rather than geographical, and local as much as national. From very early on he was a committed medievalist but never to the exclusion of an interest in earlier and later periods. His first publications display the close and fastidious engagement with archives that became his hallmark. The deep and enduring interest in the south-west, particularly his native county of Devon, was there from the outset, along with a concern with the micro-geography of individual places. From the research undertaken for his 1971 doctoral thesis sprang his abiding interest in field systems and early enclosure and their effects upon agricultural improvement and the adoption and spread of innovations. From this period, too, stemmed his curiosity about the nature of small towns and chartered boroughs – of which the south-west possessed a remarkably high density – and their role in a coastal society that lived by both fishing and farming. In short, the lines of historical inquiry for which Harold became renowned while at Leicester were essentially an extension of the agenda he had begun all those years before as first a postgraduate and then an assistant lecturer in the Department of Geography headed by Professor H. C. Darby at Cambridge. Even so, for all its geographical provenance, it is an agenda today more likely to excite historians than geographers, so far have these once close sibling disciplines now moved apart.

Cambridge historical geographer, Gerry Kearns, recently expressed his regret that HSAF had not been appointed to a permanent position in Cambridge following expiry of a 5-year assistant lectureship in 1974. Yet had Harold remained at Cambridge and within a mainstream department of geography very likely he would have found himself increasingly ill at ease with the direction taken by the subject in which he had been trained. He was essentially an empiricist and positivist, an intellectual position rendered unfashionable by a growing subject preference for theory – much of it cultural and post-modern – over empirical substance. Insofar as he wrote with clarity and verve but never with pretentiousness, he was decidedly old-fashioned. Historical geography, too, has changed since he succumbed to its appeal, abandoning its concern with the *longue durée*, privileging the recent almost to the exclusion of the remoter past, and substituting an eclectic and often formless internationalism for a close and rigorous engagement with the historical geographies of individual countries and regions and the spatial and temporal processes that shaped them (for HSAF was above all schooled and interested in the historical geography of England, although not in any narrow or jingoistic way). He would also have found himself at variance with the mounting obsession with a research-grants culture and the concomitant disdain for publishing in the non-prestigious, non-peer refereed, non-international journals of which he himself was such a champion. In fact, for Harold the real misfortune would surely have been to have remained entrapped at Cambridge, for that mainstream department could never have provided him with as natural a spiritual home or students as sympathetic to his own talents as a teacher as he eventually found at Leicester. English Local History was his natural niche and it is fortunate for all that he found it.

Harold and geography effectively parted company in 1979, with the result that among geographers he is remembered with fondness by a small and dwindling cohort of contemporaries, all of them either retired or approaching retirement. Today, the historical-geography research group of which he was secretary and the journal on whose editorial board he served for so long have changed beyond recognition. What he once taught has disappeared from the curriculum of most geography departments and few geographers now need to read his work. In contrast, his most substantive publications remain indispensable to medieval economic historians and all with a serious historical interest in the south-west. It will be a long time before his classic 1996 study of the *garciones* on the estates of Glastonbury Abbey – 'Exploitation of the landless by lords and tenants in early medieval England' – is superseded. His twin essays on Devon and Cornwall in the *Agrarian History of England and Wales, Volume III, 1348–1500* (1991) – 'The occupation of the land' and 'Farming practice and techniques' – remain definitive. His 2001 monograph, *The Evolution of the Fishing Village: Landscape and Society along the South Devon coast, 1086–1550*, cuts entirely new ground.

Geography has changed profoundly since 1963 when, fired by his schooling at Churston Ferrers Grammar School near Brixham in Devon, Harold enrolled to study it at UCL. At that time, given his talents and academic inclinations, it was obviously natural for him to prefer geography over history, although as events turned out it proved to be in history rather than geography that he built his career and established his reputation. It was, however, historical geography that first inspired Harold, shaped the paradigm within which he operated, formed his personal research agenda and equipped him with the skills that he used so expertly to make his very individual mark as a historian. Harold Fox was not alone in making the crossover from geography to history; Tony Wrigley, Richard Smith, Michael Turner, Mark Overton, and myself (among others) have made the same journey. But we belong to much the same academic generation and, with the exception of Michael Turner, like Harold, spent time in the same Cambridge stable. In terms of the pre-industrial past, geography and history then shared more in common than, sadly, they do today. Nevertheless, Harold Fox's many publications – all but the last, left incomplete at his death, enriched with wonderfully erudite footnotes containing many a scholarly aside for others to follow – demonstrate what rich insights can be obtained from a true fusion of the skills of the geographer with those of the historian.

Appendix 1. Harold Fox's career as a Geographer/ Historical Geographer, 1963–79

1963   left Churston Ferrers Grammar School near Brixham.

1963–6   read Geography at University College London, where he studied historical geography with H. C. Darby and Hugh Prince (Richard Smith recalls that HSAF's undergraduate dissertation dealt with some aspect of hedgerows and hedgehogs).

1966   graduated with 1st class honours.

1966–69   postgraduate, Department of Geography, University of Cambridge, and member of St Catherine's College: PhD supervisor, Professor H. C. Darby (who had recently taken up the chair of Geography at Cambridge).

1969–74   Assistant Lecturer in Geography, University of Cambridge (historically minded colleagues in the Cambridge department included Alan Baker, Clifford Darby, Robin Donkin, Jack Langton, Brian Robson, David Stoddart, Tony Wrigley; quantitatively minded colleagues included Richard Chorley and Andrew Cliff; postgraduates included Peter Atkins, Bruce Campbell, Richard Denis, Mark Overton, Susan Shaw nee Blake, Richard Smith, Charlie Withers).

1971   awarded PhD for his thesis, 'A geographical study of the field systems of Devon and Cornwall'.

1972–6   secretary of the Historical Geography Research Group of the Institute of British Geographers.

1972   authored *Geography: a degree course guide, 1972–3*, Careers Research Advisory Centre, Cambridge (50 pp.).

1974   authored *Geography: a degree course guide, 1974–5*, Careers Research Advisory Centre, Cambridge (58 pp.).

1974–5   freelance college tutor, University of Cambridge.

1975–6   Lecturer in Geography, The Queen's University of Belfast (replacing Robin Glasscock, a previous doctoral student of Darby's during the latter's time at UCL, who moved to a permanent lectureship at Cambridge in 1975). His immediate colleague at QUB was Bruce Campbell, with whom he taught a final-year course on 'The Historical Geography of England': Fox lectured on medieval agricultural technique, medieval field systems, the expansion and contraction of settlement, the evolution and functions of towns and markets, towns before the Industrial Revolution, and agricultural change 1500–1900 (including implements, under-drainage, crops, crop nutrition, animal husbandry, and farm transport).

1975–81   book review editor, *Journal of Historical Geography*.

1975–97   member of the editorial board, *Journal of Historical Geography*.

1976   appointed Research Fellow in Topography, Department of English Local History, University of Leicester.

1979   co-edited with Robin Butlin, Institute for British Geographers, Special Publication, 10: *Change in the countryside: essays on rural England, 1500–1900*.

Appendix 2. Harold Fox's published papers to 1979

Fox, H. S. A. (1970) Going to town in thirteenth-century England. *Geographical Magazine* 42, 658–67 (reprinted in A R. H. Baker and J. B. Harley (eds) 1973. *Man Made the Land: Essays in English Historical Geography, a Series from the Geographical Magazine*. Newton Abbot: David and Charles).

Fox, H. S. A. (1970) The boundary of Uplyme. *Transactions of the Devonshire Association*, 102, 35–47.

Fox, H. S. A. (1971) Subdivided fields in south and east Devon. *Transactions and Proceedings of the Torquay Natural History Society*, 16 (a note).

Fox, H. S. A. (1972) The study of field systems. *Devon Historian* 4, 3–11.

Fox, H. S. A. (1972) Field systems of east and south Devon. Part 1, east Devon. *Transactions of the Devonshire Association*, 104, 81–135 (Part 2 was drafted but never published).

Fox, H. S. A. (1972) *Geography: a Degree Course Guide, 1972–3*. Careers Research Advisory Centre, Cambridge (50 pp.).

Fox, H. S. A. (1973) Outfield cultivation in Devon and Cornwall: a reinterpretation, in M. Havinden (ed.) *Husbandry and Marketing in the South-West*. Exeter Papers in Economic History, 8, 19–38.

Fox, H. S. A. and Stoddart, D. R. (1973) The original *Geographical Magazines*, 1790 and 1874. *Geographical Magazine* 47, 482–7.

Fox, H. S. A. (1973–6) Historical Geography Research Group (Secretary's annual reports). *Area* 5–8.

Fox, H. S. A. (1974) *Geography: a Degree Course Guide, 1974–5*. Careers Research Advisory Centre, Cambridge (58 pp.).

Fox, H. S. A. (1975) The chronology of enclosure and economic development in medieval Devon. *Economic History Review*, 2nd series, 28, 181–202.

Fox, H. S. A. (1976) *Register of Research in Historical Geography*. Institute of British Geographers, Belfast.

Fox, H. S. A. (1977) The functioning of bocage landscapes in Devon and Cornwall between 1500 and 1800, in M. J. Missonnier (ed.) *Les Bocages: Histoire, ecologie, economie*, 55–61. Institut National de la Recherche Agronomique, Rennes.

Fox, H. S. A. (1978) The origins of the two- and three-field system in England: past conjectures and future research, in M. Kielczewska-Zaleska (ed.) *Rural Landscape and Settlement Evolution in Europe*, 109–18. Polish Academy of Sciences, Warsaw.

Fox, H. S. A. (1979) Local farmers associations and the circulation of agricultural information in nineteenth-century England, in H. S. A. Fox and R. A. Butlin (eds), *Change in the Countryside: Essays on Rural England, 1500–1900*. Institute of British Geographers, Special Publication, 10, 43–63.

Fox, H. S. A. and Butlin, R. A. (eds) (1979) *Change in the countryside: essays on rural England, 1500–1900*. Institute for British Geographers, Special Publication, 10.

Reviews for *Archives, Geographical Magazine, Devon and Cornwall Notes and Queries, Proceedings of the Suffolk Institute of Archaeology, Times Literary Supplement, Journal of Historical Geography*.

CHAPTER TWO

Harold Fox: his Contribution to our Understanding of the Past

Christopher Dyer

Anyone writing about Harold Fox is tempted to lapse into anecdote, because his idiosyncrasies and witty conversation made a strong impression on all who came into contact with him. His well-entrenched prejudices, eccentric behaviour, inspiring teaching, strong loyalties, kindness and courtesy all made him unforgettable, and led to many amusing situations and occasionally to unfortunate incidents. Others in the aftermath of his early death have recorded his complex personality (Baker 2008), but this is a book about his scholarly interests and his influence in the academic world, and this essay will be devoted to his contribution to our understanding of the past.

His career began in geography, and he maintained connections with the discipline. He was a student of geography at University College London, and went on to Cambridge to complete a PhD with the renowned H. C. Darby. His first job was as a lecturer in the geography department of Queen's University Belfast, and he took a leap into the unknown when he moved to a historical environment in the Department of English Local History at Leicester in 1976. He adapted quite easily, and came to think of himself as a local historian as well as a geographer. For many years he served as reviews editor and a member of the editorial board of the *Journal of Historical Geography* and he was active in the Historical Geography Research Group. His ideas and methods were always influenced by his geographical training. He was devoted to maps, and occasionally wrote about them: had he lived he looked forward to a project on a sixteenth-century map of the south coast.

As with any scholar who engages with a number of disciplines – geography, history, archaeology, and place-name studies, and who was influenced by literature and art history – it is difficult to place him in any specific pigeon hole. He was slightly wary of the phrase 'landscape history', and preferred to call himself a 'topographer', though he knew that by using that word he was exposing his 'old fogy' tendency. When required to devise the title for his personal chair he opted for Professor of Social and Landscape History, which reflected his interests in his later years.

My qualification for making this contribution is not just that I was Harold's colleague in the years 2001–7, but that I knew him throughout his career. I was a referee for his first article in a major journal in *c*.1974, and encountered him at various seminars and conferences from *c*.1978. I appreciated and respected his contributions on these occasions, and I enjoyed meeting him. We were engaged in projects in parallel, and attended meetings of such bodies as the Medieval Village Research Group, later the Medieval Settlement Research Group, and the Agricultural History Society. We both contributed to the third volume of the *Agrarian History of England and Wales*, the *festschrift* for Beresford and Hurst, and Joan Thirsk's book on the English landscape.

This essay will be a journey through his writings, and is informed by knowledge of his contributions to conferences and private conversation. His published work was based on thorough research, as became very apparent to those of us who sorted his papers after he died. He meticulously collected data from printed books and archives, and analysed it by assembling large card indexes and pages on which thoughts were gathered and arguments marshalled. A general comment is needed on his writing. Most academics hammer out some functional prose, with the help of a typewriter in former days, or now on a computer, but Harold's works were careful compositions in long hand, which were constantly revised and rewritten. They were then typed professionally, and radically revised again two or three times. They had a literary character, and he was capable of occasional passages of rather lyrical prose. He also incorporated into his writing literary allusions and phrases from, for example, Evelyn Waugh, and he may have derived some mischievous pleasure from the failure of his rather prosaic peers (who were not well read) to notice the references. The careful preparation and rephrasing of each piece of writing inevitably took a long time, and his failure to meet the deadlines for contributions to collective works caused editors and fellow authors some anguish. Harold himself, in these intervals between the date when an essay or chapter was due and its actual completion, was also in a state of distress and guilt, and would provide the editor with a running commentary on progress by letter and telephone. The process could culminate in a late-night drive to the editor's home or office, six months or a year after the supposed date of delivery. He was usually forgiven because of the quality of the piece of writing when it eventually appeared. His outputs (to use the unlovely jargon now favoured by academic bureaucrats) were not exceptionally numerous, amounting in almost forty years to around sixty works (including obituaries, forewords and other short pieces) (Jones 2007), but about sixteen of them must be judged to have been really memorable contributions, which changed the way in which the subject was viewed. This essay will concentrate on the most influential and significant works, subdivided into the categories of fields, landscapes and society.

An important theme running through Harold Fox's work was his ambition to understand the form and organisation of fields. Field systems, sometimes regarded as an old-fashioned subject, are still central to the landscape and agrarian history of the Middle Ages. Our assessment of agricultural production, social organisation and regional cultures depends on understanding fields and their management, just as factories, warehouses and shops are essential components in our world. Harold worked initially on Devon fields, and came to the conclusion that in the fourteenth and fifteenth centuries there had been a tendency to enclose that county's considerable areas of open field (Fox 1975) This movement, achieved piecemeal and by agreements among cultivators, differed from those high profile impositions of enclosure in the midlands, and had received little attention from scholars because it had to be painstakingly reconstructed from documents and post-medieval maps. The discovery of this process opened up fundamental questions about the formation of open fields in the period before the fourteenth century.

This second train of thought about the origins and early development of open fields was stimulated further by his move to Leicester and his consequent investigations of the midland field systems, which culminated in a long and thoughtful essay on the adoption of the midland system which was originally conceived for a seminar held in 1978 (Fox 1981). In this he put special emphasis on the importance of grazing on the fallows and stubbles, and he related the growth of fields to other developments in the pre-Conquest countryside such as the fragmentation of the 'multiple' estates and the nucleation of villages when the earlier hamlets and farms were abandoned. His thinking about fields continued, and in 1983 he presented a conference paper on the change from two- to three-field systems (Fox 1986). He was sympathetic to Joan Thirsk's approach to fields which saw them as the product of evolution, but in this paper he expressed scepticism which was justified about the assumption that population pressure in the thirteenth century led to a widespread agricultural intensification, in which two-field villages with half the land fallowed each year were reorganised so that a three-course rotation reduced the fallow area to a third of the land. His point was that the cultivators were wise enough to avoid a change which reduced the grazing area and might threaten crop yields.

His thinking about fields culminated in two important general works, one of them a long essay about the agriculture of open fields in a publication produced for a conference debate (Fox 1992), in which he focussed on the pre-Conquest period and visualised very effectively the sequence of changes which led to the formation of midland field systems attached to nucleated villages. His contribution to the *Agrarian History* discussed fields in the wider context of agrarian change and developing markets in the fourteenth and fifteenth century in the south-west region which he knew so well (Fox 1991).

This account of his work on field systems has selected the most important contributions, but there were a number of conference papers, the conclusions of which were incorporated into the major writings. But much of his exploration of other themes was underpinned by his extensive knowledge and profound understanding of the agricultural management practised by medieval communities.

His first published venture into the study of settlements and landscapes came when he surveyed the history of dispersed settlement in the south-west, and in particular he showed how hamlets had shrunk down to single farms in the later Middle Ages (Fox 1983). He enlarged on this work on settlements and landscapes in the region in an essay published in a collective work on the south-west (Fox 1989a), which pointed the way towards the rounded picture of settlement, farming and rural society he provided for the *Agrarian History* (Fox 1991). Later he made a study of settlement, fields and landscapes in Cornwall, which formed part of the introduction to texts that he edited with Oliver Padel. Here he showed how small hedged fields co-existed with areas of arable subdivided into strips, and went on to link the land to hamlets, farmsteads and small towns (Fox and Padel 2000).

One of the strengths of his interpretation of landscapes was his comparative approach, because in parallel with his research into the south-west he was also thinking about the east midlands. The 'big idea' that had emerged from Leicester around 1980 had been the concept of *pays*, that is a classification of sections of countryside which shared similar characteristics in settlement, farming, society and culture. 'Champion' country, woodland, moorland, downland and so on were relatively easily identified and characterised, but 'wolds' retained some mysteries. Why did landscapes now known for their bare rolling limestone hills carry the German name for woodland – because English wold derived from wald? He argued that in the east midlands the wolds of Leicestershire, Northamptonshire and Nottinghamshire were high countries, which had been wooded and pastoral in the early Middle Ages. Names like Somerby showed that they had once been pastures to which animals were driven in the summer season. Around the end of the first millennium these grazing grounds were colonised for arable and villages were established. Clues like the relatively small size of the villages, and their vulnerability to depopulation, differentiated the wolds from the champion country which they had grown to resemble (Fox 1989b).

Two related lines of enquiry extended from Fox's exploration of the south-west and the midland wolds. He became interested in the idea of 'seasonal settlement', firstly because he had noticed that hamlets on the south Devon coast had grown up at a time when the peasant fishermen lived inland (in villages like Stokenham) but kept their boats and nets in seaside 'cellars', a local name for storage buildings in which those engaged in the fishing could stay overnight. Gradually in the fifteenth century the seasonal cellar settlements became permanent, specialised fishing villages (Fox 2001). While preoccupied with fishing villages he organised, chaired and published a symposium on 'seasonal settlement' which brought together researches on temporary upland pastoral shielings as well as on fishing settlements, though in his introductory essay he was able to bring into the picture huts temporarily occupied by industrial workers, such as tinners (Fox 1996b)

Harold Fox was already aware of the seasonal occupation of huts on the south-western moorlands, and this took him on to an investigation of the pastoral exploitation of Dartmoor, which in the later Middle Ages had been elaborately organised so that large numbers of cattle were sent from the lowlands into the care of officials who did not live on the moor. In an earlier period – before the eleventh century – he believed that herdsmen and dairy maids had occupied small huts on the moor alongside their beasts (Fox forthcoming). Place-name evidence revealed these

> early medieval activities on the uplands, as names containing the elements butter and *smer-* show that dairying was practised, presumably based in shieling settlements (Fox 2008).

By analogy with recent rural life in Ireland and other countries which practised transhumance, Fox could imaginatively reconstruct life in the shielings. The young men who herded the cattle, and young women who milked the cows and made cheese, spent the summer productively, but also enjoyed the freedom of a spell away from their parental homes (Fox, forthcoming). This was not the first of his ventures into social history, as he had always envisaged the fields, villages, hamlets and landscapes as populated spaces, and he enjoyed naming the inhabitants when the sources allowed. Even in the necessarily solemn pages of the chapters for the *Agrarian History* he found room for the striking phrase from early topographers, like the commentator on Cornwall who compared ale brewed from oats to 'wash as pigs has wrestled in' (Fox 1991). He also picked up fragments of folklore, like the local ditty in Hartland in Devon referring to the decayed hamlet of Hendon, thought by the local population to have had a glorious past : 'Hendon was a market town, When London was a fuzzy down' (Fox 1989a).

He had noticed that in the rentals compiled by manorial lords in Devon in the late fourteenth and fifteenth centuries that better-off tenants would add cottages to their substantial holdings of land, for no obvious purpose as there was little useful land attached to many cottages. This was revealing the origin of the tied cottage, as it seemed likely that the smallholdings were sublet to labourers who would be duty bound to work for their landlord (Fox 1995). Fox was pursuing the subject of agricultural workers also in the early 1990s when he investigated the *garciones* ('lads') listed in the manorial court records of Glastonbury Abbey. He was able to show that these were single men, many of them young, who were employed by the peasants as casual labour. They represented an underclass, without any land, who lived in outhouses or cabins or in corners of their employers' houses. Their low status was indicated by disparaging nicknames like Pig and Dustybeard (Fox 1996). Both of these explorations of the lowest ranks of village society were in accord with a revisionism of the time, which instead of regarding the lords as the only oppressors of the peasantry, also recognised that the peasants were capable of exploiting each other.

This survey has not attempted to summarise or even mention every publication of Harold Fox. Brief reference should be made to his interest in towns, because although he did not write about them at length, he realised their importance and interest. In particular, he celebrated the multiplicity of small boroughs in Devon, and defended them against detractors who denied that they could be called urban, by showing that even a community of twenty or thirty houses could still have a special character (Fox 1999). Finally, his sense of place was a quality which brought together his geography and local history: he could write with real warmth and evocative skill about Hound Tor in Devon, a Dartmoor hamlet abandoned by its inhabitants in the fourteenth century, Podimore, the village in lowland Somerset which had the layout of its fields changed by its lord with the active participation of the peasants in 1333, and the Devon coast to the east of Stokenham where, in about 1360, Richard Still 'will watch on the beach … waiting for the coming of the mullet' (Fox 2001, 123). Harold Fox's great achievement was to make us look at people and places in new ways.

Bibliography

Baker, A. R. H. (2008) Obituary. Harold S. A. Fox, 1945–2007. *Journal of Historical Geography* 34, 171–4.

Fox, H. S. A. (1975) The chronology of enclosure and economic development in medieval Devon. *Economic History Review* 2nd series 28, 181–202.

Fox, H. S. A. (1981) Approaches to the adoption of the midland system, in T. Rowley (ed.) *The Origins of Open-field Agriculture*, 64–111. London: Croom Helm.

Fox, H. S. A. (1983) Dispersed settlement. *Medieval Village Research Group Annual Report* 31, 39–45.

Fox, H. S. A. (1986) The alleged transformation from two-field to three-field systems in medieval England. *Economic History Review* 2nd series 39, 526–48.

Fox, H. S. A. (1989a) Peasant farmers, patterns of settlement and *pays*: transformations in the landscapes of Devon and Cornwall during the later middle ages, in R. Higham (ed.) *Landscape and Townscape in the South-West*, 41–74. Exeter: University of Exeter Press.

Fox, H. S. A. (1989b) The people of the wolds in English settlement history, in M. Aston, D. Austin and C. Dyer (eds) *The Rural Settlements of Medieval England: Studies Dedicated to Maurice Beresford and John Hurst*, 77–101. Oxford: Blackwell.

Fox, H. S. A. (1991) The occupation of the land: Devon and Cornwall; Farming practice and techniques: Devon and Cornwall; Tenant farming and tenant farmers: Devon and Cornwall, in E. Miller (ed.) *The Agrarian History of England and Wales III, 1348–1500*, 152–74; 302–23; 722–43. Cambridge: Cambridge University Press.

Fox, H. S. A. (1992) The agrarian context, in H. S. A. Fox (ed.) *The Origins of the Midland Village*, 36–72. Leicester: Department of English Local History.

Fox, H. S. A. (1995) Servants, cottagers and tied cottages during the later middle ages: towards a regional dimension. *Rural History* 6, 125–54.

Fox, H. S. A. (1996a) Exploitation of the landless by lords and tenants in early medieval England, in Z. Razi and R. Smith (eds) *Medieval Society and the Manor Court*, 518–68. Oxford: Clarendon Press.

Fox, H. S. A. (1996b) Introduction: transhumance and seasonal settlement, in H. S. A. Fox (ed.) *Seasonal Settlement*, 1–23. Leicester: Vaughan Papers 39.

Fox, H. S. A. (1999) Medieval urban development, in R. Kain and W. Ravenhill (eds) *An Historical Atlas of South-West England*, 424–31, Exeter: Exeter University Press.

Fox, H. S. A. (2000) The Cornish landscape in the sixteenth century and later, in H. S.

A. Fox and O. Padel (eds) *The Cornish Lands of the Arundells of Lanherne, Fourteenth to Sixteenth Centuries*, lxviii–c. Exeter: Devon and Cornwall Record Society.

Fox, H. S. A. (2001) *The Evolution of the Fishing Village: Landscape and Society along the South Devon Coast, 1086–1550*. Oxford: Leopard Head's Press.

Fox, H. S. A. (2008) Butter place-names and transhumance, in O. J. Padel and D. N. Parsons (eds) *A Commodity of Good Names. Essays in Honour of Margaret Gelling*, 352–64. Donington: Shaun Tyas.

Fox, H. S. A. (forthcoming) *Alluring Uplands. Transhumance and Pastoral Management on Dartmoor*. Exeter: University of Exeter Press.

Jones, G. (2007) Harold Fox: an appreciation. *Landscape History* 29, 5–15.

CHAPTER THREE

Working with Wood-pasture

Andrew Fleming

Meetings with remarkable trees

Just outside Canon Pyon, in Herefordshire, an ancient pollard oak stands in the middle of a field (Fig. 3.1). If I were to tell a fellow landscape historian that this tree represents all that remains of an extensive tract of wood-pasture, I would undoubtedly be rewarded with an old-fashioned look.

Rightly so. And yet we would both be aware of the processes of attrition that would have gradually diminished an old wood-pasture. Hypothetically, there might once have been a couple of hundred pollards here. Yet as agrarian priorities, economic conditions and legal entitlements changed, such a tract of wood-pasture would have been exposed not only to disease and stormy weather, but also to managerial neglect and the possibility of deliberate destruction. Of course the older the pollards, the greater their capacity for resistance. Their thick trunks, short stature and relatively attenuated crowns would have given them more protection from strong winds than was enjoyed by taller maiden trees in the vicinity; most would also have benefited from the shelter provided by their upwind neighbours. And the thicker and more hollow they were, the more daunting and costly the work of removing them, especially when weighed against the benefit to be obtained by so doing. It might be better to let them be, providing shelter for livestock, and occasional supplies of firewood. Thus in some places at least, more pollards may have died from natural causes than by fire or the axe. In such cases, the decline of wood-pasture would have been extremely slow, slower than we might at first imagine. But one day, according to the inexorable process of attrition, there would be just one pollard standing alone in a field – exactly like the one at Canon Pyon. Some day, this tree too will be gone; will a local historian have thought of photographing such a 'natural artefact', and putting the record into the public domain?

My friend would be less sceptical if we were to travel some 45 km to the west-north-west, near Gaufron, in the parish of Nantmel, in the old district of Gwerthrynion (in west Radnorshire, now part of Powys) (Fig. 3.2a). Here stand some thirty oak pollards in an eleven-acre (4.5 ha) field, much of which features a steep slope facing north-east, sheltered to some degree from south-westerly gales. The disposition of these trees reminds me of neglected old orchards in Herefordshire (which are also wood-pastures of a sort). The oaks of Gaufron are scattered unevenly, often in groups of two or three which protect each other

FIGURE 3.1. Pollard oak, Canon Pyon, Herefordshire

from the wind. By measuring the distances between obvious neighbours it is possible to make a reasonable estimate of the average 'original' spacing of the pollards on this hillside (about 8m, or *c.*10–11m centre to centre). These trees display a good deal of variability in height and girth (and presumably age); understanding their 'lopping history' (a useful piece of terminology in Powys) is not altogether a straightforward matter.

What we see in this field has not changed much in recent decades. Mature individual trees are marked on the first edition of the six-inch Ordnance Survey map, surveyed in 1888 (Fig. 3.2b). Most of the trees marked on the map can still be identified. Those few which are missing must have fallen in the intervening period; two recently fallen trees are visible now. More puzzling are four or five trees present today, but not marked on the map. The girths of the trees concerned suggest that these were not trees too small to qualify as mature in 1888, so these omissions have to be regarded as map-makers' 'mistakes'. In the tithe map schedule of 1842 this field was named 'Old Wood' (with no entry under 'state of cultivation'). Given that many of the trees are visibly or presumably hollow, it seems that the only way of estimating the minimum age of this old wood-pasture is to measure the girth of the oldest tree, or trees. The girth range of the trees here, and by inference their age range and 'survivorship curve', is unsurprising; that is to say, there are quite a few relatively young trees, fewer older ones and only one or two in what is evidently the oldest age class. In terms of its size and venerable appearance, the oldest tree here (Fig. 3.3) looks very like the famous Hypebaeus Tree, a redoubtable oak pollard in Moccas Park (Herefordshire). Its girth is *c.*9–9.2m, compared with a remarkably precise 9.27m for its Herefordshire rival (Wall 2000, 83), whose date of germination has been estimated as 1406 (Wall and Harding 2000b, 121). On this basis, our oak too should date from the 15th century.

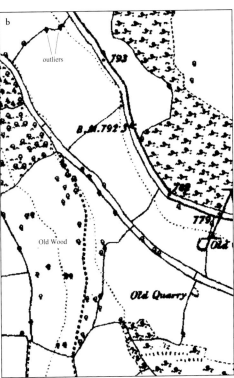

FIGURE 3.2. a. pollard trees in Old Wood field at Gaufron, Nantmel, Radnorshire; b. the trees on the First Edition Six Inch map (1888)

FIGURE 3.3. The oldest of the Gaufron oak pollards

The hillside north-west of Old Wood and immediately adjacent to it is now shrouded in younger woodland. This raises the possibility that the whole hillside was once used as wood-pasture, before being sub-divided into parcels of land which then experienced different land-use histories. Near the edge of a field about 200m north of the Old Wood stand two further old oak pollards, some 30m apart; it looks as if the dog-leg in the adjacent boundary has been created in order to include both in the same parcel of land. These trees are marked as 'outliers' on Figure 3.2b. It is hard to believe that these two were not once part of the tract of wood-pasture now represented by the pollards in Old Wood field. But what would we have concluded if, two hundred years ago, the tenant farmer had cut down all the pollards in Old Wood field, leaving just these two outliers? Would we have dared to postulate an extensive tract of former wood-pasture here, on the basis of just two standing pollards?

As a matter of fact, this kind of situation occurs some 8km to the north-east of Gaufron. Not far east of Abbeycwmhir, and close to the old farm of Tyvaenor, two old-looking pollards (with girths of *c*.5.3 and 5.85m) stand fairly low on a hillside, near the edge of an enclosed pasture (Fig. 3.4). Much of the steeper, lower part of this hillside, on the other side of the road leading up to Tyvaenor, and further west, is occupied by a tract of woodland which is perhaps best described as 'decadent' wood-pasture. That is to say, animals still browse among the trees today, as they do in many tracts of woodland in mid-Wales; the trees are mostly quite young, but there are also one or two pollards, and a few not very young coppice stools of oak and alder. Immediately west of this wood, just across a stream and on the same hillside, one or two older oak pollards are to be found, on the fringes of enclosed pasture. It is tempting to conclude that the lower slopes of this hillside once carried an extensive tract of wood-pasture, and that what we see now are two occurrences of old oak pollards, flanking a wood which has preserved indicators of only the more recent phases of its use as wood-pasture. But it is also possible that these pollards are survivors from a once much larger tract of wood-pasture called Tyvaenor Park; one with an even bigger girth (*c*.6.5m) is to be found about 800m to the north-east, above Llidiart y Dwr (Fig. 3.5). Some 17km to the south-south-west, in Llanfihangel Brynpabuan, is another pair of lopped oaks in a field (Fig. 3.6). The tithe map, however, shows that in the early nineteenth century these were both in a wood (albeit near its northern edge). Immediately outside the *southern* edge of this wood was an open common which survives to this day.

Just west of Tyvaenor, the Cistercian monastery of Cwmhir Abbey owned two parks, the Great Park and the Little Park, where Roger Mortimer was granted the right to hunt in 1241 (Rees *et al.* 2005, 147, fig. 9). In his *History of Radnorshire*, Jonathan Williams (1905, 162) mentioned 'the oaks of immense size which grew in the parks of Abbey-cwm-hir within the recollection of many persons now living, and which were planted by the hands of the monks, whose indolence is often unjustly condemned'. Williams died in 1829, so he was referring to oaks which were venerable in the late eighteenth century, and must have first sprouted in the later Middle Ages, in the time of the Cistercians.

These parks are now swathed in conifers. Williams' text is probably the only documentary record of this kind for Gwerthrynion; perhaps counter-intuitively, it may be harder to trace old wood-pasture in the archives than in the modern landscape.

This is not the place to offer a systematic summary of my work on the survival of wood-pasture in north Breconshire and west Radnorshire in its regional context; in any case, this research is still in progress. However, the area is a good place to choose in order to illustrate and discuss the *taphonomy* of ancient wood-pasture – the relationship between former wood-pasture landscapes and what is visible today. In my view, we should be approaching this question from both chronological directions. That is to say, we need to think about what may, indeed should, be observed in the field, and what may be implied historically by such observations. What kinds of evidence and argument should be assembled before a tree like the Canon Pyon pollard oak could be claimed as the last survivor of a tract of wood-pasture? As is often the case, it is necessary to work with as much information as possible, in a region large enough to provide both patterning and variability. Looking at the problem in terms of chronological sequence, we have to imagine complex, nuanced trajectories of attrition and decline in old wood-pastures. And we also have to consider the survival of customs associated with wood-pasture in recent and present-day farming practice. In mid-Wales, for instance, wood-pastures still exist, in the sense that livestock still browse in woodland; sometimes in winter they are kept in woods, or at least in pastures furnished with clumps or belts of trees, which provide them with shelter when necessary. The photograph used for Figure 3.7 was taken near Rhayader on February 1st, 2009. And there is still plenty of tree-lopping going on in the region, an expression of a 'cut and come again' approach to trees, woods and hedges, a faint but persistent echo of older traditions of wood-pasture management.

Ancient wood-pasture: the challenge

Of all the components which make up the complex history of the British landscape, ancient wood-pasture is arguably the least well understood. Palaeobotanists are fairly sure that from the Mesolithic period, from around perhaps 8000 BC, humans were changing the character of the 'wildwood' by various means. When hunter-gatherers burned undergrowth, they altered patterns of vegetation, and brought about local differences in the distribution and density of wild animals. This would in turn have had a further impact on the vegetation, and so on, with some species poised and ready to exploit any opportunities created by changes operating within complex ecological systems. Among groups of human hunter-gatherers, unintended consequences will at first have been opportunistically exploited, wherever possible, before becoming the *intended* result of deliberate, strategic actions. The introduction of farming *c.*4000 BC would in due course have increased human population levels. Browsing by domestic livestock, continued hunting and gathering, and growing

FIGURE 3.4. Two oak pollards near Tyvaenor, Abbeycwmhir, Radnorshire

FIGURE 3.5. Pollard oak at Tyvaenor Park, Abbeycwmhir, Radnorshire

demand for timber and firewood would have put further pressure on woodland. These processes took time. In the language of pollen analysts, over the period from the Mesolithic to the later Iron Age and Romano-British periods, episodic 'interference episodes' give way to 'clearance phases' and then 'major clearances' and the spread of more permanently open country. Increasingly, palaeobotanists focus on traditional agricultural practices, asking how, say, hay-making, or the harvesting of leaf fodder, or coppicing, would reveal themselves in pollen diagrams.

It seems hard to avoid the inference that wood-pasture, in the broadest sense, was the prevalent landscape component over much of later prehistory. It is not difficult to imagine how, in the Middle Ages, with much spatial and temporal variability and differences of emphasis, this form of land-use would have made the transition from an abundant, extensively used, 'background' to a more intensively managed, claimed and contested array of scarcer, if sometimes critical, resources. And landscape historians have documented the third phase in this story – the decline of common, managed wood-pasture over the course

FIGURE 3.6. Two lopped oaks at Llanfihangel Brynpabuan, Breconshire

FIGURE 3.7. Cattle in a wood near Rhayader, Radnorshire (February 2009)

of the later Middle Ages. Finally, at around the turn of the eighteenth and nineteenth centuries, both the commons and the habit of pollarding trees became the object of adverse comment by the opinion-formers of the day (Petit and Watkins 2003).

Arguably, then, landscape historians ought to know a good deal about wood-pasture and its history. At present it is hard to contend that we do. Prehistorians concerned with landscape history, and the palaeobotanists who sometimes work with them, rarely use the word wood-pasture, let alone put the topic on their agenda. Ironically, the most illuminating discussions about prehistoric people's treatment of woodland, and the ecological and behavioural complexities involved, have concerned the Mesolithic – the period when the use of the term 'wood-pasture' is perhaps least appropriate. Landscape historians concerned with the Middle Ages are at least familiar with the concept, because they are aware of the outstanding work of Oliver Rackham (*e.g.* 1976, 1980 and 2006). However, the re-emergence of woodland history as a distinct research area carries the risk that landscape historians will regard it as peripheral, a specialist topic looked after by others. Unfortunately such specialists are thin on the ground.

At present there are notable gaps in our knowledge and understanding. Within England, Rackham has provided a national overview, discussing documentary evidence for the rise and fall of medieval wood-pasture and describing woodlands where this form of management survives in some sense. The focus of Della Hooke's work (*e.g.* 1989, 2008) has mostly been on the earlier Middle Ages in the English Midlands, where she has defined several large tracts of wood-pasture which were of regional importance (such as Arden, Wychwood and Sherwood) and noted the patterns made by the lanes and droveways which led to them. This is a phenomenon which has also been observed further east, where other landscape historians (*e.g.* Warner 1996, 49; Williamson 2000, fig. 24; Harrison 2002; Bryant *et al.* 2005) have discussed the possibility that these long, roughly coaxial route-ways were involved in the re-working and adaptation of coaxial field systems dating back to the later Iron Age or the Romano-British period. Does long-distance transhumance go back to those times too?

However, to read the work of Rackham and Hooke is to become aware of a gap in our perception, in the space lying between the regional overview and descriptions of local detail. It is rather as if we have just two sets of maps of former wood-pasture, one at the old one-inch scale (1:50,000 now), the other at 1:2,500 (the old twenty-five inch scale) with little at the scales which landscape historians find most useful (1:10,000 and 1:25,000). Arguably, local landscape historians should be operating at these levels, following the leads provided by Rackham and Hooke. But I am not sure that much progress has been made. There may be several reasons for this, apart from the perception of woodland history as a separate, specialist area of research. Much of the literature on old wood-pasture happens to be quite heavily dependent on case-studies and examples from south-east and central England. It is debatable whether this historically rich and densely populated area makes an entirely satisfactory 'reference region' for the history of wood-pasture in England as a whole, still less Britain. In such a region, the historical trajectories of wood-pasture, and the context and character of its 'survival', may well have been different from those of other regions. This is not a simple matter, a contrast between an area where dense populations, intensely competitive social hierarchies and a high demand for access to land and its resources led to the early extinction of rights in common wood-pasture – and other regions where the opposite historical tendencies often held sway. On the contrary, it may be that it was precisely in the more 'competitive' regions (in the sense sketched above) that common rights were most tenaciously fought for and preserved, and that rights and responsibilities, including those pertaining to wood-pasture commons, were most frequently written down and then preserved in archives. And it may also be the case, ironically, that it was such 'competitive' historical conditions which best enabled the 'survival' of sample areas of common wood-pasture, first as privatised deer-parks and then as components of polite landscapes. Lords and landowners sought exclusive access to what sometimes came to be seen as ideal landscapes, affording intimations of Paradise – their own exclusive wood-pastures, secured at the expense of the wood-pasture rights of others.

Apart from special areas like the New Forest and Epping Forest, these are the landscapes of wood-pasture which are extant today, as a search of the works of Rackham for examples to visit will soon reveal. Where common rights in wood-pastures have been extinguished, there may be little to be seen today; the pollards are usually long gone. Nevertheless, even in the absence of documentation it may not be too hard to work out the whereabouts of former common wood-pasture. Somewhere on the fringes of a parish there may well be steep ground, where woodland is essentially the only viable form of land-use. Today such a wood may well contain fairly young maiden trees, and perhaps pheasants will be reared here; trespassers will be prosecuted. But it may also be the case that the wood carries the name of the parish or township, and there may be an obvious lane or droveway leading not to the home of the wood's owner, but into the heart of the village (which will once have held more farmers than is the case today). Such observations would lead most landscape historians to conclude that the traditional common wood-pasture had been satisfactorily identified. There may be other clues, such as the name of the access road. Also certain field-names, and/or the patterns made by their boundaries, may imply that the common wood-pasture was once more extensive than the woodland of today.

Alternatively, it may be possible to argue that the creation of the earliest version of the park around the great house involved the enclosure of a piece of the local wood-pasture, along with the extinction of common rights. There may be scope for debate here. Rackham has recently described Moccas Park (in west Herefordshire) as 'a famous and mysterious park, in which extensive research, and even the publication of a book, has failed to elucidate its origin' (2006, 141). Recently, taking part in a trip organised by Natural England, I was informed that this park was a Norman deer-park. In fact, the first documentary evidence that Moccas was a deer-park dates from no earlier than 1617 (Whitehead 2000, 45). It may indeed be the case that Moccas was emparked in the late Middle Ages, as suggested (without conclusive evidence) in the main work of reference on the subject (Whitehead 2000). However, one cannot help noticing that *Moccas Park* (Harding and Wall 2000a) contains aspects of a philo-Norman, Cymrophobic perspective not entirely unknown in Herefordshire. The book finds room for no less than seven coats of arms, plus a photograph of a medieval knight's tomb and an extract from Domesday Book – material which strikes a slightly incongruous note in a book published by English Nature. And the coda of the book's title establishes its central theme: 'an English deer park'. Deer are still shot ('culled') in Moccas Park today.

Yet there may be good reason to believe that Moccas Park started life as a Welsh wood-pasture. After all, Moccas lies in the former Welsh district of Erging (Coplestone-Crow 1989, 2); its name comes from Welsh *Moch-rhos*. The park itself ran from low-lying Moccas up onto a ridge which separated Erging from Ewyas (or the Golden Valley). This long ridge is well-wooded today, and it is tempting to suggest that it was once a zone of common wood-pasture shared by communities settled on each side of it. Certainly the parish boundary between Moccas and Dorstone allocates much the greater share of the park to Dorstone (Whitehead 2000, fig. 2.2.5), and there is a gate which provides access from the Dorstone side. Moccas Park itself once contained a celebrated pollard, the 'Moccas Oak', whose girth measurements imply that it started growing in the mid-eleventh century (Wall 2000, 83). There are also one or two old oak pollards which stand *outside* the park boundary. As a matter of fact the forestry expert George Peterken has recently recognized that the park 'developed out of wood-pasture commons' (2008, 135, 153); independently, I have come to the same conclusion.

The North and the West: scope for further investigation?

I have briefly described two guises which old wood-pasture may take – the park, and the big wood on the hillside at the edge of its eponymous parish. In many parts of central and south-east England, these may be virtually the sole manifestations of former wood-pasture. But there are areas of western and northern England, not to mention Wales and Scotland, where landscape history had different trajectories, arguably more diverse and less well understood. Here, in more thinly populated regions, with fewer and smaller nucleated settlements, in places where landowners were absent, or preoccupied with promoting their own mineral rights, the decline of wood-pasture may have been a slower process. In some regions the impact of mining, and perhaps of other rural industries such as charcoal-burning and tanning leather, may have had various consequences – for instance, hastening the decline of local woodland, or promoting the development of coppice at the expense of wood-pasture. Such historical relationships need to be borne in mind by the landscape archaeologist. In my work in Swaledale in North Yorkshire (Fleming 1997, 1998a, 1998b) I took an agrarian approach to the history of wood-pasture, although I suspect that there is a good deal more to be said about coppicing, and the impact of the lead-mining industry in general.

Swaledale is now a landscape of stone walls, field barns and family farms, and it requires some effort of the imagination to think about the more wooded landscapes of the more distant past, and more communal ways of managing access to critical resources. However, taking advantage of the fact that land-use choice in Swaledale is quite closely constrained by the terrain, it was possible to examine the former daleside 'cow pastures', township by township, to work out where woodland had survived longest, and to suggest that such woodland had once been common wood-pasture, with pollard trees. There were several indicators of the probable former presence of woodland, or wood-pasture. Perhaps the most surprising 'survival' was the field-name element 'plain', found seven times on Upper Swaledale's tithe maps (Fleming 1997, fig. 1) and evidently indicating the former sites of open spaces often known in other parts of the country as lawns or launds. One intriguing discovery – which I have not previously commented upon – was that in one locality with a field called 'plain', Low Whita, five fields were called 'cow pasture', one was called 'cop pasture' and four were called 'cow or cop pasture' (Fleming 1997, fig. 5). One has to ask whether the surveyor asking about these field-names was confused by the tenant farmer's pronunciation, and did not get the matter cleared up. Perhaps the two names when spoken sounded very similar, which raises the possibility that some, or even all, of Swaledale's eighteenth or nineteenth-century 'cow pastures' were formerly called 'cop pastures' (that is, pastures with pollard trees, as seen at Watendlath in Cumbria: Fleming 1998, fig. 6.3). And one would not rule out the possibility that the farmer at Low Whita understood this in some sense, and refused to reject one of the alternatives furnished by history, as Swaledale people did with several other place-names, including the name for the upper dale itself (Fleming 1994; 1998, 22). The fantastic old elm pollard at Low Whita survived long enough for me to photograph it (Fleming 1998, fig. 6.2), although it has since been destroyed. I was relatively fortunate to work in Swaledale in the late 1980s, before most farmers had got round to clearing up the casualties of the most recent epidemic of Dutch elm disease.

In the part of Powys where I am working now, the indicators of former woods containing lopped trees, including pollards of various kinds, are as diverse as those in Swaledale. I have too little space here for more than a brief mention of them. Pollard oaks (and a few alders) may occur in woods, or outside them – as individuals, or in small clusters, or scattered as if in a decaying orchard (like those at Gaufron), or dispersed in larger numbers, either in woods composed of younger maiden trees, or in fields. Pollard oaks are not evenly distributed through the landscape; one can pass quickly from an interesting to a sterile area (from this point of view). This is mostly because pollards are not confined to woods, so that a landscape containing old, lopped oaks is not hard to recognise, between January and May at any rate. It seems unlikely that these variations reflect random differences between the tree management policies of different eighteenth and nineteenth-century estates, and/or local clusters of tenant farmers (although this matter may need more detailed research).

The traditional settlement pattern of this part of Wales involves few nucleated villages or even hamlets; many of the dispersed farms have evidently been in the same locations since at least the fifteenth century. It is not clear at this stage how tracts of wood-pasture can be understood in relation to patterns of settlement, land-use, and administrative and political geography. Some obvious possibilities are summarised on Figure 3.8. In terms of the study region, it may be worth pointing out that Gwerthrynion itself was divided between Is-coed (Below the wood) to the south and Uwch-coed (Above the wood) to the north, so it is possible that once there was a large central belt of woodland, perhaps accessible to anyone in the district who held common rights there. However, it does not seem that such a zone is detectable on the map, or through place-name studies; although there *are* sites of former wood-pasture here, their density or areal coverage do not command attention. At the other end of the 'commons' scale, I know of one case where a large wood of 40.55 acres (16.4ha), which evidently once contained numerous oak pollards, some of which survive today, was shared by neighbouring farms at the time of the tithe map (Cae Melin and Brondorddu, in Llanwrthwl, north Breconshire). A further complexity involves the distribution of rights in woodland, as between landowner and tenant farmers/commoners. It seems that it was the landowner who had the right to sell bark to tanners, though this should mostly have involved coppice rather than wood-pasture.

By the time of the tithe maps, in the 1830s and 1840s, most parcels of land suspected of having been former wood-pasture (whether shared or subject to more widely distributed common rights) evidently belonged to individual farms. Those parcels not converted to enclosed pasture must have continued in use either as wood-pasture in gradual decline, as at Gaufron, or, much more frequently, as browsed woods, old pollards in due course being eliminated (sometimes gradually) and replaced by maiden trees. Appearances may be deceptive. Today, Old Wood at Gaufron is well within enclosed farmland. However, the farm above it, Upper Esgair-rhiw, is surrounded by straight, surveyed boundaries. This suggests that two or three hundred years ago Old Wood lay very close to the edge of the upland common of Gwastedyn, and arguably once occupied its lower fringes.

The tithe maps leave a good deal to be desired. Sometimes, for instance, the names of parcels of land, or their 'state of cultivation' have not been entered on the schedules. And I suspect that woodland on land subject to common rights, for example on the lower fringes of upland commons, was not indicated on these maps. On the other hand, the tithe map for Llanwrthwl, a very large parish at the northern tip of Breconshire, is a remarkable document. The surveyor evidently employed the 'woodland' convention not only to indicate woods; he also used it to mark clusters of trees or patches of woodland within fields (often along their edges or tucked into corners). At the same time, entries in the 'state of cultivation' column often try to reflect the mixed character of each parcel. Thus a field may be described as 'Pasture and Wood', or 'Meadow and Wood' and the map may cover part of it with the woodland convention; a field described as 'Rough Pasture' may be marked as woodland. There are three or four parcels described as 'Woody Pasture', including one field called 'The Coppy', making one wonder whether a Welsh 'coppy' might have been a wood-pasture rather than a coppice, sometimes at least. Consistency of recording was not achieved, so that working out how much 'woodland' was attached to each farm, and its character, is a problematic exercise. However, the map does show the sheer 'boskiness' of the enclosed land in Llanwrthwl parish in the early nineteenth century. The widely scattered, one might say ill-disciplined, distribution of clusters of trees here, potentially fragments of former

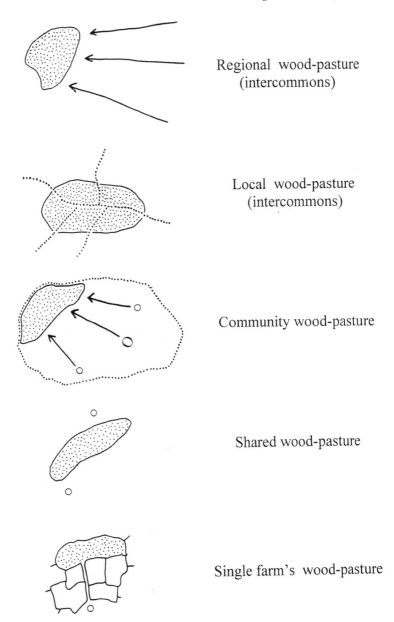

FIGURE 3.8. Models of wood-pasture. Scales are variable; stipple represents woodland; dotted lines indicate parish or township boundaries

wood-pasture (though in most cases we simply cannot know) is echoed by the frequency of old oak pollards in the parish today. In short, the Llanwrthwl tithe map is much more ecologically revealing than its fellows in the research area. There is a marked contrast with the map of Llansantffraed Cwmdeuddwr, just across the Elan, which is highly schematic, and also has noteworthy gaps in its schedule entries. The best corrective to the sterility of most of the tithe maps is to compare them with the much more tree-endowed First Edition six-inch maps (which were surveyed only four or five decades later) and also with the evidence of one's own eyes (in the case of older trees).

I have already argued that we need to think more about the taphonomy of wood-pasture, and to reconstruct the processes which led towards the final manifestations of wood-pasture traditions. In quantitative terms, really old pollards represent the diminutive 'tail' of a survival curve. But we also need to understand more qualitative matters – where, why and how such trees have persisted in the landscape. One interesting question is this: what lies behind the existence/survival of single old alder pollards (Fig. 3.9)? Both in Swaledale and Powys, examples include one or two located at high altitudes; the Abbey Wood, near Strata Florida in Ceredigion, contains just one old alder pollard. Pollards in most woodlands would have included a few alders, most commonly but not exclusively in the wetter spots. I suggest that when the time came to get rid of the pollards, such alders would have been left alone; they were not the species mentioned in the wood-cutters' instructions. There may just have been positive reasons for leaving such trees standing; alder wood has specialist uses. However, I doubt that the makers of clogs or musical instruments would have expected to obtain their wood from a single alder pollard high on a remote hillside! Such alders, then, should be seriously considered as potential remnants of wood-pasture.

Similar considerations apply to old coppice stools, which may be spotted clinging to rocky bluffs and crags in woodlands otherwise characterised by the prevalence of relatively young maiden trees. Removing such stools would often be judged too dangerous and time-consuming to make the effort worthwhile; no ground for fresh plantings would have been cleared by such an operation. It is in any case likely that steep rocky bluffs would have held stubs or coppice stools rather than pollards. Thus old coppice stools (Fig. 3.10) which cling to rocks in woods containing much younger trees are indicators of older woodland, but not necessarily representative of its composition. Such considerations apply, for instance, in the Abbey Wood at Strata Florida.

Pace Monty Python's Flying Circus, wood-cutting is hard and dangerous work; ease of operation, weighed against the advantage to be gained, will always be an important consideration. Several centuries ago, given the tough task presented by each ancient pollard, I suspect that there was often an obvious choice between firmly leaving them alone and ordering (and thus investing in) a mass cull – involving variously a holocaust, a holocopt, or a holoscapt (burning, cutting, or digging out). On Powys farms, one or two oaks which have continued to be lopped in quite recent times, and may still be lopped today, will often be found at the edge of the farmyard (Fig. 3.11) or just behind the farm, at the edge of a wood otherwise containing maiden trees. Within a single farm's wood-pasture, it is likely that most of the tree-lopping, whatever form it takes, will be in the zone closest to the access gate (as I have noticed at Eggworthy, in the parish of Walkhampton in Devon: see the chapter by Rosamond Faith in this book).

In Powys, diversity is very evident, and lopped trees defy easy categorisation. Surviving cut oaks include not only pollards cut at 'conventional' height, just above the reach of browsing animals, but also trees cut much higher (Fig. 3.12)

FIGURE 3.9 *(left)*. An ancient alder pollard beside the Mwyro, below Coed Troed-y-Rhiw (formerly Yr Allt Goch), Caron Uwch Clawdd, Ceredigion

FIGURE 3.10 *(right)*. An older 'stub' surviving on a difficult site, Abbey Wood, Strata Florida, Ceredigion

FIGURE 3.11 *(left)*. A 'farmyard' pollard, Cefn-coed, near Llandrindod Wells, Radnorshire

FIGURE 3.12 *(right)*. A 'giraffe pollard', Gaufron, Radnorshire

– Rackham's 'giraffe pollards' (1980, 5) – and trees which have evidently been shredded – that is, their side-branches have been removed (Rackham 1980, fig. 1.2), in a style more commonly seen in rural France in more recent years. Recently shredded trees, French style, are clearly visible on an old photograph taken near New Radnor about 100 years ago and shown at the National Library of Wales's recent exhibition of the photographic work of P. A. Abery. One or two of the trees at Gaufron look as if they may have started life as conventional pollards before becoming 'giraffe pollards' – that is to say, at some stage the lopping policy was changed, and a central 'leader' was promoted. It seems likely that 'giraffe pollards' and the thicker shredded trees were 'timber pollards', in the sense that the landowner was intending to have them felled eventually to make money from the sale of their trunks. There are even trees which look as if they have been deliberately formed into curving shapes by being pulled over and lashed down with ropes when young. This is a tradition which may have originated with the need for crucks (for which there is good evidence in sixteenth-century Powys – Suggett 2005) and continued as a response to the demand for ships' timbers of particular shapes, in the seventeenth and eighteenth centuries (Harris *et al.* 2003, 56; 110). As Oliver Rackham has pointed out (2006, chapter 18), given changing market forces and the longevity of trees, 'economic management' of woodland is an inexact science, to say the least; one might even say a mug's game. It may be that traditional wood-pasture, in relatively sparsely populated regions (and often in prehistory?) was heterogeneous in character, more subject to informal 'cut and come again' events than the object of rigorously enforced or enacted 'management policy'. Certainly the evidence from Neolithic Somerset, involving the 'draw-felling' of coppice woodland, seems to reflect such practices (Rackham 1977).

Conclusion

I would very much like to think that Harold Fox would have approved of this article, which is intended as a manifesto for the reconstructive study of ancient wood-pasture – a neglected topic, which deserves more concentrated research. Wood-pasture was, after all, of considerable importance until quite recent centuries. And although it is just possible that Powys happens to be the best area in the west of southern Britain for doing this kind of research, I suspect that more opportunities exist elsewhere than are generally recognised.

Bibliography

Bryant, S., Perry, B. and Williamson, T. (2005) A 'relict landscape' in south-east Hertfordshire: archaeological and topographic investigations in the Wormley area. *Landscape History* 27, 5–16.

Coplestone-Crow, B. (1989) *Herefordshire Place-names*. Oxford: British Archaeological Reports British Series 214.

Fleming, A. (1994) Swadal, Swar (and Erechwydd?): early medieval polities in Upper Swaledale. *Landscape History* 16, 17–30.

Fleming, A. (1997) Towards a history of wood-pasture in Swaledale (North Yorkshire). *Landscape History* 19, 31–47.

Fleming, A. (1998a) *Swaledale: Valley of the Wild River*. Edinburgh: University Press.

Fleming, A. (1998b) Wood pasture and the woodland economy in medieval Swaledale, in M. Atherden (ed.) *Woodland History and Management*, 26–42. Leeds: Leeds University Press.

Harding, P. T. and Wall, T. (eds) (2000a) *Moccas: an English Deer Park*. Peterborough: English Nature.

Harding, P. T. and Wall, T. (2000b) The trees: species, numbers, growth forms, ages and dead wood, in P. T. Harding and T. Wall (eds), 115–26.

Harris, E., Harris, J. and James, N. D. G. (2003) *Oak: a British History*. Oxford: Windgather Press.

Harrison, S. (2002) Open fields and earlier landscapes: six parishes in south-east Cambridgeshire. *Landscapes* 3, 35–54.

Hooke, D. (1989) Pre-Conquest woodland: its distribution and usage. *Agricultural History Review* 37, 113–29.

Hooke, D. (2008) Early medieval woodland and the place-name term *lēah*, in O. Padel and D. N. Parsons (eds) *A Commodity of Good Names: Essays in Honour of Margaret Gelling*. Donington: Shaun Tyas.

Peterken, G. (2008) *Wye Valley*. London: Collins.

Petit, S. and Watkins, C. (2003) Pollarding trees: changing attitudes to a traditional land management practice in Britain 1600–1900. *Rural History* 14.2, 157–76.

Rackham, O. (1976) *Trees and Woodland in the British Landscape*. London: J. M. Dent.

Rackham, O. (1977) Neolithic woodland management in the Somerset Levels: Garvin's, Walton Heath, and Rowland's Tracks. *Somerset Levels Papers* 3, 65–72.

Rackham, O. (1980) *Ancient Woodland*. London: Edward Arnold.

Rackham, O. (2006) *Woodlands*. London: Collins.

Rees, S., Jones, N. and Silvester, R. (2005) Conservation and investigation at Cwmhir Abbey, Powys. *Archaeologia Cambrensis* 154, 133–51.

Suggett, R. (2005) *Houses and History in the March of Wales*. Aberystwyth: Royal Commission on the Ancient and Historical Monuments of Wales.

Wall, T. (2000) A landscape of remarkable trees, in P. T. Harding and T. Wall (eds), 81–9.

Warner, P. (1996) *The Origins of Suffolk*, Manchester: Manchester University Press.

Whitehead, D. (2000) The de Fresnes, Vaughans and Cornewalls: 1160–1771, in Harding, P. T. and Wall, T. (eds), 41–8.

Williams, J. (1905) *A History of Radnorshire*. Brecon: Davies & Co.

Williamson, T. (2000) *The Origins of Hertfordshire*. Manchester: Manchester University Press.

CHAPTER FOUR

'Wealdbāra & Swina Mǣst': Wood Pasture in Early Medieval England

Della Hooke

Introduction

Links between areas of more intensive cultivation and seasonal pastures in more marginal zones of woodland or moorland were fundamental features of many early British societies. Wood pasture, especially, played a significant role in the economy of early medieval England, with marginal areas associated with such land use influencing the demarcation of territories and the administrative patterns of the period. In time, some pastoral areas gave way to new arable landscapes but many wooded regions were to be taken into the new Norman forests. The case study presented here illustrates one example of the latter kind of area, showing the legacy of place-names which reflect early usage and the subsequent development of the region.

The pre-history and history of wood-pasture landscapes

The old adage that a squirrel might cross Britain from tree to tree without touching the ground has long since been abandoned, especially following the observations of Rackham (1998) and Vera (2000) in the late 1990s. Even before the advent of man, wild herbivores such as aurochs, red deer and, early in the Holocene, European elk would have opened up the woodland by foraging, except in the most inaccessible places, and wild boar would have opened up land by rooting. Subsequent studies (Kirby 2004; Hodder *et al.* 2009) have shown how a cycle of woodland/open land might develop over time, with clearance undoubtedly affected by the activities of prehistoric man. It was not only that farmers would have felled woodland to make fields but that domestic stock were seen as an indication of wealth and status by Bronze Age and Iron Age times. Not only did increased numbers of cattle, sheep and goats hinder tree regeneration but the removal of the tree cover would have led to increased podsolisation of the soil or peat formation in marginal areas that were climatically or geologically vulnerable (Walker and Taylor 1976; Chambers *et al.* 1999). The collection of leaf fodder, too, for domestic stock may also have helped to hinder tree regeneration. Throughout Britain, tree cover seems to have been in decline by the late Iron Age, a situation apparently confirmed by pollen and archaeological evidence, with the consequent 'demise of major uncleared landscapes' (Hodder *et al.* 2009, 11).

The social context of Iron Age land management is not fully understood but the importance of cattle rearing, in particular, is undoubted. Enclosures on the southern downlands and elsewhere have been linked to stock management (Cunliffe 1978, 165–6, 186–9, 214–16), and in the Welsh borderland it has been suggested that many hillforts were located in order to control resource management, including stock rearing. Many hillforts dominate the surrounding plains and valleys with excellent views over their respective territories. Clearly, enforceable rights over land were in place in prehistoric times. Moreover, the use of complementary resources may already have been an influential factor in defining territories.

There is clear evidence that land was being parcelled out at an early date, but even customary use may have given rise to patterns of land use that persisted over the centuries. Much of the land division that has been recognised appears to have linked heavily cultivated zones with areas of seasonal grazing, offering complementary regions linked by parallel, linear road patterns which served as droveways. The movement of stock, sometimes over considerable distances, was necessary because pastures used in the winter and spring would need resting before they produced the essential hay crop or were used for crop cultivation, so that in the late spring/early summer stock would be moved to higher pastures (in the uplands) or areas of marshland (especially in parts of southern and eastern England such as the Fens or the Somerset Levels). It is the date of this form of land management that has yet to be clarified.

The droveways bear little relation to later Anglo-Saxon or medieval settlement foci and may have arisen in many cases not so much through the strict apportionment of land but as a result of the need for access by individual communities, established over a long period of habitual use (Harrison 2002, 43). There is evidence to suggest that they were present by later Anglo-Saxon times and were probably much older.

The practice of transhumance can be related to the folk regions of early medieval England, groupings that were already being subsumed into larger kingdoms by the seventh century (Hooke 1985a). In the southern half of the later county of Staffordshire, for instance, the Pencersæte and the Tomsæte occupied the valley territories of the rivers Penk and Tame, but their territories ran southwards to take in parts of the south Staffordshire/Birmingham plateau; in Warwickshire links between the more heavily wooded Arden and the more intensively cultivated Feldon persisted into medieval times (Ford 1976; Hooke 1985b). The central Weald was a frontier region between the men of Kent and the south Saxons, continuing to serve as an area of seasonal pasture for regions to the north and south throughout the early medieval period.

Not only were the boundaries of early folk regions, and even of kingdoms, influenced by such arrangements but the use of seasonal pastures, especially in wood-pasture regions, frequently underlay the later administrative patterns that became established and which, in their general outlines, have lasted to the present day. Fragmentation of these regions into the townships and subsequent manors and ecclesiastical parishes of later Anglo-Saxon/post-Conquest England broke the functional links of transhumance but gave rise to linked estates in which estates or areas of land in less developed regions – whether these were woodland, marshland, heathland or moorland – might become attached to manors in the more developed regions, links which are sometimes traceable through pre-Conquest charters, Domesday Book and medieval ecclesiastical chapelries. Such links perpetuated resource management, if not by the actual movement of flocks and herds, then through the interchange of resources (Hooke 1985b, 75–94). Indeed, the markets of medieval England continued to operate such resource interchange, acting as the means of exchange between different regions with varying economic strategies producing different surpluses.

The use of seasonal wood pasture in early medieval England

Early Anglo-Saxon charters show quite explicitly how the seasonal pastures were used at this time. The Kentish charters are some of our earliest documents of this type and describe the arrangements for accessing the pastures, or 'dens' as they were called. The Wealden dens of Kent seem at first to have belonged to specific folk groups established along the more fertile coastlands or the inland Vale of Holmesdale region, as land held in common, only gradually being appropriated by individual manors as the administrative pattern of manors and then parishes evolved (Hooke 1998, 143). For example, swine pastures added to an eighth-century charter granting land by the river Lympne to Mildred, abbess of Minster, include those in the *Limenwearawalde* 'the wood of the men of the *Limen* region/district', and in *Weoweraweald*, 'the wood of the men of Wye' (*Limen* was the name of the old East Rother River that flowed out to the sea at Lympne and the district became recognised as the lathe of the *Limenwara*) (Sawyer 1968, S 1180; Kelly 1995, no. 47, 163). The pattern of droveways is perhaps clearest in this region (Everitt 1986).

The word commonly used for swine pastures was *denbǣra*, although occasionally they are referred to as *wealdbǣra* or, more specifically, as *pascua porcorum*, 'pasture for pigs'. It is clear that the pasturing of herds of swine was one of the most important uses of woodland regions in the early medieval period, and sometimes the number of pigs that could be pastured is spelled out in the charters; numbers might vary from one herd to twelve herds, or might be quoted by number, as in the 120 pigs noted in the woods of *Hostringedenne* and *Ægelbyrhtingahyrst*, probably Asherden in Tenterden and a wood in High Harden (Sawyer 1968, S 1623). Other charters refer to cattle, one to 'pigs and cattle or goats', and another to 'common of pasture for cattle and sheep', but do not specify that these pastures lay within the Weald. Yet others refer to pannage and pasture for draught animals. The dens that can be identified often lay along the actual droveways.

There is another point that may be made about the Weald and its use as a transhumance area. The ancient name of the Weald, given in the Anglo-Saxon Chronicle in 477, was *Andredesleah*, and it was said to extend 120 miles from east to west and 30 miles from north to south (Swanton 1996, 14). Old English place-names could suggest a visual characteristic but might also indicate an economic interest and it may be argued that the *lēah* term, normally translated by place-name scholars as 'wood or clearing', can most closely have represented the type of open woodland used as wood pasture (Hooke 2008a). Wood-pasture woodland was kept relatively open by grazing stock but with thicker stands of trees in less accessible places and, although the species of tree might vary, in many regions it was the oak and the ash which most easily withstood the pressures of grazing. Much of this ancient wood-pasture environment was, therefore, a mosaic of open lawns and heath with scattered woods (Fig. 4.1). This is a perfectly sustainable environment unless grazing pressure is pushed too hard. Leaf fodder could be taken from pollarded trees such as ash, oak or elm, and the upper leaves of the holly were particularly valuable during the winter when other nutrients might be in short supply (the numerous 'hollin' place-names in the north of England probably reflect the importance of this practice). Too many animals in the woods in winter might lead to poached or damaged soils but the rooting of pigs has been found actually to aid tree regeneration. If grazing becomes neglected, then this landscape will revert, firstly getting clogged with bracken and bramble, before giving way to denser woodland.

Woodland cover undoubtedly varied over time, reflecting the pressures upon it. Woodland regeneration can, of course, reflect many factors – there seems little doubt that the amount of land under cultivation receded at the end of the Romano-British period, but former arable seems frequently to have reverted to pasture rather than woodland, perhaps implying a return to traditional native systems of farming favouring stock rearing (Hooke 1988; Hooke 2010). In some regions woodland regeneration seems to have occurred at a much later date (see below). The evidence which might help to identify regions of early wood-pasture usage is drawn from documents, place-names and particular patterns of routeways.

A well-wooded region lay along the western frontier of the Hwiccan kingdom in what is now Worcestershire and north-west Gloucestershire, extending southwards from the Wyre Forest on the Shropshire border through an area then known as *Weogorena leah* to the future forests of Malvern and Corse (Hooke 2008b). This was the least developed part of the kingdom. Charter evidence reveals that wood pasture was a valuable asset in at least parts of this zone for there is, indeed, ample reference to the pigs being taken into the woodlands west of the River Severn. There were disputes between the king and the Church, for instance, about the right to mast in the woods below the Malverns at Sinton in Leigh (S 1437; Hooke 1990, 96–7). In 855 an estate at Bentley in Holt, within *Weogorena leah*, was exempted from the duty of pasturing the king's swine *quod nominamus fearnleswe*, 'which we call "fern-pasture" ' (Sawyer 1968, S 206; Hooke 1990, 100–1). Other Worcestershire charters noting mast were associated with an island in the River Severn and estates at Spetchley and Wolverley, the woods belonging to the former providing mast for 100 swine in AD 967 (S 54 – spurious, S 1315, S 212; Hooke 1990, 36, 150, 120–1). The value of trees in

FIGURE 4.1. A wood-pasture environment: the New Forest, Hampshire

wood-pasture regions is illustrated by a seventh-century law of Ine of Wessex that imposed a fine of 60 shillings on those found cutting down a tree that could shelter thirty swine (Attenborough 1922, 50–1).

Moreover, an extensive area to the north-west of Worcester was known as *Weogorena leah*, the *lēah* of the *Weogoran* tribe whose territory was focused upon Worcester itself. Again, as with *Andredesleah*, this reveals the use of the *lēah* term at an early date for an extensive area of known wood pasture. There were also estate linkages in west Worcestershire beyond that revealed in the name of *Weogorena leah*, for a number of estates in the plains below the Malverns were attached to others in the more heavily cultivated areas to the east of the Severn. When these links were formed is not known (all were Church of Worcester estates), but the third indication of possible transhumant activity is also present in this part of Worcestershire, both to the north and south of the River Teme: the familiar pattern of parallel routeways leading from the Severn Valley westwards (Fig. 4.2). That this pattern was already established by at least the later part of the early medieval period is confirmed by the naming of many of the routes in Anglo-Saxon charter boundaries. Within *Weogorena leah*, one of these routeways is called the *wudu herpaþ*, 'highway to the wood'. Although Wyre to the north and Malvern/Corse to the south were to become royal forests in the full legal sense under the Normans, it may have been because the region to the north of the River Teme belonged to the powerful Church of Worcester that it remained free of such control; it had also been an area of colonisation and considerable development in the early medieval period.

It may be relevant to enquire whether any other large areas seem initially to have borne *lēah* names. The Weald (*Andredesleah*) itself was described as a *mycclan wudu*, 'great wood' in 893 (Swanton 1996, 84). That part of Hormer Hundred in Berkshire (now taken into Oxfordshire) was initially known as

Ærmundeslea; Straddle in Herefordshire may be a *lēah* name; and Groveley, Digherlye and Finkley all became forests or parts of forests in Wiltshire and Hampshire (Hooke 2008a, 370).

The landscape was, however, gradually changing and inevitably more land was cleared and permanently settled as time progressed and as the nature of landholding also altered. The *lēah* term became applied to smaller woods that in some areas appear only along the boundaries of early medieval estates. Within *Weogorena leah* numerous individual *lēah* names are subsequently recorded, some associated with settlements but others now surviving only as field-names. The settlements may have taken their names from a pre-existing wood – several in this region certainly began as assarts – or adopted a term characteristic of the area. The nature of the *lēah* vegetation, too, might change over time, for the woods within the pastures were also used for their products and both felling and replacement might take place (Hooke 1978–9). By the early medieval period most *lēah* woodland probably consisted of secondary woodland (Wager 1998, 155).

Place-names, wood pasture and seasonal grazing

The droveway pattern is another strand of evidence that recurs in other wood-pasture regions like the Warwickshire Arden and the Chilterns. It has recently been described, too, by Williamson in the territory of the Wuffingas in the region of south Suffolk which contains the Sutton Hoo burials (Williamson 2008, 86–94). All the types of evidence do not always occur together, however. We can see regions like Wychwood in Oxfordshire or Whittlewood in Northamptonshire serving as areas of wood pasture for surrounding estates (Schumer 1984; Jones and Page 2006, 63). Swineherds, oxherds, cowherds and shepherds all figure in Old English prose, but it was probably the swineherds that travelled most often with their animals to the distant pastures. The animals taken into the woods would not have been turned out loose to fend entirely alone for, as in many parts of Europe to this day, the herdsman and his dogs would have kept a watchful eye:

> *On forewerdne morgen ic drife sceap mine to heora lease, and stande ofer hig, on hǣte and on cyle, mid hundum, þe-lǣs wulfas forswelgen hig, and ic agen lǣde hig to heora loca, and melke hig tweowa on dæg, and loca heora ic hæbbe þǣrto, and cyse and buteran ic do, and ic eom getrywe hlaforde minon (Ælfrici Colloquium; Thorpe 1846, 20).*

> 'In the early morning I drive my sheep to their pasture, and in the heat and in cold, stand over them with dogs, lest wolves devour them; and I lead them back to their folds and milk them twice a day, and move their folds; and in addition I make cheese and butter; and I am loyal to my lord' (*Ælfric's Colloquy*; Swanton 1975, 109).

Beyond the Weald, with its numerous den names, Old English place-names are less specific in indicating seasonal settlement. The West Saxon term for swine pasture, *bǣr* (or *denbǣr, waldbǣr* and *wudubǣr)*, is most common in southern England. Bere Farm in Bramdean in Hampshire, for instance, is located upon the site of the *hnut leage bǣre* 'the pastures of nut wood', noted

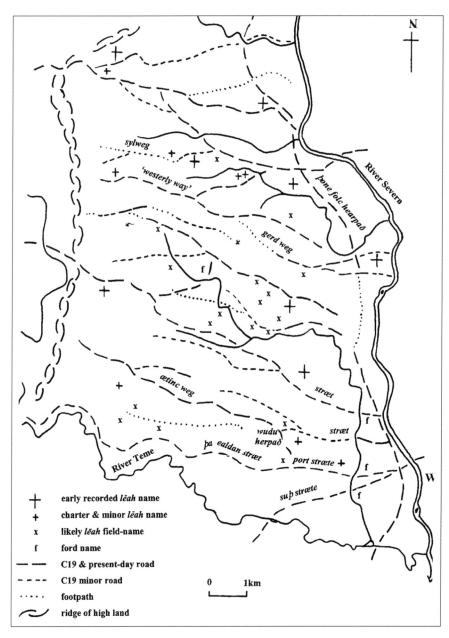

FIGURE 4.2. Possible droveways in *Weogorena leah*, west Worcestershire

in a tenth-century boundary clause (S 417). The term does not seem to have given rise to many settlement names outside this region, although Scandinavian seasonal settlements, often in an upland location, might be referred to by the term *skáli* (a possible OE *scela, sceling* 'shield, shieling', referring to a 'hut' or 'shed' is similar) and Old Norse *sǽtr* and *erg*, which seem to have referred to the pastures rather than the huts themselves (*erg* pehaps borrowed from a Gaelic word); Old English names of this kind are less directly helpful. While the *tūn* settlements – the proto-manorial centres and villages – usually lay outside the regions of wood pasture, the seasonal settlements that gradually gave way to more permanent farms, or the farms that were later established as assarts, have no common terminology. A *wīc* might be a 'specialised farm', and both 'herd' wicks and 'cheese' wicks are common; single farms in wooded areas were often termed 'worths' but others acquired the *lēah* name, indicating a wooded or wood-pasture landscape, often coupled with a personal name. Sometimes the *feld* term appears, suggesting a cleared area in an otherwise wooded landscape, perhaps even an area of common pasture. A cluster of such names have been noted in Whittlewood, perhaps along a regional boundary, and others occur in the Malvern region of Worcestershire. *Fyrth* (modern 'thrift') is another term that begs further study. While Gelling and Cole (2000, 224) have interpreted this as 'land overgrown with brushwood, scrubland on the edge of forest', fields bearing this name occur throughout western Wales between the cultivated zone and the open uplands and it seems to have been used in a quasi-legal sense (as *ffridd*) to refer to the 'common waste' until much of this was enclosed in about the sixteenth century, often being used as summer pasture in the first instance. It probably was overgrown with small trees and shrubs, with occasional patches of open woodland, until stock numbers increased in Tudor times. 'Thrift woods' are not uncommon in England today.

The use of seasonal pastures was a subject that greatly interested Harold Fox and, in addition to his many studies of Devon, he examined the use of the *wald*/wold regions of midland England, finding 'evidence of a once more pastoral orientation on the wolds of the Nottingham-Leicestershire border and in High Leicestershire'. In this region, too, he was able to identify a pattern of eastwards-running tracks leading up from the Soar valley and the subdivision of once intercommoned land (Fox 1989, 87–9, fig. 5.2). In this region, however, this type of land use had been virtually superseded by more typical arable systems by the twelfth century, perhaps reflecting an intensification of settlement between the end of the ninth century and the eleventh (Fox 1989, 93). It is therefore likely that the old arable/seasonal pasture system was much more widespread in pre-medieval England.

Hunting and its relationship to seasonal pastures

Wooded regions were also used by Anglo-Saxon times for hunting, the drive with dogs being the most common method of catching game. Forests had been introduced into the Frankish kingdoms by the seventh century and the concept would certainly have been known in England. Hunting rights are sometimes allotted in pre-Conquest charters, or estates relieved from the duties of maintaining huntsmen, falconers and dog-handlers, while the Old English term *haga* is likely to indicate enclosures for deer. Such enclosures, whether used for capturing deer or protecting does and their young, are found to have been concentrated in many of the areas over which the Norman kings were later to impose forest law (Hooke 1998). While forest law imposed heavy restrictions upon those who lived beneath its enforcement, the use of forest land as seasonal pasture was rarely suppressed and local communities continued to benefit from the practice. The benefit was, however, twofold for grazing kept the woodland open with scattered groves and more open launds – essential for the successful hunting of deer whether with dogs or on horseback.

Post-Conquest wood pasture

Swine pastures remained so important at the time of the Domesday survey that woods in some Domesday Book circuits were assessed according to their capacity to support herds of swine or the renders that could be obtained in return for the right of pannage (Darby 1977, 175–8). Among the latter were the five counties of the south-eastern circuit: Kent, Sussex, Surrey, Hampshire and Berkshire, although individual entries might vary. At Wrotham in Kent a render was due when the wood bore mast: *silva quando fructificatur quingentis porcis*, 'woodland, when fruitful, 500 pigs'. The renders themselves varied from only one pig to as many as 500 (the latter usually from grouped entries), but it is impossible to know how many swine they represented: in Surrey it was 1 in 7 for grass (*herbagio*)-fed swine at two places and 1 in 10 at another two; in Sussex often 1 in 7, but renders of mast-fed and grass-fed swine may not have been the same. In Herefordshire it is said that each villein on the king's vill of Leominster who had ten pigs gave one for pannage. For the Bedford-Middlesex and Eastern circuits swine totals are recorded. In the rest of the Domesday Book record woodland is usually recorded by its extent, and wood pasture often referred to as *silua pastilis* (or just *silua*) but there are occasional references to mast: the manor of Stoneleigh in Warwickshire, lying within the well-wooded Arden, had, in its amassed woods which measured in total four leagues long and two leagues wide, sufficient pasture for 2,000 pigs.

Harold Fox, in his introductory paper to *Seasonal Settlement* (1996) examined the different kinds of 'transhumance' that persisted in England. Although the 'greater transhumance' necessitated by the need to find upland pasture for herds in areas where lowland pastures were desiccated in summer owing to the climate was not a factor in England, movement between regional *pays* appears to have existed at an early date (above). However, it was what Fox called 'lesser transhumance' that remained a dominant feature in some parts of Britain in the Middle Ages with landowners 'moving their animals from manor to manor as part of a well thought out system of livestock husbandry', especially in the north of England where the practice persisted into the seventeenth century (Fox 1996, 3–4). Dyer has also shown how flocks were moved to upland Cotswold pastures in the summer in the early Middle Ages (Dyer 1996). In these regions it was often upland pastures that continued to be used, but the practice of moving stock to lowland woodlands to forage also remained a feature of many royal forests. Many forests were no longer upheld as wooded hunting reserves as their boundaries were pushed back after a period of medieval expansion, but where they survived so did the practice of moving stock into their wood pastures. The Statute of Merton, passed in 1235, allowed lords to enclose their wastes providing sufficient pasture was left for their tenants and, although undoubtedly this led to severe inroads into the commons, commoners' rights continued to be jealously guarded.

The following case study looks more closely at the wood-pasture environment of a particular wooded region of midland England in the early medieval period, its recognition as a royal forest in the post-Conquest period and the subsequent demise of the forest area, summarising the historical evidence of its role throughout as a region of wood pasture.

Wood pasture in a medieval forest: a case study of Wychwood, Oxfordshire

Wychwood, 'the wood of the Hwicce', is first recorded by name in the ninth century (S 196) by which time it lay outside the Hwiccan kingdom. If the Hwiccan kingdom perpetuated the tribal grouping of the late Iron Age Dobunni, as seems likely (Hooke 1985b, 5–8), then this region had probably lain within their territorial sphere at the end of the Roman period. However, the border area with the Catuvellauni to the south-east is likely to have been a heavily contested frontier region (Laycock 2008, 19).

There is evidence of considerable Romano-British settlement in this area, indicating at least some open land, for, in addition to the enigmatic Iron Age earthwork known as Grim's Ditch, several Roman villa sites have been identified within the heart of Wychwood. The regeneration of woodland in this region may have been relatively late. A recent pollen core from Shotover in the forest of Shotover and Stowood to the east of Oxford dates the post-Roman regeneration there to the late Anglo-Saxon period (Day 1991; Dark 2000, 120–1). It is likely that a growing royal interest in hunting was helping to protect woodland and promote such regeneration (Hooke 2010).

By the time of the Domesday survey, however, the woods of Shipton-under-Wychwood and of Wootton to the east had been put 'within the King's enclosure', *i.e.* declared royal forest, and the wood of Shipton had already been producing 50 shillings yearly in King Edward's reign (Caldwell 1978, 1.5). It was stated that Woodstock, Cornbury and Wychwood were also 'the lordship forests of the King' in 1086 (Caldwell 1978, 1.10). Before 1086 a forester had held Bampton, and in 1086 a forester had a holding in Chadlington in Wychwood. The town of Oxford paid towards the upkeep of a hawk and hounds for hunting. Perhaps the interest of the king in hunting had really protected and strengthened the presence of the woodland of Wychwood. A 'hunter's way' is recorded in 969, in a boundary clause of Witney (S 771).

Reference has already been made to the Old English term *haga*, 'an enclosure', which seems to have been a kind of proto-deer-park; initially most were established upon royal lands. The term implies 'enclosure', often in a protective capacity, but it is unlikely that the early medieval mind saw any contradiction between the safeguarding of deer and taking them for venison. There are a number of *haga* features recorded in the pre-Conquest charters of Oxfordshire (Fig. 4.3): one of them at Ducklington close to Home Wood and another in Shipton-on-Cherwell, both in the greater Wychwood region.

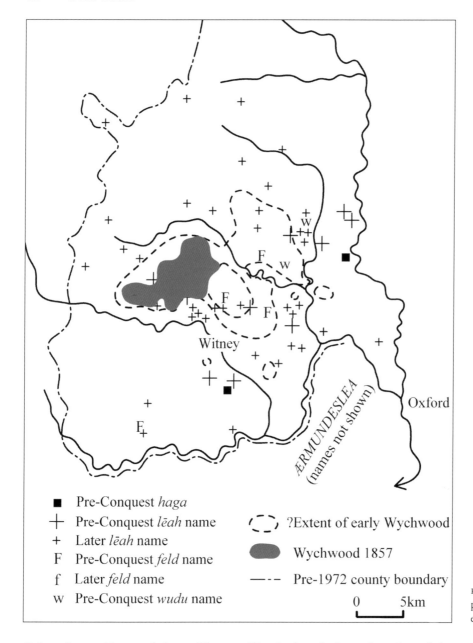

Legend:

- ■ Pre-Conquest *haga*
- + Pre-Conquest *lēah* name
- + Later *lēah* name
- F Pre-Conquest *feld* name
- f Later *feld* name
- w Pre-Conquest *wudu* name
- (⁻) ?Extent of early Wychwood
- ● Wychwood 1857
- — - - Pre-1972 county boundary

0   5km

FIGURE 4.3. Wychwood: place-name and charter evidence

Others lay in *Earmundeslea* in Hormer Hundred and along the edge of the Chilterns.

Place-name evidence suggests that the woodlands of north-west Oxfordshire were initially more extensive than the area of the later forest (Schumer 1984). Many of the *lēah* names are likely to have originated in the pre-Norman period and are prolific well beyond the medieval forest margins (Fig. 4.3), but with the majority falling within the region known to have been wooded in 1086. The names in this region correspond with the naming of such features noted elsewhere (Hooke 2008a). Some were associated with named individuals, a common feature; trees mentioned include the aspen, willow and oak; among the animals noted the horse appears most frequently – studs were often maintained in woodlands – but include sheep. The use of woods for timber is indicated by names referring to the taking of logs (Stockley) and wood for wheel-rims (Felley in Spelsbury), and to wood shavings or chips (the *sponleah* of Crawley).

Wychwood remained a royal forest throughout medieval times and was at its most extensive in Henry II's time (Hooke 1993). In medieval times the woodland extended across a large area between the rivers and stretched north-eastwards almost as far as Woodstock and the River Glyme; it also included a number of woods detached from the main area of forest. Within the forest, lodges were established for its management; High Lodge, probably one of the oldest and a moated site, was the residence of the park ranger when this was a Crown estate. Woodstock Park was an ancient royal forest park, allegedly enclosed by a stone wall by Henry I according to the fifteenth-century chronicler John Rous (and said to be the first such wild-animal enclosure of its kind in England) and certainly walled much earlier than Rous' time, at least by the early thirteenth century (Bond and Tiller 1987, 28). The park was usually held in dower by queens from 1281, but Henry built a palace or hunting lodge here and the park was regularly visited by royalty. Cornbury Park was also a medieval deer-park which still belonged in 1244 to the Crown but in 1339 was granted to John Solers. This, too, was also to be walled in 1664 and was later known as Blandford Park.

Within the forest, the hunting of fox, hare, wild boar and deer is recorded in medieval documentation, the last being mainly the fallow deer with only rare references to red deer; roe deer were of lesser importance and, if taken, were rarely recorded. The 200 fallow deer in Cornbury Park in 1905 were said to be descendents of the wild deer of Wychwood. Forest law was especially directed towards the protection of deer but also covered the management of the vert and guarded timber rights. The law also ensured a rich source of revenue, not only for the king but also for his officials.

Around the forest were the manors of landed families, several of them erecting castles at their manorial centres, as at Ascott d'Oyley and Ascott-under-Wychwood. The forest interior remained for the most part lightly settled, although assarting upon the fringes gave rise to a number of hamlets at the forest gates, especially in the south-east, and several hamlets in Hailey, such as Delly End and Poffley End, developed where assarts were recorded in 1279. 'End' and 'green' names are common in similar areas of woodland settlement elsewhere. The forest villages here tend to have developed as straggling settlements set along irregular lanes and tracks, in contrast to the more nucleated villages on its fringes and beyond.

The use of this area for wood pasture before it became recognised as a royal forest would seem to be attested by several *lēah* place-names (Fig. 4.3; Table 4.1). In the heart of the forest lay Leafield, but this was an open area known simply as *la Feld* in the thirteenth century and the 'Lea' here is from the French definite article; the *feld* term does, however, indicate land in close proximity

Core area:	Asthall Leigh, Asthall (C13: '*lēah* of the people of Asthall')	Wychwood (*Huiccewudu* 840: 'wood of the Hwicce')
	Stockley Copse, Asthall (*Stochelie* 1086: ?' *lēah* producing logs')	Leafield (C13: 'the *fēld*')
	Studley Copse, Leafield (1300: 'wood-pasture for horses')	
	Crawley (C13 'crow *lēah*')	
	Henley Knapp, FN in Crawley (C10: *on hean leage* 'to the high *lēah*')	
	Spoonley Copse, FN in Crawley (C10: *on swon leage* 'to the *lēah* producing chips, shavings')	
	? Great & Little Smalley, FNs in Crawley (C17: 'narrow island' or '*lēah*')	
	On lungan leage weg, Crawley (C10: 'to the long *lēah* way')	
	Hailey (C13 'hay *lēah*')	
	Delly pool. Hailey (C13: 'valley *lēah*')	
	North Leigh (*Lege* 1086: *lēah*')	
	Sullesleye, FN in North Leigh (C15: '?*lēah*')	
	Lamburleye, FN in Shipton-under-Wychwood (C10: 'lamb's pasture')	
	Whitley Hill, Wychwood (1300 'white' or 'fair *lēah*')	
	Asperleyehurn, FN in Wychwood (1300: 'corner by the aspen wood')	
	Hodleye, FN in Wychwood (1300: ?*Hūda*'s *lēah*')	
	Bradeleye, FN in Wychwood (C13: 'broad *lēah*')	
	Widley Copse, Swinbrook & Widford ((*on) wiðilea*, 1059: 'willow *lēah*')	
	?*Lays*, FN in Milton-under-Wychwood (C19)	
	?*Lay Ground*, FN in Chastleton (C19)	
West:	Langley, Shipton under Wychwood	
	Tangley Bruern (C12: '*lēah* by the River Teign')	
North:	Cleveley, Enstone (C12: '*lēah* on a cliff')	Stonesfield (*Stvntesfeld* 1086: '*Stunt's *fēld*'
	?Leys Farm C19), Enstone	
	Asterleigh (C12: 'eastern *lēah*')	
	Pedersle, FN in Asterleigh (C13: '?pedlar's *lēah*')	
	Ditchley, Spelsbury (C13: '*lēah* by the ditch', referring to Grim's Ditch	
	Felley, Spelsbury (C12: '*lēah* where fellies – wheel rims – are cut')	
	Lockesleghe, Taynton woods (a hermitage)	
	Horse Lays, FN in Sandford St Martin (C18: 'pasture for horses')	
	Nine Lays, FN in Chadlington (C19)	
	Lays under the Heath, FN in Swerford (C19)	
	Leycroft, FN in Rollright (C14: North Leigh (*Lege* 1086: *lēah*' croft)	
East:	Foxley Farm, Eynsham (C13: 'fox *lēah*')	Wootton (*at Wudutune* 958: 'wood village')
	Tilgarsley, Eynsham (1200: '*Tilgār's *lēah*')	Woodstock (*Wudestoce* c.1000: 'place in the woods')
	Acheley, FN in in Eynsham (C14: 'oak *lēah*'	
	FN in Eynsham, (C13: 'horse *lēah*')	
	Bodesle, F N in Gosford & Water Eaton 9C13: '*Bode*'s *lēah*')	
	? Woodleys Copse, Eynsham (C17)	*on hæðfeld*, Eynsham ch. (1005 'to heath *fēld*')
	Pinsley Wood, Hanborough (C13: '*Pin*'s *lēah*')	
	Murzeley Closes, FN in Hanborough (C13: 'mouse or *Mūsa's *lēah*')	
	Roweleye, FN in Hanborough (C24: 'rough *lēah*')	
	Tackley (*Tachelie* 1086: '*Tæcca's' or 'tag's *lēah*' i.e. *teg tag* 'young sheep')	
	Weaveley Farm, Tackley (1005: *to wiðigleas gemaero* 'to willow *lēah*'s boundary')	
	Hordley Farm, Wootton (C12 'treasure *lēah*')	
	Woodleys, Wootton (*Widelei* 1086 'wide' or 'willow *lēah*')	
	Farley Lane, Wootton (C17)	
	Benteleye, FN in Wootton (1300 '*lēah* full of bent-grass')	
	Poddeleye, FN in Wootton (1300: '*Podda*'s *lēah*')	
	?Chapel Leys, FN in Wootton (C19)	
	Burleigh Farm/Wood, Cassington (C13: 'earthwork' *lēah*')	
	Hureleye, FN in Cassington (C18: '*lēah*' in a corner')	
South:	South Leigh (*Stanton lege* 1190)	Clanfield (*Chenefelde* 1086: 'clean *fēld*')
	Barleypark Farm, Ducklington (C10: *Byrnan lea* 'Beorna's *lēah*')	Claywell Farm, Ducklington (*Welde* 1086:
	Hastelegefurlong, FN in Shifford (C14: 'east *lēah*')	Weald, Bampton (C12: 'wood')
	Burthemeleye, FN in Black Bourton (C13: '*lēah*' of the people of Bourton'	
	?The Lay(s), FN in Clanfield (C19)	

TABLE 4.1. *Lēah* names around Wychwood (the hundreds of Wootton, Bampton and Chadlington) (listing those names accepted by Gelling 1954; column 2 shows only selected 'wood' and *fēld* names.)

to woodland. Many of the real *lēah* names are found around the central forest core, indicating a greater extent of woodland by the late Anglo-Saxon period than that included within the later forest. A tenth-century boundary clause of Witney (S 771) notes the *hean leage*, 'high wood', approached by a routeway from Langley, noted as the *lunga leage weg*, 'Langley way', and a *swon leage*, which may be a corruption of OE *spon*, *i.e.* 'wood-chipping wood' (mapped in Blair 1994, 131, fig. 77).

Other early recorded *lēah* names are found to the south of the Windrush beyond the main area of Domesday woodland. In an authentic charter of 958 Edgar of Mercia granted an estate at Ducklington to Eanulf, minister (S 678; Kelly 2001, no. 82, 332–6), which included the 'old church' at *Æstlea*, 'east *lēah*', identified as Cokethorpe in the east of the parish, and *Byrnanlea*, '*Beorna's lēah*', represented by Barleypark Farm and Wood in the west of the parish, both representing *lēah* features here that were by the tenth century surviving close to the parish boundary (the two Ducklington estates recorded in Domesday Book each held woodland measuring three furlongs by two (Caldwell 1978, 28,20; 59,6). It was the easternmost of these, the 'east *lēah*', that seems to have been bounded by a *haga* boundary. Other *lēah* names also lay further away from the later forest core (Fig. 4.3 and Table 4.1). Only a few *lēah* names became those of parishes, the majority occurring as minor names that only found their way into later records.

Within Wychwood, the Domesday survey records the value of the extensive woods of the Bishop of Winchester's manor of Witney (three leagues by two) when they bore mast (as with the Domesday manors of Eynsham and Bloxham with Adderbury, the latter rendering both pigs and pannage). Renders from the pannage are also entered for Shipton-under-Wychwood and for Bampton to the south.

Within the forest the inhabitants of many of the surrounding settlements continued to enjoy common of pasture in later times (Fig. 4.3; Schumer 1984, 41). Many of these had the right to pasture their horses and cattle, but only the forest settlements of Leafield, Langley and Shorthampton enjoyed the right to pasture sheep upon particular areas of waste. The pasturing of pigs was still allowed in Woodstock Park in the thirteenth century but in the Middle Ages no swine pasturage was permitted in Wychwood. Later rights of common are specified for horses and sheep but not for cattle or pigs. Holdings within the woodland might remain attached to their home manors – either as whole townships, in the case of the Warwickshire Arden, or as individual patches of woodland and heath. There are several references to 'wood ways' in the region: a *wudestret* is already mentioned on the boundary of Witney in 1044 (S 1001; Blair 1994, 131, fig. 77) and later ones occur in Hook Norton, Broadwell, Swinford and Widford. Within the forest, stands of woodland alternated with more open areas of pasture, as still in the New Forest today.

Trees in wood pasture regions were often pollarded in order to produce timber that was out of the reach of animals, and one of the earliest references to such a practice may be revealed in the tenth-century Ducklington charter where

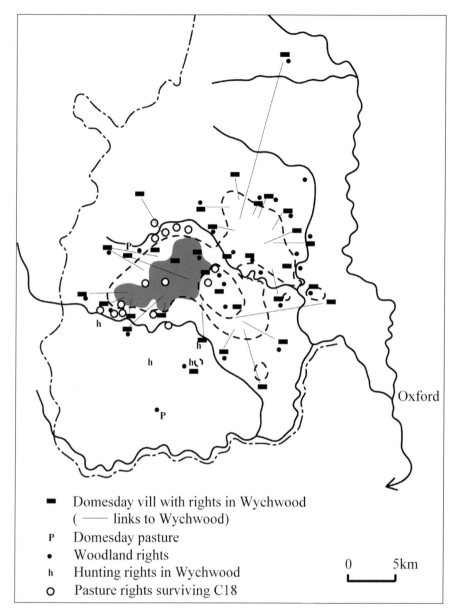

- ■ Domesday vill with rights in Wychwood
  (—— links to Wychwood)
- P Domesday pasture
- • Woodland rights
- h Hunting rights in Wychwood
- o Pasture rights surviving C18

0   5km

FIGURE 4.4. Rights
of pasture within
Wychwood

two meadows lay *æt loppede þorne* (another 'copped thorn' is later recorded in
Hailey: S 678). Parks, too, often helped to conserve wood-pasture landscapes
and ancient trees: of the woods associated with medieval parks, Pinsley Wood
in Hanborough survives and Blenheim Park, the successor to the royal park
of Woodstock, had, in 1907, 'much fine timber, particularly oaks and elms',
and 'a noble belt of beeches' (Page 1907, 300). The much later Ditchley Park,
enclosed in 1603, was described in 1907 as 'exceptionally well wooded with every
variety of English tree, some of which are of venerable age, and supposed to
be older than the park'; Glympton Park, another late emparkment, was also
'well-timbered' (Page 1907, 300).

By the eighteenth century the woods themselves were divided into groves of spring woods, woods of timber and underwood, and coppices with only underwood (Report to the Board of Agriculture 1794: Page 1907, 293–301). In 1813 coppices covered just over 3,000 acres of the total 5,593 acres of the forest and over 1,000 acres in addition in the Chase Woods and Cornbury Park, with nearly 2,500 acres remaining as 'open forest' – described as producing nothing but brushwood used for fuel and browse for deer. Although oak was the dominant tree within the forest, Arthur Young, the agriculturalist, visiting the forest in the early nineteenth century, observed 'not one very fine tree of navy oak in a ride of 16 or 17 miles', although he did remark upon the presence of some young oaks which might be of value in the future . Despite the 'many very beautiful scenes' within 'this fine wild tract of country' he felt obliged to recommend immediate enclosure (Young 1813, 237–9). The final enclosure of Wychwood was not completed until 1862 but much of the woodland core fortunately survived.

Much of Wychwood, like other forests, had been subjected to extensive assarting from medieval times onwards and, in spite of attempts to revive the forests under the Stuarts and the survival of some valuable coppices scattered throughout the region, relatively little remained unscathed after enclosure in 1857/62: the trees on the 2,000 acres of the Crown allotment were conscientiously felled and sold, the ground cleared for new farmsteads and fields (Emery 1974, 160–1). Nevertheless, some 1,500 acres passed to the owner of Cornbury Park and escaped destruction. Beyond this central core some other patches of ancient woodland have also survived: as well as Pinsley Wood, mentioned above, Burleigh Wood in Bladon, Cogges Wood in Cogges and Stockley Wood in Asthall are examples of woods classed today as 'ancient or replanted woodland'. Yet this represents only a fraction of the original royal forest that had extended over some 102,400 acres (Jessup 1975, 76). Ancient or replanted ancient woodland is limited in Oxfordshire but is still most prevalent in the areas known to have been well wooded in 1086 – Wychwood, Hormer Hundred, the claylands to the north-east of Oxford and along the northern edge of the Chilterns.

As the woodlands of this region passed into private ownership, areas of common available for grazing by the tenants' stock became limited, confined almost entirely to relatively small patches on the south-eastern margins of the forest; it was only beyond the forest core that more extensive commons survived in North and South Leigh, Freeland, Eynsham and Newland (Hooke 1993). Here the commons, by now open heath, were finally enclosed only in the eighteenth and early nineteenth centuries. After a series of riots and fence-breaking by the dispossessed commoners, especially in North Leigh and Eynsham, most of the area became enclosed farmland with commoners' rights extinguished.

No longer do most of the surviving woods of this region resemble an open wood-pasture habitat for this was an environment which was to lose its *raison d'être* almost entirely, with modern farming practices and different uses for the woodland. Nevertheless, to the south, remnants of the ancient *lēah* areas of Ducklington survive as Barleypark Wood and Home Wood. The largest area of woodland remains Wychwood itself, its ancient walks and copses, most not even falling under the umbrella of 'replanted', still extending for over 3km from east to west and nearly 4km from north to south. Still, from some angles, it still provides an image of what the ancient forest may have looked like.

Bibliography

Attenborough, F. L. (1922) *The Laws of the Earliest English Kings*. Cambridge: Cambridge University Press.

Blair, J. (1994) *Anglo-Saxon Oxfordshire*. Stroud: Alan Sutton.

Bond, J. and Tiller, K. (eds) (1987) *Blenheim. Landscape for a Palace*. Stroud: Alan Sutton.

Caldwell, C. (1978) *Domesday Book, 14, Oxfordshire*. Chichester: Phillimore.

Chambers, F. M., Mauquoy, D. and Todd, P. A. (1999) Recent rise to dominance of Molinia Cerulea in environmentally sensitive areas: new perspectives from palaeoecological data. *British Ecological Society* 36, 719–33.

Cunliffe, B. (1978) *Iron Age Communities in Britain*, 2nd edition. London: Routledge and Kegan Paul.

Darby, H. C. (1977) *Domesday England*. Cambridge: Cambridge University Press.

Dark, P. (2000) *The Environment of Britain in the First Millennium AD*. London: Duckworth.

Day, S. P. (1991) Post-glacial vegetational history of the Oxford region. *New Phytologist* 119, 445–70.

Dyer, C. (1996) Seasonal settlement in medieval Gloucestershire. in H. S. A. Fox (ed.), *Seasonal Settlement*, 25–33. Leicester: University of Leicester.

Emery, F. (1974) *The Oxfordshire Landscape*. London: Hodder and Stoughton.

Everitt, A. (1986) *Continuity and Colonization: the Evolution of Kentish Settlement*. Leicester: Leicester University Press.

Ford, W. J. (1976) Settlement patterns in the central region of the Warwickshire Avon, in P. H. Sawyer (ed.), 274–94. *Medieval Settlement, Continuity and Change*. London: Edward Arnold.

Fox, H. S. A. (1996) The people of the wolds in English settlement history, in M. Aston, D. Austin and C. Dyer (eds) *The Rural Settlements of Medieval England: Studies dedicated to Maurice Beresford and John Hurst*, 77–101. Oxford: Basil Blackwell.

Fox, H. S. A. (1996) Introduction: transhumance and seasonal settlement, in H. S. A. Fox (ed.), *Seasonal Settlement*, 1–23. Leicester: University of Leicester.

Gelling, M. (1954) *The Place-Names of Oxfordshire, Parts I and II*, English Place-Name Society, Vols XXIII and XXIV. Cambridge: Cambridge University Press.

Gelling, M. and Cole, A. (2000) *The Landscape of Place-Names*. Stamford: Shaun Tyas.

Harrison, S. (2002) Open fields and earlier landscapes: six parishes in south-east Cambridgeshire. *Landscapes* 3, 35–54.

Hodder, K. H., Buckland, P. C., Kirby, K. J. and Bullock, J. M. (2009) Can the pre-Neolithic provide suitable models for re-wilding the landscape in Britain? *British Wildlife* (supp. edn., June), 4–15.

Hooke, D. (1978–9) Anglo-Saxon landscapes of the West Midlands. *Journal of the English Place-Name Society* 11, 3–23.

Hooke, D. (1985a) Central places. Central areas?, in E. Grant (ed.) *The Concept of Central Places*, 79–93. Sheffield: University of Sheffield.

Hooke, D. (1985b) *The Anglo-Saxon Landscape. The Kingdom of the Hwicce.* Manchester: Manchester University Press.

Hooke, D. (1988) Regional variation in southern and central England in the Anglo-Saxon period and its relationship to land units and settlement, in D. Hooke (ed.) *Anglo-Saxon Settlements*, 123–52. Oxford: Basil Blackwell.

Hooke, D. (1990) *Worcestershire Anglo-Saxon Charter-Bounds.* Woodbridge: Boydell.

Hooke, D. (1993) Oxford historical landscapes project'. Unpublished report for English Heritage.

Hooke, D. (1998) *The Landscape of Anglo-Saxon England.* London: Leicester University Press.

Hooke, D. (2008a) Early medieval woodland and the place-name term *lēah*, in O. J. Padel and D. N. Parsons (eds) *A Commodity of Good Names. Essays in Honour of Margaret Gelling*, 365–76. Donington: Shaun Tyas.

Hooke, D. (2008b) Recent views on the Worcestershire landscape. *Transactions Worcestershire Archaeological Society*, 3rd series 21, 91–106.

Hooke, D. (2010) The nature and distribution of early medieval woodland and wood-pasture habitats, in H. Lewis and S. Semple (eds) *Perspectives in Landscape Archaeology*, 55–65. Oxford: British Archaeological Reports, International Series 2103.

Jessup, M. (1975) *A History of Oxfordshire.* Chichester: Phillimore.

Jones, R. and Page, M. (2006) *Medieval Villages in an English Landscape, Beginnings and Ends.* Oxford: Windgather Press.

Kelly, S. E. (ed.) (2001) *Charters of Abingdon Abbey, Part 2.* Oxford: British Academy and Oxford University Press.

Kirby, K. J. (2004) A model for a natural wooded landscape in Britain driven by large herbivore activity. *Forestry* 77, 405–20.

Laycock, S. (2008) Britannia: a failed state? *Current Archaeology* 219 , 18–25.

Page, W. (ed.) (1907) *The Victoria History of the County of Oxford, Vol. II.* Oxford: Institute of Historical Research and Oxford University Press.

Rackham, O. (1998) Savanna in Europe, in K. Kirby and C. Watkins (eds) *The Ecological History of European Forests*, Wallingford: CABI.

Sawyer, P. H. (ed.) (1968) *Anglo-Saxon Charters: an Annotated List and Bibliography.* London: Royal Historical Society.

Schumer, B. (1984) *The Evolution of Wychwood to 1400: Pioneers, Frontiers and Forests.* Leicester: Leicester University Press.

Swanton, M. (ed. and trans.) (1975) *Anglo-Saxon Prose.* London: Dent.

Swanton, M. (ed. and trans.) (1996) *Anglo-Saxon Chronicle.* London: Dent.

Thorpe, B. (ed.) (1846) *Ælfric, Colloquium ad Pueros Lingua Latinae Locutione Exercendis an Ælfrico Compilatum, Analecta Anglo-Saxonica.* London, 18–36.

Vera, F. W. M. (2000) *Grazing Ecology and Forest History.* Wallingford: CABI.

Wager, S. J. (1998) *Woods, Wolds and Groves: the Woodland of Medieval Warwickshire.* Oxford: British Archaeological Reports.

Walker, M. F. and Taylor, J. A. (1976) Post-Neolithic vegetation changes in the western Rhinogau, Gwynedd, northwest Wales. *Transactions of the Institute of British Geographers* (new series) 1, 323–45.

Williamson, T, (2008) *Sutton Hoo and its Landscape. The Context of Monuments.* Oxford: Windgather Press.

Young, A. (1813) *General View of the Agriculture of Oxfordshire.* London: Board of Agriculture.

CHAPTER FIVE

Brent's Waterways, Walls and Works, *c.* Twelfth–Fourteenth Centuries

Jem Harrison

The southbound traveller emerging from the Mendips between Loxton and Crook Peak cannot fail to notice Brent Knoll. This hill of volcanic appearance, 137 metres high, rises above the Somerset Levels that lie just six metres above Ordnance Datum (Fig. 5.1). On a grim day, viewed from a distance, it is easy to imagine Brent Knoll being surrounded by a giant marsh. Yet in the Domesday Book, Brent was among the most valuable of Glastonbury Abbey's estates, and in the Lay Subsidies of 1327 and 1334, the tax yield of its component manors of East Brent, Lympsham, Berrow and South Brent was among the highest in Somerset (Thorn 1980, 8–33, 34; Dickinson 1889, 249–51; Glasscock 1975, 264; Harrison 1997, 66–88, 361–7). A clue to the medieval value of such an unprepossessing landscape can be observed from the summit of Brent Knoll after heavy rainfall, when the most striking aspect is hundreds of ditches brimful of water. If this landscape was to have a utility superior to marshland in the past, then management of the water was vital.

FIGURE 5.1. The landscape of Brent. Photo courtesy of Nick Corcos

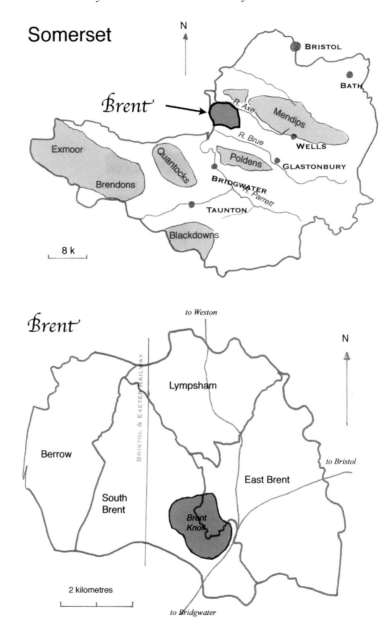

FIGURE 5.2. Maps showing the location of Brent within Somerset, and the four component manors of Brent

Water is a defining feature of Brent in its charter dated AD 693 (Sawyer 1968, S.238), as the bounds are waterways: *terra autem hec sita est in monte et curcum montem qui dicitur Brent habens ab occidente Sabrinum, ab aquilonem Axam, ab oriente Ternuc, ab austro Siger* (Watkin 1952, 527). The Bristol Channel is evidently the western boundary. The River Axe is on the north, although Bell (1990, 82–3, 105) concluded that this river originally followed the course of Brean Cross Pill (A–B in Figure 5.3), marking the boundary between Brean and Berrow. Tarnock Stream represents the eastern boundary (C–D), flowing from Plash Rhyne (E–D) to join the River Axe (C–B). Our knowledge of the extinct

River Siger has been enhanced by the analysis and mapping by Brunning and Farr-Cox (2005, 11), based on the Environment Agency's Light Direction and Ranging (LIDAR) of the Somerset Moors and Levels, in which they revealed that the Siger had a number of tributaries, the northern one following the north-east/south-west course of Blind Pill Rhyne (P–O in Fig. 5.3) to join the main course of the Siger by White Cross (G).

Brent Marsh and inter-manorial responsibilities

The estate boundaries are generally followed by parish boundaries in Figure 5.3 which is based on the first edition of the 6-inch Ordnance Survey, except in the south-east corner where the bounds of the Ordnance Survey map vary

FIGURE 5.3. Ditches in Brent. In the shaded area boundaries are marked by hedgerows, fences and walls. The main course of the defunct River Siger is shown by a thicker line following the course of Brent Broad Rhyne, and its northern tributaries align with a number of existing ditches, especially Blind Pill Rhyne

from those shown by the South Brent Tithe Map of 1840, which reveals an intermingling of holdings belonging to East Brent, Allerton, Mark, Weare and Wedmore, stretching south into Vole (Fole) Moor (Fig. 5.5). In the absence of clear demarcation by rivers, boundaries tended to be zonal rather than linear (Squatriti 2002, 33–4), lending themselves to inter-commoning, a feature which is especially noticeable in Thurlemere, *alias* Mark Moor, the subject of parliamentary enclosure in 1770. Common rights to Thurlemere were restricted to landholdings in fourteen Brent Marsh parishes (Croot 1981, 6, 17). The conceptual extent of Brent Marsh is variable over time and in context. In Figure 5.6, Christopher Saxton's map of Somerset (1575) shows Brent Marsh to be south of Brent Knoll and stretching beyond the River Brue, and may indicate why Brent in the Charter of 693 is physically separate from the main block of Glastonbury properties. In Domesday Book, Brent is named *Brentmerse*, posing the question as to how much land or marsh in its south-east corner was included. The manor adjacent to Brent in that corner is Mark, but it is not mentioned in Domesday, although it probably formed part of Wedmore, held by the Bishop of Wells. An Inquest recorded in the Abbot Beere Survey of 1515 (BL Egerton Ms.3034) revealed that the Abbot of Glastonbury rendered annually 'five cheeses and three quarts of oats and two bushels' to the Dean of Wells so that the Abbot and all his men of the four villages had rights in common in Thurlemere, with all their animals, and that the Dean did not have the right to improve the aforesaid pasture without the agreement of the Abbot and the commoners. Other lords, such as Richard of Santa Barba who was living *c*.1300, had a similar arrangement, which had existed for years 'for which there is no customary memory', so the practice of inter-commoning on Thurlemere was centuries old. In the Soliaco Survey of 1189 (Jackson 1882, 64–8), the name *Brentmareis* is used only for South Brent, while East Brent, Lympsham and Berrow appear as separate components, lending weight to the concept of South Brent being the only one of the Brent manors physically adjacent to the moors. *Brentmareis* is not used for South Brent in later documents.

Two other medieval documents, one in the Great Chartulary (Watkin 1952, 544) and the other in Geoffrey of Fromond's survey *c*.1307 (BL Egerton Ms.3321), provide a list of lords and the respective watercourses for which they were responsible. The one in the Great Chartulary is undated, while the one in the Fromond survey is located just before the beginning of the South Brent survey, but in a different hand, indicative of an early fifteenth-century addition. Despite their different locations, the two documents are virtually identical. As many of the place-names in these documents are unrecognisable, it is difficult to trace the watercourses on a modern map. Included were two watercourses from Meare: *ab ore Mere usque in mare* and *ex alia parte ab all Blakewelleshende (Alleblakespilleshende* in Fromond*) usque in mare,* a probable reference to the site of Meare Pool and the routes of its two outlets to the sea. If two of the Brent Marsh watercourses did commence at Meare Pool, then this stretches the concept of Brent Marsh further east than Saxton's map indicates. However,

FIGURE 5.4. Brent Broad Rhyne on the left, Applewithy Rhyne on the right. ST 329506

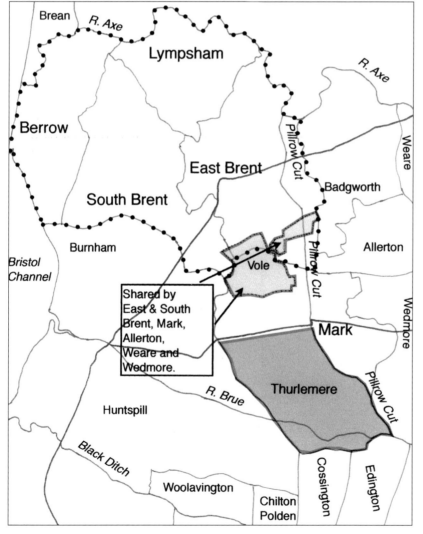

FIGURE 5.5. Map showing the mixing of landholdings in the south-east corner of Brent revealed by the Tithe Map of 1840, and Thurlemere according to the Enclosure Map of 1770

FIGURE 5.6. Part of Christopher Saxton's Map of Somerset (1575) © British Library Board (C.7.c.1.) showing the Pillrow Cut joining the Rivers Brue and Axe, and the location of Brent relative to Brent Marsh and the large lake at Meare

there is enough recognizable content to ascertain that the Lord of Badgworth's watercourse from *Blakelake* to the sea ran through, or adjacent to Badgworth in the north of Brent Marsh, while a watercourse from Burtle Pool via Chilton Polden, Edington, Cossington and Huntspill marked the southernmost of Brent Marsh's waterways, perhaps the modern Black Ditch being one remnant of that watercourse.

Despite the difficulty in tracing old watercourses across Brent Marsh on modern maps, there are features of the two documents that are quite revealing. The survival of the same register in two different contexts indicates the importance of the subject matter to the compilers of both the Great Chartulary and the Survey of Geoffrey of Fromond. They illustrate the political, economic and environmental significance of the waterways, not just to the Abbot of Glastonbury, but to all the ten lords listed therein, who shared a responsibility and interest in their maintenance, by means of scouring, embanking and bridging. As one of the lords, Ralph of Santa Barba, is recorded in the Soliaco Survey of 1189 (Jackson 1882, 2) as holding a substantial amount of land in Brent as part of his knight's fee, the arrangements among the lords must have been generally accepted at that time. Whether this responsibility dates from the time of Henry de Soliaco's abbacy, or was already in existence, we do not know. That it was copied at a later date reflects its continuing significance from the time it was first recorded, when Henry de Soliaco determined to strengthen his grip on the Abbey's assets; but because a written record of these arrangements has not survived from before that time, it would be unwise to assume that a similar arrangement was not already in place.

The extent of Brent Marsh and its availability for inter-commoning, with ten lords having responsibilities for watercourses, had a major impact on the local economy. The provision of this large area of common pasture enabled tenants to maintain larger numbers of livestock than if they were locked into the constraints of a strict open-field system with a significant dependency upon the grazing available from fallow fields. The absence of any mention of pasture for *Brentemerse* in Domesday, indicates that either the scribes were unaware of any possible value of Brent Marsh, as marsh or moor, or that it was too wet to render it of use, and that some concerted effort to improve existing watercourses and dig canals took place between the Conquest and 1189 to turn large tracts into rough pasture. Perhaps a more fundamental motive behind the maintenance of these watercourses was simply to speed the evacuation of surplus water and reduce the hazard of flooding, whether caused by heavy and prolonged rainfall, marine inundation, or a combination of high tides and heavy rain.

Ditching Work in Brent

Feeding those major watercourses, whether they were natural or canalised rivers, or long continuous rhynes, were hundreds of ditches in Brent alone. In Figure 5.3, ditches form all the field boundaries, except on Brent Knoll where fences, walls or hedgerows sufficed. Hedgerows also accompany the ditches on most of the boundaries on the alluvium. Ditches are essential in this landscape, both to drain and to provide a balanced water supply to facilitate growth of grass for good pasture. They form substantial boundaries that remain permanent until interested parties summon the motivation and labour involved in alteration; thus they become markers of agrarian units and put parameters upon the uses to which the field can be put. Running parallel, the spoil from the ditches can be used to create raised ways, or walls, providing the basis of roads and tracks which usually have ditches on either side. Ditches are not discrete, for they have to connect with other ditches so that surplus water can run off into the larger ditches or rhynes, and thence to rivers and the sea. Landholders on either side of a ditch should have a mutual interest in its efficiency, not just in voiding surplus water, but also in penning the water by the use of water-gates, or sluices, to maintain a required water level. The possibility of disputes, perhaps over selfish penning, or lack of maintenance, required recognition of communal responsibility and its oversight, arbitration and enforcement in local courts.

Manorial court rolls contain numerous examples of presentations for failure to scour ditches, such as that of Andrew Springhoese whose shortcomings in 1311 had led to the obstruction of the watercourse at *Paperscrofte* and *Edyngwie* (Longleat Ms.10767 m.21v), but it is manorial account rolls that reveal more about the amount of work that could be done year by year. The table in Figure 5.7 shows watercourses scoured, as revealed in three account rolls, and a comparison of the length of perches with the dayworks allocated gives a relative impression of the amount of work involved in each watercourse. Most medieval place-names cannot be found on modern maps, but by plotting

Watercourses scoured 1312–16

Date	Perches	Watercourse	Dayworks
1312–13	76	C[urs]us de Saltebrodemere	76
	29	C[urs]us apud Lytelcrofte	29
	66	Curs[um] de Henacre us[que]thetam ad sclug	40
	60	Curs[um] de Burmede	20
	34	Fossat[um] jux[t]a Bythenham	12
	54	Curs[um] juxt[a] Bolewall	18
	85	Curs[um] apud Netelworth	42
	224	Fossat[um] apud Natelonde	112
	154	Fossati[s] ap[u]d Gavelondesvilles	60
1314–15	11	In Pullenedich	11
	40	In Saltbrodemere	44
	20	Juxt[a] dom[us] Ad[a]m Slug	
	208	Int[ra] Lytelnywenh[a]m & Muchelemywenh[a]m, Warpool & Salt[er]hulle	215
	1	In Werh[a]masrewe	
	34	Curs[um] jux[ta] Bolewelle	
	30	Curs[um] int[ra] Wythenh[a]m & Albodesmede	
	170	In Ganellanndepulle	216
	130	In La Heypulle	
	70	atte Wewepull	
	80	Rowewor[th]espulle jux[ta] Cathulle	
1315–16	?	Curs[us] jux[ta] dom[us] Ad Slug, Killyngewurth, Estewhithenh[am], Henacre, Croftesbrigg, Thoendich	202
	?	Curs[us] Theta de Rokesmulle – Danyelesrine, Nywenh[a]mesrine – Pedredeh[a]m, curs[us] jux[ta] dom[us] William Batecock	395
	?	Curs[us] jux[ta] dom[us] Ade atte Wyk – Ganellondespull – Bozepull, Herepulle	232
	?	Cursu[s] de Welpesh[a]m – Werh[a]m – Salterehulle – Warepol – Nywenh[a]m – Bradewhurth, Winthenh[a]m	430

FIGURE 5.7. Table of water-courses scoured

significant field-names from the Tithe Map schedule in Figure 5.8, in which shorter field boundaries have been eliminated (following Williamson's method: 1984, 225–30), some watercourses may be located. The sixty-six perches scoured in the *cursus de Henacre* must have been either in Pitland Rhyne or in the long watercourse between Henacre and Summerleaze in South Brent. The sixty perches of the *cursus de Burmede* were either in the north-south ditches running through Burmede, or in the waterway bounding Burmede and Bearcroft on the

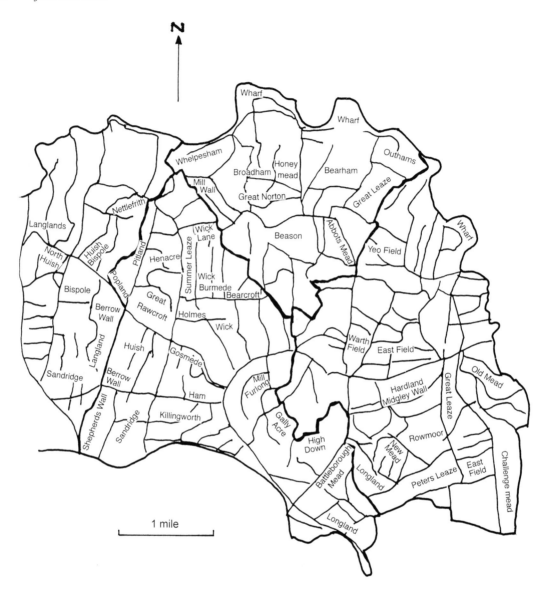

FIGURE 5.8. Longer
boundaries and
significant names from
the Tithe Map schedule

south. It is possible that the scribe used *cursus* and *fossatum* indiscriminately, but if not, perhaps *cursus* referred to the longer rhynes such as those in Figure 5.8, while *fossatum* was ditching in a particular area. The ditches shown in Figure 5.3, based on the Ordnance Survey map of 1888, were present at the time of the Tithe Survey. A detailed map of Berrow indicates that most of its boundaries in 1888 were there in 1773 (Somerset Record Office DD/CC 11467), so it seems likely that the ditches of the other three manors were also there at that time. As to how much further back in time most of those ditches existed, we can do little more than speculate. It is probable that many of the ditches in Figure 5.3 were there in medieval times, especially the longer ones and those with a natural sinuous course.

The most significant of the rhynes in Brent is the Mark Yeo *alias* the Pillrow Cut (Figure 5.3, S-R-T-U). In Saxton's map it is delineated as a river connecting the rivers Axe and Brue, but study of Ordnance Survey maps and observation on the ground clearly indicates the artificial nature of this watercourse. To follow its course on Google Earth, one cannot but be impressed by the scale of the civil engineering and labour involved in the construction of this canal, the strategic importance of which is reflected in surviving documents.

Whereas manorial court rolls can expose failures to keep watercourses open, and account rolls reveal some expenditure on maintenance, their chance and intermittent survival provides only an occasional glimpse of the work involved. Just as the Domesday survey enabled the king to register his assets and their potential, so did a number of Glastonbury's abbots initiate surveys of their fiefdom, partly to tighten control over their estates, but also to have a record of their resources in order that the requirements of the monastery could be met, its interests defended, and the demands of Rome and the Crown satisfied. The surveys of Henry de Soliaco *c.*1189, Michael de Amesbury *c.*1235, Roger de Ford *c.*1260 and Geoffrey de Fromond *c.*1307 set out the feudal services expected of every category of tenant, and these include work on ditching, scouring and walling, which for Brent tenants was both within and beyond the estate, emphasizing the importance of this work to all of the Glastonbury barony.

There are not many references to ditching in the Soliaco survey. Simon de Berga, a free tenant of Berrow, was expected to *adjuvit ad gulet* (help with the ditch). In South Brent, Richard de Wica, a ferdeller (customary tenant holding nominally ten acres), had custody of a *thetam* and one *gulet*. John de Greitona, a five-acreman, had responsibility for a *gulet*. The three-acremen of South Brent were required to scour the *Gulet Maris* (moor ditch). It is possible that others had ditching responsibilities under inclusive terms such as *servicia sicut alii* (the same service as others) (Jackson 1882, 65–9). Such minimal references to waterway maintenance may suggest that 1189 was before the Abbey took a pro-active interest in controlling the waterways of the Somerset Levels. However, it is important to understand that the Soliaco survey was compiled at a time when many manors had been farmed out and consideration was being given in the survey as to whether it would be better to bring them back under direct management. In these circumstances it is possible that the services recorded were those that were intrinsic to the manor. Thereafter, control becomes tighter and each survey is more detailed than its predecessor, so that in reference to waterways, this does not necessarily reflect more civil engineering activity so much as increasing attention to detail by Glastonbury scribes as part of the desire to maximize the potential of their estates.

Mordich and *Cursum Aque*

Work on the *Mordich* was a common service for most tenants in all four manors in 1235. By 1260 the service alternated with ditching in Thurlemere, except that South Brent tenants had to work once every three years in the *Mordich* and once every four years in Thurlemere. Between 1235 and 1307 the most work that was required of a tenant at each of these locations was one day a year, indicating that these services were connected with maintenance rather than building. If the *Gulet Maris* in the 1189 survey was the same waterway as the *Mordich*, then the fact that it was tenants of South Brent and Berrow involved in its maintenance would suggest that perhaps it was one or more of the rhynes between those two manors, such as Applewithy, Pitland or Wick Rhynes (H, I, J, K, L, M, N in Fig. 5.3). If, as Williams (1970, 69) suggests, the *Mordich* was the Mark Yeo/Pillrow Cut, then tenants in East Brent ought to have been included among those responsible for its maintenance.

The case for the *Mordich* being the Pillrow Cut is diminished by the reduction in its prominence by the time of the 1307 survey, when it is only the tenants of Lympsham, Berrow and just the five-acremen, three-acremen and twelve-acremen of South Brent who are obliged to scour the *Mordich*. There is another waterway, the *Cursum Aque*, which from 1235 was of greater significance than the *Mordich*, as half-virgaters (customary tenants holding nominally twenty-acres each) and ferdellers of East Brent were each required to dig 10 perches, five-acremen 5 perches and three-acremen 2½ perches, all of which would have required more work than the one-day requirement for the Mordich. This work was not required of South Brent, Lympsham or Berrow, and the specified amount of digging is not repeated in 1260, so perhaps this marked the actual construction of the Pillrow Cut in East Brent.

By 1307 all four manors were involved in scouring the *Cursum Aque*, lengths of which were described as from *Brockesdore* as far as *Rokesbrigg*, from *Rokesmulle* as far as *Lockesbrigg*, from *Brockesdore* as far as the house of Simon Bulion, a ferdeller and the messor (hayward) of East Brent. *Rokesbrigg* must be the medieval spelling of Rooksbridge, and it would seem likely that *Rokesmulle* would have been adjacent, thus the watercourse involved in this service has to be the Pillrow Cut. If the *Cursum Aque* was the Pillrow Cut, then where was the *Mordich*? The possible association with the *Gulet Maris* of 1189 and Applewithy, Pitland and Wick Rhynes is only logical if the labour attached to each manor was limited to its geographical bounds, but various services were required beyond Brent, whether for carrying as far as Ashbury in Berkshire, walling around the vineyards at Pilton and Meare, building in Glastonbury, or ditching and walling in Thurlemere. These forensic services provided flexible resources essential for the cohesion of the Glastonbury barony: concentrating labour resources when required on capital schemes or emergency repairs, maintaining lines of communication, enhancing the economy of the Abbey and providing a sense of common purpose.

Whereas surveys differentiated between Brent's four manors, manorial court and account rolls tended to deal with Brent as one unit. Brent is not confined by its boundaries, but is set in a landscape bordered by other estates with similar economic interests, and required to participate in the service of the wider Glastonbury barony. In setting down feudal services, the requirements

FIGURE 5.9. Pillrow Cut/
Mark Yeo looking south
from ST367522

from different manors, especially for work outside the bounds, would require balancing in the light of fairness, potency and practicality. So, could the *Mordich* be beyond Lympsham, Berrow and South Brent? There is a clue to its whereabouts in an amercement of 1348 in which Michael Wilecock and six others were charged with failing to scour 'the ditch at the *Morwall* next to Thurlemere as much as they should' (Longleat Ms.11179 m. 45r–v.). If 'the ditch at the *Morwall*' was the *Mordich*, then it appears that this ran alongside Thurlemere. As the Pillrow Cut and its adjacent wall form the eastern boundary of Thurlemere, and other waterways bounding Thurlemere are natural courses followed by parish boundaries, then perhaps the *Mordich* was the continuation of the Pillrow Cut alongside Thurlemere as far as the River Brue, whereas the designated lengths of the *Cursum Aque* to be scoured were on the same waterway, but within Brent.

Attempting to locate medieval features is fraught with difficulty. The use of generic terms, such as *gulet* and *cursum aque* raises the possibility that these were all references to the same waterway. The significance of the Pillrow Cut is evident from the scouring duties set out in the Fromond Survey, from Saxton's map, and also from the Amesbury Survey of *c.*1235 in which Robert Malerby of Sowy was responsible for providing a boat capable of carrying eight men and the Abbot to a number of manors, including Brent, and he also had custody of the waterway between Mark Bridge and Glastonbury (Elton 1891, 176–7), illustrating that this waterway is not just a drain, but a vital transport artery linking Glastonbury and the River Brue through Brent to the River Axe and the sea.

Sea-defence and *Thetas*

Work on sea defence was written into services expected from tenants of Berrow and Lympsham in 1307. Sand dunes provided direct protection from high tides on the coast, but protective banks had been built along the tidal stretches of the River Axe. In Berrow, even free tenants were required to maintain walls at *Bitwynewyk,* east of the *Wykschete* (the same service was for north of the *Wykesthete* in 1515) and *Schyprokeswalle*. Half–virgaters had to maintain seven perches of sea-wall and seventeen perches in *Schyprokeswalle*, ferdellers four perches of sea-wall and four perches of *Schyprokeswalle*, the smaller landholders being required to do proportionally less. The banks close by Wick Farms evident in Figure 5.10, lend weight to *Bitwynewyk* and *Wykeschete/Wykesthete* being located in that area. River embankments, or levees, may seem to be more appropriate descriptions of these banks today, but to the medieval scribe, terms such as *sustinebit cont[ra] mare* (maintain sea-defences) and *muro marino* (sea wall), indicate his awareness of the vulnerability to flooding caused by high tides along this tidal stretch of the river in close proximity to the Bristol Channel.

The same three account rolls that yielded information on the scouring of watercourses between 1312–16 provides similar information on walls, including 160 works for maintaining 80 perches of 'sea-wall' at *Nywelonde at Wyke*, suggestive of reclamation, while 240 works for maintenance of the 'sea-wall' between *Whelpesham* (see Fig. 5.8) and *Justinheye* also locates work on sea-defence in the areas adjacent to the River Axe, as highlighted in Figure 5.10. Winter Work on 215 perches of 'sea-wall' in Lympsham in 1314–15, followed by a further 602 perches the following year and 300 perches of 'sea-wall' in Berrow emphasizes the hazard from high tides. It may stretch our concept of sea defence to include Berrow Wall (see Fig. 5.10), as it seems to be the road formed from the spoil of its adjacent rhyne, between Middle Street and Berrow Lane, and forming a boundary between Berrow and South Brent. Walls such as Berrow Wall represent an awareness that the forces of nature can overpower human endeavour from time to time. Thus the wall also served a damage limitation function to pen floodwater, and as the tide receded, sluices could be opened so that the adjacent rhynes could evacuate water to Brent Broad Rhyne or the River Axe, and on to the sea. In the Fromond survey, when there was a major threat from the sea and the cry was raised, tenants of Lympsham and Berrow were expected to work from day to day until the danger was averted, suggesting that flooding following the breaching of 'sea-walls' was fresh in the local memory in 1307.

Incorporated into the obligations for sea-defence was the requirement to maintain *thetas*. The origin of *theta* and its variations of *thete, thetam, thetarum,* and in earlier documents, *þeta*, is elusive. As a letter of the Greek alphabet,

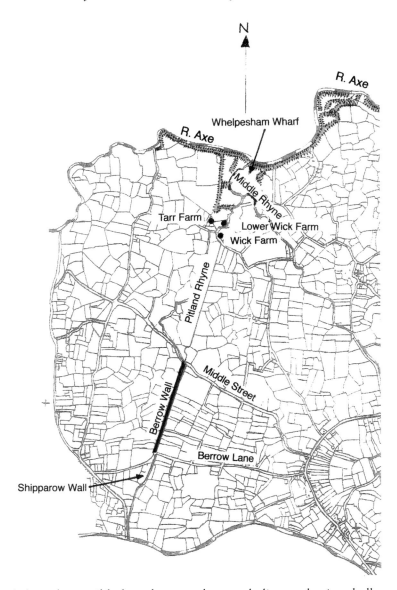

FIGURE 5.10. Sea defences

Theta (Θ) might possibly have been used to symbolize a valve in a hollowed-out tree trunk. This form of sluice, as a culvert in an embankment, was used in classical times (TeBrake 2000, 114). Occasional substitution of *exclusam* for *theta*, in the case of the *theta* associated with Henry Slugg in 1260 (BL. Add. Ms. 17450) and 1304 (Longleat Ms. 11215 mm.35–37), and the context in which references to *thetas* appear, suggest that the probable meaning is sluice, or watergate. *Thetas* appear in manorial accounts, the costs of their maintenance frequently justifying their own section for the 'upkeep of *thetas*' and occasionally 'upkeep of bridges and *thetas*'. All those fields bounded by ditches in Figure 5.3 would have required causeways or bridges, or just a few planks, to facilitate access. Repairs to bridges resulting in expenditure appearing in the accounts are suggestive of bridges more substantial than a few planks and thus formed crossings of larger rhynes. Fifteen place-names in the Brent documents have the final element *–brigg*, repairs to six of them being accounted for in 1314 alone: *Croftesbrigg, Bendenesbrigg, Hornesbrigg, Danielsbrigg, Comesbrigg* and *Vordesbrigg* (Longleat Ms. 10766 mm.29–32). While the location of these bridges is unknown, their existence and the recorded costs involved in their upkeep announces the presence of waterways and the importance of their crossings in the local economy.

Thetas enabled the level of water in the waterways to be controlled and also protected Brent from the sea. The *theta* that was the responsibility of Richard de Wica in 1189 was probably the same *theta* being repaired in 1300 next to the house of Edith atte Wyke (Longleat Ms.11272 m.41–4) and in 1311–15 next to the house of Richard atte Wyke (Longleat Mss.11216 m.12–5; 10656 m.19–24; 10766 m.29–32). Occupancy of a house by the same family can indicate the same *theta* being the subject of separate appearances in documents over time, but different names could mean either a change of occupancy, or a reference to a different *theta,* so precision in enumerating them is not possible, but there were at least five, perhaps as many as nine, mentioned in the Brent documents. Costs included iron for nails and hinges, boards for mending sluice gates, wages for carpenters and smiths, and in 1333–4 the allocation of twenty-one day-works for repairing and raising the sea wall *sup[er] duas thetas de Warpole et iux[t]a dom[u]m Henr[y] Spark* (by the two *thetas* of Warpole, and next to the house of Henry Spark) (Longleat Ms.10632 m.12).

The most frequent of documentary references to *thetas* in Brent apply to the one at *Rokesmulle*, a water-mill (Longleat Ms.11273 m.23). *Rokesmulle* was also a transhipment point. There are numerous references to the carriage of barrels of wine from Bristol to *Rokesmulle*, (Longleat Ms.11272 mm. 41–44 of 1300–1 is just one reference). This was probably Bordeaux wine imported into Bristol, where a portion of the cargo was transferred to a smaller vessel that sailed via the Bristol Channel and the River Axe to *Rokesmulle* where the casks were transferred to continue their journey by barge to Glastonbury. Other imports unloaded at *Rokesmulle* included salmon, herring, millstones and honey. In the opposite direction hundreds of poles and scores of hurdles were brought from Hartimore, Beckery and Meare for sea-defence work between 1312 and 1316, including work on 171½ perches of 'sea-wall' adjacent to *Rokesmulle c.*1312 (Longleat Ms.11216 m.12–15; 10656 m.19–24). Timber was brought in for repairs to the mill, *thetas* and bridges; on several occasions there are references to eight boatloads of timber; from Westhay in 1274–5 and Glastonbury in 1303–4 (Longleat Mss.11244 m.20–1; 11271 m.1–4).

Some understanding of the importance of a *theta* can be gained from the details recorded of the construction of the new stone *theta* and mill-dam at *Rokesmulle* in 1333–4. The old wooden *theta* had to be raised and foundations dug, cement made, a lodge measuring 20ft by 14ft erected for the mason, and stone quarried at South Brent, Shiplate, Bleadon, Badgworth and Allerton.

FIGURE 5.11. Rooksbridge.
Note the stone footings
to the structures on the
eastern bank

Reeds, faggots and poles were brought in to make a landing stage. The major carting operation was concentrated into four days, involving as many as 80 men with 40 wagons and 14 boats. Elms were brought in from *Palmeresmore* and Meare. A large boat was hired for five days to carry stone, and one cart was employed for five weeks carrying stone from Allerton. Twenty-four barrows were used for carrying stone, presumably on site. Forage and grass was required for eight oxen for twelve weeks and three horses for four weeks. Expenses were provided for the Cellarer, the Rector of Wrington and others who supervised the works; compensation was given to the men of Bleadon and Shiplate whose crops were damaged by the wagons carrying stone across their fields, and wages paid to 'the men who carried earth to the new wall, filling in the outside part of the new *theta*'. Some work was allocated as sixty day-works for six workers helping to make the sea-wall on both sides of the new *theta* for ten days. The reconstruction of the *theta* at *Rokesmulle* was clearly a civil-engineering project of some magnitude. Details of the maintenance of demesne buildings are commonplace in the account rolls, and sections on the upkeep of mills are particularly detailed, but nothing matches the drama evident behind the building of the new *theta* at *Rokesmulle*. The mill was out of action for fourteen weeks, the fishery of *Rokesmulle* relinquished for a year, foal production was down because most of the mares were working on the *theta*; even the Abbot came to see the new work (Longleat Ms. 10632 m.12).

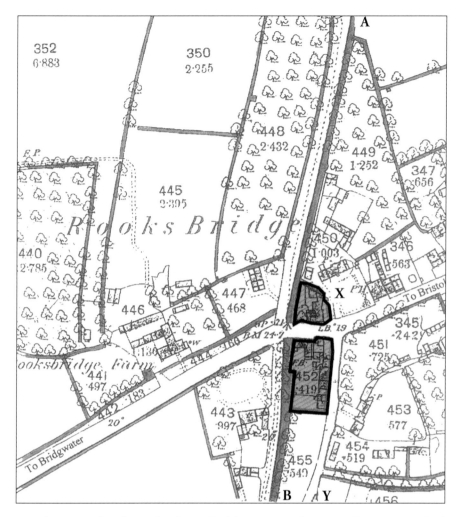

FIGURE 5.12. Shaded area on either side of the main road represents a possible site for *Rokesmulle* at Rooksbridge. The Pillrow Cut is shaded between points A and B. The route X–Y serves as a service road to the properties in the shaded area. Based on reproduction of part of the 1888 OS map

Where was the *theta* of *Rokesmulle*? The Fromond survey of 1307 prescribed lengths of watercourse to be scoured from *Brokesdore* to *Rokesbrigg*, and from *Rokesmulle* to *Lockesbrigg*, plus their equal weighting of dayworks, suggesting that *Rokesmulle* and *Rokesbrigg* were adjacent to each other, because it is unlikely that a length of watercourse between the two lengths would be left without a scouring service. A mill as important as *Rokesmulle* ought to enjoy good access, and the crossing of the Pillrow Cut (A–B in Fig. 5.12) by the main road from Bridgwater to Bristol at Rooksbridge would seem to fit that requirement. The stone footings on the eastern bank to the north of the bridge in Figure 5.11 and the function of the route X–Y in Figure 5.12 as a service road to properties abutting the Cut, would facilitate a commercial interchange between waterway and road at Rooksbridge. There is also a modern sluice gate south of the bridge. Yet the reference to maintaining 171½ perches of 'sea-wall' between *Rokesmulle, Saltelonde* and the house of Thomas Foghel (1311–12 Longleat Ms.11216 mm.12–15), and a reference to works spent on the 'sea-wall', *muro*

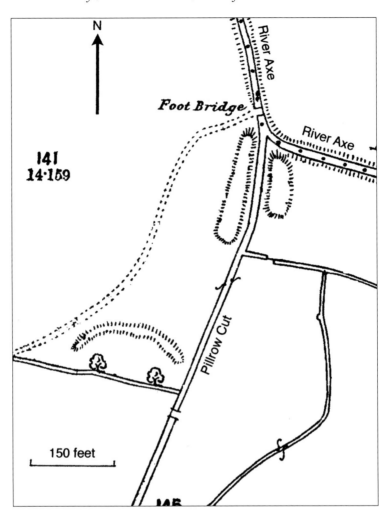

N

River Axe

Foot Bridge

River Axe

141
14·159

Pillrow Cut

150 feet

FIGURE 5.13. Another possible site for *Rokesmulle Theta*. Reproduction from part of the 1888 OS map

marino sup[er] theta lignea[m] (the sea wall by the wooden *theta*) and associated digging of foundations for the stone *theta* (1333–4 Longleat Ms. 10632 m.12) suggests a location closer to the sea.

The observation by the M5 Research Committee of two mounds marked on the first edition of the large scale Ordnance Survey maps, close to the confluence of the Pillrow Cut and the old River Axe, has the appearance of being an alternative location for the *theta* (Fig. 5.13). Fourteenth and fifteenth-century potsherd finds close by add to the intrigue, as do two pieces of dressed stone dredged up nearby from the Pillrow Cut (Somerset HER 10051). The curved feature marked in Figure 5.13 could possibly have formed a dam for a mill-pond and may have contained the stone *theta*. If the curved feature was the *Rokesmulle* mill-dam, perhaps the new stone *theta* was part of this feature. However, the reference to work on the *muro marino ut[ra]q[ue] p[ar]te* (sea wall on each side) of the new stone *theta* (Longleat Ms.10632 m.12), raises the possibility of the *theta* being situated between the two banks on either side of the Pillrow Cut at its confluence with the Old River Axe. Some weight is lent to this possibility by Stephen Rippon's reference to a 'stonework' constructed during the time of Abbot Sodbury (1322–34) at *Rokusmille* 'to shut out the sea waves' (Rippon 2007, 220). At this point the *theta* could maintain a desired level of water in the Pillrow Cut, offer protection from high tides, and enhance the value of the fishery between *Rokesmulle* and Mark Bridge which could be farmed for £1 6s 8d prior to 1347 (Longleat Ms. 11179 m.44). In Figure 5.14 some impression can be gained of the height above the water level that a masonry structure would reach to form a dam incorporating a sluice gate, while the contrast between the height of the mounds and the river banks at the confluence can be seen in Figure 5.15.

Limitations of sources

Archives associated with the Glastonbury Abbey estates contain scattered snippets about waterways and walls, especially concerning the necessity for their maintenance. The sort of detail included for the rebuilding of the *theta* at *Rokesmulle* is exceptional. From references to lengths of wall, the number of perches and dayworks allocated, we can infer that considerable effort was involved in raising the height of those defences. To what extent these were new walls or maintenance of existing walls is debateable. If there was already a wall in existence, accountants of a later time might classify such work as 'renewal', as the additions and replacements may obliterate the original work, but in essence it is still the same wall. Occasionally one can question if a waterway or wall mentioned in the document is the subject of new work, but the context in which it is set is generally indicative of maintenance.

Dating the construction of new walls and waterways from information in the Brent documents is not possible. The surveys set out continuing requirements from the tenants; therefore capital work would not be included, apart from references to building a wall when required. Surveys represent surges of interest in the Abbey's resources by administrators intent on improving the economic well-being of Glastonbury Abbey. Each survey contains more detail than previous ones and by 1307 the Fromond survey has each type of work costed, reflecting the trend among many tenants to commute their services. The detail of a specific ditching requirement in one survey that is absent from previous surveys, may be an indicator that the waterway had been constructed between the dates of the two surveys, but of itself this is not a reliable indicator. It may be that what had been deemed sufficient to be covered under unspecified winter-works, could, in the light of experience, and as a consequence of increasing proficiency, be set down in detail in later surveys, to remove any doubt as to the services owed.

Account rolls can provide specific information, but they are technical documents associated with a sophisticated method of accountancy, reflecting the degree of engagement in the direct management of the estate. This appears to have been at its height during the abbacy of Geoffrey of Fromond, from

FIGURE 5.14. High banks of Pillrow Cut/Mark Yeo at ST367535

FIGURE 5.15. Junction of Pillrow Cut/Mark Yeo with Old River Axe at ST367536

whose time the rolls of 1312–13, 1314–15 and 1315–16 are the closest we have to a continuous run. The lengths of waterway to be scoured and the work on the walls are detailed under *Opera Yemali* (winter works), but in the next roll, sixteen years later in 1331–2, the scribe has only entered the total number of winter-works performed. Prior to 1312, winter-works are not set down in the accounts. Our understanding of work on waterways and walls is hindered by the intermittent survival of documents and changing attitudes to the detail required.

References to waterways and walls occupy a very small part among the surviving Brent documents, the priorities of which were to assess the resources of the estate, to maintain its cohesion as a functioning social and economic unit, and to calculate, and keep a tight rein upon, profit and loss. That we gain some insight into waterways and walls may seem fortuitous considering how little information survives. Whether we see ditches on the ground, or in maps, they tend to be just part of a picture in which our gaze is concentrating on some other subject. Maps of Brent show that most ditches were there by the 1780s and had probably already been there for a long time. The survival of documentary sources from the twelfth to the fourteenth centuries has concentrated historians' attention on a period of time when monasteries such as Glastonbury held vast swathes of land. A working knowledge of hydraulic engineering was essential for the health of a monastic community, so it is not surprising that such knowledge should be applied to gaining access to rivers and improving their navigability (Aston 1993, 21, 60, 80–1, 91, 93 and 96). The ability and resources were there to construct canals such as the Pillrow Cut, to co-operate with greater and lesser lords for digging and maintenance, plus the tacit compliance of the tenantry who provided most of the labour, for their mutual benefit.

To confine our perception of the construction of so many waterways to the twelfth century onwards is to ignore what may have been achieved previously. Some knowledge of the remarkable achievements in water technology, especially concerning lifting devices and mills, ought to have survived from the classical world (Oleson 1984). Some relics of the Iron Age and Romano-British landscape must survive in Brent, if the hill-fort and the villa at Lakehouse Farm were sustained (Harrison 1997, 25–35). Neither could Glastonbury Abbey have remained isolated from the application of water technology across medieval Europe (Squatriti 2000 and contributors). Archaeological work by the Holinrakes (2007, 235–43) demonstrates the construction of a canal to serve Glastonbury Abbey and also diversions of the River Brue during the Anglo-Saxon era. Castles, cathedrals and monastic ruins are admirable medieval icons, but their construction was dependent to a large extent on wealth arising from agrarian produce and trade facilitated by the drainage and transport provided by the diggers and scourers of waterways. In terms of utility and longevity, the humble ditch is worthy of greater attention.

Acknowledgements

Thanks are due to a number of people who assisted in various ways, especially Nick Corcos, Sam Turner, Chris Webster, Richard Brunning, Ann Nix and Kate Harris, for providing encouragement, leads, photocopies and checking details in sources that were difficult for me to access. Local library staff in Basildon, Vange and Southend libraries were especially helpful in obtaining books and journal articles via inter-library loan. The British Library Board and H. M. Ordnance Survey granted permission to reproduce maps. Mike Thompson kindly read some of my drafts, prior to our enjoying a working lunch, a method I recommend to any writer.

None of this would have been possible had not Harold Fox supported my wish to pursue a medieval topic for my MA dissertation back in 1987. He had sown the seed with an aside about Brent that had resonated and provided me with a challenge. My studies were sustained by his interest as my supervisor for the MA and later for the part-time study towards the PhD. Supervision meetings were always worthwhile. The first twenty to thirty minutes were usually occupied by Harold putting the world of academe to rights, after which we would settle to sorting out my naïve attempts at transcribing and interpreting documents, causing him much hilarity. He would exercise patience with my unconventional ideas. There would be moments of quiet contemplation and analytical thought, resulting in cogent discussion and paths to pursue. Behind the scholastic eccentricities lay a warm, sympathetic and professional personality, with a determination to uphold the highest standards of historical research and writing. The world of History has been diminished by his passing.

Bibliography

Manuscript Sources

British Library: Egerton Mss.3034, 3321.
British Library: Add. Ms. 17450
Longleat Mss. 10767 m.21v., 11179 m.45r–v., 11216 m.12–15, 10656 m.19–24, 10766 m.29–32, 11215 m.35–7, 10632 m.12, 11273 m.23, 11272 m.41–4, 11214 m.20–1, 11271 m.1–4, 10761 m.22

Maps

Ordnance Survey (1888, surveyed 1884) Somerset 6 inches to 1 mile sheets XVII SW, XVI SE, XVI SW, XXVI NW, XXV NE, XXV NW, XXV SE, XXVI SW. Southampton.
Ordnance Survey (1965 rev.) 1 inch to 1 mile, sheet 165. Southampton.
Ordnance Survey (1980) 2½ inches to 1 mile, sheets ST24/34 and ST25/35, Southampton.
Parliamentary Enclosure Award Map (1784) Mark Moor *alias* Thurlemere, Q/RDe 115, Somerset County Record Office, Taunton.
Tithe Commutation Act 1836 (1840) Maps and Schedules: D/D/Rt/105, D/D/Rt/213, D/D/Rt/264, D/D/Rt/339, Somerset County Record Office, Taunton.
Map of Berrow (1773) DD/CC 11467, Somerset County Record Office, Taunton.

Published Sources

Aston, M. (1993) *Know the Landscape; Monasteries.* London: Batsford.
Bell, M. (1990) *Brean Down Excavations 1983–7.* London: English Heritage.
Brunning, R. and Farr-Cox, F. (2005) The River Siger rediscovered: Lidar survey and relict landscape on the Somerset Claylands. *Archaeology in the Severn Estuary* 16, 7–15.
Croot, P. E. C. (1981) *Aspects of Agrarian Society in Brent Marsh, Somerset, 1500–1700.* Unpublished PhD thesis, University of Leeds.

Dickinson, F. H. (ed.) (1889) '*Exchequer Lay Subsidies, 1327*', *Kirby's Quest for Somerset*. Taunton: Somerset Record Society 3.

Elton, C. (ed.) (1891) *Rentalia et Custumaria, Michaelis de Amesbury 1235–52 et Roger de Ford 1252–61*. Taunton: Somerset Record Society 5.

Glasscock, R. E. (ed.) (1975) *The Lay Subsidy of 1334*. London: British Academy.

Harrison, J. D. (1997) *The Composite Manor of Brent. A Study of a Large Wetland-edge Estate up to 1350*. Unpublished PhD thesis, University of Leicester.

Hollinrake, C. and Hollinrake, N. (2007) Glastonbury's Anglo-Saxon canal and Dunstan's Dyke, in J. Blair (ed.) *Waterways and Canal-Building in Medieval England*, 235–243. Oxford: Oxford University Press.

Jackson, J. E. (ed.) (1882) *Liber Henrici de Soliaco, Abbatis Glaston, an Inquisition of the Manors of Glastonbury Abbey, of the Year 1189*. London: Roxburghe Club.

Oleson, J. P. (1984) *Greek and Roman Mechanical Water-Lifting Devices: the History of a Technology*. Toronto: Springer.

Rippon, S. (2007) Waterways and water transport on reclaimed coastal marshlands: the Somerset Levels and beyond, in J. Blair (ed.) *Waterways and Canal-Building in Medieval England*, 207–227. Oxford: Oxford University Press.

Sawyer, P. H. (1968) *Anglo-Saxon Charters, an Annotated List and Bibliography*. London: Royal Historical Society.

Saxton, C. (1575) *Map of Somerset*, 1981 reprint. London: British Library Board.

Squatriti, P. (ed.) (2000) *Working with Water in Medieval Europe; Technology and Resource-Use*. Boston: Brill.

Squatriti, P. (2002) Digging ditches in medieval Europe. *Past and Present* 176, 11–65.

TeBrake, W. H. (2000) Hydraulic engineering in the Netherlands during the Middle Ages, in P. Squatriti (ed.) *Working with Water in Medieval Europe; Technology and Resource-Use*, 101–128. Boston: Brill.

Thorn, C. and Thorn, F. (1980) *Domesday Book, 8, Somerset*. Chichester: Phillimore.

Watkin, Dom A. (ed.) (1952) *The Great Chartulary of Glastonbury*. Taunton: Somerset Record Society, 63.

Williams, M. (1970) *The Draining of the Somerset Levels*. Cambridge: Cambridge University Press.

Williamson, T. (1984) The Roman countryside: settlement and agriculture in N. W. Essex. *Britannia* 15, 225–230.

CHAPTER SIX

Some Devon Farms
before the Norman Conquest

Rosamond Faith

Harold Fox combined an artist's appreciation of the landscape with an intense interest in the day-to-day workings of the farms within it. This small study follows him with some trepidation onto Dartmoor, his home territory both personally and professionally. The farms considered here lie along the east bank of the Walkham Valley between the area of Dartmoor known as Walkhampton Common and the east bank of the river Walkham, a tributary of the Tavy which it joins south of Tavistock (Fig. 6.1). They are all in the ancient, although not the modern, parish of Walkhampton. To the river name *Wealca* 'the rolling one', and *hæma*, dwellers, was added *tūn* to give Walkhampton its name, which first appears in the written record in 1086 (Gover *et al.* 1931–2, 243; Smith 1956, i.216–7). An alternative name for the river Walkham was the Stoure or Store, a form of the common river name Stour and an 'ancient' river name (Coates and Breeze 2000, 366). For people to have a name which associates them with a river and its territory is to assume, or to be given, a kind of cultural identity rooted in the environment. This was common in early Anglo-Saxon England where territories associated with rivers were found on both a large and a small scale. To rename a river in this way is a considerable cultural shift, and provides a good reason (although by no means the only one) for thinking that the 'Walkham people' considered themselves in some way a community, with rights or control over their territory. As well as a physical boundary, which had to be crossed by fords and clapper bridges, the river was an administrative one: it separated the parishes of Walkhampton and Sampford Spiney, and was probably the western boundary of the royal manor of Walkhampton. In 1086 Domesday Book records land there for four ploughteams, six *villani*, four bordars and two slaves with four teams (Thorn and Thorn 1985, 1.19) Walkhampton was probably granted to the Redvers family by Henry I. Together with the manors of Bickleigh and Buckland it became part of the original endowment of Buckland Abbey in 1278, following a grant by Isabella de Fortibus, Countess of Devon and a member of the Redvers family (Moore and Birkett 1890, 105–7). After the Dissolution this estate became Crown land. The various farms were leased separately under Elizabeth and these leases are recorded in a survey of 1585 when the estate went

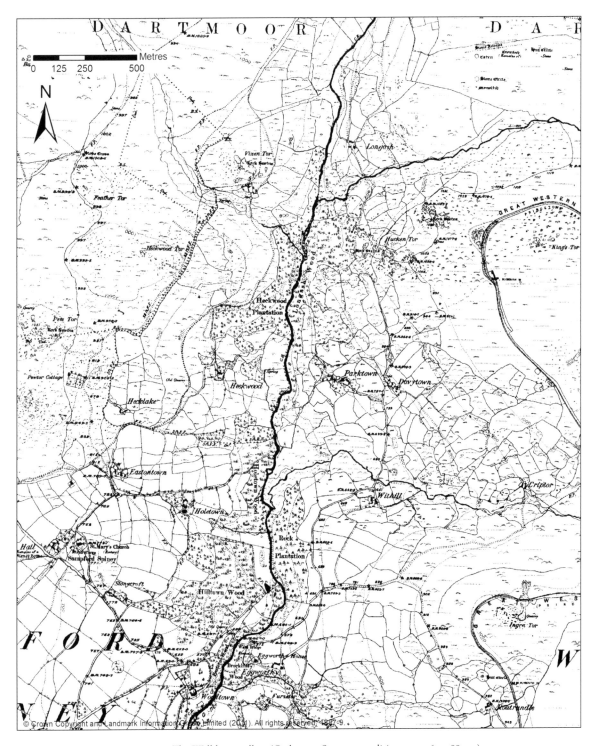

FIGURE 6.1. The Walkham valley. (Ordnance Survey 1st edition 1:10,560, 1887–9)

to a new owner. This survey of Walkhampton, which records details of these leases, and the map accompanying the Tithe Award for 1839 are the principal written sources of detail about the individual farms considered here (BL Add. Ms. 21605, 46r–50r; Tithe Award, Walkhampton). The broad similarity between the names and acreages of the farms given in the survey, and their boundaries in the Tithe Award map and at the present day give a strong impression that these boundaries marked farms with a solidly-established and long-lasting identity.

All these farms lie between the east bank of the Walkham and the moor and each has a long sinuous boundary on the moor, a massively built stone wall sometimes incorporating large boulders. These outer boundaries have been rebuilt over time and most are now 'cornditches', with a sloping bank on the farm side and a ditch on the outer side. The cornditches helped prevent deer escaping onto private land and made it easier to drive them out if they did so. During the period in which Dartmoor was royal forest, from perhaps the Conquest, possibly before, until it was deforested in 1204, it was compulsory to cornditch land which bordered the moor. Cornditches continued to be kept up and even today it is expected, although it is not compulsory, that farmers will fence their moor-edge land. The original farm and field boundaries were very likely turf banks, or low stone banks which became turfed over, and were either deliberately planted with a quickset hedge, or colonised by thorn and gorse. Boundaries of this type are visible at Hucken Tor Farm. It was deserted sometime between the mid-fourteenth and the sixteenth century, though the foundations of its buildings are still visible. Hucken Tor Farm's land was not cornditched, perhaps because the whole farm was taken over sometime after the mid-fourteenth century by a neighbouring farm and was incorporated within Long Ash's cornditch. The farm's original boundary may well have been laid out before Dartmoor became forest or in the twelfth or thirteenth century.

It is not just the walls of the valley farms which give an impression of antiquity, but also their names. Several contain Old English personal names or elements: 'Ecca's *worðig*' at Eggworthy, 'Wit(t)a's *halh*' at Withill, *crype* (a 'creep' through the vast rock) at Criptor, Long *ersc* (ploughland) at Long Ash, *holoc* (hollow) at Hucken Tor, and Rountrundle's *ruh tryndle*. Two have elements which could be either Old or Middle English: *crabba* at Crabbaland, *stoccen* at Stockingtown (these terms are discussed further below). There are farms with Old English names elsewhere round Dartmoor, many with the suffix *worðig* (pronounced 'worthy'). A brief tour round the edge of the moor will sketch them in and show that as well as sharing common features, they operated in very varied physical and economic environments. This will help in trying to understand the farm economy of the Walkham farms, to which we will return.

On the western side of the moor between the Walla Brook and the Tavy, *Wifel's worðig* at Willsworthy has a long curve in one section of its boundary on the moor edge at Peter Tavy Common. Between the Tavy and the Walkham *Wæbeorht's worðig* at Wapsworthy and *Goda's worðig* at Godsworthy similarly have a boundary which has a curving section quite distinct from its later rectangular intake (the farms in the Walkham Valley are considered in detail below). Between the upper waters of the Meavy and Walkhampton Common the farmsteads of *Leofa's worðig* at Lowery and Norsworthy have disappeared under Forestry Commission plantations, but their curving outer boundaries and field walls are still visible (Fig. 6.2). Between the Meavy and the Plym *Eadswith's worðig* at Essworthy is now under the waters of the Burrator Reservoir and there are *Beorhtwine's worðig* at Brisworthy, *Bella's worðig* at Belliver, *Cada's worðig* at Cadover, and a possible *Goda's worðig* or an equivalent name at Godameavy (Gover *et al.* 1931–2, 232, 235). All have sinuous outer boundaries.

All these farms were operating in quite a harsh environment, on the wettest, windiest and rockiest side of the moor. It is true that some were relatively sheltered and arable farming was viable enough to make it worthwhile to expand onto the moor as Godameavy and Willsworthy did. Those in the Meavy-Plym group with access to Wigford Down and *Eanna's dun* at Yennadon had good open grazing nearby, on land from which a hay crop could be taken. An eleventh-century charter mentions the 'hay-way of the Buckland people' which was leading to Yennadon and the lower slopes of Peek (OE *peac,* peak) Hill (S 963; Hooke 1994, 195–200). The lower slopes of the moor here are sheltered enough to have been used as a 'fore-down' where young stock were put out, and cows with new calves are there today. But to walk up onto the moor above any of the Walkham or Meavy farms is a steep climb to boulder-strewn hillsides where you catch the full force of the wind.

When we reach the south side of the moor we are in a much milder and more benign countryside: the moor itself is less rocky here, the climate softer, and the prospects for arable farming much more hopeful than in the Walkham Valley. Farms here have become embedded in field systems abutting the moor, which was much more suitable here for conversion to arable than on the western side. The south side of Harford parish, and of adjoining Ugborough parish, has a series of long, furlong-shaped fields whose junction with the moor is a fairly even 'moor hedge' (Moorhedge Farm is among these fields), not an individual farm boundary (Fig. 6.3). Harford Arrish (from OE *ersc,* 'ploughed land') may have originated as an arable intake, and between the Glaze Brook and the upper Dart, of which it is a tributary, *Bada's worðig* is embedded in a field system with long strip fields/furlongs through which a short lane or 'stroll' leads to the moor. The same seems to be true of *Binna's mor* at Binnamore.

This part of the moor provides the pasture which was most immediately available to the cattle driven up from the 'down country' of the South Hams: here one can see the relics of old drove roads, now so hemmed and hedged in by the fields which have been laid out alongside them that they have become deep hollow-ways. Only their occasional 'Gates' indicate the traditional entrances to the moor, through Harford Ash Farm and Harford Moor Gate onto Harford Moor, and by Leigh Lane through Wrangaton Moor Gate or Peek Moor Gate or Owley Moor Gate onto Butterdown Hill. By contrast with these long-distance

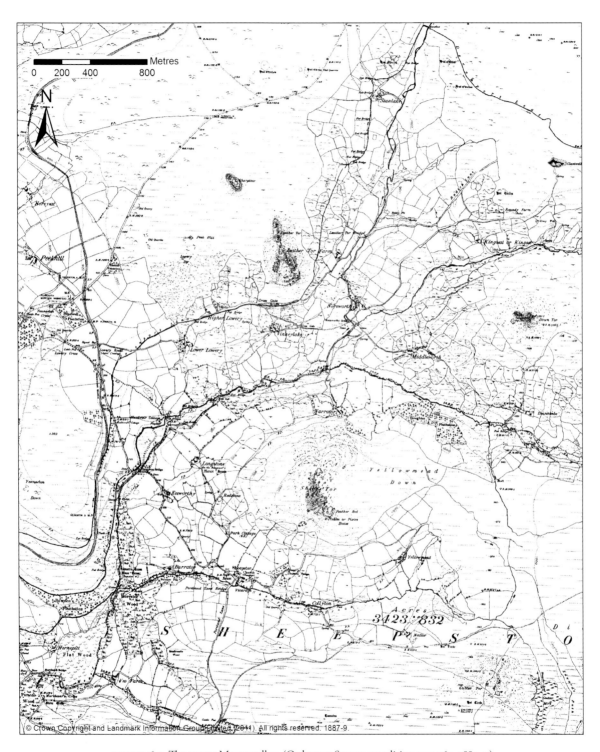

FIGURE 6.2. The upper Meavy valley. (Ordnance Survey 1st edition 1:10,560, 1887–9)

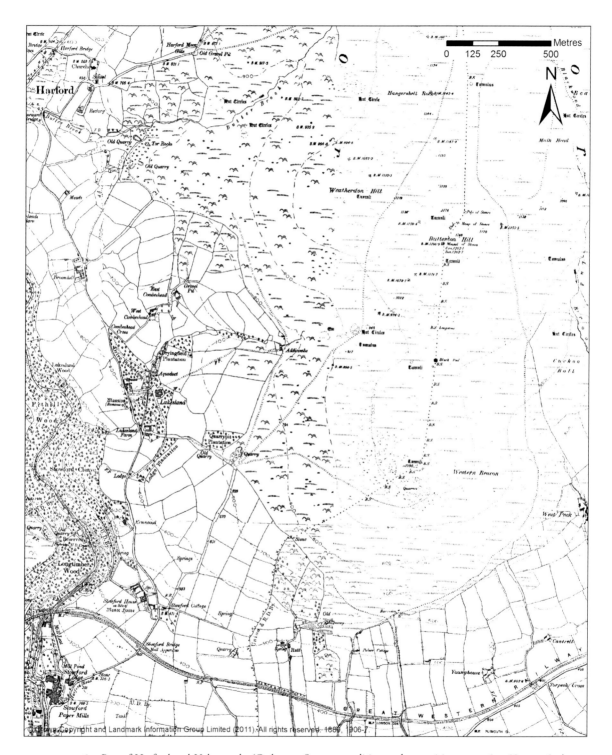

FIGURE 6.3. Part of Harford and Ugborough. (Ordnance Survey 1st edition and 1st revision, 1:10,560, 1889, 1906–7)

travellers the moor edge farm stock went to the moor by a stroll leading to the farm and the farm alone. Examples include one at Yadsworthy (*Eadda's worðig*) leading onto Stall Moor, the stroll at Broomhill Farms and those at Lukesland, Rutt Farm, Cheston and Higher Badworthy.

On the east side of the moor rather the same pattern emerges. Cattle and arable farming have both made a strong impact on the landscape and while a *worðig* on the edge of the eastern moor could well have been enclosed by a ring-fence, it evidently would have had a very different character from those on the west. Between the Avon and the Dart *Dudda's worðig* at Didworthy has no very convincing moorland boundary and this farm and *Dun's tor* at Downstow and the 'old cultivated land', *eald land* at Yalland are embedded in field systems. Buckfast and Holne parishes do not appear to have any *worðig* farms with a moorland boundary. A double enclosure on Holne Moor, thoroughly investigated by Andrew Fleming and Nicholas Ralph, had boundaries that enclosed two large 'lobes' of land within which arable strip-fields were laid out – very different from anything found on the western moor-edge (Fleming and Ralph 1988). Challaford's *cealf-loca*, 'calf-enclosure ford', and Challacombe's *cealfa dun*, 'calf-hill', show that we are now well into cattle country rather than sheep country. *Afan's worðig* at Ensworthy and *Bitela's worðig* at Bittleford (crossed by two long-distance routes), have no very obvious moor boundary, while *long worðig*, Langworthy, is a strikingly long enclosure but the date of its name is uncertain. Hexworthy is not recorded before the fourteenth century but this appears to be the same name that elsewhere derives from the OE personal name Heca (Gover *et al.* 1931–2, 439). *Hnott's worðig* at Natsworthy, *Bada's* at Batworthy, *Eada's* at (another) Yadsworthy and *Afan's* at Ensworthy are the last enclosed farms with Old English names until we come round again to the western side of the moor.

It seems that farms containing Old English personal names can be found around the edge of Dartmoor apart from the north-eastern, northern and north-western sides. Some but not all have a continuous curved boundary on the moor, and they are different in different areas. On the southern stretch, eastward from the river Erme, these farms are embedded in field systems which run right up over the moor edge. Here there was a more favourable climate and more land suitable for incorporation into arable field systems.

This was a very different environment from the Walkham Valley, where as we shall see the possibilities for arable were limited, and cereal crops played a very minor role in farming strategies. There is another difference too in their relationship with the moor. The southern and eastern farms were part of a much larger economy than that of the family farm. This was the world of long-distance transhumance systems so well described by Harold Fox. In spring and autumn the south and east sides of the moor provided the nearest access to the moor for 'down-country' flocks and herds on their way to the High Moor, driven up for summer pasture – the major theme of *Alluring Uplands* (Fox, forthcoming).

Walkham Valley Farms

Apart from Hillside, whose field boundaries all look comparatively modern, the farm highest up the Walkham Valley is *Long Ash* (Fig. 6.1). It is likely that the second word was originally *arrish* and derived from OE *ersc*, ploughed land. This survives in dialect form as *arrish* and *earsh* and as the common Devon place-name Ash or Aish. This term has slightly different connotations in different parts of the country and has been broadly interpreted as land which was difficult to work, but here it looks more likely to be an isolated patch of ploughland, distinctive because it was not contained within the farm boundary, as at Long Ash (Smith 1956 i.157–8; Gelling and Cole 2000, 267–9). It is probably represented in the 1585 survey, by a compiler unfamiliar with local terms and accents, as a thirty-acre farm called High Hestent (Hemery 1983, 1051). Long Ash's fields are bisected by the valley road which appears to run into a notch between two of its fields. Its land abuts the land of Hucken Tor farm and they were later combined. Long Ash does not apparently have the same direct access to the moor as the other farms and this may have been one of the advantages of the acquisition (it now has a large intake of moor called Long Ash Newtake). Its original assets were probably that it had much more potential arable, hence its name. Its boundary runs along a long stretch of gently open sloping land above the river, still cultivated today and very different from the steeper wooded slopes of the other farms.

Hucken Tor Farm. Holc(a), holoc is an OE term for hollow or cavity and may have rather the same connotations as the *halh* in Withill, a sheltered place in which case the tor would have taken its name from the farm. But any visitor to this dramatic assemblage of mighty boulders up the hill from the farm, four of which enclose a sheltered space, might wonder if it was the other way about. In the first half of the fourteenth century Agnes atte Holk and her son Richard atte Holken leased Hucken Tor Farm from the Buckland Abbey estate, but sometime after this, possibly between 1520 and 1585, the farmhouse was abandoned and its thirty acres were farmed from Long Ash, with which it is contiguous (Hemery 1983, 1051).

Daveytown took its name from a fourteenth-century tenant of a croft there. It does not appear under that name in the 1585 survey but is mentioned in a deed of 1576. Down Gate, north of the boundary wall might suggest an old stroll (TA 562; Gover *et al.* 1931–2, 245).

Adjoining Daveytown is *Crabbaland*, 'crab-apple land', of eight acres in the survey, ten in the Tithe Award, which is now a mix of wet wood-pasture and land extending up the gap between Davytown and Criptor. Richard Kitchin has found medieval pottery among the foundations of a deserted farmhouse here and it may well have been a small farm.

Criptor, twenty acres in the 1585 survey, thirty acres (excluding two small possible add-ons) in the Tithe Award, was in place by 1317. The present day farm, on an open bench on the hillside above a small stream, is overlooked by the deeply cleft Criptor, from OE *crype* a narrow passage like the 'creep' for sheep in many upland field walls (*pace* Gover *et al.* 1931–2, 244).

Withill and *Stockingtown*. Although 'white hill' is the favoured local etymology, Withill may, by analogy with Pithill in Cornwood parish, be a much older name, combining the personal name Wit(t)a with OE *halh* or *healh,* 'a sheltered place' or 'nook', and it is snugly tucked into a little valley. Although medieval pottery has been found near the present farmhouse, Withill does not appear under that name in the 1585 survey but was entered as Stockyn (information from Richard Kitchin). This was later Stockington, a deserted medieval settlement named from its *stocs* (stumps), indicating an area of managed woodland of some kind. Andrew Fleming suggests it originated as a kidney-shaped enclosure, still detectable, which was later expanded by acquiring enough of Withill's arable to make it into a viable farm. In the Tithe Award they were separate farms of fifty-three and fifty acres respectively and held by the same tenant. Withill within its old ring-fence measures twenty-nine acres but it also has land west of the road reaching down to the river. A short stroll connects it to the moor

Eggworthy, Heca's worðig, 'Hirkworthie' in the 1585 survey with no acreage given, is now the largest of the valley farms with seventy acres. Its land extends down to the Walkham and is crossed by the Ashburton-Tavistock road just below the farmstead at Ward Bridge. This was an important route which runs up to the moor between the fields of Eggworthy and Withill. At this point it was once a broad stroll, much wider than the present day roadway, which has broad verges. On the moor-edge but within Eggworthy's ring-fence was a little farm called *Babeland*, possibly OE Babba's land. This was a smallholding of four acres in 1585 (and thirteen in the Tithe Award), which could have originated as a dependency of Eggworthy. The foundations of its homestead and garden walls are still visible. Another outlier, Routrundle (twenty acres in 1585, fifty-one in the Tithe Award), was named from one of two circular prehistoric enclosures within the farm boundary, its OE *ruh tryndle* meaning 'rough circle'.

The land of Holewell, 'holy spring', runs down to a broad area of flat valley land enclosed by a bend of the Walkham, and is separated from Eggworthy by a dramatic fast-running stream fountaining down a steep rocky slope. Its farmstead sits on a long, sheltered bench on the west side of the valley road and the farm has a stretch of very substantial boundary bank where its land meets the road. On the other side of this road the fields of Wayton look late medieval, or perhaps early modern, so it seems that Holewell was originally on the edge of the moor like the other valley farms. This is confirmed by the name of the little farm tucked in between it and Eggworthy, Furzetor ('Fostor' in the 1585 survey). Furze or gorse is a moorland plant and the little gorse-covered tor now embedded in one of Furzetor's fields must once have been on the open moor.

Each farm is separated from its neighbour by a small stream running down heavily wooded, rocky little valleys. Although there may once also have been more woodland on the commons than there is now, these wooded valleys were an essential part of the farm economy. If livestock were wintered on the farm in the past they must have been fed on a wide range of rough fodder from the moor including holly, as well as hay and straw from cereal crops. Woodland may have been valued more as a source of fodder than of fuel, as turf and furze were so plentiful. Wood pasture was a vital supplement to hay, for which suitable land was limited. It provided leaf fodder, either cut for the stock or grazed by them on lower branches, bushes and undergrowth. The only named 'hay land', Filice (from OE *filið*), is down the valley where it opens out. The name Stockington denotes an area of managed woodland (*stoc*). Andrew Fleming has found signs of pollarding and coppicing in its now overgrown woods, although tinning became common in the area in the later Middle Ages and may have altered their character. Along the overgrown banks and the lower slopes of the Walkham it is not always easy nowadays to distinguish wet meadow – which cows relish – from wood pasture. This river land could have been divided between individual farms or it may have been common pasture.

The primary reason that the farms were established on the margin of the moor must surely have been that it provided an unlimited supply of pasture, where sheep, cattle and goats could be turned out free of cost. During the period of the royal forest the central or High Moor which comprised the forest area was defined by a boundary; it remained after deforestation in 1204 and was incorporated into parish and manorial boundaries, whose other lengths were the rivers which ran off the moor. The moorlands between this boundary and the private boundaries of the marginal farms became the commons of the township and the manor: Walkhampton parish and Common are bounded by the Forest, the Walkham and Narrator Brook. Before these administrative divisions of the landscape the 'Commons of Devon' were open to all, and there must have been a much less formal way of laying claim to moorland which gave *de facto* priority to the stock of the neighbouring farms. It is possible that it was not people who originally established these claims but animals, which are very unlikely to have recognised any formal invisible lines. Both sheep and cattle have strong territorial instincts, preferring to graze and shelter in accustomed places and passing this local geography on to their young. In other words they become, in the northern phrase, 'hefted to the fell'. The Dartmoor word for an established place where sheep habitually graze is a 'lair', from the OE *leger*, a 'lying-place'. The lairs above a particular group of farms could well have established an early *ad hoc* version of common rights.

Yet if this was a pastoral economy it was one on a household or domestic scale in which only a couple of cattle were needed for pulling the plough, a pony or two for transporting people and panniers, sheep for homespun, milk and cheese, and pigs and poultry for household needs. A major source of protein in the Anglo-Saxon diet was cheese and in Devon as elsewhere this is much more likely to have been made from sheep's rather than cows' milk (Banham 2004, 53–7; Finberg 1969, 138). Butter and cheese making need running water and coolth and, as Harold Fox's work on 'butter' place-names has shown, milking and making butter and cheese were often done on a sheltered part of the moor rather than in the farmyard. There is a local example at Peter Tavy, whose common adjoins Walkhampton's, on Smeardon Down. But on small farms like Hucken Tor Farm, where the water supply is close to the farmyard and probably very small flocks were kept, milking near to home seems more likely. If Anglo-Saxon housewives made clotted cream, which involved heating the milk, it seems more likely still (Fox 2008).[1] We have no livestock figures for the valley farms, but on two very similar farms in the Meavy area we know the largest had twenty sheep, nine cattle and ten pigs on the demesne, the other only seven sheep. (Thorn and Thorn 1985, 17.79–82; 29.9) As *Alluring Uplands* shows, the big stock owners using moorland grazing in the medieval period were off-moor landholders who had enough winter fodder, on stubbles and from straw and hay, to keep large numbers through the winter. This was true in late Anglo-Saxon Devon too. There were lords like the landowner Brictmer, whose vast landholdings included estates in the fertile South Hams as well as land in the Roborough area adjacent to Walkhampton. His manor at Buckland alone had 130 sheep, 20 cattle and 40 pigs (Faith 2004, 69–71; Thorn and Thorn 1985, 21.20). In our area the major droveway running between Eggworthy and Withill and leading to a 'funnel' onto the moor looks as if it served much larger and longer-distance stock movements than the valley farms would have given rise to.

If they had ample grazing on the moor and in the woodland, there was less pressure on farmers to use livestock as fertilisers of arable by turning them onto the fallow or close-folding them once the crop had been taken off, as was necessary in other parts of England. In post-Conquest Devon the traditional method of maintaining soil fertility was 'convertible husbandry', a system of long 'leys' in which part of the land was periodically left uncultivated to recover its fertility naturally and to grow a covering of nitrogen-fixing weeds which could then be ploughed in when the land was taken back into cultivation, giving a useful 'nitrogen boost'. In Sussex this was neatly termed 'taking the plough round the farm' (Fox 1991; Hatcher 1988; Adams 1976, 154). One form or another of sporadic cultivation, whether an outfield was combined with a permanently cultivated infield or whether all the land was cultivated at one time or another in what amounted to a long-term rotation, may have been widespread and remained so outside the areas that went over to common-field farming. In this part of Devon it would have had many advantages: it was suitable for areas where land was both plentiful and hard to work, and where relatively little improvement in yields could be expected from a heavy investment in labour and manure. As long as the essential minimum of cereals was produced, arable was probably not of prime importance. The three acres that C. C. Dyer has shown supported a thirteenth-century Gloucestershire family could easily have been provided from the thirty or so acres of the valley farms (Dyer 1989, 117–8, 134–5).

The system puzzled outsiders. Darby pointed to the frequency of Domesday

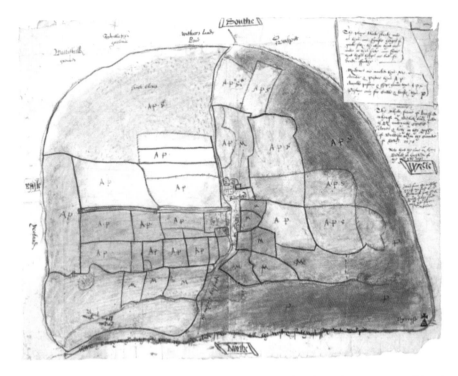

FIGURE 6.4. Kersford Farm, Bridestow, 1574. Devon Record Office 189M add 3/E4/4. Reproduced by kind permission of Mr J. B. Wollocombe

entries for Devon in which the number of ploughlands – the amount of land which *could* be ploughed – was greater than the number of ploughteams actually on the manor (Darby 1977, 98–9; Darby and Finn 1967, 98–9 and fig. 38). A plausible explanation is that the commissioners were accustomed to recording 'land for *x* teams' as representing a fixed arable area, part of which was always in cultivation. This is much the same mind-set as the Tithe Commissioners who firmly recorded all the valley fields as arable *or* pasture. A more realistic picture is given by a sixteenth-century map of Kersford Farm, Bridestow, in north-west Devon (Fig. 6.4). This distinguishes meadow and pasture as distinct categories but all the other fields are labelled 'arable and pasture' or 'arable and pasture and shepe grond'. Even the strip fields, which in many parts of England would suggest permanent arable, are labelled 'arable and pasture' (Ravenhill and Rowe 2000, 10–11). Before the Conquest Kersford had belonged to a thegn called Saewin Tuft and was considered to have arable enough for a single ploughteam. I think it is likely that Saewin's farm then had much the same size, layout and land-use as it had in the sixteenth century and was worked in much the same way (Thorn and Thorn 1985, 16.7 and note).

One very common form of convertible husbandry, perhaps the oldest of all, was infield-outfield cultivation. H. P. R. Finberg was able to trace a version of this in medieval Devon. The 'in-ground' of a farm was intensively cultivated, the 'middle ground' consisted of enclosed pasture, and the 'out-ground' was moor, furze or downland which was attached to a particular farm. Parts of the outfield were taken into periodic cultivation and this episodic cultivation was still practised into the seventeenth century (Finberg 1969, 32–4). An example from the Walkham area is Lynch Common where slight ridges are still visible which may have been where the arable of nearby *Leofa's tūn* at Lovaton was extended onto the moor.

The earliest of Finberg's examples is from the twelfth century but there are some indications that this was already the practice in pre-Conquest Devon. Recently pollen analysis has made the case for pre-Conquest convertible husbandry significantly stronger. A change in the pollen deposits in mires on four mid-Devon sites suggested to the author that convertible husbandry was a new introduction there, part of an agricultural regime that developed or was introduced in the eighth century (Fyfe 2006). Such an important change in farming technique need not necessarily prove the influx of new farmers, but it must indicate something. Its association with farms with pre-Conquest names, in areas very different from what little evidence can be gathered of Romano-British sites, must indicate something too. Three of the tested sites were on open (and wet) ground not now under cultivation, in the parish of Rackenford, west of Tiverton on the Culm Measures. Several of the farms with access to this open ground or to small patches of moorland nearby have names very similar to the Dartmoor-edge farms in that they contain an Old English personal name or term: Rackenford, Brownsford (which may have originally contained the element *worðig*), Canworthy, Bulworthy (which certainly did), Mogford, Tidderson and Bickham. However, there were differences. These farms do not seem to have had the long continuous boundaries of the western Dartmoor-edge farms and the Culm Measures were much more suitable for arable. The mires were outside the farm boundaries, so what the pollen records show may well be episodes of the kind Finberg described – taking a piece of open moor into cultivation. If these were contemporary with the moor-edge farms described earlier, they seem to have been farmed with an eye to expanding the arable. The possibilities for this in the Walkham Valley were very much more constrained and their continuous boundary walls do not appear to have many openings onto the moor through which a ploughteam could pass, apart from the funnelled droves from the farm. If Walkham farmers before the Conquest were practising convertible husbandry, it was more likely to have been within the farm boundary. If so, how were they organising it?

Within the outer boundary on the moor the farmland is internally divided into smallish fields – some have been thrown together – by stone walls, some of which are so substantial as to suggest that they could well have been an integral part of the farm and its management system from the start. The field would have been used at one time for stock, at another for arable, and at other times left uncultivated. This certainly appears to be the case at Hucken Tor Farm where the internal walls are low banks of much the same character as the ring-fence. This would have led the surveyor of Kersford Farm, Bridestow, if he had visited before the Conquest, to label them as 'arrable and pasture and shepe grond'. Most are pasture nowadays and grow much better grass than is found on the moor. In his evidence in a tithe case heard in 1611 the vicar of Walkhampton noted that his parishioners put their sheep 'as well in their ingrounds as also in the said [Walkhampton] commons' (Moore and Birkett 1890, 51). Nearest the farmstead were probably small enclosures kept for young animals, or those milked on the farm. But cultivation could also have been extended more gradually, with areas being cleared of stones and walled (perhaps part of the same process). At Cadworthy on the Meavy all the fields are grazed nowadays but those nearest the farm are more cleared, those further off less so and they tail away, growing increasingly overgrown, into the outer boundary in dense woodland on cliffs. Possibly the further, higher or more stony land was always grazed. This is the case at Kersford Farm, where the 'Pasture only for cattle and beasts' lies on the perimeter.

Conclusion

Trying to reconstruct ancient farming systems is a foolhardy business, but we can get some indication of what people's priorities were. Some, like water and fuel are obvious and universal. Perhaps most important was a sheltered spot for the farmstead and its outbuildings. A boundary was needed to divide the farm both from neighbours and from the moor, to mark ownership as so many names of the 'Ecga's *worðig*' kind emphasise, and to keep livestock in its proper place. Within that boundary enough reasonably fertile land was needed to make possible a very 'extensive' husbandry system that saw no need to extract the maximum from the soil in cereal crops, leaving nature to replenish it. But most important of all was access to open pasture.

Neighbours were important too. We should not visit or envisage any kind of farm at any period, however isolated, without being aware of the invisible networks in which it was enmeshed. The great boundary walls speak of communal effort. So does the management of the moor: this literally goes with the territory. Theft of livestock was a preoccupation of the late Anglo-Saxon law codes but we hear of it in the tenth century because the means of dealing with it through local authorities, notably the hundred, had become formalised, not because the problem was a new one. A long period of rough justice in which neighbours took the law into their own hands lay in the past (and no doubt continued). The 'drifts' in which ponies are today driven off the moor to be sorted and claimed, some helter-skelter down the Walkham Valley road, are a dramatic continuing expression of a longstanding need to control and check the use of a common resource. Such drifts are old enough to have given an Old English name to the 'gate' through which the ponies are still driven off Walkhampton Common, Horseyeatt.

The Dartmoor moor-edge farms were only 'marginal' in the most obvious sense. They are still there today. As Harold Fox emphasised, they do not represent a 'journey to the margin' but were small enterprises successfully adapted to their environment (Fox, forthcoming). To early medieval farmers, who had not had the pleasure of reading 'The Hound of the Baskervilles', the moor was not a place of 'otherness' and terror, but a highly valued resource, where it was proudly claimed that 'all the men of Devon' had rights of common. To the moor-edge farmers it was the moor that made self-sufficiency and independence possible.

Acknowledgements

I am grateful to Andrew Fleming for his guidance on the archaeology of the region, during our continuing work together on the Walkham Valley farms, for the provision of information from the Walkhampton Tithe Award, and for his observations on Holwell; to Sam Turner who kindly pointed out to me the medieval fields within the boundary at Godameavy; to Peter Herring for elucidating the Bridestow map for me; and to Pam and Richard Kitchin who have been enormously helpful in explaining the nature of the drift to me.

Abbreviations

BL	British Library
ME	Middle English
OE	Old English
S	Sawyer, P. (1968) *Anglo-Saxon Charters: an Annotated List and Bibliography*, London: Royal Historical Society.
TA	Tithe Award, Walkhampton, Devon Record Office, Exeter.

Bibliography

Adams, I. H. (1976) *Agrarian Landscape Terms: a Glossary for Historical Geography*. Institute of British Geographers Special Publication 9, London.

Banham, D. (2004) *Food and Drink in Anglo-Saxon England*. Stroud: Tempus.

Coates, R. and Breeze, A. (2000) *Celtic Voices, English Places: Studies of the Celtic Impact on Place-names in England*. Stamford: Shaun Tyas.

Darby, H. C. (1977) *Domesday England*. Cambridge: Cambridge University Press.

Darby, H. C. and Finn, R. W. (1967) *The Domesday Geography of South-west England*. Cambridge: Cambridge University Press.

Dyer, C. C. (1989) *Standards of Living in the Later Middle Ages: Social Change in England c.1200–1520*. Cambridge: Cambridge University Press.

Faith, R. (2004) Cola's *tun*: rural social structure in late Anglo-Saxon Devon, in R. Evans (ed.) *Lordship and Learning: Studies in Memory of Trevor Aston*, 63–78. Woodbridge: Boydell.

Finberg, H. P. R. (1969) *Tavistock Abbey: a Study in the Social and Economic History of Devon*. Newton Abbot: David and Charles.

Fleming, A. and Ralph, N. (1988) Medieval settlement and land use on Holne Moor, Dartmoor: the landscape evidence. *Medieval Archaeology* 25, 101–37.

Fox, H. S. A. (1991) Farming practice and techniques: Devon and Cornwall, in E. Miller (ed.) *The Agrarian History of England and Wales* iii. 1348–1550, 303–23. Cambridge: Cambridge University Press.

Fox, H. S. A. (2008) Butter place-names and transhumance, in O. J. Padel and D. N. Parsons (eds) *A Commodity of Good Names: Essays in Honour of Margaret Gelling*, 352–64. Donington: Shaun Tyas.

Fox, H. S. A. (forthcoming). *Alluring Uplands: Transhumance and Pastoral Management on Dartmoor, 950–1550*. Exeter: University of Exeter Press.

Fyfe, R. (2006) Paleoenvironmental perspectives on medieval landscape development, in S. Turner (ed.) *Medieval Devon and Cornwall: Shaping an Ancient Countryside*, 10–23. Oxford: Windgather.

Gelling, M. and Cole, A. (2000) *The Landscape of Place-Names*. Stamford: Shaun Tyas.

Gover, J. E. B, Mawer, A., and Stenton, F. M. (1931–2) *The Place-Names of Devon*. Cambridge: Cambridge University Press.

Hatcher, J. (1988) Farming techniques: south-western England, in H. E. Hallam (ed.) *The Agrarian History of England and Wales* ii 1042–1350, 383–98. Cambridge: Cambridge University Press.

Hemery, E. (1983) *High Dartmoor: Land and People*. London: Hale.

Hooke, D. (1994) *Pre-Conquest Charter Bounds of Devon and Cornwall*. Woodbridge: Boydell.

Moore, S. and Birkett, P. (1890) *A Short History of the Rights of Common*. Plymouth: Dartmoor Preservation Society.

Ravenhill, M. and Rowe, M. (2000) *Early Devon Maps*. Exeter: Friends of Devon's Archives.

Smith, A. H., 1956. *English Place-Name Elements*, 2 vols. Cambridge: Cambridge University Press.

Thorn, C. and Thorn, F. (1985) *Domesday Book: Devon*. Chichester: Phillimore.

Note

1. Finberg, something of a gourmet and whose wife was a cookery expert, has an eloquent description of this at Finberg 1969, 138.

CHAPTER SEVEN

Shadows of Ghosts: Early Medieval Transhumants in Cornwall

Peter Herring

Appreciating pasturing supports understanding of all aspects of prehistoric and medieval rural life in south-west Britain (see Fox 1972; 1981; 1996; Herring 2004; 2008). Transhumance and the more attenuated forms of summer grazing that succeeded it, probably from around AD 1000, were important elements of the mixed farming systems that exploited the varied land of Cornwall: rolling lowlands in which lay most home farms and fields, and the deep wooded valleys, numerous marshes and scattered blocks of upland and coastal rough ground.

Transhumance, the movement of people with their livestock to seasonal pastures, can be seen as a risk-reduction strategy that maximised grazing by exploiting seasonally available rough grass and herbage on the uplands, coast and wetlands, while removing livestock from open and unprotected home fields where crops and hay were being grown and saved (Ó Dhubhthaigh 1983–4, 49; Davies 1984–5, 77; Bil 1990, 45; Herring 1996a, 39; Fox 1996, 3; Ward 1997, 103–4). The Irish also maintained that the summer's 'change benefited the health and well-being of both the cattle and their guardians' (Ó Danachair 1983–4, 36; Kelly 1998, 43; and see Gaffney 1959, 21). For a period in which the farming community is particularly difficult to pin down, the exploration of an activity that took communities and individuals to the landscape's margins greatly enriches understanding of early medieval society. But owning and sharing, tending and caring, milking and shearing, knowing and fearing, living and moving among domesticated ungulates creates worlds and world views like no others, and it is these as much as the agrarian practice itself that this paper explores.

It interweaves six strands of material studied broadly sequentially: toponymy, archaeology, palaeoecology, landscape history, cultural geography and ethnography. The last may seem least relevant, but early modern Irish transhumance had close similarities with that of the seventh to twelfth centuries (Ó Danachair 1983–4, 40; Kelly 1998, 43–5).

Historians would have feeble confidence in identifying early medieval Cornish transhumance were it not for the strength and breadth of the place-name evidence. Cornish names suggest a practice established as early as the seventh century. *Hendre* and *havos*, pre-Norman compound words applied to the permanent and summer dwellings respectively, had their equivalents *hendre* and *hafod* in the fellow Brittonic Celtic language, Welsh. *Havos* contains *haf* 'summer' and *bos*, 'dwelling', and *hendre* has *hen* 'ancient' and *tre*, 'farming estate, homestead' (Padel 1985, 127; 129). Using 'ancient' for 'winter' or 'home' settlement in the *hendre* name is 'odd', but it is the commonality of these words and especially the shared unusual development of the meaning of *hendre*, which suggests that both Cornish and Welsh used them to describe the main transhumance habitations by the later seventh century when the westward growth of Wessex separated the two countries (*ibid.*, 129). Evidence for such early dating is strengthened by two Cornish *havos* places, Hamatethy (St Breward) and Hammett (Quethiock), being recorded in Domesday Book (1086). These seasonal settlements had been permanently occupied and then become centres of large estates before 1066 (Padel 1985, 127). A Welsh *hendre* near Mold in Flintshire, Hendrebifau, was also recorded in Domesday Book (Beamont 1863, 73; Davies 1977, 50–51).

To contextualise the Cornish *hendre* places, we should note that there are in the region of 1300 surviving places whose names contain, like it does, the early medieval element *tre*, 'farming estate' (Padel 1985, 223–232). From their spacing, typically half a kilometre apart where they lie in clusters (see Preston-Jones and Rose 1986, figs 4 and 5; Turner 2006a, figs. 19, 30, 34 and 38), it appears that these *tre* 'estates' contained around 50 hectares. They therefore probably supported small groups of households rather than single farmsteads; four or five if each household worked anything like the thirty acres (12 hectares) of a typical early modern Cornish mixed farm. Archaeological evidence also suggests that later first millennium households were grouped into hamlets, with fields open and worked in common (Herring 2006a, 71–3), close in concept and form to the ancient Irish townland (Glassie 1982, 19; Aalen 1997, 21; Herring 1999, 4). Hamlet and constituent households and individuals were probably relatively autonomous, despite being part of larger landholding units, broad equivalents of multiple estates, represented unevenly as manors in Domesday Book. If Welsh *hendre* compositions can guide interpretation, it is possible that there were kinship links among such a townland's households (Davies 1984–5, 76).

While individuals may have been more or less free than each other (and Domesday Book makes such differences visible, if not wholly understandable), there is little to suggest that the individuals living in hamlets like that excavated at Mawgan Porth (Bruce-Mitford 1997), with extensive provision for privately held property, were slaves owned and directed by members of higher levels of rural society (and see Fox 2006, xii–xiii). In the following discussion it is, however, assumed from current knowledge that those who practiced transhumance did so within the confines of broader proprietorial, customary and cultural structures. Indeed, close examination of lives lived in both *hendre* and *havos* provides powerful independent evidence for both freedom and the various legal, social or customary constraints upon it (Pearce 2004, 210).

Understanding of Cornish transhumance can be extended by plotting

FIGURE 7.1. Locations of places whose Cornish names indicate the practice of transhumance plotted on a simplified historic landscape characterisation of Cornwall. Early medieval summer grazings were in the two darker toned landscape types, rough ground and recently enclosed land (improved and hedged in the post-medieval period). Here transhumants established seasonal homes: *havos* ('summer dwelling') and *kyniaf-vod* ('autumn-dwelling'), the latter at the edges of commons. Permanent homes in anciently enclosed land included those named *hendre* ('ancient farming estate') and *gwavos* ('winter dwelling'). Later medieval settlements named *lety* ('milk house'), edging west Cornish anciently enclosed land, appear to represent revised pastoral arrangements. The nine unusually large and possibly prehistoric Cornish hundreds neatly subdivide Cornwall's rough ground (and each also has access to the coast and its resources). The four western hundreds meet at a single upland point, suggesting coordination by a larger political entity whose roles probably included overseeing access to extensive resources. The three northern and two south-eastern hundreds are also likely to have constituted similar political units. (Thanks to Bryn Tapper of Cornwall Council)

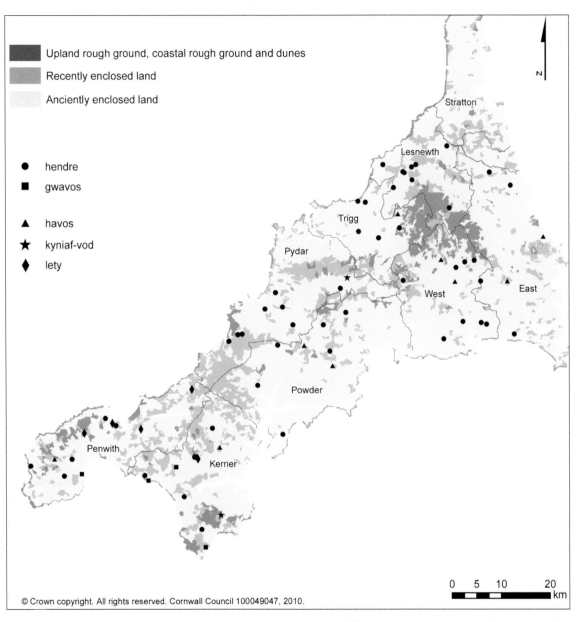

Upland rough ground, coastal rough ground and dunes

Recently enclosed land

Anciently enclosed land

● hendre

■ gwavos

▲ havos

★ kyniaf-vod

◆ lety

related place-names against a simplified historic landscape characterisation that emphasises anciently enclosed land (settled and farmed since at least the later medieval period and probably since later prehistory) and the probably even more ancient rough ground (Cornwall County Council 1996; Fig. 7.1). The nine known *havos* settlement names follow an upland-edge pattern similar to distributions of *hafod* names in Wales (Davies 1982, fig. 17). They are not confined to the larger uplands like Bodmin Moor, the Lizard, West Penwith and Carnmenellis. Smaller and lower downlands like those now enclosed in Ladock, St Ewe, Phillack, Liskeard and Quethiock (Herring 2004) were also used for transhumance. Hampt in Stoke Climsland suggests that lowland marshland was also resorted to, as were the Irish bogs and the Denbighshire marshes (Ó Danachair 1983–4, 36; Davies 1977, 58). We should also expect seasonal exploitation of coastal rough ground, including that on cliffs and dunes.

Two other early Cornish place-name elements might also be derived from transhumance. The four examples of *gwavos*, 'winter dwelling' (Padel 1985, 116) all edge west Cornwall's anciently enclosed land; three are on the coast. Habitations called *kyniaf-vod*, 'autumn-dwelling' (*ibid.*, 59) may have been used while exploiting intermediate pastures when returning from summer ones and could suggest that in some cases the distance between summer and winter homes was great. Two documented survivals are indeed in an intermediate zone: Bosneives on St Breock Downs' southern flanks and Kernewas on Goonhilly Downs' eastern side.

Hendre names, found throughout lowland Cornwall, range from being over 10 kilometres from extensive rough ground (in Gerrans, Pelynt, Morval and St Germans) to being, especially on the edges of Bodmin Moor and the Davidstow Moors, as close to rough grazings as some *havos* names. Many others are where they might be most expected, four or five kilometres from rough grazing (judging from transhuming distances elsewhere in Britain; Ó Danachair 1983–4, 36; Bil 1990, 50–57; Davies 1984–5, 82). The impression gained is that each early medieval townland in Cornwall's anciently enclosed land could be regarded as a *hendre*, as would be expected when recalling the importance of clearing livestock from summer fields.

Replacement of early place-names by Saxon and English ones in Devon (Padel 1999, 88) and counties further east possibly conceals the extent to which transhumance may have been part of life in other areas where communal agriculture and extensive rough land existed. Harold Fox examined similarly early transhumance in Devon (Fox forthcoming) and there is evidence in Dorset, the Weald, Warwickshire and the East Midlands, as well as the well-known practice in northern England (Taylor 1983, 186–7; Hooke 1989, 10; Fox 1989, 86–7; Winchester 2000).

Archaeological remains of scores of small sub-rectangular huts have been recorded on Bodmin Moor in the last thirty years. They are similar in scale and form to shielings, bothies, booleys and hafotai known elsewhere in upland Britain (*e.g.* Evans 1957; Miller 1967, 202; Ward 1997). Most form loose groups on open downs, the huts around 20m apart, 'within calling distance of one another' (Evans 1957, 38), and sometimes associated with a single small pen. Most are distant from tin streamworkings and therefore probably not associated with the Moor's other principal medieval use. Many are like their Donegal equivalents, 'crouching in the shelter of a lumpy rock outcrop' (Robinson 2007, 12). Some of the dozens on Brockabarrow Common are clearly defined by low banks of small stones, with entrance gaps on the downhill long sides (Fig. 7.2). They may originally have had stone-faced turf walls (as in North Lochtayside; Miller 1967, 208), the turf having gradually eroded away. Many others, however,

FIGURE 7.2. Aerial view of transhumance settlement on the east side of Brockabarrow Common, Blisland, Bodmin Moor. North is to the right and a Bronze Age platform cairn on the hill's summit is above and to the right of the small granite tor. Both would have been significant local presences for occupants of several small sub-rectangular transhumance huts scattered in two rough lines below them. Those huts appear to represent a coherent hamlet sharing the squarish pen towards the left hand (southern) end of the higher line. (Photograph by Emma Trevarthen. HES F96,100; © Cornwall Council)

are ephemeral, little more than ovoid scoops, and may have been built entirely of turf (compare Houndtor's apparently early medieval 'shielings'; Beresford 1979). None of these Bodmin Moor huts has been excavated, but their round-cornered rectangular shape is typical of early medieval Cornish buildings and where relative chronology is detectable, as on Roughtor and Brown Willy, they fall between the field and boundary patterns associated with prehistoric round houses and later medieval longhouses (Herring 1996, 37). Similar structures on Dartmoor have not yet been systematically recorded though some are plotted, like many of those on Bodmin Moor once were, as 'hut circles'.

The Bodmin Moor huts could not have housed whole families. Typically around 4m by 2m internally, they had room for a single-person bed, a small hearth (if any fire at all), a spinning wheel and some storage for cheeses, etc. (Herring 1996, 37–39; Johnson and Rose 1994, 80–83, fig. 53). While small and simple, the more recent summer huts elsewhere in Britain were well built, their occupants 'as untroubled inside these as if they were in a king's castle' (Ó Dubhthaigh 1983–4, 43), enjoying the 'healthiest bed anyone ever slept in' (Robinson 2007, 13). The size of hut groups suggests upland activities were labour-intensive; just one or two huts might be expected if transhumants simply watched over grazing animals. Instead it seems there was plenty of work for each household. Twice-daily gathering in of livestock, then milking, and butter and cheese making, and carding, spinning and knitting wool sheared on the summer grounds, probably accounted for the bulk of the time (Gelling 1962–63, 170; Ó Danachair 1983–4, 38; Herring 1996, 39; Robinson 2007, 14). Excavations of transhumance huts in northern Wales and England produced vessels and jugs (Astill and Grant 1992, 58).

Maintaining the open unwooded, largely grassy cover that apparently prevailed over most of Bodmin Moor's 20,000 hectares throughout later prehistoric and early medieval times (see Gearey *et al.* 1997; 2000), required at least 5000 cattle, or 50,000 sheep (Herring 2008, 81). Those stocking rates, based on modern prescriptions for encouraging scrubby growth, are likely to be low, and more realistic may be those allowed to the twelve eighteenth-century commoners of Twelve Men's Moor (for which see Spooner 1942, 53). If extended to all Bodmin Moor these would produce 92,880 sheep, 1857 horses and 1857 bullocks, or, if a milking cow were equivalent to a horse, a bullock or ten sheep, then 13,002 cows. Figures might have been even higher (say 15,000 cows) if account were taken of the native Cornish cattle and sheep's small 'mould' (Carew 1602, 106; Worgan 1811, 140). Later medieval longhouses and inventories may suggest household herds of between five and ten cattle (Herring 1986, vol. 2, 157), similar to those of early modern Irish households (Ó Danachair 1983–4, 38). If so, animals from up to 3000 households or around 750 townlands might have been required to maintain Bodmin Moor's open character. This would take in everyone living in the lowland parts of those estates that became the parishes which reach finger-like onto the Moor, plus at least another ring beyond this, taking the area using Bodmin Moor close to the south coast, similar to the pattern identified for Dartmoor by Harold Fox (forthcoming).

While such calculations should of course be treated with caution, they do suggest an order of magnitude of Cornish early medieval transhumance and the agricultural settlement of which it was part. Historic landscape characterisation indicates that around 120,000 hectares of rough ground (upland, coastal and marsh) existed in early medieval Cornwall (Fig. 7.1); using the Bodmin Moor formula, this suggests around 90,000 cows (or equivalents in sheep, goats, horses etc.) kept them relatively open: yielding around 18,000 households and 4500 townlands. That this figure is tenable is suggested by the 1300 Cornish settlements with *tre* names, 49 with *hendre* names, 130 with *ker* and 230 with *bod* elements, and many more with the numerous, less common, early medieval roots (Padel 1985). Settlement pattern reconstructions also show evenly spaced *tre*, hendre and other townlands throughout lowland Cornwall (Preston-Jones and Rose 1986).

Cornish transhumance's origins may be pursued back beyond the seventh century AD and into later prehistory. Small sub-circular huts, again housing just one or two people and again distant from tin streams, were tucked inside ruins of earlier structures on Bodmin Moor. One hut inside an older round house at Leskernick, produced a radiocarbon date of cal BC 1030–810 (Bender *et al.* 2007, 171), while another reusing a ring cairn at Stannon Down gave dates of 370–160 cal BC and 350–40 cal BC (Jones 2004–5, 36–40). There was also Iron Age and Romano-British reuse of earlier houses on Garrow Tor (Herring 1986, vol. 1, 92–97). Unlike the larger round houses before them, the later Bronze Age and Iron Age settlements were not associated with field systems; they were apparently the homes of pastoralists.

Even earlier, by the mid-second millennium BC, large open areas of rough grazing, undivided, treeless proto-commons apparently shared by several prehistoric communities, extended over much of central Bodmin Moor. Pastoralist settlements within them lack fields, but have small pens, and may be the summer dwellings of early transhumants whose principal, permanently occupied settlements were among more sheltered lowland and down-edge fields (Herring 2008, 82–4).

Abandonment of the south-western uplands around 1000 BC has recently been interpreted as a reorganisation of common pastures reflecting the continuing significance of summer grazing into later prehistory. Transhumance and commons, already central to the region's economy and society, became increasingly important as rising population levels placed pressure on grazing through the Iron Age, the Roman period and into the early medieval period (Herring 2008, 87–91). Prehistoric communities had established over a period of around two thousand years sustainable ways of organising a viable mixed farming system in which transhumance played a crucial role.

The early medieval transhumant hut groups on Bodmin Moor typically contain between two and a dozen huts, probably reflecting similar clustering of households in the *hendre* hamlets; the single pen, presumably for securing sick animals or for weaning (see Allen 1979, 55–6), was apparently shared by several huts (Herring 1996a, 37). In early modern Irish transhumance, 'the townland was the unit; the people of a townland had the right of pasture in common in a certain area' (Ó Danachair 1983–4, 36; see also Gaffney 1959, 23). Commentators on north-west European transhumance have noted connections between the movement of representatives of households grouped into hamlets and the communal organisation and working of open strip fields (Graham 1953–4, 75; McCourt 1953, 81; Uhlig 1961, 287; Davies 1984–5, 76); the need to remove livestock from unprotected fields would have been urgent. (See Ó Dhubhthaigh 1983–4, 49, for wintering livestock wandering around open fields searching for a bite). Cornwall's own strip fields may have early medieval origins (Herring 1999).

While hut-grouping, pen-sharing, and open-field agriculture suggest communalism and cooperation, the primacy of the individual household economy over that of the hamlet can also be detected in transhumance hut groups. Sharing fewer larger buildings would have been more cost-effective, more sociable, and possibly safer than maintaining for each household a single-person hut in which was stored the produce (cheese, butter, *etc.*) of owned animals. The wide spacing between huts also probably reflects private property, the land around each hut being privately used for overnight tethering, ready for morning milking, of those owned animals (see Ó Dubhthaigh 1983–84, 50).

Private space for storing privately held livestock and deadstock confirms separation between constituent households in late prehistoric and medieval Cornish hamlets. Each courtyard house in a west Cornish Romano-British hamlet had its own sub-circular rooms opening into a central private space, the courtyard (Christie 1993, 10–11), as did the rectilinear rooms of tenth-century houses at Mawgan Porth (Bruce-Mitford 1997). Later medieval longhouse farmsteads on Bodmin Moor were less rigid, but still had clusters of buildings and enclosures (yards, mowhays, gardens etc) closely set around each dwelling. The dynamics between the communal hamlet (in which cooperation and sharing kept rural society viable) and the basic economic and social unit, the semi-autonomous individual household, already evident in later prehistory, continued through the early medieval period. Their unravelling in the later medieval period brought great changes in favour of the individual (Herring 2006a, 73–75).

Transhumance and society

Hefting and herding probably kept animals close to particular slopes, 'quiet and peaceful all day' (Ó Dubhthaigh 1983–4, 43), to which households and hamlets can be expected to have become customarily attached. The lack of stock-proof boundaries dividing commons, however, meant that animals from many hamlets and estates could have intermingled. The organisation of access to extensive grazings probably included well-defined rules regarding rights and limits regarding numbers of animals turned out. Later medieval Cornish arrangements, possibly with prehistoric or early medieval roots, usually depended on the wintering capacity afforded by the home fields' grass and hay: only over-wintered animals could be summered on the commons (Herring 1986, 119; McCourt 1954–55, 375; Thomas 1975, 26).

On larger upland areas 'drifts', in which all grazing animals were rounded up and checked to prevent over-stocking and trespass, would have required administration and an authority higher than estates. Cornwall's unusually large and early hundreds, possibly later prehistoric and perhaps supporting groups from which armies could be mustered (Thomas 1964), neatly subdivide Cornwall's rough ground (Fig. 7.1). Three of the four hundreds between which Bodmin Moor was split contain large pounds into which trespassing livestock could have been driven: King Arthur's Hall in Trigg; Crowspound in West Wivelshire and Stowe's Pound in East Wivelshire (Herring 1986, vol. 1, 127–30).

As Bodmin Moor's hundreds were undivided, a still higher authority may have coordinated timings of drifts and dealt with trespass across hundredal boundaries. Names of the Cornish hundreds and the ways they are arranged, especially in relation to upland rough ground, suggest there might have been three small units, akin to kingdoms: Trigg, comprising the three north-eastern hundreds; Wivelshire (*i.e.* East and West Wivelshire together); and the four western hundreds which neatly divide the uplands west of Truro and meet at a single point, known in 1580 as Assa Govranckowe, from *keverang* 'hundred' (Padel 1985, 12, 56–7 and 244) (see Fig. 7.1). If Pydar hundred's name really is derived from *petuar-ija*, the 'fourth quarter' (Thomas 1964), then this may confirm that these four were a unity. Transhumance can thus either reveal or confirm at least five interdependent levels of early medieval Cornish rural society, with a sixth, equating with the 'community' of estate, parish and tithing visible in other contemporary historical and archaeological evidence, and whose study often dominates models of medieval society and economy. Transhumance therefore helps reassert the value of studying each of the other levels. It shows their potential for either stimulating or containing change, enriching our interpretative models by involving a wider range of active agents, each with concerns and motivations that are otherwise rarely made visible and thus rarely considered (Herring 1986, 130–31).

TABLE 7.1. Levels of society in early medieval Cornwall

Individual	in *havos* hut	
Household	in *hendre* farmstead	
Hamlet	transhumant group	
Community	*estate/parish*	? *kindred*
Hundred	drift and pound	
Kingdom	coordinator of drifts	

In more recent north-west European transhumance the household member accompanying animals to summer pastures was typically either a teenage girl or a young woman. Men, boys and older women stayed behind to work fields, harvest hay and crops, care for children and the sick, and maintain the homestead and its ways (Graham 1953–54, 74–75; Gaffney 1959, 30; Miller 1967, 196; Ó Danachair 1983–4, 38; Ó Dubhthaigh 1983–84, 42). In Norway, young women, *budeie*, moved off to the higher ground and islands with the household's animals (Dr Karen Syse, pers. comm.), barefooted 'with their many milk pails, suspended from yokes on their shoulders' (Hamsun 2007, 323). With similar imperatives, we may predict that it was also the young women who summered with cattle, sheep, goats, dogs and each other in prehistoric and early medieval Cornwall. Two artefacts found associated with light, probably seasonal use of north-western Bodmin Moor are an Iron Age decorated bead from Garrow (Herring 1986, fig. 20) and a post-Roman blue glass bead from Stannon Down (Jones 2004–5, 40).

Experiencing transhumance

Transhumance was not just an economic practice; it was also a way of being within an inherited rural world (Tilley 1994; Altenberg 2003). We may attempt to re-create the physical and emotional journeys made with livestock in early summer and early winter. Yearned-for distant hills, the young woman's summer home, were being approached; excitement mounted as remembered trees, rivers, settlements and monuments were passed. In early modern Ireland she was accompanied by the whole family, carrying the summer's equipment to the pastures, but they turned and left her at the end of that long tiring day. 'The women had nothing to carry up to the pastures, except that each woman took her spinning wheel behind on her shoulders, and they were as airy as if they were going to a wedding' (Ó Dhubhthaigh 1983–4, 45). 'The day of moving to the pasture was something of a holiday occasion' (Ó Danachair 1983–84, 38). Superstitions were attached to such momentous movements of valued stock and beloved people. In County Donegal blood was drawn from the animal's tail and red thread bound into its hair – to ward off the evil eye; Monday was a bad day for moving (Ó Dhubhthaigh 1983–4, 47).

Six months on, in late autumn, winter approaching, colours changing, nutritious grazing for their animals diminishing, the women might have started anticipating the journey home: to a world filled with memories, but changed since spring by another season's growth, decay and activities. The hills were left behind for another year and ahead were shorn fields, familiar tracks and shrieks of welcome from family and friends. Although early modern Irish women 'looked forward with delight to the pastures [and] left them with regret in the autumn' they also enjoyed their return to family and community, having 'a very merry time for a week' (Ó Dhubhthaigh 1983–4, 49).

Those two great journeys' importance may be reflected in the significance of the festivals developed on the two traditional dates for transhumance movements in Britain, May Day and Hallowe'en, Beltane and Samhain. Often now seen as marking relatively abstract concepts of summer and winter, renewal and continuity and the seasonal cycle, they probably also marked the great transformative and emotional events transhumance brought annually to rural society.

We may also consider how the summers themselves were experienced; how women responded to encounters with fellows and animals on the closely known downlands. Here were various weathers, animals and plants; bogs, tors and tumbled rocks; and perhaps most intriguingly, the remains of structures created by earlier people. We should expect each to have had stories attached, to explain and to allay fears. Encounters, experiences, stories and knowledge must have affected how transhumants perceived their world and their place within it. We look beyond functionalist economies of structural reuse when we wonder whether later prehistoric transhumants installing themselves in the shells of earlier dwellings and cairns were creating associations with much earlier people, possibly their ancestors, or their spirits (see Franklin 2006, 146–8).

Does the establishment of many early medieval transhumance hut groups on Bodmin Moor within prehistoric settlements, as at Roughtor, Brockabarrow Common and Leskernick reflect similar motivations? Those who camped within and around Leskernick's ruined Bronze Age round houses may have chattered about the hill they had grown to know so well, inventing or reiterating stories relating themselves to the creators of those earlier houses and the stone circles and stone row on the plain below (Herring 1997; Ó Danachair 1983–4, 39) (Fig. 7.3). It may have been them who gave Leskernick its Cornish name, derived from those very ruins: *Lis carn* (adj), 'the court (or ruins) in the rocky place' (Padel 1985, 150, 38–40).

Social and economic relations within and between households would have been exposed and negotiated in the summer pastures. Imagine the young woman's pleasure when family or friends visited to deliver provisions or take away butter and cheese and consider how her household position would have been strengthened. Also of interest is how the women responded to each other, as seasonal representatives of routinely cooperating households: appreciating the lightening of a shared work load and enjoying each other's company, but being irritated by those not pulling their weight, or threatening the flock and herd by poorly treating animals. Some women would display special qualities. Una Sile, of nineteenth-century County Donegal, was 'as strong as a stag…no man in the glen as strong. If a horse or cow went in a marsh, Una could go to that horse or whatever it was and pull it out by herself' (Ó Dhubhthaigh 1983–4, 47). For each Una there would be others capable of tending sick animals, spinning yarn, or spinning a yarn (*ibid.*, 50). The grouping together of women would have also helped deal with dangers in the hills – wild animals and wandering, thieving men (Ó Danachair 1983–4, 39; Kelly 1998, 44–5; Robinson 2007, 15).

Modern writers, concerned that romanticism might distort understanding of transhumance's economic and social importance, emphasise the damp and danger that must have also been experienced, eliciting concerns about whether it is 'just nostalgia that dresses those damp hillsides in the golden light of Arcadia?' (Robinson 2007, 14). But Robinson's own beautiful Irish work provides a vivid example from an ample literature confirming how people adapt to and become one with their place. If early modern Irish accounts provide accurate guides, those long summers were looked back on longingly as the woman's best years. While taking pride in being responsible for the household's valuable livestock, she had enjoyed freedom from close family control and the pleasures of the company of other girls and women. Again with more recent British arrangements as models, we may also expect that young men (brothers or future partners) would have been those bringing provisions up and taking dairy products back home. They also brought musical instruments and much fun was had before they turned to leave. 'It was good to be alive! There was the joy, the fun, the pleasure, the singing and the music. The hills were alive' (Ghuairim (1937), cited in Ó Danachair, 1983–84, 39).

Harold Fox was aware of the importance of recreating experience when composing history:

> 'A stranger coming into a wold one evening in the seventh century or the eighth would have entered a wood pasture … [and] seen clumps of wood casting long shadows over the great open spaces and, everywhere on the pastures, domestic animals of all kinds. Now people come into view, the keepers of those animals returning to their summer dwellings as night closed in. Everywhere traces of older landscapes, all the stranger in the evening light, showed that people had been there before in times long distant even in the seventh century, had buried their dead there, and divided up the land' (Fox 2000, 51).

The splitting of households for half the year suggests a secure society in which there were high levels of trust. Nineteenth-century Donegal transhumance

depended on cooperation, openness and integrity: 'There was nothing but honesty then. Nobody did treachery or harm to another, and they lived as Christians should, with nothing between them but what was right and just' (Ó Dubhthaigh 1983–4, 47). Obligations developed through transhumance were clearly defined; if a girl looked after another man's cows on the hills he would help her household throughout the year. Such arrangements became part of the rural economy; a man climbing to the summer booley grounds to collect milk 'might take three tankards with him, to oblige two other men' (Robinson 2007, 14). Close bonds tightened by long summers of cooperation and comradeship often remain unloosened until death (Ó Dubhthaigh 1983–4, 47).

Actions, such as drawing out the household's own cattle, sheep and goats from the common herd, tethering them round the hut, milking them, and then making butter and cheese all reinforced the contrast between owned and shared. The social distance between household and hamlet might have been most keenly felt when settling down in your own hut at dusk, alone and vulnerable. Drifts benefited households, safeguarding their common and individual rights, but drift days were also probably exhausting and tension-filled: precious animals were rushed together with hundreds of others (see Gaffney 1959, 26). While participating in securing the household's interests the women probably had various social relationships exposed and tested.

Here on the commons a person appreciated the balance between the interests and needs of their household and of the cooperating hamlet and community and

FIGURE 7.3. Imaginary early medieval Cornish late summer upland scene. Archaeological reconstructions extend presentation of the known and unknown by concentrating the thoughts of artist and adviser and pushing interpretation of evidence to its limits. Here we represent most confidently the strength of character to be expected in those people, probably young women, who for many months moved with the household's livestock from the home farmsteads to the upland groups or hamlets of huts, such as those in Figure 7.2. These huts are shown roofed with turf, having single entrances, and lying at shouting distance from each other. (Reconstruction © Phoebe Herring)

kingship to which it belonged, and negotiated maintenance and development of both rights and duties. Many of the great changes that Cornwall and other mixed farming areas experienced in the medieval period derived from significant shifts within such relationships.

An ending

Examination of transhumance reveals, or rather predicts or suggests, sophisticated farming practice and quite complex tenurial and administrative arrangements in early medieval Cornwall. If it really was ubiquitous and essential, transhumance's apparently universal abandonment some time after the seventh century becomes of pressing importance in terms of understanding the development of Cornwall's economy and society. Neither documentation nor any other evidence suggests that transhumance involving members of the farming household accompanying the livestock to the seasonal grazing grounds continued into Norman and later periods in Cornwall. Cattle and sheep were of course summered on hills, cliffs and marshes from the later medieval period to the twenty-first century, but nothing suggests they were accompanied by their owners. They were either occasionally checked through the summer months, as by William Carnsew of Bokelly in the 1570s (Pounds 1978, 39–50), or large numbers belonging to many households were overseen by professional summer-only herders (Herring 2004).

From the eleventh century the Cornish hills, including those of Bodmin Moor, became more widely settled and increasingly enclosed with field systems and divided by long pasture boundaries confining or excluding grazing animals (Johnson and Rose 1994, 101–106; Herring 2004). Some of this colonisation and enclosure of the pastures may have been initiated by transhumants themselves. Occupants of huts on Brown Willy laying out straggly strip fields may have been experimenting in taking a crop (Herring 1986, fig. 25). The much-manured ground immediately around transhumance sites would have been particularly favourable sites for establishing mixed farms. However, such tentative piecemeal nibblings at the boundary between lowland and upland worlds and ways cannot explain the universality of transhumance's abandonment.

More fruitful may be a consideration of the impact of establishing convertible or ley husbandry apparently some time in the second half of the first millennium, if Cornwall's unusually high ratios of Domesday ploughlands to ploughs (or ploughteams) is a guide (Herring 1996b). Palaeoenvironmental evidence from north Devon also supports such a date (Rippon *et al.* 2006). Open strip fields may have been first partially enclosed then to form what we have recently termed cropping units, the blocks of land whose use was rotated through convertible husbandry (*e.g.* Herring 1998; 2006a). They might just as usefully be seen as grazing units.

Three things flowing from the closer organisation of lowland farmland grazing may each have hastened the end of a two-thousand year old tradition of transhumance in Cornwall (and the wider south-west). Firstly, milked animals could be kept close to home throughout the year, together with their milk, butter and cheese, and of course their former summer minders, the young women. Secondly, intensified use of fields allowed a reduction in the intensity of use of commons, enabling their margins to be pushed back through gradual colonisation. Finally, enclosure of cropping/grazing units made it easier to grow autumn-sown grain crops such as wheat securely. Autumn sowing made best use of land deturfed, dressed, ploughed and harrowed through the summer as part of convertible husbandry's beat-burning process (for which see Herring 2006b, 96–98). Wheat yielded higher nutrient levels and a higher price if sold than the spring-sown oats and barley that farmers probably grew when livestock, summered on the hills, were wintered on the open fields. Manuring by grazing sheep was also more carefully controlled through the grazing units.

Some support for this model may be found in an interpretation of place-names with the element *lety*, 'milk-house' (Padel 1985, 148). Its *ty* 'house' suffix suggests a coining in the early part of the later medieval period, significantly later than transhumance's *hendre* and *havos*. As most *lety* settlements are not in summer grazings, but near the edges of medieval field systems, they seem part of post-transhumance arrangements. They may be interpreted as permanent settlements developed from milking sheds set up for convenience in more distant parts of home field systems.

Transhumance, located at the farming world's edges, is too easily dismissed as of marginal interest, however exciting and enjoyable its experience. This paper has suggested its practice by most if not all Cornish farming households made it central to economy, society and life. It was for a long time a fundamental part of being Cornish. Its close study exposes dynamic relationships whose elucidation helps explain significant change in early rural society.

Acknowledgements

Thanks to Bryn Tapper for preparing the map and providing HLC material. I have enjoyed discussing Cornish, British and European transhumance with numerous people, including Oliver Padel, Cathy Parkes, Peter Rose, Graeme Kirkham, Phillipe Planel, Sam Turner, Karen Syse and Kieran O'Conor, but especially the late Professor Harold Fox. I take responsibility for each kite flown in the pages above. Some were also launched in a recently published more fully illustrated, but shorter version of this paper (Herring 2009).

Bibliography

Aalen, F. H. A. (1997) The Irish rural landscape: synthesis of habitat and history, in F. H. A. Aalen, K. Whelan and M. Stout (eds) *Atlas of the Irish Rural Landscape*, 4–30. Cork: Cork University Press.

Allen, D. (1979) Excavations at Hafod y Nant Criafolen, Brenig Valley, Clwyd, 1973–4. *Post-medieval Archaeology* 13, 1–59.

Altenberg, K. (2003) *Experiencing Landscapes; a Study of Space and Identity in Three Marginal Areas of Medieval Britain and Scandinavia.* Stockholm: Almqvist and Wiksell.

Astill, G. (1992) Rural settlement: the toft and the croft, in G. Astill and A. Grant (eds) *The Countryside of Medieval England*, 36–61. Oxford: Blackwell.

Beamont, W. (1863) *Domesday Book, Cheshire, Lancashire and parts of Flintshire and Denbighshire, Cumberland, Westmoreland and Yorkshire.* Chester: Minshull and Hughes.

Bender, B., Hamilton, S. and Tilley, C. (2007) *Stone Worlds; Narrative and Reflexivity in Landscape Archaeology.* California: Walnut Creek.

Beresford, G. (1979) Three deserted medieval settlements on Dartmoor: a report on the late E. Marie Minter's excavations. *Medieval Archaeology* 23, 98–158.

Bil, A. (1990) *The Shieling 1600–1840. The Case of the Central Scottish Highlands.* Edinburgh: John Donald.

Bruce-Mitford, R. (1997) *Mawgan Porth. A Settlement of the Late Saxon Period on the North Cornish Coast. Excavations 1949–52, 1954 and 1974.* London: English Heritage.

Carew, R. (1602) *The Survey of Cornwall*, 1969 reprint, F. E. Halliday (ed.). New York: Augustus M. Kelley.

Christie, P. M. L. (1993) *Chysauster and Carn Euny.* London: English Heritage.

Cornwall County Council (1996) *Cornwall Landscape Assessment 1994.* Truro: Cornwall County Council.

Davies, E. (1977) Hendre and hafod in Denbighshire. *Denbighshire Historical Society Proceedings*, 26, 49–72.

Davies, E. (1984–5) Hafod and lluest, the summering of cattle and upland settlement in Wales. *Folklife* 23, 76–96.

Davies, W. (1982) *Wales in the Early Middle Ages.* Leicester: Leicester University Press.

Evans, E. E. (1957) *Irish Folk Ways.* London: Routledge and Kegan Paul.

Fox, H. S. A. (1972) Field systems of east and south Devon. *Transactions Devonshire Association* 104, 81–136.

Fox, H. S. A. (1981) Approaches to the adoption of the Midland system, in T. Rowley (ed.) *Origins of Open Field Agriculture*, 64–111. London: Croom Helm.

Fox, H. S. A. (1989) The people of the Wolds in English settlement history, in M. Aston, D. Austin and C. Dyer (eds) *The Rural Settlements of Medieval England*, 77–101. Oxford: Blackwell.

Fox, H. S. A. (1996) Introduction: transhumance and seasonal settlement, in H. S. A. Fox (ed.) *Seasonal Settlement*, 1–23. Leicester: University of Leicester.

Fox, H. S. A. (2000) The Wolds, in J. Thirsk (ed.) *Rural England, an Illustrated History of the Landscape*, 50–61. Oxford: Oxford University Press.

Fox, H. S. A. (2006) Foreword, in S. Turner (ed.) *Medieval Devon and Cornwall; Shaping an Ancient Countryside*, xi–xvi. Oxford: Windgather.

Fox, H. S. A. (forthcoming) *Those Alluring Uplands.*

Franklin, L. (2006) Imagined landscapes: archaeology, perception and folklore in the study of medieval Devon, in S. Turner (ed.), *Medieval Devon and Cornwall; Shaping an Ancient Countryside*, 144–161. Oxford: Windgather.

Gaffney, V. (1959) Summer shealings. *Scottish Historical Review* 38, 20–35.

Gearey, B. R., West, S. and Charman, D. J. (1997) The landscape context of medieval settlement on the south-western moors of England. Recent palaeoenvironmental evidence from Bodmin Moor and Dartmoor. *Medieval Archaeology* 41, 195–208.

Gearey, B. R., Charman, D. J. and Kent, M. (2000) Palaeoecological evidence for the prehistoric settlement of Bodmin Moor, Cornwall, south-west England: Part II – land-use changes from the Neolithic to the present. *Journal of Archaeological Science* 27, 493–508.

Gelling, P. S. (1962–63) Medieval shielings in the Isle of Man. *Medieval Archaeology* 6–7, 156–172.

Glassie, H. (1982) *Passing the Time; Folklore and History of an Ulster Community*. Dublin: O'Brien Press.

Graham, J. M. (1953–54) Transhumance in Ireland, *Advancement of Science* 10, 74–79.

Hamsun, K. (2007) *Growth of the Soil*. (first published 1917, new translation S. Lyngstad). London: Penguin.

Herring, P. (1986) *An Exercise in Landscape History: pre-Norman and Medieval Brown Willy and Bodmin Moor*. Unpublished MPhil thesis, University of Sheffield.

Herring, P. (1996a) Transhumance in medieval Cornwall, in H. S. A. Fox (ed.) *Seasonal Settlement*, 35–44. Leicester: University of Leicester.

Herring, P. (1996b) *Pastoralism in Medieval Cornwall*. Paper presented to the Economic History Society, Lancaster University, 30 March 1996.

Herring, P. (1997) Early prehistoric sites at Leskernick, Altarnun. *Cornish Archaeology* 36, 176–185.

Herring, P. (1998) *Presenting a Method of Historic Landscape Assessment*. Truro: Cornwall County Council and English Heritage.

Herring, P. (1999) Farming and transhumance in Cornwall at the turn of the first millennium AD. *Journal Cornwall Association of Local Historians* 37, 19–25 and 38, 3–8.

Herring, P. (2004) Cornish uplands: medieval, post-medieval and modern extents, in I. D. Whyte and A. J. L. Winchester (eds) *Society, Landscape and Environment in Upland Britain*, 37–52. Society for Landscape Studies, supplementary series 2.

Herring, P. (2006a) Cornish strip fields, in S. Turner (ed.) *Medieval Devon and Cornwall; Shaping an Ancient Countryside*, 44–77. Oxford: Windgather.

Herring, P. (2006b) Medieval fields at Brown Willy, Bodmin Moor, in S. Turner (ed.) *Medieval Devon and Cornwall; Shaping an Ancient Countryside*, 78–103. Oxford: Windgather.

Herring, P. (2008) Commons, fields and communities in prehistoric Cornwall, in A. Chadwick (ed.) *Recent Approaches to the Archaeology of Land Allotment*, 70–95. Oxford: British Archaeological Reports International Series 1875.

Herring, P. (2009) Early medieval transhumance in Cornwall, Great Britain, in J. Klapste (ed.) *Medieval Rural Settlement in Marginal Landscapes, Ruralia VII*, 47–56. Turnhout, Belgium: Brepols.

Hooke, D. (1989) Early medieval estate and settlement patterns: the documentary evidence, in M. Aston, D. Austin and C. Dyer (eds) *The Rural Settlements of Medieval England*, 9–30. Oxford: Blackwell.

Johnson, N. and Rose, P. (1994) *Bodmin Moor: an Archaeological Survey. Vol. 1, The Human Landscape to c.1800*. London: English Heritage.

Jones, A. M. (2004–5) Settlement and ceremony. Archaeological investigations at Stannon Down, St Breward, Cornwall. *Cornish Archaeology* 43–4, 1–140.

Kelly, F. (1998) *Early Irish Farming. A Study Based Mainly on the Law-Texts of the 7th and 8th Centuries AD, Early Irish Law Series, Vol. IV*. Dublin: School of Celtic Studies.

McCourt, D. (1953) Traditions of rundale in and around the Sperrin Mountains. *Ulster Journal of Archaeology* (3rd series) 16, 69–83.

McCourt, D. (1954–55) Infield and outfield in Ireland. *Economic History Review* 7, 369–376.

Miller, R. (1967) Land use by summer sheilings. *Scottish Studies* 11, 193–221.

Ó Danachair, C. (1983–84) Summer pasture in Ireland. *Folk Life* 22, 36–41.

Ó Dubhthaigh, N. (1983–84) Summer pasture in Donegal. *Folk Life* 22, 42–54.

Padel, O. J. (1985) *Cornish Place-name Elements*. Nottingham: English Place Names Society.

Padel, O. J. (1999) Place-names, in R. Kain and W. Ravenhill (eds) *Historical Atlas of South-West England*, 88–94. Exeter: University of Exeter Press.

Pearce, S. (2004) *South-western England in the Early Middle Ages*. London: Leicester University Press.

Pounds, N. J. G. (1978) William Carnsew of Bokelly and his diary, 1576–7. *Journal Royal Institution Cornwall* 8.1, 14–60.

Preston-Jones, A. and Rose, P. (1986) Medieval Cornwall. *Cornish Archaeology* 25, 135–185.

Rippon, S. J., Fyfe, R. M. and Brown, A. G. (2006) Beyond villages and open fields: the origins and development of a historic landscape characterised by dispersed settlement in south-west England. *Medieval Archaeology* 50, 31–70.

Robinson, T. (2007) *Connemara. Listening to the Wind*. London: Penguin.

Spooner, B. C. (1942) The boundaries of Twelve Men's Moor in the parish of North Hill. *Devon Cornwall Notes Queries* 22.2, 49–55.

Taylor, C. C. (1983) *Village and Farmstead. A History of Rural Settlement in England*. London: George Philip.

Thomas, A. C. (1964) Settlement history in early Cornwall: 1, the hundreds. *Cornish Archaeology* 3, 70–79.

Thomas, C. (1975) Peasant agriculture in medieval Gwynedd. *Folk Life* 13, 24–37.

Tilley, C. (1994) *A Phenomenology of Landscape*. Oxford: Berg Publishers.

Turner, S. (2006) *Making a Christian Landscape. The Countryside in Early Medieval Cornwall, Devon and Wessex*. Exeter: University of Exeter Press.

Uhlig, H. (1961) Old hamlets with infield and outfield systems in Western and Central Europe. *Geografiska Annaler* 43, 285–312.

Ward, A. (1997) Transhumance and settlement on the Welsh uplands: a view from the Black Mountain, in N. Edwards (ed.) *Landscape and Settlement in Medieval Wales*, 97–111. Oxford: Oxbow Monograph 81.

Winchester, A. J. L. (2000) *The Harvest of the Hills*. Edinburgh: Edinburgh University Press.

Worgan, G. B. (1811) *General Review of the Agriculture of the County of Cornwall*. London: Board of Agriculture.

CHAPTER EIGHT

Time Regained: Booley Huts and Seasonal Settlement in the Mourne Mountains, County Down, Ireland

Mark Gardiner

The subject of this paper might appear to be a considerable distance from Harold Fox's field of interest, but there are two reasons for contributing a study of seasonal settlement in the north of Ireland to his *Gedankschrift*. Harold lectured early in his career at Queen's University in Belfast where he taught for eighteen months. Later, when established at Leicester, Harold developed an interest in the issue of seasonal settlement, edited a book on the subject in 1996 and at his death was working on a volume on transhumance on Dartmoor. The subject therefore links the beginning and the end of his professional career.

The Mourne Mountains, some forty miles to the south of Belfast, rise dramatically from the rolling drumlin clay lands to the north and east, Carlingford Lough to the west and the sea to the south. In strict terms, and from a European perspective, the area barely merits the title of mountains since the highest point at Slieve Donard is only 850m high, but the region is marked by an abrupt contrast with the surrounding land and by its rocky terrain (Fig. 8.1). The *Archaeological Survey of County Down* published in 1966 had little to say on the area and the uplands were believed to contain few archaeological traces (Ministry of Finance 1966). That view was also implicit in the work of the Belfast geographer, Estyn Evans, who knew the area well and wrote a book on the region (Evans 1951). In succeeding decades there was a gradual realization, in Britain at least, not only that the uplands had been extensively used in the past, but also that they contained some of the finest surviving prehistoric landscapes and extensive historic remains (Darvill 1986). That has not, on the whole, been reflected in the pattern of archaeological research in Northern Ireland. The uplands there have remained little investigated and the extent of archaeological survival is still uncertain.

The landscape around the Mournes and in the lower valleys is largely the product of improvements in the later eighteenth and nineteenth century, when 'ladder fields' were laid out. Farms comprised long strips of land running from the valley bottoms to the tops of the hills and were subdivided into fields by boundaries running at right-angles (Evans 1951, 119–20). The optimism of land surveyors was not always borne out by the realities of the soil, and some of the higher fields or, in some cases, all of the lands of upland farms, have since been abandoned to a moorland of heather and coarse grass. Land in the Mournes at a greater elevation was never divided in this way and remained open moor exploited only for peat-digging, granite-cutting and for grazing (Evans 1951, 130–32, 155–65). The trackways in the Mournes also seem to have been laid out at this time and they can often be related to routes followed for the extraction of peat and granite. No trackways can be identified on the ground which are definitely of an earlier date.

The most detailed study of the history and landscape of the Mourne Mountains remains that by Estyn Evans (1951). He was interested in all periods of activity in these areas of uplands and drew attention to groups of huts in the Mourne Mountains which he recognized as probably associated with transhumance (Evans 1951, 128–30). A wider survey of the practice of booleying in Ireland – the seasonal movement of stock from the lowlands to the uplands – was made by his student, Jean Graham, though she seems to have undertaken only limited fieldwork in the Mournes (Graham 1953; 1954). In 1957 Estyn Evans and Bruce Proudfoot excavated one of the transhumance huts before it disappeared beneath the waters of the newly constructed Spelga reservoir. No dating evidence was identified, although they found that the floor was marked by intense burning. Charcoal from an earlier phase of occupation was also discovered running beneath the walls of the excavated hut. The excavation and survey indicated many of the features which have been observed subsequently in other huts. The buildings were constructed of layers of sods, sometimes with stone edging, and were found alongside streams, on mounds to raise them well above the level of the water. They occurred in groups and later buildings seem to have overlain earlier structures (Evans and Proudfoot 1958).

Approaches to transhumance

It is hardly possible to discuss the practice of transhumance in Ireland without first considering the framework of understanding which is implicit in the earlier studies of the subject. Booleying – the Irish term for the seasonal movement of stock from the lowlands to the uplands – has generally been regarded as a traditional practice and one which continued in the west of the island until recent times. It is regarded like other traditions in Ireland as having very ancient roots, reflecting a perception that this was a society in which such practices had endured for many centuries. Ireland has been imagined as a country which somehow existed out of time, or was at least barely affected by the great social and economic movements of feudalism and commercialisation which had such an impact elsewhere in Europe.

The association of booleying with the west of Ireland is particularly significant. The west has had a particular place in the formation of Irish identity since that area was considered to have preserved the essence of a culture which in the east of Ireland had been compromised by the influences of urbanisation

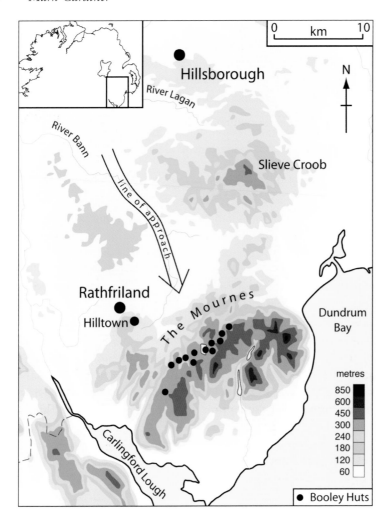

FIGURE 8.1. Location of the Mourne Mountains and other places mentioned in the text. Arrows show suggested lines of approach to the Mourne booley huts

and Anglicization (Nash 1993). With the establishment of the Irish Free State in 1922, attempts were made in this area to foster the culture of 'Irish Ireland' and encourage the continuing use of the Irish language. But it was not only in Ireland that the unique character of the west was recognized. Between the two world wars folklorists and anthropologists in many other countries considered the west of Ireland to be the last surviving area of an ancient Indo-European culture which had once been found throughout Europe (Johnson 1993). In 1931 the Anthropology Department at Harvard initiated a survey of the social anthropology and archaeology of Ireland because it 'presented a distinctive and characteristic variant of western European civilization and a long, relatively unbroken tradition dating back to pre-Christian and pre-Roman times' (Arensberg and Kimball 1968, xxxi). The Harvard Archaeological Expedition which resulted was to refer to the 'tenacious conservatism that characterizes Ireland in nearly every period' (Hencken 1941, 4). In 1934 the Swedish ethnographer Åke Campbell came to record the structure of Irish farmhouses for similar reasons (Lysaght 1993). The Irish themselves, aware of the importance of tradition, established the Irish Folklore Commission in 1935 with funding from the government to ensure that there was a permanent record of folk practices (Almqvist 1979).

It was imagined that the culture of Ireland and of the west of Scotland had been arrested in a primitive and almost pristine state. Estyn Evans wrote that,

> In the north of Ireland the culture-lag, already apparent in the northeast, increases towards the west: the centuries fall away as one approaches the Atlantic, and to journey from east to west is to travel into the past (Evans 1939, 207).

In much the same way and at about the same time, the prehistoric archaeologist, Cecil Curwen wrote concerning Scotland,

> The observations and information set forth in this paper illustrate the extraordinary culture-lag which has existed, even in so small a region as Britain, between the Lowland Zone and the more remote parts of the Highland Zone…. If we had visited [the Isle of] Lewis even fifty years ago, we should have been able to study the life and manners of a Celtic-speaking race emerging from roughly the same state of culture as the Celtic people of pre-Iron Age Wessex (Curwen 1938, 288–89).

These views of Ireland, particularly the west, and of Scotland were based on the perception that these were places with a 'timeless past'. Rural life was imagined as existing outside time (Bell 1998; Gardiner forthcoming). This perspective had the effect of creating an ahistorical view of the traditions of the country. It was thought possible, therefore, for historians to use the evidence from any period to provide an insight to any other time since nothing had altered. This approach proved particularly attractive to some historians because the sources of rural history before the modern period are so few. As a result, the patterns of rural Ireland in the eighteenth or nineteenth centuries were projected backwards to provide evidence for a distant and unchronicled Gaelic past (Nicholls 1978, 4).

The study of transhumance has been affected by all of these assumptions, for although the view of Ireland's timeless past is no longer enunciated as such, it is still held that Ireland is a country with long traditions which have survived with little change (Gardiner forthcoming). The practice of booleying has, therefore, almost invariably been discussed with reference to two types of evidence – the oral records of the last herders practising transhumance, and the accounts of English colonial administrators of the late sixteenth and early seventeenth century. Both sources, of course, may be relevant, but they need to be treated with considerable caution. Booleying had effectively ceased even in the west of Ireland by the late nineteenth century, and when visited by the Irish Folklore Commission's field recorders in the later 1930s and early 1940s, memory of it was only recalled by a few elderly people (Danachair 1945; 1983; Graham 1954, 16–17, 21–23, 26; Ó Moghráin 1944). In other areas it had disappeared even earlier, in the early or mid-nineteenth century, or before. It was, however, regarded as a practice typical of traditional Irish society, and it was assumed that it had persisted unchanged until it eventually died out. Ethnographic evidence is, of course, of considerable importance in understanding the operation of transhumance, but the evidence of informants cannot be applied to a period apart from their own. To project their experience into the past is to perpetuate a view of a static past.

The historical evidence has proved to be no less problematic, largely because of the way it has been employed. Sweeping conclusions have been drawn from the comments of Elizabethan and seventeenth-century English observers of Ireland who did not regard transhumance simply as a form of land-usage, but indicative of something fundamental. They considered it a primitive practice and almost invariably deemed it to be a sign of the backward nature of the country and its inhabitants (Harding 2005, 43). It was part of the creation of difference between Ireland and England which contributed to the ideology underpinning the colonization of the former by the latter (Neill 1994, 3–10). Spenser, for example, wrote,

> there is one use amongst them to keep their cattle and to live themselves the most part of the year in Bollies, pasturing upon the mountain and waste wild places.... Moreover, the people that live thus in these Bollies grow thereby more barbarous, and live more licentiously than they could in towns, using what means they list, and practising what mischiefs and villainies they will (Spenser 1596, 49–50).

The English settlers, as Spenser indicated, were hostile to the movement of stock. In 1610 Sir Arthur Chichester, the Lord Deputy of Ireland proposed that the Irish should be 'drawn from the course of running up and down the country with their cattle which they term 'creating' and are to settle themselves in towns and villages' (*Calendar of State Papers Relating to Ireland 1608–10*, 65). In a similar vein, Sir Thomas Phillips in 1623 proposed that laws should be enacted for reasons which closely resembled those given by Spenser. He said that the Irish should 'be drawn out of remote places and compelled to live in town reeds [clusters of homesteads] and the 'creteing' be abolished being the nursery of all idleness and rebellion' (*Calendar of State Papers Relating to Ireland 1615–25*, 412).

It is not clear whether this practice of creaghting which so upset these administrators was really transhumance, that is the seasonal movement of stock, or a year-round nomadism, and if the English administrators could or even wished to distinguish between the two. Rural society in the early seventeenth century was much disturbed by the Plantations and the response of some of the Irish to their dispossession was to take their cattle and goods and move to wherever they could settle (see for example, Moryson 1907, 416). Nicholls, in particular, has interpreted this to conclude that late medieval Gaelic Irish society was also highly mobile and the population lived in insubstantial buildings. This seems unlikely. It is more probable that it was a particular response to the arrival of English and Scots settlers and their expropriation of land (Andrews 2000, 153; Nicholls 1987, 403–04; Nicholls 2003, 136–37; Prendergast 1854–55, 423; Quinn and Nicholls 1989, 35; Simms 1986).

This brief summary of the conceptual framework should be sufficient to demonstrate the lack of clarity surrounding the issue of booleying. It has been variously regarded as a quintessential age-old Irish practice, as in some way related to the Elizabethan and Stuart attempts to conquer Ireland, and as a reflection of the nomadic character of traditional society. Field survey offers a chance of providing an alternative perspective on booleying, enabling the subject to be reconsidered and placed in a historical perspective.

Field evidence

Only five groups of huts in the Mourne Mountains are noted on the Northern Ireland sites and monuments record. Three of these were recorded by Evans at Deer's Meadow. He also alluded to five other areas where booley huts were to be found (Evans 1951, 129). The paucity of recorded sites led to the perception that they were not common in the Mournes: Estyn Evans had an intimate knowledge of the area and it seemed probable that he would have recorded other groups of huts, if they had existed. Casual observation while walking in the Mournes showed, however, that there were also a number of unrecorded examples of booley huts and, once the characteristic earthworks of the buildings had been recognized, it was possible to undertake systematic survey work to locate others.

The fieldwork was undertaken between autumn 2007 and autumn 2009, particularly during the winter months when the grass had died back (Figs 8.2, 8.3). Some of the work was done by Michael Newell as part of his undergraduate dissertation (Newell 2008). The remainder was done at weekends over the period of two years. The survey sought not only to identify the location of sites, but also consider the form and the number of huts in each group, and to examine the relationship of the hut sites to the surrounding landscape. Fuller details of the sites have been published elsewhere (Gardiner 2010).

The survey showed that the buildings were not randomly situated, but could be found in almost predictable positions. They did not occur at high altitude or on exposed mountain sides, but protected sites were chosen wherever possible. They were invariably situated near streams. Huts were often built on mounds which stood up to one metre above the surrounding ground. This seems to have been done deliberately to ensure the interior of the huts remained dry, but there is also evidence discussed below to show that the same sites were used over a number of years and that the ground-level was raised through the progressive introduction of building material. The earthworks were often marked by lusher growth of grass which assisted their identification from a distance. Huts were also built on boulder berms – banks of stones and gravel deposited when mountain streams were in spate. The tops of boulder berms are well above the normal level of streams and, because of the presence of gravel and other coarse debris, the land is well drained. The huts were generally in groups, sometimes comprising as many as fifteen or more buildings.

As a consequence, it was possible to survey fairly large areas on foot quite rapidly, directing work only to the most likely sites. There was little point in examining peat bogs which were too wet, or the upper slopes of the mountains. There was, of course, a danger that such an approach to survey can be self-

FIGURE 8.2. Surveying a hut site on the Yellow Water River in winter 2008–09. See also Figures 4 and 6

FIGURE 8.3. The Mourne Mountains showing the location of booley huts

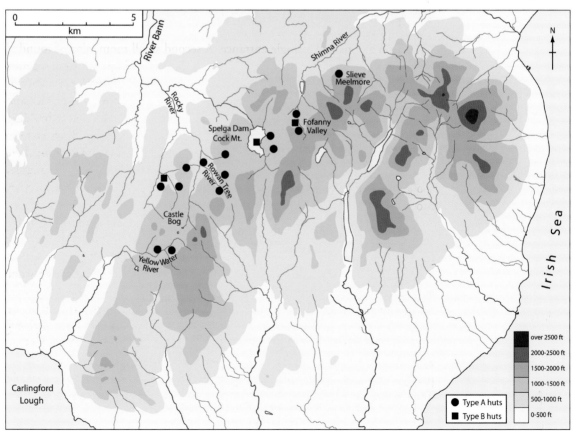

confirming, since the only areas examined are those in which sites are expected. However, a sufficiently large area was examined during the course of work to ensure that a suitably critical approach was taken. Hut sites could not be readily located on any of the aerial photographs studied and so all the main valleys in the Mournes were examined on foot. When huts were identified, they were recorded and their location was determined by navigation-grade GPS which gives a precision of 6–10 m. A number of examples of individual huts were surveyed in detail using a Total Station to produce digital elevation models of representative buildings. Examples were also surveyed using the same equipment to produce general plans of hut groups.

The position of the walls of the huts was marked by a raised band, sometimes only a few centimetres above the interior level, but in a few buildings up to half a metre or more. The exact limits of the walls could be difficult to determine because they were built of sod which has since spread, but it is clearer where stone has been incorporated. Some walls appeared to have been faced in stone, though this was dependent entirely on the availability of materials in the immediate vicinity. Huts near to streams with abundant stone were more likely to incorporate this in the walls. The entrances were commonly revetted with stone.

Evans (1951, 129) had noted that the booley huts vary in shape from circular to rectangular, but in fact most can be placed firmly in one of two categories. The first type (Type A) has a low bank marking the outline of a building of near circular or oval plan, with internal dimensions along the long axis of little more than 2–3 m and a single entrance. A second small room, also of rounded form, was generally attached to one end of the main building and had a separate external entrance (Fig. 8.4). To judge by the surviving earthworks, the sod walls of the buildings cannot have extended higher than 0.5m above the interior and external ground surface and therefore the upper part of the walls of the building must have been constructed out of some other material. The buildings were so small that they can only have provided accommodation for one person; there would barely have been room for a second person to lie down. The smaller room attached to the end of the building may well have been for storing dairy products, as Evans suggested (1951, 130).

As fieldwork proceeded, it became clear that it was possible to distinguish a second type of building (Type B) which was square in plan and seemed to have had sod walls which were greater in height (Fig. 8.5). The square buildings had a single doorway which was set, not in the centre of the wall, but towards one end. Some square buildings had a single room, but in other cases they were found in rows of up to three conjoined and identical structures. The buildings in such rows may not have been built all at one time, but developed through the addition of extra rooms. One example in the Fofanny valley (Irish Grid J 28496 27707) had one room built entirely of sod and a conjoining room constructed partly of stone and partly of sod, suggesting that the two were erected separately. The square buildings generally lie at lower altitudes than the Type A buildings and are found in smaller groups

The upper part of the walls of Type A huts must have been made from a perishable material which allowed the construction of a roof with a circular or oval-shaped plan. It is hard to envisage how a building like this could have been constructed using either cruck timbers which are found in the earliest surviving vernacular buildings in Ireland, or using post-and-truss construction which became more common in the seventeenth century (Gailey 1984). Instead, we must conclude that the building belongs to an entirely different tradition of construction. A possible indication of the form of the structure is given in a series of maps of the north of Ireland drawn up in the years around 1600 which show oval-shaped buildings with a central doorway, sometimes flanked by windows. Such buildings are depicted in both urban and rural situations. They are shown, for example, to the rear of the tenement plots at Carrickfergus (Co. Down) in a map of *c.*1560 where they are clearly inferior to the stone buildings which line the streets (British Library, Cotton MS. Augustus I ii 42, reproduced in Harvey 1993, 99). They appear to be domed structures with no distinction between the walls and roofs. Similar buildings are shown in a near contemporary illustration by Robert Bartlett of the ruined city of Armagh. These depict what are apparently structures with wicker walls and with roofs of a different material (Ó Danachair 1969, 95; Hayes-McCoy 1964). A building apparently of this type has been excavated by Horning (2001, 385–95) in the former village of Movanagher (Co. Londonderry). These buildings, however, appear to have been larger than the booley huts, though they were evidently constructed in a similar manner.

Type B buildings appear to have been built in a different way. Judging by the surviving earthworks (even after their partial collapse) they seem to have been constructed to full height with sod walls. Permanently occupied buildings of this form survived into the twentieth century, demonstrating that this type of construction is perfectly possible (Evans 1969). They were presumably roofed with turfs laid over timber couples. The other feature which sets them apart from Type A buildings is the construction of identical conjoined buildings. These were evidently for accommodation and not for the separate storage of dairy products as in Type A huts. Each room seems to have been a separate living space.

It is often difficult to determine the shape of the buildings since they seem to have been replaced on a number of occasions on the same spot, so that the latest buildings sit on mounds formed from the decayed debris of earlier structures. In some places the walls of earlier buildings appear to protrude beneath those of the last building on the site. One example can be seen in Fig. 8.4 which shows a cell to the west projecting from beneath what appears to be a later building. The earthworks do not allow certainty on this point and excavation would be necessary to clarify the history of development of individual hut mounds.

Many of the huts occurred in groups of ten or more. The number of huts seemed to be generally related to the extent and quality of the rough pasture in the immediate locality, and also the altitude of the sites. The greater the altitude, the smaller the number of huts. Accessibility was a further factor and areas of pastures at a greater distance from the main valleys had fewer buildings and were evidently less heavily used. An example of this can be found in the Yellow Water River valley where the broad valley bottom seems to offer fair pasture, but the difficulty of access, which requires a steep climb from the Kilbroney valley, appears to have discouraged more extensive use (Fig. 8.6). The largest cluster of buildings discovered was on the shoulder of Cock Mountain where there were at least twenty-three huts, many with a number of cells. These lie in two groups, one to the west on the flatter ground beyond the confluence of streams and the second on the slope up the valley along one of the watercourses (Fig. 8.7). Of course, the huts may not have all been occupied simultaneously. However, an already existing site would have been higher than the surrounding ground level because of the introduction of building material, and therefore would have provided an attractive location for a later occupation. It is therefore unlikely that the buildings at Cock Mountain represent successive sites. If only half of the hut sites were occupied at any one time, there would have been a considerable community in this spot.

The most striking thing about the distribution of hut sites (Fig. 8.3) is that they are limited almost entirely to the north side of the Mournes. This is not a result of the scope of fieldwork and Evans (1951, 128) made the same observation. Diligent searching in suitable locations on the south slopes has failed to find any remains. The only possible exception is on the slopes of Rocky Mountain, and south and east of Millstone Mountain where Evans (1951, 129) asserts that there were some huts, though no sites were located in either place in the present survey. The latter site is rather doubtful, as Evans admits, and adds in a footnote that they may have been the foundations for stacks for cut peat. That seems a more likely explanation. The other notable aspect of the distribution of booley huts is that they are also not found in the north-east of the Mournes. Again the area was carefully examined. For example, not a single example was located in the Tullybranigan River valley to the south of Tullymore Forest, or along the Trassey River which seem in every way suitable.

It is possible to suggest a number of reasons for this distribution. The huts were occupied by herders who did not have sufficient rough pasture near to hand, but had to drive their animals such a distance that they could not return home in the evening. Farmers on the south side of the Mournes had abundant rough pasture on the slopes close to hand and would not have had to stay away from home overnight. Evans (1951, 96–98, 109) has noted that the townlands there took the form of long strips extending from the shore to the mountains. Irish townlands, at least in their general pattern, seem to date to the pre-Norman period, suggesting that a system combining land closer to the sea with that near the mountain is an ancient one (McErlean 1983). The huts on the north of the Mournes were occupied by those who travelled a greater distance, but the absence of huts on the north-east is more difficult to explain. Two possibilities might be put forward. The area of upland around Slieve Croob to the north of the Mournes may have provided an alternative and perhaps a closer area of hill pasture for those coming from that direction. Alternatively, it

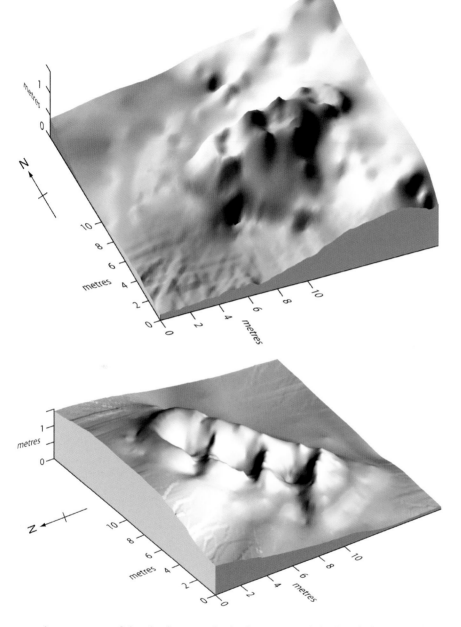

FIGURE 8.4. Digital elevation model of a Type A booley hut at Yellow Water River

FIGURE 8.5. Digital elevation model of three conjoined Type B booley huts at Leitrim Lodge

was the presence of that high ground which prevented the herds from reaching the north-east side of the Mournes and diverted the drovers to the west (Fig. 8.1).

Limited fieldwork was undertaken on the slopes of Slieve Croob to investigate the first of these possibilities. Much of the lower slopes of the mountain had been taken into farmland during the nineteenth century and traces of huts that might have been there will have been removed. The area examined was the valley on the northern side of the mountain from which the River Lagan descends

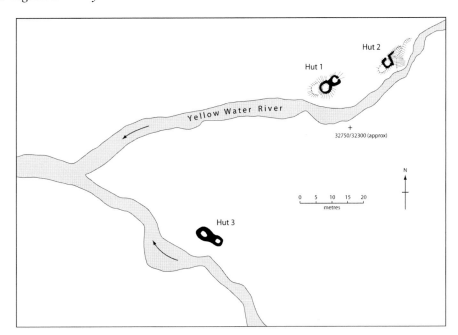

FIGURE 8.6. Plan of booley huts on the upper reaches of the Yellow Water River

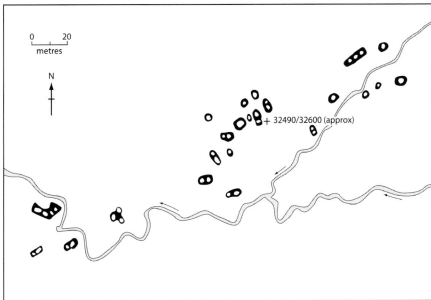

FIGURE 8.7. Plan of hut groups on the south side of Cock Mountain

towards the hamlet of Finnis. Nothing was found in the area examined by the streams, except for the trace of one building (at J 30150 45728) which seemed most likely to be connected with the mid-nineteenth-century cultivation of a small part of the valley.

There is only limited written evidence for the origin of the people who occupied the booley huts on the Mournes. Harris in 1744 recorded that many poor people came in the summer months to Deer's Meadow, bringing their wives and children and constructing huts where they lived for two months or more (Smith and Harris 1744, 125). In her thesis Graham reports a tradition, which she had second-hand, that people came from as far away as Hillsborough to use the pasture at Deer's Meadow (Graham 1954, 27). If correct, it would suggest that the movement of animals could indeed be over a considerable distance since Hillsborough lies 18 miles (29km) away. The distribution of huts does imply a line of approach from the upper reaches of the River Bann to the east of Rathfriland and Hilltown, which would be consistent with drovers coming from the Hillsborough direction (Fig. 8.1).

Discussion of field evidence

The buildings discussed here have been identified as booley huts and it has been assumed that they are associated with seasonal settlement, but that needs further examination. The buildings are extremely small and many of them would have been unable to accommodate more than a single person because the floor area was simply insufficient. It is also notable that there was no evidence of cultivation around the huts, though this was carefully sought around all the buildings identified in the Mournes. Typically in Ireland, this would be represented by lazy beds, ridges produced by throwing up the soil by spade with intervening

FIGURE 8.8. Plan of booley huts on Rocky River

ditches to aid drainage. Lazy beds are found in the formerly enclosed land at the lower end of Rocky River below Hen Mountain, but, on the evidence of the successive editions of the Ordnance Survey maps, they date to the mid-nineteenth century. No lazy beds are found in association with the huts, so it is very unlikely that any cultivation was practised. While these factors do not prove absolutely that the huts were only occupied on a seasonal basis, they point firmly in that direction.

The other notable absence is of any enclosures. There are no ancient land divisions marking territories within the Mournes or animal pens close to the booleys, with the single exception of a possible example near huts at the confluence of Rowan Tree River and Rocky Water (Fig. 8.8). Neither territorial enclosures, nor small pens were necessary to prevent animals from straying if they were hefted – that is, habituated to graze within a certain area. Hefted stock would graze within a wide area around the huts and would return there in the evening. The fact that neither pens nor enclosure were used argues strongly for the repeated use of the same hut sites in successive

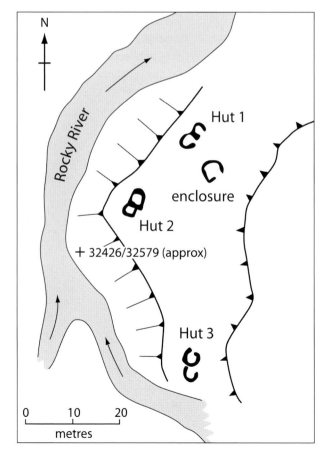

years. If herders tried to use different locations, hefted livestock would have been confused and liable to stray. This argues that the booley huts represent communities which returned to the same places year after year. The nature of such communities is more difficult to establish. In Redesdale in the borders of England and Scotland it was noted in 1604 that the pastures were held in common and 'they sheylde together by surnames' (Ramm *et al.* 1970, 4, citing TNA, E178/4294, 104). This indicates that those summer pastures were occupied by groups of related people who in the winter lived in similar proximity. We cannot know whether there were similar arrangements in the Mournes, though it does seem possible. Certainly, in the early sixteenth century land was held by kindred groups, but the progressive introduction of British practice to Ulster eroded such Gaelic concepts of land rights (Nicholls 2003, 64–76).

This explains the groups of booley huts. The strings of more isolated huts, occurring in ones, twos or threes up the Yellow River and Fofanny valleys, must imply different sorts of communities. Here, the herders chose not to settle close together, although there were no geographical reasons not to do so. Neither the shape of the valley floor, nor the distribution of pasture in the upper part of the Yellow River would have prevented the dispersed huts from occupying a single spot (Fig. 8.6). This is even more clear in the Fofanny valley where the huts strung out over a distance of 450 m might have all been located in just two or perhaps three groups. It is possible that this arrangement of booley huts also reproduced the home communities: the smaller groups of huts in these valleys was a reflection of a series of quite separate groups.

Conclusions

It has been argued that interpretations of booleying have been influenced by oral records of the final period of transhumance which have been uncritically used for earlier periods to create an impression of a 'timeless past'. A further influence on interpretation has been the views of the Elizabethan and Jacobean planters who saw booleying as a manifestation of the primitive customs of an uncivilized people. The field evidence allows an alternative perspective by placing the huts within an historical context. The date of the huts is crucial to our understanding. The only excavated building has provided no evidence for this, but it is possible to suggest at least a likely date for the cessation of the practice. It is clear that it survived until the mid-eighteenth century when Harris was able to see the booley huts in Deer's Meadow, but it was not recorded in the Ordnance Survey memoirs in the 1830s (Smith and Harris 1744, 125). No buildings are shown on the first-edition six-inch Ordnance Survey maps, though less weight can be placed on that because their record is in outline only. The comments in the Ordnance Survey memoirs for the Sperrins, another area of upland in the north of Ireland may be relevant. In 1821 they recorded that in the parishes of Ballynascreen, Desertmartin and Kilcronaghan (Co. Londonderry) many families used to take their flocks and herds to the uplands in the summer where they lived on a little oatmeal and abundant butter, curds and cream.

However, the practice had been given up since the area had been brought under the plough almost sixty years previously (*Parishes of Co. Londonderry XI*, 119). It suggests that transhumance died out in that area in the 1760s. It is likely that booleying in the Mournes was curtailed by similar developments. The Ordnance Survey map of 1835 shows that fields had been carved out of the rough ground, for example, to the west of Hen Mountain, as well as in a number of other places.

We may be able to provide further evidence for date by considering the type and distribution of buildings. Type A huts belong to a long tradition of building in wattle work which stretches back into the Middle Ages and still persisted into the seventeenth century. For example, an excavated medieval house at Glenmakeeran seems to have had this sort of structure to judge from the rounded walls (Williams and Robinson 1983). The building dug by Horning at Movanagher, apparently dating to the seventeenth century, was of similar construction (Horning 2001, 385–95). The building type was closely associated with the Irish in the seventeenth century and their rude huts were unfavourably contrasted with the houses of the Scots and English settlers (for example, Petty 1691, 79, 116, 130). In reality, the Plantation settlers were in some instances quite happy to occupy Gaelic-style dwellings (Horning 2001, 388–89). Wattled buildings were still used for transhumance near Newry in the later seventeenth century according to Story (1693, 16). In 1705 an Act was passed by the Irish parliament ostensibly to conserve the use of wood and timber, but perhaps in fact to discourage traditional building customs. It forbade the use of 'wattling the walls of houses, or cabbins, or outbuildings', and this may well have enforced a change in building practice with the replacement of Type A huts with the sod-walled Type B structures (4 Anne c. 9: *Statutes at Large in Ireland* 4, 87). Type B buildings occur in smaller numbers and are found generally at lower altitudes, that is on the better pasture. It seems, therefore, that these later buildings were introduced as booleying was already in decline and there was less pressure on the pasture. Significantly, they are found at Deer's Meadow, where we have Harris' account to show that booleying persisted into the mid-eighteenth century.

Rathbone (2009) reached a similar conclusion about the development of the plan of transhumance huts in his more general survey of the practice in the area around the Irish Sea. He argued that small, square buildings emerged in a number of areas at about the same time, and ascribed this change to the early modern period. We might question whether similarities in huts in different areas around the Irish Sea really represent what Rathbone calls a 'shared cultural heritage'; however, we can accept the argument that there was a general change in building form around this time. Type A huts identified here belong to an earlier phase which stretch from around 1700 back into the later Middle Ages, while the Type B buildings represent the final phase of seasonal settlement in the eighteenth century.

Three themes have emerged from this field study of remains of booley huts in the Mournes. The first has been the identification and the distribution of buildings associated with transhumance. The second has been the recognition of the historical context of the practice of booleying and the way in which the field evidence might be set within that. Insofar as is possible without further excavation, transhumance in the Mournes has been removed from the 'timeless past', that ahistoric limbo of folk practice into which an earlier generation of scholars had consigned it. While the origins of booleying remain unclear, the end of the practice in the later eighteenth century is now a little better understood, and the typology of buildings proposed here allows them to be dated in broad terms.

This is associated with a third aspect which has been only touched upon. It is the issue of the inter-ethnic tensions surrounding booleying. The English settlers of the late sixteenth and early seventeenth century regarded Irish pastoralism as primitive and contrasted it with the industrious arable cultivation of the British settlers. Spenser, as we have seen, viewed booleying in a very hostile manner, not only as barbarous, but as wanting in proper supervision. Sir Henry Wallop, who participated in the plantation of Wexford, said his actions had led to 'better civility, inhabitation and plough-going than heretofore', connecting arable agriculture with a superior existence (Canny 2001, 111, citing TNA, SP63/94/55). In much the same way, the type of buildings used by the herders was unfavourably compared with the 'proper' structures being erected by the Scots and English settlers. As Edwards (2001, 78) has expressed it, 'essentially in place of an Ireland that was semi-nomadic, heavily militarised and dominated by autonomous native lords, the crown and its advisers wished to create an Ireland that was sedentary, peaceful and regulated by crown officials'. Transhumance thus formed an element of the colonial discourse of reform by which Ireland was to be improved by the British.

Some historians have accepted without question some elements of this discourse and in particular have agreed that booleying was an essentially Gaelic Irish practice in contrast to the arable agriculture of the Plantation settlers (Gardiner forthcoming). In spite of the colonial rhetoric, there is no evidence that any such contrast was sharply drawn along these ethnic lines. Plantation farmers in early seventeenth-century Ulster were happy to let their cattle graze across the unfenced countryside, much as their Irish contemporaries did (Canny 2001, 350). We do an injustice to the evidence if we regard transhumance in Ireland in ethnic terms. We must remember that transhumance was still practised in some parts of the homelands of those English and Scots settlers who came to settle in Ireland. Transhumance was not a uniquely Gaelic Irish practice, nor was it certainly an age-old tradition. We need to set booleying in its historic context and regard it as a particular manifestation of the widespread practice of transhumance found across Europe and Scandinavia in the medieval and early modern periods.

Acknowledgements

I am grateful to Shannon Allison, Sarah Burns, Jill Campbell, Michael Newell and particularly Mary Ozanne who shared the work of surveying the sites in the Mournes, mostly in the cold and sometimes in the wet days of the winters of 2008–09 and 2009–10. Michael Newell also drew my attention to the booley huts in the Fofanny valley.

The sites were surveyed using a Leica 705 Total Station and the plans prepared in AutoCAD 2004. The final maps and surveys were re-drawn for publication by Libby Mulqueeny in Adobe Illustrator. The digital terrain models were prepared from the original survey data using Surfer 8.

Bibliography

Unpublished

The National Archives (Kew)
TNA, E178/4294. Surveys of lands in Northumberland leased to George, late Earl of
    Dunbar.
TNA, SP63/94/55. State Papers Ireland, Miscellaneous Letters and Papers.

Published

Almqvist, B. (1979) *The Irish Folklore Commission: Achievement and Legacy* (Folklore
    Studies pamphlets 3 (reprinted from *Béaloideas*, 45–47 (1977–79), 6–26). Dublin:
    Comhairle Bhéaloideas Éireann.
Andrews, J. H. (2000) Plantation Ireland: a review of settlement history, in T. B. Barry
    (ed.) *A History of Settlement in Ireland*, 140–57. London: Routledge.
Arensberg, C. M. and Kimball, S. T. (1968) *Family and Community in Ireland* (second
    edition). Cambridge, Mass.: Harvard University Press.
Bell, J. (1998) Concepts of survival and revival in Irish culture. *Ulster Folklife* 44,
    100–09
Calendar of State Papers Relating to Ireland 1608–10. London: HMSO.
Calendar of State Papers Relating to Ireland 1615–25. London: HMSO.
Canny, N. (2001) *Making Ireland British 1580–1650*. Oxford: Oxford University Press.
Curwen, E. C. (1938) The Hebrides: a cultural backwater. *Antiquity* 12, 261–89.
Danachair, C. (1945) Traces of the buaile in the Galtee Mountains. *Journal of the Royal
    Society of Antiquaries of Ireland* 75, 248–52.
Danachair, C. (1983) Summer pasture in Ireland. *Folk Life* 22, 36–41.
Darvill, T. (1986) *The Archaeology of the Uplands: A Rapid Assessment of Archaeological
    Knowledge and Practice*. London: Royal Commission on the Historical Monuments
    of England.
Edwards, D. (2001) Collaboration without anglicisation: the MacGiollapadraig lordship
    and Tudor reform, in P. J. Duffy, D. Edwards and E. Fitzpatrick (eds) *Gaelic Ireland:
    Land, Lordship and Settlement*, 77–97. Dublin: Four Courts Press.
Evans, E. E. (1939) Some survivals of the Irish openfield system. *Geography* 24, 24–36.
Evans, E. E. (1951) *Mourne Country*. Dundalk: Dundalgan Press.
Evans, E. E. (1969) Sod and turf houses in Ireland, in G. Jenkins (ed.), *Studies in Folk
    Life: Essays in Honour of Iorweth C. Peate*, 75–90. London: Routledge.

Evans, E. E. and Proudfoot, B. (1958) Excavations at the Deer's Meadow. *Ulster Journal of Archaeology* 3rd series, 21, 127–31.

Gailey, A. (1984) *Rural Houses of the North of Ireland*. Edinburgh: John Donald.

Gardiner, M. F. (2010) A preliminary list of booley huts in the Mourne Mountains, County Down. *Ulster Journal of Archaeology* third series, 67 (for 2008), 142–52.

Gardiner, M. F. (forthcoming) Folklore's Timeless Past, Ireland's Present Past, and the perception of rural houses in early historic Ireland. *International Journal of Historical Archaeology*.

Graham, J. M. (1953) Transhumance in Ireland. *Advancement of Science* 10 (37), 74–79.

Graham, J. M. (1954) *Transhumance in Ireland, with Special Reference to its Bearing on the Evolution of Rural Communities in the West*. Unpublished PhD thesis, Queen's University Belfast.

Harding, D. (2005) Objects of English colonial discourse: the Irish and native Americans. *Nordic Irish Studies* 4, 37–60.

Harvey, P. D. A. (1993) *Maps in Tudor England*. London: Public Record Office and British Library.

Hayes-McCoy, G. A. (1964) *Ulster and Other Irish Maps, c. 1600*. Dublin: Stationery Office.

Hencken, H. O'N. (1941) The Harvard Archaeological Expedition in Ireland. *American Journal of Archaeology* 45, 1–6.

Horning, A. (2001) 'Dwelling houses in the old Irish barbarous manner': archaeological evidence for Gaelic architecture in an Ulster Plantation village, in P. Duffy, D. Edwards, and E. Fitzpatrick (eds) *Gaelic Ireland c.1250–c.1650: Land, Lordship, and Settlement*, 375–96. Dublin: Four Courts Press.

Johnson, N. C. (1993) Building a nation: an examination of the Irish Gaeltacht Commission Report of 1926. *Journal of Historical Geography* 19, 157–68.

Lysaght, P. (1993) Swedish ethnological surveys in Ireland 1934–5 and their aftermath, in H. Cheape (ed.) *Tools and Traditions. Studies in European Ethnology Presented to Alexander Fenton*, 22–32. Edinburgh: National Museums of Scotland.

McErlean, T. (1983) The Irish townland system of landscape organisation, in T. Reeves-Smyth and F. Hammond (ed.), *Landscape Archaeology in Ireland*, 315–339. Oxford: British Archaeological Reports.

Ministry of Finance (1966) *An Archaeological Survey of County Down*. Belfast: HMSO.

Moryson, F. (reprinted 1907) *An Itinerary containing his Ten Yeeres Travell through the Twelve Dominions*. Glasgow: James MacLehose.

Nash, C. (1993) Embodying the nation – the west of Ireland landscape and Irish identity, in B. O'Conor and M. Cronin (eds) *Tourism in Ireland: A Critical Analysis*, 86–112. Cork: Cork University Press.

Neill, M. (1994) Broken English and broken Irish: nation, language, and the optic of power in Shakespeare's Histories. *Shakespeare Quarterly* 45, 1–32.

Newell, M. (2008) *Study on the Booley Huts in the Mourne Mountains*. Unpublished BA thesis, Queens University Belfast.

Nicholls, K. W. (1978) *Land, Law and Society in Sixteenth-Century Ireland* (O'Donnell Lecture). Dublin: National University of Ireland.

Nicholls, K. W. (1987) Gaelic society and economy, in A. Cosgrove (ed.) *A New History of Ireland: II. Medieval Ireland 1169–1534*, 396–438. Oxford: Oxford University Press.

Nicholls, K. W. (2003) *Gaelic and Gaelicized Ireland in the Middle Ages* (second edition). Dublin: Lilliput Press.

Ó Danachair, C. (1969) Representations of houses on some Irish maps of *c.*1600, in G. Jenkins (ed.) *Studies in Folk Life: Essays in Honour of Iorweth C. Peate*, 92–103. London: Routledge.

Ó Moghráin, P. (1944) Some Mayo traditions of the *buaile*. *Béaloideas. Journal of the Folklore of Ireland Society* 13, 161–71.

Parishes of Co. Londonderry XI, 1821, 1833, 1836–7. South Londonderry (Ordnance Survey memoirs of Ireland 31), ed. A. Day and P. McWilliams. Belfast: Institute of Irish Studies, Queen's University Belfast.

Petty, W. (1691). *The Political Anatomy of Ireland* (introduced by John O'Donovan, 1970). Shannon: Irish University Press.

Prendergast, J. P. (1854–55) The Ulster creaghts. *Proceedings and Transactions of the Kilkenny and South-East Ireland Archaeological Society* 3, 420–30.

Quinn, D. B. and Nicholls, K. W. (1989) Ireland in 1534, in T. W. Moody, F. X. Martin and F. J. Byrne (eds) *A New History of Ireland: III Early Modern Ireland 1534–1691* (revised edition, 1–68. Oxford: Oxford University Press.

Ramm, H. G., McDowall, R. W. and Mercer, E. (1970) *Shielings and Bastles*. London: HMSO.

Rathbone, S. (2009) Booley houses, hafods, and shielings: a comparative study of transhumant settlements from around the northern basin of the Irish Sea, in A. Horning and N. Brannon (eds) *Ireland and Britain in the Atlantic World*, 111–29. Dublin, Wordwell.

Simms, K. (1986) Nomadry in medieval Ireland: the origin of the creaght or caoraigheacht. *Peritia* 5. 379–91.

Smith, C. and Harris, W. (1744). *The Antient and Present State of the County of Down*. Dublin: Edward Exshaw.

Spenser, E. (1596) *A View of the Present State of Ireland* (edited by W. L. Renwick, 1970). Oxford: Oxford University Press.

Statutes at Large Passed in the Parliaments held in Ireland, 4: (1703–1719). Dublin: Boulter Grierson.

Story, G. W. (1693*) An Impartial History of the Wars of Ireland: Together with Some Remarks upon the Present State of that Kingdom*. London: printed for R. Chiswell.

Williams, B. and Robinson, P. (1983) The excavation of Bronze Age cists and a medieval booley hut at Glenmakeeran, County Antrim, and a discussion of booleying in north Antrim. *Ulster Journal of Archaeology* 46, 29–40.

CHAPTER NINE

Seasonal Settlement in Northern England: Shieling Place-names Revisited

Angus J. L. Winchester

One of the themes which Harold Fox highlighted in his masterful overview of transhumance practices in the introduction to *Seasonal Settlement* (Fox 1996) was the wide range of distances involved in systems where the movement of livestock resulted in the erection of seasonal dwellings. This paper picks up that theme by using an analysis of minor place-names to explore some of the evidence for seasonal settlement in northern England and (to a lesser extent) the Scottish Borders. It drills more systematically into the body of toponymic evidence that has been drawn on before in work on shieling practices and published elsewhere (Winchester 2000, 84–93). Harold Fox revelled in the potential of minor place-names as a source allowing us to recapture what might be termed the folk culture of past landuse, peopling the landscape with countrymen and women and helping us to see the medieval countryside through their eyes. Almost the last paper he published (Fox 2008) used place-names recording the making of butter to explore some of the themes touched on below, so I hope that this paper is a fitting tribute to his scholarship.

On the face of it, the evidence for transhumance involving the use of summer shielings in northern England and the Borders is overwhelming (McDonnell 1988). Documentary evidence records the organised migration of pastoral communities to summer pastures in the Borders and in the North Pennines in the late sixteenth and early seventeenth centuries, where the herdsmen dwelt in huts referred to as 'shiels' or 'shielings' (Winchester 2000, 85–90). The remains of small, single-celled stone structures, often clustered in groups on upland pastures, and with little evidence of associated field systems, have been identified as the shieling huts themselves (Ramm *et al.* 1970, 9–43), and the widely distributed minor place-names incorporating elements signifying summer pasture grounds (ON *saetr* and *erg*) or huts (ME *shele*; ON *skali*) appear to point to the same feature of pastoral farming in the uplands (Whyte 1985).

The place-names and the physical evidence usually attributed to seasonal settlement are found over a much wider area than the few locations for which a written record of shieling practices survives, and it is generally assumed that the documentary evidence describes the last vestiges of a system of transhumance that was much more widespread in medieval times. The linkages between the three types of evidence have often been assumed without question: the place-names refer to places where there were shieling huts, which were used in a system akin to that described in the documentary evidence. In this paper, I wish to argue that we have perhaps been over-ready in identifying seasonal settlement sites in northern England and southern Scotland and to suggest that a more critical approach is required. The focus is on the most extensive group of place-names which are generally interpreted as evidence of past shieling practices – those containing the elements *shele* and *skali* – and it is suggested that the assumption that these names invariably refer to huts occupied seasonally in association with transhumance practices needs to be questioned.

Shieling practices recorded in the late sixteenth and early seventeenth century

Transhumance survived longest in northern England in the Border hills, where the documentary evidence for the use of summer shielings is the most detailed. William Camden's description of transhumance in Gilsland [Cu] and Redesdale [Nb], apparently written after he visited the area in 1599, is well known: 'every way round about in the wasts', he wrote, 'you may see as it were the ancient *Nomades*, a martiall kind of men, who from the moneth of Aprill unto August, ly out skattering and sommering (as they terme it) with their cattaile in little cottages here and there, which they call *Sheales* and *Shealings*' (Camden 1610, 806). The organisation of the shieling system is recorded in most detail in Redesdale, where the Border Survey of 1604 listed sixteen 'summering places', each consisting of a side valley or a named bank of hillside, at the head of the valley beyond the permanent 'wintersteads' lower down the valley. Each summering ground belonged to men of a particular surname, the Reed family occupying Bateinghope and Coomsdon; the Halls Spithope and Cottonshope; the Hedleys Deadwood and Blakehopeburn haugh, for example. Each tenant paid a separate sum of rent for their share of the 'summer grounds' (Winchester 2000, 86–8).

In a handful of manors in the Borders and the North Pennines manor court presentments and byelaws recording the regulations governing the shieling season enable us to recapture the workings of the shieling system in more detail. It is clear that going to the summering grounds was a communal activity, organised and policed by the manor courts, but it is also clear that the system was collapsing by the later sixteenth century, as the court records include presentments of large numbers of individuals for failing to go to the shieling grounds in the summer. The courts required the whole community to leave for the shieling grounds after the crops were sown and individuals were not to return until a specified date. Moving stock to the summer pastures had a double benefit: it enabled the exploitation of distant (and, on the Border, dangerous) hill grazing grounds, taking pressure off more heavily-grazed pastures closer to home; while the physical removal of livestock to the shieling grounds also offered protection to crops growing at the 'winterstead', as illustrated by the case of the man from Redesdale who was taken to court

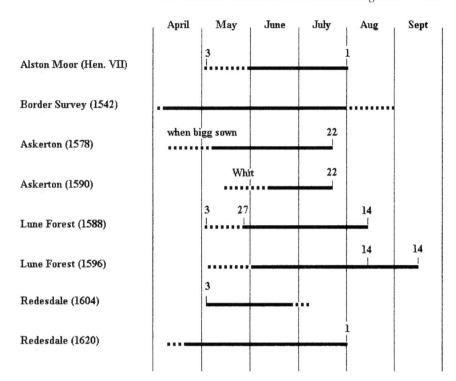

FIGURE 9.1. The shieling season recorded in late sixteenth-/early seventeenth-century sources from northern England

by a neighbour in 1624 for 'sitting all the year at home and eating his grass at unlawful times between St Tillinmas [Ellenmas, 3 May] and Michaelmas'. The dates of the shieling season (Fig. 9.1) reflected its place in the agricultural system: the community left to go to the shieling grounds after the 'bigg' (barley) was sown, returning in time for the hay harvest in late July or early August (see Winchester 2000, 85–90).

The central question of this paper is whether the assumption that shieling place-names are evidence of similar systems in the medieval period is, in fact, justified. A closer analysis of the place-name evidence suggests that the shieling practices recorded in the Border hills and north Pennines in the decades around 1600 represent only one of several types of seasonal settlement associated with livestock rearing.

shele and *skali* place-names

The place-name elements most frequently taken to be evidence for seasonal settlement on summer pastures are the related terms 'scale(s)' (from the Old Norse *skali*) and 'shiel(s)' or shield(s)' (from the Middle English *shele*), both of which are often interpreted as 'shieling hut'. Almost 400 names containing these elements appear on the mid-twentieth century Ordnance Survey One-Inch maps of the six northern counties of England and Scotland south of the Forth-Clyde isthmus.[1] It is not surprising that names derived from the Old Norse *skali* (usually in the form *scale(s)*, but taking the form *schole(s)* in

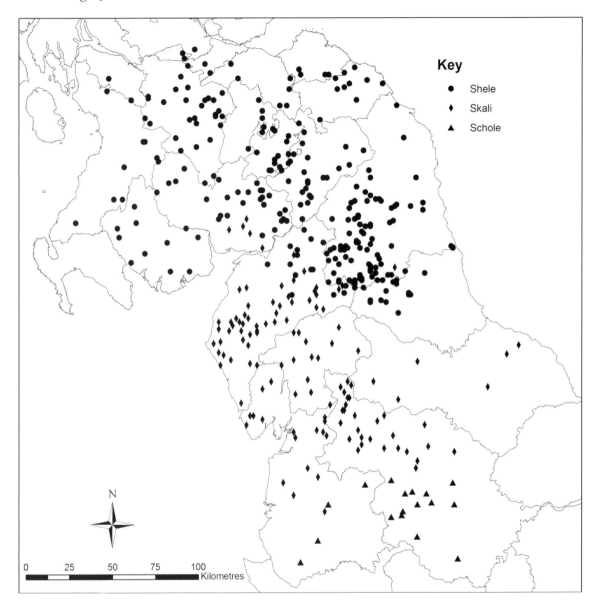

FIGURE 9.2. Distribution of *shele*, *skali* and *schole* place-names on One Inch maps of northern England and southern Scotland (map: Caron Newman)

the more southern parts of Lancashire and the West Riding of Yorkshire) are found across the areas of Scandinavian settlement in Yorkshire and north-west England, while *shele* names are found in Northumbria and southern Scotland. The greatest concentrations of the names are in Northumberland and the Borders and in Cumbria, with the scatter thinning out as one moves south into Lancashire and Yorkshire and west into Galloway (Fig. 9.2). As has been noted elsewhere, the names are noticeably less frequent in the heartland of demesne stock-rearing, the vaccary country of the central Pennines and Bowland fells (Winchester 2000, 90–1).

The total assemblage of 405 names (see Appendix) may be sub-divided into

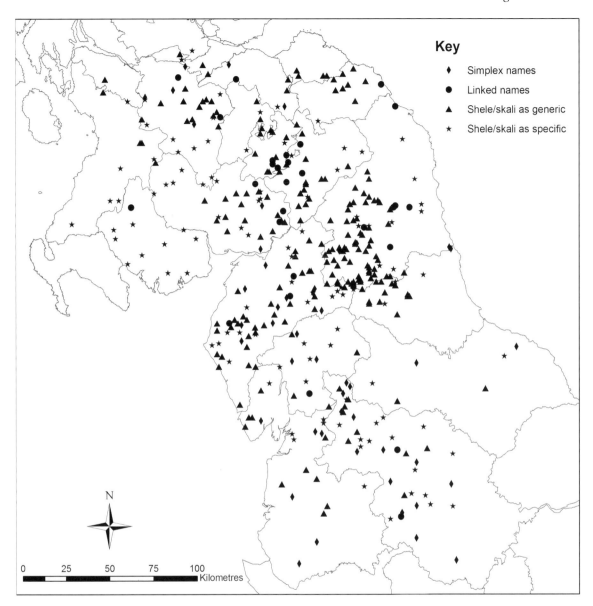

FIGURE 9.3. Classification of *shele*, *skali* and *schole* place-names on One Inch maps of northern England and southern Scotland (map: Caron Newman)

four categories, according to how the *skali/shele* element is used (Fig. 9.3). As will be shown, these are found in different topographical contexts, suggesting that they may reflect differences in meaning and chronology. Group 1 (forty-seven examples) consists of simplex names, normally in the plural: Scales or Shields; Group 2, has twenty-eight instances of a *skali/shele* name being linked to the name of a 'parent' township or farm (as Deanscales, in the parish of Dean [Cu]). Group 3, by far the most numerous (occurring 218 times), comprises those names in which *skali/shele* is the generic element, as in Rogerscale or Foreshield. Also numerous (112 occurrences) are Group 4 names in which *skali/shele* is the specific element, as in Scalehill or Shield Burn.

Groups 1 and 2, the simplex names and linked names, may be taken together, not least because simplex names are not infrequently also recorded in forms linking them to a parish or township name. Examples from Cumberland include the Scales place-names at Bromfield, Lorton and Skelton, which are recorded as 'Broomefielde Skailes', 'Lortonscales' and 'Skelton Skailes' respectively in sixteenth-century sources, and Scalehouses at Renwick, recorded as 'Ravenwik Scalez' in 1485 (Armstrong *et al.* 1950–2, i, 236, 242; ii, 273; Winchester 1987, 148). Conversely, Holmescales [We], the *scales* belonging to the township of Holme, was recorded simply as 'Eschales' in 1201 (Smith 1967, I, 127). It is striking that the element *scale/shiel(d)* is in the plural in almost two-thirds (thirty-one out of forty-seven) of the Group 1 names, suggesting that most refer to clusters of buildings rather than individual huts. This is reflected on the modern map, where places bearing such names are often hamlets or groups of farms. They frequently lie in a peripheral location within a township: Scales, in Kirkoswald [Cu] is on rising ground at the eastern extremity of the township; the hamlet of Deanscales on the edge of the parish of Dean [Cu], for example. Most Group 2 names are outlying settlements linked by name to a farm or hamlet: examples include Braithwaite Shields [Cu], which lies within 1 km of Low Braithwaite and 2 km of Braithwaite Hall; East and West Rothley Shields [Nb], on rising ground on the northern margin of the parish, a couple of miles from Rothley itself; and Witton Shields [Nb], 2 km from Nether Witton. Most names in this category are located in the lowlands or on the edges of the hills, rather than in the heart of the uplands. An exception is provided by a handful of linked names in the Southern Uplands, which are deep in the hills, linking a 'shiel' name (often in the singular) to a farm a mile or so downstream (for example Finglandshiel [Dmf], in a side valley a mile from the farm of Fingland in Eskdalemuir). In each case, such names imply that these were secondary settlements, in some sense subsidiary to the principal settlement in the township and generally within a couple of miles of it.

In contrast to many of the simplex names, the Group 3 names, in which *skali/shele* is the generic element (as in Southerscales [YW], Carp Shield [Du] and Gutherscale [Cu]), are generally single steadings rather than nucleated settlements, a scatter of farms bearing names of this type often being found in the same area. The names themselves reflect this, a much smaller proportion (35%; 77 of the 218 names) containing the plural form *scales/shiel(d)s* than is the case among the simplex names. The distribution of Group 3 names shows a concentration in Northumberland and the eastern Borders and also in the Lake District, generally on the fringes of the uplands and running up the valleys into the heart of the hills. A number of defining adjectives recur, most strikingly a group of specifics suggesting decay or poverty. The prefix *burnt* (Burntshiel(d)) occurs six times; *old* (Auld/Old Shiel(d), Old Scale(s)) occurs five times. Names implying dirt (Foulshield; Sosgill ('sour scales')) and chilliness (Coldshield; Cauldshield) are found, while the most numerous prefix is *wind* (Winskill; Windscales; Windshield), occurring eleven times. Although only a minority of the total group, these names are strongly suggestive of impoverished dwellings in inclement locations, a description which would fit many seasonal settlement sites.

The final category, Group 4, consists of topographical names in which *skali/shele* is the specific, as in Shiel Hill or Scale Beck. Although some are now the names of settlements (presumably taking their name from the topographical feature so named), the category also includes the names of numerous features in the landscape – indeed, by using the One-Inch maps as a filter, this analysis under-represents this category of name; the 1:25,000 maps of northern England augment the numbers considerably. In this category, *skali/shele* is combined with a wide range of generics, but three particular groups of names stand out. By far the commonest, occurring forty-seven times in the corpus, are names in which the specific *skali/shele* is combined with a term meaning 'hill', such as *hill* (twenty-one occurrences), *rig(g)* ('ridge') (ten occurrences); *ber/bar* (OE *beorg*) (6 occurrences); and *howe, bank, knowe,* or *dod*.[2] Second, accounting for twenty-three names in Group 4, are names where the generic is a term meaning 'stream', most commonly *burn* or *gill* (ten occurrences each). Third are names denoting open ground of some description, including *green* (six occurrences), *hope* (a valley), *field* and *moor*. In each case, we may assume that the presence of 'scales' or 'shields' was the salient feature of the place and gave its name to the hill, stream or open area. Indeed, names in this category confirm the types of location where archaeological remains identified as shielings are found, clusters of huts on hills or by streams, often on an interfluve where two streams meet. In several instances it is possible to link such names directly with archaeological evidence for shielings. The Royal Commission's survey of shielings in northern Cumbria included huts at Shiel Knowe and Shiels Brae in Bewcastle, on the flanks of the Shield Water valley on the northern slopes of Cross Fell, and at Scale Close in Borrowdale (Ramm *et al.* 1970, 18, 35, 36–8). Furthermore, names in this category are found in areas for which the documentary evidence for shieling practices, discussed above, occurs. The Shield Water valley, for example, forms the boundary of the manor of Alston Moor [Cu], where there is evidence for organised removal to shieling grounds in the sixteenth century (Winchester 2000, 162–3).

Taken as a group, the *skali/shele* names of northern England and the Scottish Borders are thus found in a wide range of contexts: subsidiary hamlets on the periphery of lowland townships; poor dwellings in remote locations; and hills and streams where huts were built. Only the last of these three categories of names links obviously to the shieling practices recorded in the sixteenth and seventeenth centuries. A closer look at the meanings, use and chronology of the words *scale* and *shiel(d)* strengthens the impression of a diversity of origins given by this initial analysis of the place-names.

Meaning, use and chronology of *shele/skali*

What did medieval northerners mean by the terms *scale* and *shiel(d)* and how were they used? There can be no doubt that they were used of summer shielings (the term derives, of course, from *shele*), and *shiel(d)* or *sheal* is found specifically in connection with transhumance practices in sixteenth- and seventeenth-century documents. The related Latin term *scalinga* is usually translated 'shieling', though 'summer pasture' or 'shieling ground' might be a preferable translation, in view of the high valuations and large acreages assigned to some *scalingae* in medieval documents (Winchester 2000, 93). However, *scale* and *shiel(d)* were certainly used to refer to a much wider range of features than just shieling huts on summer pastures.

It is clear that they had the general sense of 'a hut or cottage' and were applied to clusters of cottages housing the labouring or non-agricultural elements of society, and presumably occupied permanently rather than seasonally. These included non-agricultural settlements, such as those devoted to fishing or mining. Harold Fox noted the phrase *scalingas piscatoribus* ('shielings for fishermen') in a twelfth-century charter from Paisley, and it seems highly likely that North Shields [Nb] and South Shields [Du] at the mouth of the Tyne were fishing settlements (Fox 2001, 179). A comparable usage is recorded in the north Pennines, where the lead miners of Alston Moor [Cu] were said to dwell together in their own *shelis* in the fourteenth century (*Cal. Inq. Misc.* iii, no. 222). Some of the lowland settlement names incorporating *shiel(d)* or *scale* and lying close to villages may have originated as lower status clusters of huts – communities of the landless perhaps – rather than being specifically associated with seasonal herding of stock. Such an interpretation may be particularly likely for the simplex names, 'Scales' or 'Shiel(d)s', a significant number of which were recorded before 1300 (see Appendix), and which, as we have seen, often took the form of clustered hamlets in peripheral locations within a township. One documented example of such a name is the lost vill of 'Shelom' (OE *scelum*, 'at the huts') at Kirk Merrington [Du], which was a dependant, servile settlement, physically adjacent to, but distinct from, the mother settlement (Roberts 1972, 44–5).

When names which might refer to such non-agricultural contexts are put to one side, the remaining place-names suggest that the terms could refer to huts associated with uses other than the specific forms of transhumance recorded in the sixteenth- and seventeenth-century documentary evidence. First, it is immediately apparent that the distribution of names containing *skali*/*shele* is not restricted to the uplands, the scatter extending from Seascale [Cu] on the Irish Sea coast to Cheswick Shiel [Nb] on the Northumberland coast near Lindisfarne. If these are not fishing settlements, they presumably record coastal huts associated with something other than transhumance to upland pastures: writing *c.* 1600, the antiquary John Denton interpreted Seascale as 'a Skale or Sheele for cattle & sheep-cott att the sea' (Winchester 2010, 43). His suggestion that 'scale' could refer to a sheepcote tallies with the evidence of some of the place-names themselves, which, while clearly telling of an association with livestock management, link 'scales' or 'shields' with a much wider range of animals than milk cows. We find shielings associated with pigs (Swinescales), sheep (Lambshield) and goats (Gatescale, Gaitsgill), as well as cattle. Other place-name interpretations offered by Denton confirm that he did not consider 'scales' and 'shields' to have been restricted to milk cattle. He explained Gaitsgill [Cu], near Carlisle, as 'a whinny place where the inhabitants of Raughton made skales and sheeles for their goates, which pastured on the blossomes of the whins [gorse] there'. Assuming wrongly that the place-name Skelton [Cu] contained the element *skali*, he interpreted it as the 'place where of auncient tyme the country people that had their sheepe, swine and milk-beasts agghested in [Inglewood] forrest, had certaine sheeles and little cottages to rest in, whiles they gathered the summer profitts of such goods' (Winchester 2010, 131, 171). Not only might shielings be built where sheep and pigs, as well as milk cows, were tended on summer pastures but Denton could conceive of a 'scale' as a shelter for goats, rather than humans.

This leads to a third dimension of the meaning of *scale* and *shiel(d)*: they were used in the early modern period for a variety of outbuildings, particularly when built in isolated locations. 'Peat scales' (huts in which peat was stored to dry) were found on the Lake District fells and recorded from the sixteenth to the nineteenth centuries (Winchester 1984) – the use of 'scale' in this context mirrors the use of the Welsh term for a summer shieling, *hafod*, in the name of structures called *hafodtai mawn*, which were almost identical peat stores in Caernarvonshire (RCAHMW 1956, lxxviii). Sheds for sheltering cattle or for lambing, in use at the end of the seventeenth century, appear to have given their name to Ayle Shield [Nb] (PRO, E134/14 Geo. II/Hil. 6). Incidental references to 'sheles' or 'scalings' (such as the shiel (*shela*) in Weardale [Du], where Border sheep thieves were given ale and pasties in 1513, or the *scalings* on the common in Loweswater [Cu], where thieves were suspected of lurking in 1519) may relate to sheds and huts such as these, rather than to seasonal dwellings (Fraser 1991, 70; Cumbria RO, D/Lec/299/16, m. 15). In summary, it seems that both *shele* and *skali* are probably best interpreted simply as 'hut', the sense extending from 'cottage' at one extreme to 'shed' or 'outbuilding' at the other. The over-ready assumption that they invariably record the past presence of seasonal dwellings on summer pastures should be abandoned.

In the context of this wide range of meanings, what can be said about the chronology of the place-names and of the use of the terms *scale* and *shiel(d)*? As an assemblage, the *skali/shele* names cannot be assigned to any one period. At one end of the timescale are those names, particularly the names of hamlets, which are recorded as permanent settlements well before 1300. Seascale [Cu], on the Irish Sea coast, is recorded in a personal name *c.*1165 and as a settled, cultivated vill by *c.*1210 (Armstrong *et al.* 1950–2, ii. 433; Wilson 1915, no. 56); men were living in the hamlet of Scales near Ingleton [YW], by 1251; Winscales, near Workington [Cu], is recorded from 1227; Scalehouses (at Renwick) [Cu], Deanscales (Dean) [Cu] and Scales (Orton) [We] are all recorded during the second half of the thirteenth century (see Appendix). At the other end of the spectrum are the minor topographical names, some of which are likely to be of much more recent origin, since, as we have seen, both *shiel(d)* and *scale* continued in use as vernacular terms well into the early modern period.

The received interpretation of the origins of settlements bearing *skali/shele* names is that they originated in the permanent occupation of summer huts on former shieling grounds. How many of the names recorded as settlements before 1300 are to be interpreted in this way is unclear. After all, even the poverty and bleak isolation of places bearing names like Windscales and Foulshields do not necessarily imply that they were occupied only seasonally – they may have originated as low-status cottage or squatter settlements, rather than transhumance huts. Nor is the documentary evidence necessarily unambiguous: in 1315 an extent of the manor of Alston Moor [Cu] in the North Pennines included thirty-three tenants at Garrigill in the upper Tyne valley and a further twenty-two in the Nent valley who each held a *scalinga* for which they paid sums of rent averaging between 3*s* and 5*s* per annum (PRO, C134/35 (16)). Some of the strings of farms up these valleys, which are presumably the successors of these *scalingae*, bear 'shield' names (Foreshield, Loveladyshield, Shieldhill) – but were they summer shielings or permanent hill farms in 1315?

A range of evidence does suggest a process of colonisation of former seasonal dwellings, however. The 'old' *shields/scales* place-names presumably refer to former shielings, and a date for the transition to permanent occupation can occasionally be determined. At Wythop [Cu], for example, on the northern edge of the Lake District, it is possible to trace the transition from summer grazing ground to the establishment of permanent farms in the later thirteenth century. The settlement name Old Scales is probably to be interpreted as the site of shielings used to exploit the summer pastures, a reminder of Wythop's previous function (Winchester 1987, 39–40). Likewise, it seems probable that the handful of names where *scale* or *shiel(d)* is combined with 'winter' are to be interpreted as recording a move to year-round occupation. The distinguishing feature of Winter Shields on the Border wastes at Askerton [Cu], and the three Winterscales names on the western fringes of Yorkshire [YW] (in Garsdale, on bleak moorland on the slopes of Whernside in Ingleton, and at Rathmell on the edge of the Bowland fells) was presumably that each was occupied all year round, perhaps where other *scales* were not. From their location, high up and deep in the hills, reverse transhumance – the movement of stock to winter pastures – is highly unlikely. In one case (the Winterscales by Whernside), the reference to a 'house' (*domum*) there in 1346 implies that it was inhabited and settled permanently before the Black Death (Brownbill 1916, 332).

There is also some evidence for a transition from seasonal to permanent settlement in the economic recovery of the late fifteenth century. The settlements at the head of Allendale [Nb], which bear *shield* names (Carrshield; Turney Shield; Farney Shield) and were recorded as holdings by 1547, probably represent the six areas of demesne grassland called 'lez Shelez' in 1421 (PRO, SC6/1123/12; *NCH* iii, 72–3). It is plausible that a transition to permanent settlement took place between these dates. More explicit evidence of a similar process comes from the edge of Inglewood Forest [Cu], where rent paid for 'lodges or scalings' at Westward, near Wigton, in 1492 was explained as the result of their having been 'approved' in the winter time (Lancs. RO, DDMa, box 28, Cockermouth honour compotus 1492–3).

The different categories of place-name identified above thus probably have different histories and record different types of hut in use at different periods. Some (perhaps especially the simplex names) may have originated before the Black Death as cottager communities or squatter settlements, separate from and of lower status than the principal settlement in the township. Although the element 'cot' is found in northern England, it appears to be less common than further south and it may be that 'shiel(d)' and 'scale' sometimes took its place to describe cottage dwellings. Others are clearly associated with livestock management, but almost certainly with a wider range of practices than the sort of transhumance recorded in the Borders and North Pennines in the late sixteenth century. It is to these names that attention is now turned.

Huts close to home

The Group 4 names discussed above include topographical names (such as Scalehill and Shielburn), where *skali/shele* is the defining element, used to distinguish one hill, stream or area of open ground from others in the vicinity. Some of these names, particularly when they occur in remote locations, in the hills at a distance from settlement, can safely be interpreted as recording shieling huts on the hill grazings, particularly since, as noted above, the remains of huts have been found at some such named places. However, putting those to one side, it is striking that, across northern England, similar names (notably *scale/ shiel(d)* + 'hill') are frequently found within 1–2 km of a village, sometimes as a topographical name within an area of former open fields, elsewhere on the edges of the common moorland. To the instances recorded in the Appendix, several others may be added, from the 1:25,000 maps. A selection of examples of these 'shieling hill' names will suffice. The first of those illustrated in Figure 9.4 are on the Yorkshire/Lancashire border in the rolling country in the valley of the River Greta. Two farms named Scaleber lie out in the fields between Cantsfield [La] and Bentham [YW] – both are on rounded drumlins close to the parish and county boundary, apparently within the confines of early-enclosed farmland. A second example is Scalehaw Hill, which lies on rising ground on the edge of the moor 1 km from the village at Long Preston [YW] to which it is linked by a lane through the village fields. A comparable name and situation occur at Melmerby [Cu], where Shieldgreen Wood (NY 624 381) lies at the foot of the Pennine scarp, within 2 km of the village. Perhaps the most striking of these names are those which occur in areas of strip-like fields, almost certainly representing enclosure of furlongs in a former open field: Scalebarrs Hill (NY 53 26) in the fields of Clifton [We] and Scalehow Rigg (NZ 00 19) west of the village of Cotherstone [YN] are examples. None of the examples cited are in upland situations; all are close to 'lowland' villages, sometimes on the edge of the hills.

How are such names to be explained? The huts to which they refer would have been too close to the settlement to be shieling huts associated with transhumance proper. In the cases cited above, as in many others, they lie not far out on the common grazings but close to the head-dyke or within land

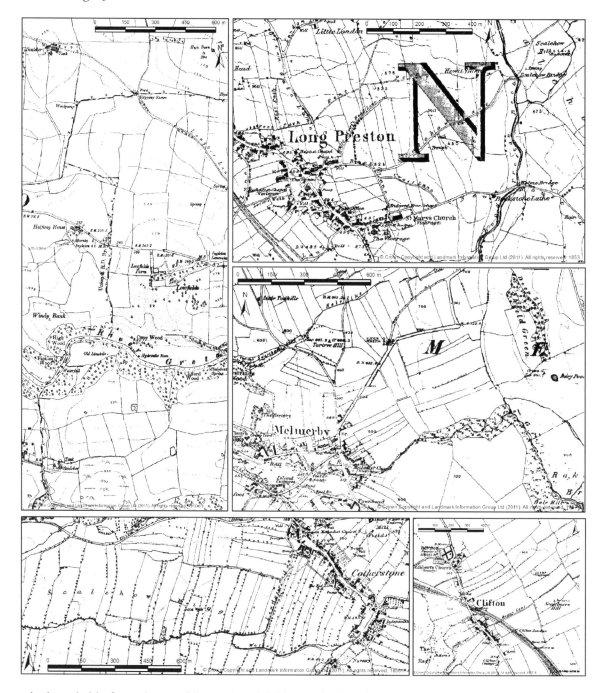

which probably formed part of the medieval fields – indeed, as has been noted, at Clifton [We] and Cotherstone [YN], the 'shieling hill' seems clearly to have lain within the open fields. Some parallels are recorded in the documentary evidence, suggesting that 'shieling hills' such as these may nevertheless have been associated with dairying. That shielings might be built at a short distance from permanent settlement is made clear in late medieval evidence from several areas. In 1465 a man from Consett [Du], erected a 'shele to dwell in in somer' when tending his cattle at Horsleyhope, a valley on the edge of Muggleswick common, no more than *c*.5 km away. In Westward [Cu], men from Thursby and Micklethwaite, settlements a similar distance away, held 'scalings' in 1517. Those belonging to Thursby were still in use in 1638 when the tenants were said to 'have had Sheildes there and milked there Kye theire it beeing aboute 2 myles from Thursbye' (Greenwell and Knowles 1895; Cumbria RO, D/Lec/299/14, m. 2; D/Lons/L5/2/41/53).

These are late references but they provide evidence of an alternative form of seasonal settlement, involving short-distance stock movement to summer milking grounds. The huts recorded in the names such as Scalehow Rigg and Scaleber may well have disappeared by the later medieval centuries. Those names lying within the open fields presumably predate expansion of the open fields (probably in the thirteenth century) – certainly, some names in this category had been coined at an early date. 'Scaleberg' is recorded as a field name at Clifton [Cu] by the mid-thirteenth century, for example (Wilson 1915, 357n). In these topographical names are we catching glimpses of an earlier pastoral system, in which milking grounds on the margins of the village fields carried groups of seasonally occupied huts? It is instructive here to note the variety of functions and locations embraced by the term *seter* in Norway: the traditional transhumance systems included not only full *seters*, occupied across the summer, in which both milking and butter and cheese production were carried out, but also the 'milkingseter', where milking was carried out at the *seter* but cheese and butter production took place on the home farm. Some of the short-distance stock movements implied by the northern English shieling names may parallel the Scandinavian *heimseter*, a shieling ground close to home used in the first flush of grass growth in spring and when stock returned from mountain shielings at the end of summer (Borchgrevink 1977).

In summary, the *skali/shele* place-names of northern England almost certainly record a much wider range of activities than transhumance as traditionally conceived. If we strip away the names which may more likely be interpreted as recording squatter cottages, settlements of miners or fishermen, or outbuildings such as 'peat scales' and lambing sheds, the key to the remaining core is probably the need to provide shelter and temporary accommodation for herdsmen and milk-maids on milking grounds. Some, no doubt, were shielings in the conventional sense, huts on summer pastures at considerable distance from the permanent settlement, to which milking herds and their keepers were sent from May to August. But some, indeed perhaps a majority, are more likely to record the use of milking hills comparatively close to home. In a landscape with few enclosed pastures, milk cows would require close herding and their minders and milkers may well have lived with them during the dairying season. We need therefore to add an additional form of seasonal settlement to the transhumance recorded in the Border hills and north Pennines in the sixteenth and seventeenth centuries. Short-distance removal of stock and their minders to milking sheds on the margins of the village's fields may have been widespread during the

FIGURE 9.4. A selection of *scale/shiel(d)* + 'hill' place-names as shown on the Ordnance Survey 1:10560 County Series maps. Clockwise from top left: Two farms named Scaleber between Cantsfield [La] and Bentham [YW] (2nd revision, 1910–19); Scalehaw Hill, Long Preston [YW] (1st ed. 1853); Shieldgreen Wood, Melmerby [Cu] (1st ed. 1867–8); Scalebarrs Hill, Clifton [We] (1st ed. 1863–7) and Scalehow Rigg west of Cotherstone [YN] (1st ed. 1856–7). © Crown Copyright and Landmark Information Group Ltd (2011). All rights reserved. 1853–1919

medieval period, surviving into the early-modern period only in restricted areas, such as Westward. The decline of these seasonal dwellings would have gone hand-in-hand with a move to other, perhaps more intensive, pastoral systems. Of key importance would have been the enclosure of separate cow pastures, acting to contain the milking herd and allowing milking to take place close to the farm, while the transition to improved, stock-proof, field boundaries around farmland, in the form of stone walls and quick hedges, across the two centuries from approximately 1450 to 1650, would have lessened the urgency of removing stock from the home farm for the sake of protecting crops of corn and hay. Only some shielings in the northern counties were really 'out in the wilds', as in the transhumance practices of the Borders, witnessed by Camden.

Appendix: *shele/skali* names in northern England and southern Scotland

The following lists present the corpus of place-names discussed in this paper. They are based on *shele/skali* names recorded on Ordnance Survey 7th series One Inch to One Mile maps, supplemented by names recorded in county place-name surveys. Coverage is thus slightly uneven, the data from the counties covered by English Place-Name Society surveys (Cu, We, YN and YW) being more complete than those from other counties. The date of earliest record is given for those names recorded before 1600.

Name	County	Grid ref.	Earliest record	Source
Group 1: simplex names				
Scale (Hutton Roof)	Cu	NY 38 33	1562	Armstrong, 1950–2 , i. 212
Scale (Grisdale)	YW	SD 76 93		
Scale (Horton)	YW	SD 80 75		
Scale House (Farleton)	La	SD 58 66		
Scale House (Rylstone)	YW	SD 97 56	1567	Smith 1961–2, vi. 95
Scale Houses (Renwick)	Cu	NY 58 45	1278	Armstrong, 1950–2, i. 236
Scale (Roeburndale)	La	SD 62 65		
Scale, High/Low (Halton West)	YW	SD 82 55	1561	Smith 1961–2, vi. 157
Scale, High/Low (Garsdale)	YW	SD 78 91		
Scales (Aldingham)	La	SD 27 72	1269	Mills 1976, 131
Scales (Askham)	We	NY 48 20	1577	Smith 1967, ii. 202
Scales (Dent)	YW	SD 74 87		
Scales, East/West (Gretna)	Dmf	NY 27 67	1512	Fellows-Jensen 1985, 68
Scales (Ingleton)	YW	SD 73 77	1251	Brownbill 1916, 326
Scales (Kentmere)	We	NY 45 05		
Scales (Kirkoswald)	Cu	NY 57 43	1479	Armstrong, 1950–2, i. 251
Scales (Lorton)	Cu	NY 16 25	1517	Winchester 1987, 148

Scales (Newton with Scales)	La	SD 45 30	1501	Mills 1976, 131
Scales (nr Buttermere)	Cu	NY 16 16	*c.*1618	Whaley 2006, 296
Scales (Threlkeld)	Cu	NY 34 26	1323	Armstrong, 1950–2, i. 253
Scales Hall (Skelton)	Cu	NY 42 40	1316	Armstrong, 1950–2 i. 242
Scales House (Askwith)	YW	SE 16 49	*c.*1296	Smith 1961–2, v. 61
Scales, High/Low (Gilling)	YN	NZ 16 04	1137–47	Smith 1928, 289
Scales, High/Low (Bromfield)	Cu	NY 18 45	1353	Armstrong, 1950–2, ii. 273
Scales, High/Low (Orton)	We	NY 59 06	1256	Smith 1967, ii. 44
Scaling (Easington)	YN	NZ 74 13	12th cent.	Smith 1928, 139
Scholes (Barwick)	YW	SE 36 37	1258	Smith 1961–2, iv. 109
Scholes (Cleckheaton)	YW	SE 16 25	1229	Smith 1961–2, iii. 18
Scholes (Eccleston)	La	SJ 49 93	1190	Ekwall 1922, 108
Scholes (Greetland)	YW	SE 08 21	13th cent.	Smith 1961–2, iii. 48
Scholes (Holmfirth)	YW	SE 16 07	1274	Watts 2004, 531
Scholes (Oakworth)	YW	SE 01 38	1325	Smith 1961–2, vi. 8
Scholes (Rotherham)	YW	SK 39 95		Smith 1961–2, i. 187
Scholes (Wigan)	La	SD 59 05	1332	Mills 1976, 132
Shiel (Westerkirk)	Dmf	NY 28 91	1376	Johnson-Ferguson 1935, 135
Shiel, Nether/Over (Kirknewton)	Midl	NT 09 69		
Shiels, Nether/Over (Stow)	Midl	NT 41 46		
Shield [on the Wall]	Nb	NY 72 66		
Shield [on the Wall]	Nb	NY 82 70		
Shield (Burgh by Sands)	Cu	NY 30 58		
[North] Shields	Nb	NZ 35 68	1267	Watts 2004, 544
[South] Shields	Du	NZ 36 67	1235	Watts 2004, 544
Shields (Carmichael)	Lnk	NS 89 36		
Shields (East Kilbride)	Lnk	NS 61 51		
Shields (Monkland)	Lnk	NS 84 68		
Shields (Motherwell)	Lnk	NS 77 55		
Skelling (Skirwith)	Cu	NY 62 33	1292	Armstrong, 1950–2, i. 243
Group 2: linked names				
Adderston Shiels	Rox	NT 51 09		
Arkletonshiels	Dmf	NY 40 88		
Barden Scale	YW	SE 05 56	1295	Smith 1961–2, vi. 60
Biggarshiels	Lnk	NT 04 40		
Birtley Shields	Nb	NY 86 79		
Borthwickshiels	Rox	NT 43 15		
Bothwellshields	Lnk	NS 80 62		
Braithwaite Shields	Cu	NY 44 41		
Broomholmshiels	Dmf	NY 38 82		
Cheswick Shiel	Nb	NU 04 46		
Colterscleugh Shiel	Rox	NT 42 04		
Deanscales	Cu	NY 09 26	1278	Armstrong, 1950–2, ii. 366
Deloranieshiel	Slk	NT 34 16		
Elland Scholes	YW	SE 07 19	13th cent.	Smith 1961–2, iii. 50

Finglandshiel	Dmf	NT 24 03		
Halton Shields	Nb	NZ 01 68		
Holmescales	We	SD 55 87	1201	Smith 1967,, i. 127
Hoscoteshiel	Rox	NT 37 12		
Lambertonshields	Berw	NT 96 58		
Listonshiels	Midl	NT 13 61		
Mainshiel Head	Rox	NT 44 14		(associated with Borthwick Mains)
Riddelshiel	Rox	NT 50 25		
Rothley East Shield	Nb	NZ 04 91		
Rothley West Shield	Nb	NZ 03 90		
Shiel of Castlemaddy	Kcd	NX 53 90		
Todrigshiel	Slk	NT 42 19		
Wetheral Shield	Cu	NY 46 52		
Witton Shields	Nb	NZ 12 90		

Group 3: shele/skali as generic

Allenshields	Du	NY 96 49		
Appletree Shield	Nb	NY 77 49		
Arthurshiels	Lnk	NT 00 41		
Aydon Shields	Nb	NY 92 56		
Ayhope Shield	Du	NZ 05 31		
Batailshiel Haugh	Nb	NT 88 10		
Batey Shield	Nb	NY 65 60		
Beldon Shields	Nb	NY 93 49		
Bellshiel	Berw	NT 81 49		
Bellshiel Law/Burn	Nb	NT 81 01		
Billing Shield	Du	NY 95 38		
Blackshiel	Midl	NT 43 61		
Bog Shield	Nb	NY 89 79		
Bonscale	We	NY 45 20	1588	Smith 1967, ii. 218
Bowershield	Nb	NY 94 94		
Bowscale	Cu	NY 35 315	1361	Armstrong, 1950–2, i. 181–2
Brackinscal	La	SD 39 37		
Brinscall	La	SD 63 21	*c.*1200	Mills 1976, 67
Broomshiels	Du	NZ 11 42		
Brothershiels	Midl	NT 42 55		
Bruntshiel	Dmf	NY 41 82		
Bruntshiels	Dmf	NY 02 83		
Burnt Shields	Cu	NY 50 83		
Burntshield Haugh	Nb	NY 92 53		
Burntshield	Ayr	NS 59 26		
Burntshields	Renf	NS 38 61		
Byreshield Hill	Nb	NY 67 83		
Camp Shiel	Pbl	NT 34 32		
Carp Shield	Du	NZ 04 47		
Carr Shield	Nb	NY 80 47		
Castleshields	Cu	NY 43 58		
Cauldshiel	E Loth	NT 48 66		
Cauldshiels	Slk	NT 51 31		
Cawburn Shield	Nb	NY 72 68		
Cockenskell	La	SD 27 89	1284	Whaley 2006, 76
Cocker Shield	Nb	NY 89 54		

Coldshield	Nb	NY 71 58		
Colinshiel	W Loth	NS 94 69		
Conshield	Nb	NY 85 75		
Cragshield Hope	Nb	NY 73 83		
Craigs Windshiel	Berw	NT 69 61		
Craigshiel	Ayr	NS 67 15		
Craikshiel	Rox	NT 32 10		
Daddry Shield	Du	NY 89 37	1438	DUL, CC 190030
Damhead Shiel	Pbl	NT 33 33		
Davyshiel	Nb	NY 89 96		
Dronshiel	Berw	NT 70 55		
Dunshiel	Nb	NY 92 94		
Eastshield	Lnk	NS 96 50		
Elliscales	La	SD 22 74	1211	Ekwall 1922, 206
Elshieshields	Dmf	NY 07 85	1521	Johnson-Ferguson 1935, 88
Eshiels	Pbl	NT 27 39		
Espershields	Nb	NY 99 52		
Farney Shield	Nb	NY 79 48		
Farrow Shields	Nb	NY 75 62		
Feniscowles	La	SD 65 25	1276	Mills 1976, 84
Foreshield	Cu	NY 75 46		
Foulshiels	Rox	NY 49 91		
Foulshiels	Slk	NT 42 29		
Foulshiels	W Loth	NS 97 64		
Gair Shield	Nb	NY 89 55		
Gaitscale Close	Cu	NY 24 02	1398–9	Whaley 2006, 124
Gaitsgill	Cu	NY 38 46	1278	Armstrong, 1950–2, i. 133
Galashiels	Slk	NT 48 36		
Gallowshieldrigg	Nb	NY 75 68		
Gamelshiel	E Loth	NT 65 63	1505	Nicolaisen 1976, 115
Gammersgill	YN	SE 05 83	1388	Smith 1928, 254
Gapshield	Nb	NY 64 64		
Garret Shiels	Nb	NY 87 93		
Garwaldshiels	Dmf	NY 19 98		
Gib Shiel	Nb	NY 80 93		
Glenshiel Banks	Pbl	NT 27 31		
Greenshieldhouse	Lnk	NS 99 49		
Greenshields	Lnk	NT 02 43		
Greenshiels	Lnk	NS 85 38		
Gutherscale	Cu	NY 24 21	1293	Armstrong, 1950–2, ii. 370
Hangingshields Rigg	Nb	NY 68 67		
Harwood Shield	Nb	NY 90 51		
Heggerscales	We	NY 82 10	1380	Smith 1967, ii. 5
Hellot Scales	We	SD 66 80		
High Shield (Kirkhaugh)	Nb	NY 65 48		
High Shield (Henshaw)	Nb	NY 76 67		
High Shield (Allendale)	Nb	NY 85 45		
High Shield (Hexham)	Nb	NY 93 63		
Highlandshiels	Pbl	NT 28 34		
Hind's Shield	Nb	NY 83 67		
Holeshields	Cu	NY 47 66		
Howcleughshiel	Rox	NT 42 14		

Howscales	Cu	NY 58 41	1278	Armstrong, 1950–2, i. 216
Hudscales	Cu	NY 33 37	1560	Armstrong, 1950–2, ii, 279
Huntershield	Nb	NY 78 60		
Huntshield	Du	NY 89 38		
Hynam Shield	Cu	NY 56 55		
Jockey Shield	Cu	NY 55 55		
Johnscales	We	SD 46 86	1526	Smith 1967, i. 84
Keeper Shield	Nb	NY 90 72		
Keepers Shield	Nb	NY 87 66		
Keskadale	Cu	NY 20 19	1260	Armstrong, 1950–2, ii. 370
Kidshiel	Berw	NT 74 56		
Knock Shield	Nb	NY 83 50		
Lamb Shield	Du	NZ 02 48		
Lamb Shield	Nb	NY 94 61		
Landskill	La	SD 53 45	1341	Fellows-Jensen 1985, 65
Laskill	YN	SE 56 90	1170	Smith 1928, 72
Legholmshiels	Lnk	NT 03 35		
Linshiels	Nb	NT 89 06		
Longburnshiels	Rox	NT 53 04		
Longheughshields	Nb	NY 82 84		
Longscales	YW	SE 22 57	1230	Smith 1961–2, v. 131
Lonscale	Cu	NY 29 25	1566	Armstrong, 1950–2 , ii. 323
Loudscales	La	SD 59 40	1219	Ekwall 1922, 149
Lovelady Shield	Cu	NY 75 46		
Low Saugh Shield	Du	NY 89 57		
Low Scales	La	SD 15 81		
Luckie Shiel	E Loth	NT 74 64		
Lynnshield	Nb	NY 69 61		
Lyonshields	Ayr	NS 37 54		
Merry Shiels	Nb	NZ 00 81		
Middle Shield	Cu	NY 62 70	1589	Armstrong, 1950–2 i. 98
Midshiel	Rox	NT 53 17		
Mill Shield	Nb	NZ 01 52		
Munshiel Hill	Dmf	NY 31 96		
Netherscale (Embleton)	Cu	NY 17 30		
Netherscales (Hutton)	Cu	NY 44 37		
Nethershield	Ayr	NS 58 26		
Nethershields	Lnk	NS 70 48		
New Shield	Nb	NY 83 52		
Newshield	Cu	NY 71 48	1597	Armstrong, 1950–2, i. 178
Nitshiel Sike	Rox	NT 38 10		
North Scale	La	SD 18 69	1247	Fellows-Jensen 1985, 66
North Scales	Cu	NY 51 54		
Northshield	Pbl	NT 25 49		
Old Man's Sheel	Nb	NY 80 83		
Old Scale(s)	Cu	NY 19 28		
Old Shields	Dnb	NS 81 75		
Old Shields	Nb	NY 66 66		
Oldshiel	Dmf	NX 95 94		
Oldshiels Wood	Dmf	NY 07 95		
Panshield	Nb	NZ 09 54		
Park Shield	Nb	NY 89 69		

Parson Shields	Nb	NY 68 53		
Penmanshiel	Berw	NT 80 67		
Penshiel	Berw	NT 63 63		
Pirryshiel Sike	Rox	NY 50 98		
Portinscale	Cu	NY 24 23	*c.*1160	Armstrong, 1950–2, ii. 371
Prior Scales	Cu	NY 06 07		
Raff Shield	Nb	NZ 01 89		
Rammerscales	Dmf	NY 08 77	1374–5	Fellows-Jensen 1985, 67
Rashshiel	Dmf	NY 39 83		
Ridley Shiel	Nb	NY 78 92		
Riggshield	Cu	NY 47 63		
Rogerscale	Cu	NY 14 26	1260	Armstrong, 1950–2, ii. 447
Ropelawshiel	Slk	NT 31 10		
Sandscale	La	SD 20 74	1292	Fellows-Jensen 1985, 68
Sarkshiels	Dmf	NY 27 74		
Seascale	Cu	NY 03 02	*c.*1165	Armstrong, 1950–2, ii. 433
Sewing Shields	Nb	NY 81 70		
Shankendshiel	Rox	NT 53 03		
Sharnothshield	Lnk	NS 84 56		
Shepherd Shield	Nb	NY 77 75		
Shipley Shiels	Nb	NY 77 89		
Simonscales	Cu	NY 12 28	1279	Armstrong, 1950–2, ii. 363
Sipton Shield	Nb	NY 84 50		
Sosgill	Cu	NY 10 24	*c.*1203	Armstrong, 1950–2, ii. 411
South Shields	Du	NZ 12 41		
Southerscales	YW	SD 74 77	1202–8	Smith 1961–2, vi. 244
Spital Shield	Nb	NY 88 58		
Staneshiel Burn	Rox	NY 53 92		
Stanshiel	Rox	NT 77 13		
Stewart Shield Meadow	Du	NY 98 43		
Stewart Shiels	Nb	NY 86 98		
Stobshiel	E Loth	NT 49 63		
Stoneshiel	Berw	NT 87 60		
Stoneshiel Hill	Berw	NT 77 58		
Stot Scales	YW	SD 77 84	1591	Smith 1961–2, vi. 259
Stubbsgill	Cu	NY 14 44	1595	Armstrong, 1950–2, ii. 328
Stubsgill	Cu	NY 02 22	*c.*1210	Armstrong, 1950–2, ii. 376
Summerscales	YW	SE 10 54	1203	Smith 1961–2, v. 74
Summersgill	La	SD 64 63		
Swinhope Shield	Nb	NY 84 49		
Swinscales	Cu	NY 41 27		
Tamshiel	Rox	NT 64 06		
Tibbie Shiels	Slk	NT 24 20		
Tomshielburn	Dmf	NY 34 77		
Town Shields	Nb	NY 81 71		
Turney Shield	Nb	NY 80 49		
Under Shieldhill	Lnk	NS 83 49		
Wall Shield	Nb	NY 71 69		
Warnscale	Cu	NY 19 13		
Watscales	Dmf	NY 18 83	1452	Fellows-Jensen 1985, 72
Wellshields	Lnk	NS 88 39		
West Scholes	YW	SE 09 31		

West Shields	Du	NZ 11 41		
Westshield	Lnk	NS 94 49		
Westshiels	Rox	NT 62 06		
Whinscales	Cu	NY 20 03		
Whiskershiel	Nb	NY 95 93		
Whitehillshiel (Castleton)	Rox	NY 55 95		
Whitehillshiel (Kirkhope)	Slk	NT 36 18		
Whiteley Shield	Nb	NY 80 48		
Whitshiels	Dmf	NY 37 86		
Windshiel Grain	Dmf	NY 26 99		
Windshield Hill	Dmf	NY 13 98		
Windshielknowe	Rox	NT 52 00		
Windshiels	Dmf	NY 16 92		
Windshiels	Ayr	NS 59 39		
Windyshields	Lnk	NS 92 46		
Winscales	Cu	NY 02 26	1227	Armstrong, 1950–2, ii. 454
Winscales	Cu	NY 02 09	1294	Armstrong, 1950–2 ,ii. 341
Winshields	Nb	NY 74 66		
Winskill	Cu	NY 58 34	1292	Armstrong, 1950–2, i. 208
Winskill	YW	SD 82 66	1414	Smith 1961–2, vi. 147
Winter Shields	Cu	NY 55 72	1259	Armstrong, 1950–2, i. 56
Winterscale Bank (Rathmell)	YW	SD 77 61		
Winterscales (Garsdale)	YW	SD 72 90	1346	Smith 1961–2, vi. 263
Winterscales (Ingleton)	YW	SD 75 80	1379	Smith 1961–2, vi. 244
Wood Shield	Nb	NY 87 66		
Woodley Shield	Nb	NY 8476		

Group 4: shele/skali as specific

Scalebank	Cu	NY 71 44	1568	Armstrong, 1950–2 , i. 179
Scalebarrow Knott	We	NY 52 15	12th cent.	Smith 1967, ii. 177
Scale Beck (Gosforth)	Cu	NY 09 05		
Scalebeck (Asby)	We	NY 67 14	1294	Smith 1967, ii. 58
Scaleber (Bentham)	YW	SD 63 71		
Scaleber (Gargrave)	YW	SD 93 53		
Scaleber (Settle)	YW	SD 84 62		
Scaleber (Cantsfield)	La	SD 63 73	1202	Ekwall 1922, 183
Scalebor Park	YW	SE 15 45	13th cent.	Smith 1961–2, iv. 198
Scaliber (Plompton)	YW	SE 37 54	1276	Smith 1961–2,, v. 31
Scaleby	Cu	NY 45 63	*c.*1180	Armstrong, 1950–2, i. 106
Scale Cross/Foot	YN	NZ 67 08	1301	Smith 1928, 148
Scales Cross	Nb	NZ 03 56		
Scalegill (Bewaldeth)	Cu	NY 19 35		
Scalegill (Orton)	We	NY 58 05	1256	Smith 1967, ii. 48
Scalegill Hall (Egremont)	Cu	NX 99 14	1321	Armstrong, 1950–2, ii. 381
Scalegill Mill (Malham)	YW	SD 89 61		
Scale Gill Foot (Dent)	YW	SD 76 84		
Scale Green	La	SD 32 93		
Scale Hall	La	SD 46 62	1577	Ekwall 1922, 177
Scale Haw (Hebden)	YW	SE 02 63		
Scalehaw Hill (Long Preston)	YW	SD 84 58	1578	Smith 1961–2, vi. 161

Scalehowe Wood (Murton)	We	NY 71 23		
Scale Hill (Brackenthwaite)	Cu	NY 15 21		
Scalehill (Tundergarth)	Dmf	NY 16 79		
Scalehill (Lazonby)	Cu	NY 54 38	1568	Armstrong, 1950–2, i. 220
Scalelands	Cu	NY 03 15		
Scale Mire	YW	SD 72 70		
Scalesmoor	Cu	NY 08 21	1586	Armstrong, 1950–2, ii. 407
Scale Park	YW	SD 97 74	1405	Smith 1961–2, vi. 110
Scalesrigg	Cu	NY 57 43	14th cent	Armstrong, 1950–2. i. 251
Scalesceugh	Cu	NY 45 49	1272	Armstrong, 1950–2, i. 149
Scalestones	La	SD 45 65		
Scalewood	Dmf	NY 20 75		
Scalthwaite rigg	We	SD 53 94	1247	Smith 1967, i. 135–6
Schole Carr	YW	SE 01 18	1536	Smith 1961–2,, iii. 74
Scholebrook	YW	SE 21 31		
Scholecroft	YW	SE 24 26		
Scholefield	La	SD 86 36	1324	Ekwall 1922, 86
Scholemoor	YW	SE 13 32	1556	Smith 1961–2, iii. 247
Scholey Hill	YW	SE 37 25		
Shealahill (Bewcastle)	Cu	NY 51 77		
Sheillahill (Kelton)	Kcd	NX 74 54		
Shealinghill	Kcd	NX 90 73		
Shield Ash	Du	NY 98 37		
Shield Bank	Nb	NY 84 49		
Shiel Burn (Sanquhar)	Dmf	NS 82 11		
Shiel Burn (Glen Trool)	Kcd	NX 43 78		
Shiel Burn (Minnigaff)	Kcd	NX 44 73		
Shiel Burn (Dalry)	Kcd	NX 66 98		
Shiel Burn (Lamington)	Lnk	NS 97 27		
Shiel Burn (Crawford)	Lnk	NS 99 07		
Shiel Burn (Stow)	Midl	NT 37 46		
Shieldburn (East Kilbride)	Lnk	NS 61 50		
Shield Burn (Crawfordjohn)	Lnk	NS 89 23		
Shield Burn (Coylton)	Ayr	NS 47 12		
Shiel Dod	Lnk	NS 94 03		
Shiel Dykes	Nb	NU 15 06		
Shield Farm	Du	NZ 04 49		
Shielfield Wood	Berw	NT 60 38		
Shielafield	Nb	NY 83 80		
Shielgreen (Kirklinton)	Cu	NY 43 68		
Shield Green (Tritlington)	Nb	NZ 19 92		
Shield Green, Low (Birtley)	Nb	NY 89 80		
Shieldgreen (Peebles)	Pbl	NT 27 43		
Schilgreen	Rox	NT 85 21		
Shield Hall	Nb	NY 95 58		
Shielshaugh	Slk	NT 41 26		
Shield Head	Kcd	NX 83 78		

Shiel Hill (Penpont)	Dmf	NS 77 04		
Shiel Hill (Kirkmabreck)	Kcd	NX 51 59		
Shiel Hill (Kells)	Kcd	NX 61 79		
Shiel Hill (Colvend)	Kcd	NX 85 54		
Shiel Hill (Douglas)	Lnk	NS 77 28		
Shiel Hill (Colmonell)	Ayr	NX 19 81		
Shiel Hill (Straiton)	Ayr	NX 41 94		
Shielhill (Kirkharle)	Nb	NZ 02 82		
Shield Hill (Hebron)	Nb	NZ 19 88		
Shieldhill (Alston)	Cu	NY 74 42		
Shieldhill (Tinwald)	Dmf	NY 03 85		
Shieldhill (Parton)	Kcd	NX 72 70		
Shieldhill (Libberton)	Lnk	NT 00 40		
Shieldhill (Eaglesham)	Ayr	NS 51 49		
Shieldhill (Falkirk)	Stl	NS 88 77		
Shieldholm	Lnk	NS 80 21		
Shielhope (Chatton Moor)	Nb	NU 08 28		
Shielhope(Yarrow)	Slk	NT 19 22		
Shiel Knowe (Castleton)	Rox	NY 54 96		
Shielknowes (Slamannan)	Stl	NS 82 72		
Shielsknowe (Jedburgh)	Rox	NT 71 11		
Sheel Law	Nb	NY 82 85		
Shieloans	Lnk	NS 62 36		
Shiel Loch	Dmf	NS 73 03		
Shiel Moss	Dmf	NY 27 95		
Shiel Rig (Moffat)	Dmf	NT 02 05		
Shiel Rig (Eskdalemuir)	Dmf	NY 27 99		
Shiel Rig (Girthon)	Kcd	NX 59 64		
Shiel Rig (Auchinleck)	Ayr	NS 66 17		
Shiel Rig (Straiton)	Ayr	NX 46 94		
Shiel Rig/Hill (Eskdale)	Dmf	NY 26 94		
Shield Rig (Kells)	Kcd	NX 54 81		
Shields Rig (Dunsyre)	Lnk	NT 04 53		
Shieldridge (Allendale)	Nb	NY 80 45		
Shield Row	Du	NZ 20 53		
Shielstockbraes	Rox	NT 75 23		
Shield Water	Cu	NY 68 41		
Shiels Wood	Slk	NT 45 19		
Skelghyll (Ambleside)	We	NY 39 02		
Skelgill (Above Derwent)	Cu	NY 24 20	1260	Armstrong, 1950–2, ii. 371
Skell Gill (Low Abbotside)	YN	SD 92 91	1301	Smith 1928, 261
Skell Gill (Skelding)	YW	SE 20 69		
Skellgill (Alston)	Cu	NY 73 46	1473–6	Armstrong, 1950–2, i. 179

Acknowledgement

The author wishes to acknowledge the detailed and helpful comments on an earlier draft of this paper provided by an anonymous referee.

Abbreviations

Ayr	Ayrshire
Berw	Berwickshire
Cu	Cumberland
Dnb	Dunbartonshire
Dmf	Dumfriesshire
Du	Co. Durham
DUL	Durham University Library, Archives and Special Collections
E Loth	East Lothian
Kcd	Stewartry of Kirkcudbright
La	Lancashire
Lnk	Lanarkshire
Midl	Midlothian
Nb	Northumberland
NCH	*A History of Northumberland*, 15 vols, 1893–1940. Newcastle upon Tyne: Andrew Reid for Northumberland County History Committee.
Pbl	Peeblesshire
PRO	The National Archives: Public Record Office, Kew.
Renf	Renfrewshire
Rox	Roxburghshire
Slk	Selkirkshire
Stl	Stirlingshire
We	Westmorland
W Loth	West Lothian
YN	Yorkshire, North Riding
YW	Yorkshire, West Riding

Bibliography

Armstrong, A. M., Mawer, A., Stenton, F. M., and Dickens, B. (1950–2) *The Place-Names of Cumberland*, 3 vols. English Place-Name Society XX–XXII. Cambridge: Cambridge University Press.

Borchgrevink, A.-B. Ø. (1977) The 'seter' areas of rural Norway: a traditional multipurpose resource. *Northern Studies* 9, 3–24.

Brownbill, J. (ed.) (1916) *Coucher Book of Furness Abbey Volume II (part ii)*. Manchester: Chetham Society, new series 76.

Camden, W. (1610) *Britain, or a Chorographicall Description of … England, Scotland and Ireland*, trans. P. Holland. London: Impensis Georgii Bishop and Ioannis Norton.

Ekwall, E. (1922) *The Place-Names of Lancashire*. Manchester: Manchester University Press.

Fellows-Jensen, G. (1985) *Scandinavian Settlement Names in the North West*. Copenhagen: C. A. Reitzels Forlag.

Fox, H. S. A. (ed.) (1996) *Seasonal Settlement*. Leicester: University of Leicester, Vaughan Paper No. 39.

Fox, H. S. A. (2001) *The Evolution of the Fishing Village: landscape and society along the South Devon Coast, 1086–1550*. Leicester Explorations in Local History 1, Oxford: Leopard's Head Press.

Fox, H. S. A. (2008) Butter place-names and transhumance, in O. J. Padel and D. N. Parsons (ed.) *A Commodity of Good Names. Essays in honour of Margaret Gelling*, 352–64. Donington: Shaun Tyas.

Fraser, C. M. (ed.) (1991) *Durham Quarter Sessions Rolls 1471–1625*. Durham: Surtees Society 199.

Greenwell, W. and Knowles, W. H. (1895) Muggleswick, *Transactions of Architectural and Archaeological Society of Durham and Northumberland* 4, 286–315.

Johnson-Ferguson, E. (1935) *The Place-Names of Dumfriesshire*. Dumfries: Courier Press.

McDonnell, J. (1988) The role of transhumance in northern England. *Northern History* 24, 1–17.

Mills, D. (1976) *The Place-Names of Lancashire*, London: Batsford.

Nicolaisen, W. F. H. (1976) *Scottish Place-Names: their study and significance*. London: Batsford.

Ramm, H. G., McDowall, R. W. and Mercer, E. (1970) *Shielings and Bastles*. London: HMSO.

RCAHMW, 1956. Royal Commission on the Ancient and Historical Monuments of Wales and Monmouthshire, *An Inventory of Ancient Monuments in Caernarvonshire, Volume I*. London: HMSO.

Roberts, B. K. (1972) Village plans in County Durham: a preliminary statement. *Medieval Archaeology* 16, 33–56.

Smith, A. H. (ed.) (1928) *The Place-Names of the North Riding of Yorkshire*. English Place-Name Society Vol. V. Cambridge: Cambridge University Press.

Smith, A. H. (1961–2) *The Place-Names of the West Riding of Yorkshire*, 8 parts, English Place-Name Society Vols XXX–XXVII. Cambridge: Cambridge University Press.

Smith, A. H. (1967) *The Place-Names of Westmorland*, 2 parts, English Place-Name Society Vols XLII–XLIII. Cambridge: Cambridge University Press.

Watts, V. (ed.), 2004. *The Cambridge Dictionary of English Place-Names*. Cambridge: Cambridge University Press.

Whaley, D. (2006) *A Dictionary of Lake District Place-Names*. Nottingham: English Place-Name Society.

Whyte. I. D. (1985) Shielings and the upland pastoral economy of the Lake District in medieval and early modern times, in J. R. Baldwin and I. D. Whyte (eds) *The Scandinavians in Cumbria*, 103–17. Edinburgh: Scottish Society for Northern Studies.

Wilson, J. (ed.) (1915) *The Register of the Priory of St. Bees*. Durham: Surtees Society 126.

Winchester, A. J. L. (1984) Peat storage huts in Eskdale. *Transactions of Cumberland and Westmorland Antiquarian and Archaeological Society*, new series 84, 103–15.

Winchester, A. J. L. (1987) *Landscape and Society in Medieval Cumbria*. Edinburgh: John Donald.

Winchester, A. J. L. (2000) *The Harvest of the Hills: rural life in northern England and the Scottish Borders, 1400–1700*. Edinburgh: Edinburgh University Press.

Winchester, A. J. L. (ed.) (2010) *John Denton's History of Cumberland*. Woodbridge: Surtees Society Volume 213; Cumberland and Westmorland Antiquarian and Archaeological Society Record Series XX.

Notes

1. The corpus of names discussed here (405 names in all) is drawn from *shiel(d)(s)* and *scale(s)* names recorded on the Ordnance Survey 7th series One Inch to One Mile maps, supplemented by names for which earlier forms suggest derivation from *skali* or *shele*, drawn from the English Place-Name Society county surveys for Cumberland, Westmorland and the West Riding of Yorkshire. The absence of detailed place-name surveys for all the counties under study and the fact that minor topographical names are not recorded systematically on the One-Inch maps means that the corpus of names is necessarily uneven.

2. A caveat should be noted here: it is possible that some names in southern Scotland containing 'shieling' and a term meaning 'hill' may derive from the Scots term *sheeling* ('winnowing') and refer not to huts but to a 'sheeling hill', a hillock where grain was winnowed in the wind (Johnson-Ferguson 1935, 11; *Concise Scots Dictionary*, ed. M. Robinson (Aberdeen, 1985), *s.v sheel*).

CHAPTER TEN

The Significance of the Devon Country House: the End of the Medieval and Medieval Revivalism

Andrew J. H. Jackson

A reassessment of the country house in Devon

In his classic county history, *Devon,* W. G. Hoskins (1954, 276) declared that it 'is a characteristic of West Country building that it is almost everywhere on a small scale. The last of the great houses, as one goes west, is Longleat in Wiltshire'. As a Devonian, as well as a historian, Hoskins was well qualified to make such an assessment. The county does indeed lack the presence of one of the nation's richly-endowed treasure houses, such as Longleat, Chatsworth or Waddesdon. Devon does not possess any monumental edifices that rank alongside the likes of Blenheim, Castle Howard or Stowe. Hoskins' remark does not of course condemn to lowly status all of the domestic architecture of his home county. Devon features in Hoskins' 'great rebuilding' thesis, and the extent and richness of its vernacular architectural tradition is beyond doubt (Beacham 1991, 62–74; Hoskins 1963, 131–3; Hunt 1977, 76). If the county's stock of country houses has a significance, then, it is perhaps for the quantity and variety, if not 'greatness', of middling to lesser order buildings (Gray 2001, xi).

There were a number of factors that limited the level of country-house building in Devon. When John Bateman came to compile his compendium of *Great Landowners* in 1876 it was clear that Devon had not emerged as one of the more 'aristocratic' of counties (Clemenson 1982, 23; Jackson 2004, 168–70; Thompson 1963, 25–7). The county had not become the location for any of the principal homes of territorial magnates, those with the landed resources available to fund the construction and embellishment of the greatest of family seats. The county tended to contain landowners from the lower and middle orders. Few of those landowners of the late nineteenth century possessed estates of much more than 10,000 acres. The south-west peninsula was also far from the centre of politics and society in and around London. The south-west did not contain the family seats of those aristocrats who formed the basis of leading and long-lasting political dynasties. The region was also relatively detached from, and only slowly integrated into, the influential movements in taste and design that were disseminated from the metropolis.

For Hoskins (1952, 334) there 'were few noblemen in the county, few great landowners of any kind' during the period between 1485 and 1914. Pugsley (1992, 96–106) considers the sixteenth and seventeenth centuries to be a decisive phase in determining the relatively limited level of ambition for country-house building in Devon. There were certain constraints on landed estate development: the region was a landscape of old enclosures, with much division of holdings, and with owners encumbered by debt. The county did not enjoy mineral wealth on the same scale as its neighbour, Cornwall. The spoils of the Dissolution passed out of the county or were much dispersed within. The greatest of the county's landowners, the Dukes of Bedford and the Duchy of Cornwall, did not reside in the county. Devon did not attract court visits, and the greatest courtiers produced by the county, Petre and Raleigh, set up home elsewhere. For Pugsley (1992, 116) the impact of these factors on country-house building was a tendency towards 'remodelling and refurbishment' and 'conservatism and restraint'. Furthermore, these became 'well-established traits that were not easily overturned'.

Hoskins was not wrong in his overview of the country house in Devon. However, fifty years on his evaluation is open to some adjustment. Since the early 1950s archaeological, historical and art historical study, some revisionist in intent (for example: Brown 1996; Currie 2003; Presswell 2007), has greatly advanced the knowledge and understanding of the country houses of the region. Considerable private and state funding has supported much conservation, restoration and reinstatement, as well as greater public access; while the 'cult' of country house visiting has encouraged many buildings to be opened up, and has led to a wider appreciation of the diversity of houses in Devon (Child 1977; Delderfield 1968; Jackson 1998, 142–70). In addition, shifts in taste have meant that styles that had fallen out of fashion, notably Victorian and Edwardian Gothic, have acquired a renewed appeal (Cherry and Pevsner 1991, 108–11; Presswell 2007; Meller 1999). It remains the case that the county does not house any of those vast and well-endowed creations from the four centuries when country-house building was at its most prolific, the sixteenth to the nineteenth. However, new understanding and appreciation does invite fresh and alternative perspectives. The country-house heritage of the county is more than just that represented by the number, range and quality of lower to middling rank houses. It is suggested here that the county is one of the best regions in the country for studying the emergence of the country house within and soon after the end of the medieval period. In addition, the county is no less ideal as a context for examining the return to the medieval as an impulse among country-house designers in the nineteenth and twentieth centuries. Moreover, the county does serve up 'great' examples for studying the theme of the legacy of the medieval in country-house architecture, from the end of the medieval period itself to the early twentieth century. Seven houses are offered up as candidates: Dartington Hall, Berry Pomeroy Castle, Luscombe Castle, Endsleigh Cottage, Mamhead House, Knightshayes Court and Castle Drogo.

The end of the medieval period

It is possible to argue that discussion of the development of the country house in Britain can commence with a case study in Devon. The county is the home of one the country's most important early domestic houses, largely late fourteenth-century in date, Dartington Hall (Girouard 1978, 33–8, 55; Cherry and Pevsner 1991, 308–14). Dartington is the greatest medieval country house in the West of England, and the only country house in Devon to attract a major monograph. For the author, Anthony Emery (1970, 38–42, 88–101), the building is of national significance in that it is an early example of a large unfortified manor house, since most major buildings constructed by the aristocracy in the late fourteenth century were castles or fortified manor houses. Dartington is also rare for its scale. In terms of both fortified and unfortified manor houses of the time, it is indeed very large, particularly its great hall, main courtyard, and range of service accommodation. As a building it is closer in type to the royal palace or castle-palace apartments of the period, and to the early collegiate buildings being constructed in Oxford. Its pretension can be owed to the status of its owner, John Holland, Earl of Exeter and half brother to Richard II. Holland grew up in the royal court, and constructed the residence after a high-profile military and political career. The residence of this major courtier had to accommodate not only a large household, but also parties of visitors, an extensive administrative staff and a body of soldiers. The location of Dartington was near to the strategic port of Dartmouth. In addition, the site had perhaps also been selected because it was at a safer distance from the intrigues and dangers of court life. This said much of the house was built in a relatively peaceful, if short-lived interlude at the very end of the 1300s.

Dartington is also remarkable for its survival as a late medieval building. By the early 1600s this 'house standing very stately' (Risdon 1811, 161) had passed into the hands of the Champernownes. However, the relative impoverishment of these later owners meant that they did not greatly rework the structure, and eventually allowed large parts of the building to fall into disuse (see Fig. 10.1). Its survival and authenticity also owes much to the restraint and faithfulness of a major restoration programme that took place in the early twentieth century, commissioned by new philanthropic proprietors, the Elmhirsts (Bonham-Carter 1970, 27–30; Emery 1970, 3–11).

The most interesting aspect of Dartington Hall is its extensive and complex internal organisation. Its construction adopted in a grand manner the advances in medieval building planning that had been made by the end of the fourteenth century. These forms of planning had developed through the medieval period led by developments in royal palaces, and would remain influential in country-house design into the fifteenth and sixteenth centuries (Girouard 1978, 30–55). The dominant feature of the standard late medieval plan, and of particular note at Dartington, is the great hall. The hall was central to the buildings and household society of the period, and was, therefore, a showpiece (Emery 1970,

Drawn by A. Glennie.   Engraved by W. Floyd.

DARTINGTON MANOR HOUSE, DEVON.

London. Published by Robert Jennings, 62 Cheapside. Feb. 1. 1830.

FIGURE 10.1. A. Glennie, 'Dartington Manor House, Devon', engraved by W. Floyd, 1830 (reproduced with kind permission of Devon Library and Information Services from the collections held in the Westcountry Studies Library, Exeter. © Devon County Council)

117–8, 152–64). Dartington's great hall reflects this in its scale and construction. Its hammerbeam roof is a rebuild, but the original was then an innovative structure that allowed huge spaces to be spanned without the use of supporting side aisles. By the late medieval period it was typical, as at Dartington, for the central hearth to have moved to a chimneyed recess at the side or in an end wall, for a raised dais to be created for the head and senior members of the household, and for a screens passage to be created separating service areas from hall.

When the artist and diarist John Swete (in Gray 1997, 106) visited Dartington in 1792 he was inspired to describe the experience in fitting terms:

> The Ediface is quadrangular which is enter'd by a Gateway towards the East, and though many of the Antient Castellated parts are in ruin, yet enough remain to blazon forth its antient grandeur. The hall is yet in being, which in size approaches perhaps nearer to that at Westminster than any other in the kingdom. 'In feudal times here oft the Oaken table groan'd' and there appears to have been ample scope for the baron's extensive hospitality – for it is 70 feet in length, 40 in width and as many in height – this is the only part that is perfect of the antient Structure – and it towers over the meaner buildings.

By the end of the medieval period the significance of the hall had started to wane, increasingly reserved only for major gatherings and feasts. There was a demand for greater privacy for the head of the household and his or her family for the purposes of meeting, eating and sleeping. There was also the emergence of more sophisticated public ritual, with a choice of rooms available depending on the meeting's purpose and the status of those participating. The net result of these processes was for a range of new private and public rooms to emerge (Girouard 1978, 30–55). The first to appear was the great chamber, typically to the rear of the dais end of the great hall, as in the area of the upper residential block at Dartington. There then followed a series of rooms with different private and/or public functions branching off from the great chamber and great hall, for example: inner and outer chambers, privy chambers, closets, parlours and galleries. Some of these rooms, it is suggested, would have been housed in the now demolished, possibly late fifteenth to early sixteenth-century south court at Dartington (Emery 1970, 42; Currie 2002, 54–6).

In Dartington, then, created in that short peaceful spell in the 1390s, can be recognised a scale and mode of domestic planning that would become far more commonplace across the country two to three hundred years later. Indeed, the wide adoption of certain aspects of the form found at Dartington can be discerned in a second Devon case. The county houses one of the most significant buildings in Britain for examining the transition from the medieval to the early modern, a building consigned to relative obscurity because of its ruinous state, Berry Pomeroy Castle. Berry Pomeroy, if its likely scheme of works had been fully realised and the structure had survived intact to the present, would have ranked as one of the most impressive and important of the nation's country houses of the Tudor period. Its recent history has been defined more by its status as a romantic ruin than an architectural design statement, an association developed in the perception of many visitors by the structure's picturesque and haunted qualities (Seymour and Hazzard 1982, 7–10; Smiles and Pidgley 1995, 23, 74–6) (see Fig. 10.2). In the early nineteenth century its condition brought the new edition of Risdon (1811, 679) to remark upon its 'most romantic appearance'. The architectural significance of the building is difficult to discern now. Recent archaeological excavations, though, have helped to realise the ambitions to which the builders of the castle had aspired. The major report on the castle (Brown 1996, 3) acknowledges the significance of the site, observing that large Tudor buildings are generally still occupied as well as much altered.

Sections of the building date from the later Middle Ages, commencing with the fortifications erected by the de Pomeroys. These alone are of much note. In this period castles had ceased to feature prominently in warfare. Castle structures were being increasingly domesticated and defensive works preserved more for show, while the first coastal artillery fortifications were being constructed, such as at Dartmouth (Higham 1987, 40–6). However, at a local level rivalries and fear of coastal raiding could give rise to a real need for fortification; and the manner of the defences at Berry Pomeroy must make it 'one of the last private

Drawn for the Port Folio by J.W.L.Stockdale, & Eng.ᵈby J. &H.S.Storer. *Pub.ᵈby Sherwood & Cᵒ Sept.1.1823.*

BERRY POMEROY CASTLE.
(Devonshire.)

FIGURE 10.2. J. W. L. Stockdale, 'Berry Pomeroy Castle, Devonshire', engraved by J. and H. S. Storer, 1823 (reproduced with kind permission of Devon Library and Information Services from the collections held in the Westcountry Studies Library, Exeter. © Devon County Council)

castles of a traditional character to have been built in the country' (Brown 1996, 157). The castle was bought by Edward Seymour, Protector Somerset, in 1547; and his son and grandson, also named Edward Seymour, began an ambitious rebuilding programme. The important features are, or rather were, its scale and relative advance in terms of design and embellishment (Cherry and Pevsner 1991, 168–9; Brown 1996, 160–6). Sir Edward Seymour, the Protector's son, was one of a small and influential circle that included William Cecil and the Protector's former steward, Thomas Thynne. This group promoted the introduction of the classical into architecture. At Berry Pomeroy Seymour built his contribution to the first round of classically inspired houses in England, a four-storey-high, compact courtyard house of around 1560–80. An east range was added around 1590. This was followed by a north range of 213 feet, probably at four stories also, and with a gallery running the full length of one of the levels. Classicism is evident in the degree of symmetry, the design of bay and bow windows, and the addition of a loggia that appears to have drawn for inspiration upon Serlio's *Five Books of Architecture*.

The castle also gives an insight into the ongoing movements in plan design that had begun in the late medieval period and had materialised at Dartington. A greater subdivision of spaces featured, along with more sophisticated customs of procession and withdrawal (Girouard 1978, 82–110). For Brown (1996, 166–7) room form and function can not be discerned for certain, but evidence to date indicates that Berry Pomeroy adopted at a substantial scale the interior organisation expected among the elite in society: to one side of the hall was a parlour; the great chamber was to be found on the first floor and ranking in size with the great hall; indeed, there were two great chambers, one of which has a further room off it, an inner chamber; the hall remains high, but above it was a floor of further rooms, and above that a connecting long gallery; moved far from the hall are the locations of possible private and guest quarters to the east and west. The unrealised west wing may have housed further state rooms and quarters. What was achieved might have stopped just short of the 'exceptionally grand' (Brown 1996, 167), but the structure that was accomplished was without doubt substantial and at the very forefront of fashion.

The locality became home to a vicar and author of *The Worthies of Devon* of 1701, John Prince. He leaves an account that has added to the enigma that is Berry Pomeroy:

> What it was in its antique form, can hardly be calculated from what at the present remains… Before the door of the great hall was a noble walk, whose length was the breadth of the court, arch'd over with curiously carv'd Free stone, supported in the fore part by several stately pillars of the same stone of great dimensions, after the Corinthian Order, standing on pedestals, having cornices or friezes wrought; behind which were placed in the wall several seats of Frieze-stone also, cut into the form of escallop shell in which the company, when aweary, might repose themselves. The apartments within were very splendid, especially the dining room, which was adorn'd, besides paint, with statues and figures cut in alabaster, with admirable art and labour; but the chimney-piece of polished marble, curiously engraven, was of great cost and value. Many other of the rooms were well adorned with mouldings and fretwork; some of the marble clavils were so delicately fine, that they would reflect an object true and lively from a great distance… Not withstanding which, 'tis now demolished, and all this glory lieth in the dust, buried in its own ruins; there being nothing standing but a few broken walls (1811, 649).

Berry Pomeroy is 'great' as a last exercise in the construction of major fortified domestic works, and as a taste of the very latest in the classical idiom. Its fate from the seventeenth century would see it drift into obscurity. It is overlooked in popular regional surveys (for example: Child 1977; Delderfield 1968). It is not mentioned in indexes of eighteenth and nineteenth-century 'views' and 'visitations' with their engravings of leading seats of the day, although the ruins are depicted in the Bucks' *Antiquities or Vulnerable Remains* of 1774 (Harris 1979; Holmes 1986, 14). It is a curiosity, but perhaps not a surprising one, that it should be overlooked also in standard texts on British architecture. Much is made of the significance of Protector Somerset's London house, the country's first classical building, Old Somerset House on the Strand, but a house now gone. The narrative then moves onto the building of Elizabethan and Jacobean 'prodigy' houses. It is a pity such texts neglect to mention a house that forms a fascinating link in the story that runs from the construction of Old Somerset

House to the emergence of the stately homes of the later sixteenth and early seventeenth centuries (Summerson 1989, 45–82; Watkin 1990, 85–94). Berry Pomeroy survives in a much reduced form, and its state is far from glorious, but recent archaeological and architectural surveys have raised its significance to a new level.

For the seventeenth and eighteenth century, students of the history of the country house in Britain can still be forgiven for looking elsewhere, and indeed overlooking the county entirely. This is the period for which Hoskins' assessment holds force. Nevertheless, Cherry and Pevsner (1991, 710) regard eighteenth-century Saltram as the county's most impressive country house, and its design owed much to wealthy and well-connected patrons (Watkin 1990, 134–5; Stephens 1996, 172–3;). Its status arises in particular from the fine interiors created by Robert Adam. However, the building as a whole is more a story of piecemeal rebuilding and refurbishment, typical in Devon, and more substantial examples of Adam's work are to be found elsewhere (Summerson 1989, 429–442). A Devon County Council survey (Child 1977, 74–5) also touches on Castle Hill, which is notable for its scale among the region's buildings, and more recently historical and archaeological study have added to the knowledge and understanding of its impressive grounds (Fausset 1994; Havinden 1996; Wilson-North 2003, 2–3). However, this was not an age of great fortune amassing, estate building and power seeking in Devon. Houses matched the relatively modest political, economic, social and cultural ambitions of the county's resident aristocracy and gentry (Cherry and Pevsner 1991, 85–90; Hoskins 1952, 337–65; Pugsley 1992).

The return to the medieval

If at least a couple of the country houses of the county represent excellent examples for examining the departure from the medieval, other houses can be considered to be important illustrations of the impulse to return to the same age from the later eighteenth century onwards. The neo-classical movement in architecture would seek out more informed renderings of Greco-Roman style, while also allowing for eclecticism. Stylistic reference would range widely, therefore, and come to include the Gothic. Moreover, the start of the Romantic Movement in art and literature would also add to curiosity about the medieval age and Gothic style. In addition the idea of the picturesque would be refined further in order to develop the association between architecture and natural landscape setting. Country houses, villas and garden buildings in a Gothic manner would form ideal components of the picturesque garden. Interest in the aesthetic merits of the Gothic also coincided with the practical. The asymmetry of the Gothic suited the new forms of extension work being required to resolve planning issues. These arose from greater pressure being put on the use of the ground floor, for, among other things, more ready access to the gardens (Girouard 1978, 218–44). Through the later eighteenth century, neo-classicism,

Romanticism and the picturesque evolved and interrelated (Summerson 1989, 409, 485–7; Watkin 1990, 130–46), and it is against this background that the perception of Devon started to alter. A number of factors opened up the region culturally (Cherry and Pevsner 1991, 90–2; Hunt 1984, 6–10; Smiles 1995): an increase in domestic tourism dating from the closing off of the continent during the Napoleonic wars; improvements in transport and communications; an awakening interest in native and wilder landscapes, cultivated by the Romantic Movement; and also a particular appreciation of the benign climate of Devon. The growing appeal of the county during the late eighteenth and nineteenth centuries would attract members of the industrial and commercial new rich, while country-house owners, established and new, became more accustomed to importing the ideas and practices of prominent architects and garden designers into the county.

The commissioning of architects from elsewhere in order to introduce the Gothic style can be identified in various buildings. Examples include the rebuildings of Ugbrooke by Robert Adam, and, with some input from Sir Robert Soane, Tawstock; the addition of the music room to Powderham Castle by James Wyatt; and the erection of the belvederes for Powderham and Haldon House (Cherry and Pevsner 1991, 90–2). Hoskins argued that this phase did not deliver great houses to the county, but, there are two cases that can certainly be regarded as being of national significance. Important experimentation in Gothic revival architecture and picturesque aesthetics took place at the level of the villa and garden building, with a dimension of the picturesque being an appreciation of the intricate and small scale. The picturesque by definition could deliver highly regarded structures that were not necessarily large in size, and indeed two are to be found in Devon. John Nash and Humphrey Repton were responsible for Luscombe Castle (near Dawlish), built for the Hoare banking family in 1800–4 (see Fig. 10.3). A few years later, Sir Jeffry Wyatt (later Wyatville) and Repton designed Endsleigh Cottage, a summer retreat for the Dukes of Bedford, south of Tavistock. The two houses achieve the irregularity and asymmetry that was being asked for in the planning and design of early Gothic revival houses. Luscombe Castle is regarded as something of a seminal structure (Cherry and Pevsner 1991, 544; Summerson 1989, 487–8). It was the English country house where 'the castellated style first found perfection' (Morley 1993, 179). The design of this mixed Gothic building combined not only reference to the castle style, but also preferred planning features of the day. These comprised ground-floor living with ease of access to the garden, as well as ground-floor accommodation to one side for the servants (Girouard 1978, 225–8). Ready enjoyment of the landscape is also apparent in the location of the domestic rooms of Endsleigh.

A decade after completion T. H. Williams (1815–6) remarked upon the irregular and asymmetrical qualities achieved in the design of Luscombe:

> The building owes its effect to the union of several fine parts, varying in figure and in elevation… The east front, strictly speaking, is formed by a single part of an

oblong figure, within which are the pointed windows of the eating-room, and those belonging to the apartment over it, and the end of the veranda; but where there are so many projecting portions so delicately interwoven, it is hardly possible to make that kind of division, without diminishing the effect, or lessening the consequence of the whole. The view of Luscombe which is given, will sufficiently exemplify this observation, for the east end is represented; but, the side of the square, and one side of the octagon tower, and other parts, claim a share in the effect, and though not in the same plane, form the eastern aspect of the building.

Endsleigh Cottage and Luscombe Castle are not only important essays in the picturesque in their exploration of the possibilities of reviving medieval forms through the Gothic revival, but they were also provided with what would come to be celebrated romantic landscape settings. Common to both houses is the work of Humphrey Repton. T. H. Williams (1815–6) was much taken by the 'beautiful eminence' of the grounds at Luscombe, declaring it a challenge to find which viewpoint was the more perfect: 'It may be doubted, whether the prospect from this most enchanting spot, or that, on the high grounds opposite, has the greatest attraction; each would, indeed, be a picturesque treasure anywhere'. The garden at Endsleigh, with contributions by Wyatville, is much cited as one of the finest examples of the 'Reptonian synthesis' (Morley 1993, 44–55). Here irregularity and variety were achieved in the general landscape setting, as promoted by the picturesque. At the same time Repton was mindful of the desire for utility and convenience, and reintroduced close to the house the likes of terrace walks, geometrical bedding and conservatories, along with various decorative elements (Gray 2001, 112–7; Hunt 1992, 139–68; Stone 1994). *Murray's Handbook* (Murray 1859, 105) notes of Endsleigh:

> *Endsleigh,* the villa of the Duke of Bedford, deserves a paragraph by itself. It is situated on the Tamar, near *Milton Abbot* (an inn), about 6 m. from Tavistock, and may be viewed by strangers who have obtained permission at the steward's office. The house was designed by Sir G. Wyatville (yr. 1810), and is remarkable for its picturesque irregularity; but the woods and the grounds are the principal attraction, particularly the *Dairy Dell,* the *Alpine Garden* with its Swiss cottage, and the *Terrace* for the extreme beauty of the prospect.

The opening up of the county, the importing of ideas and practices of leading designers, and new heights of cultural ambition among patrons meant that there arose considerable variety and quality in nineteenth-century country-house architecture in Devon. Something of the full spectrum of neo-classical and Gothic types can be found and appreciated (Cherry and Pevsner 1991, 108–11). If not among the grandest in scale, some can be considered of great importance in charting the development of the country house in Britain. After Luscombe and Endsleigh, three more houses can be singled out. Their genesis also relates to the evolution of the Gothic revival and contemporary perceptions of the medieval period. A few decades into the nineteenth century understanding of medieval architecture and design became better informed – more 'archaeological'. In addition the moral, religious and nationalistic qualities associated with the

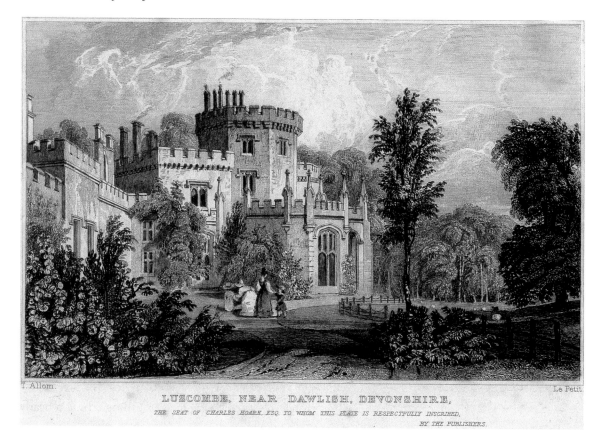

LUSCOMBE, NEAR DAWLISH, DEVONSHIRE,
THE SEAT OF CHARLES HOARE, ESQ. TO WHOM THIS PLATE IS RESPECTFULLY INSCRIBED,
BY THE PUBLISHERS.

Gothic revival became more doctrinaire. An architect who made a leading contribution to the transition in early nineteenth-century design, and the further refinement of the Gothic revival, was Anthony Salvin, a pupil of Nash. For John Harris (1985, 208) Salvin was the 'last great master of the picturesque', working in both the 'castle' style as well as in the neo-Tudor. In developing the latter style he took further the evolving preference of many patrons for a mixed or Elizabethan style of Gothic, as identified by Repton. In addition Salvin achieved this with a more scholarly approach to exterior and interior design, while also retaining something of the freedom and flair cultivated in the Regency period (Harris 1985, 206–12; Morley 1993, 180–2). Salvin's first major commission, and one that established him as a leading exponent of the neo-Tudor, is to be found in Devon at Mamhead House (Cherry and Pevsner 1991, 557–9; Harris 1985, 67; Watkin 1990, 154–6). Here his design of 1825 combines a neo-Tudor style house with castle-style courtyard and detached stable block. The planning of the house saw the adoption of a traditional courtyard plan. Inside the house a range of medieval and Tudor references include entry into a screens passage, and from there into an early example of a sculpture gallery intended to hold a series of figures from English history. It is likely that the owner, R. W. Newman MP, would have been aware of the decorative schemes intended for the Houses

FIGURE 10.3. J. Allom, 'Luscombe, near Dawlish, Devon', engraved by W. LePetit, 1830 (reproduced with kind permission of Devon Library and Information Services from the collections held in the Westcountry Studies Library, Exeter. © Devon County Council)

of Parliament. The building also features a fine cloister-like conservatory and surrounding terracing, following through the trends towards utility, formality and ornamentation set underway by Repton (Morley 1993, 31).

A few decades later more fervent renderings in the 'High' Gothic appeared, informed by closer examination of medieval architecture and design. In Devon there is a house in this manner that is undoubtedly of more than regional importance, William Burges' Knightshayes. In one respect the building materially and aesthetically falls short, in that a large corner tower was not completed (Child 1977, 73). However, as an idiosyncratic expression of the work of a master of the High Gothic, Knightshayes' significance is clear (Heathcoat 1999). This said the status of the house today owes a great deal to the restoration scheme of the National Trust. As a former owner, Joyce, Lady Heathcoat Amory (1999, 4), recalls:

> Perhaps it would be as well to admit that the Heathcoat Amorys were from early days unable to appreciate Victorian architecture, even though Knightshayes was built by a very distinguished Victorian architect. Each generation has played its part in dismantling the most eccentric and ornate features in the house… we must bear our share of 'vandalism', some of the Victoriana we destroyed between 1950 and 1970 was for the purpose of providing a suitable background for a small but very fine collection of Old Masters.

The house was built between 1869 and 1874 for John Heathcote-Amory. He commissioned one of the most extraordinary visionaries of the Gothic revival, William Burges, a man obsessed by the medieval. Burges built a nearly symmetrical and seemingly fairly standard neo-Tudor frontage, although the unrealised tower would have given the construction a more eccentric medieval appearance. The frontage that is present, however, achieves much colour in the stonework, carved in Burges' preferred French Gothic. Turning to the interior, many Gothic revival buildings returned to the medieval plan, including restoring the hall to something of its former status as a place to host events and festivities – although quite often it became an informal family living and meeting room (Girouard 1978, 288–9). Knightshayes reflects these trends. The entrance porch leads into a screens passage that cuts through the building to the garden front. Off the screens passage is a great hall, finely decorated with a now restored and richly carved screen. A stairway at the far end of the hall leads up to the private quarters. The personality of Burges and the High Victorian were intended to achieve their greatest expression in the interior decoration. However, the excessiveness and cost of the work caused the owner to dispense with Burges' services (Harris 1985, 228–9; Heathcoat 1999). Generally, Burges' designs for internal stonework and woodwork were realised, but the later stages – stained glass, wall and wood painting, and furnishings – were not. Heathcoat-Amory turned to John Dibblee Crace. Crace's work was more delicate, but also more conservative, conventional and cheaper than that of Burges. Much of Crace's work was completed, but even his designs were too exuberant for the family, and a great deal of Crace's work was painted, papered or boarded over. Since the National Trust took over the house in the early 1970s, it has been steadily restored. Both Burges and Crace left drawings; fragments of paint and woodwork have been discovered; and work by the two is evident in other houses. Referring to these sources, the Trust has been working through the rooms returning them to a late nineteenth-century appearance (Meller 1999).

By the end of the nineteenth century, the Gothic revival had mutated into the 'vernacular' revival, influenced by the arts and crafts movement. This process sustained the harkening back to the values and expressions of the medieval past. However, there was a shift of emphasis. Of importance to the arts and crafts designers, and to some extent to those working in the vernacular revival, were design tenets such as quality, simplicity, use of local materials, 'Englishness', and 'homeliness'. The aim was also to be popular in appeal, but without perpetuating the moralistic and religious associations of Gothic revivalism. Designers were relatively more relaxed, restrained, and even innovative in design; and they did not seek authentically or dogmatically to recreate, as in the revival of the Gothic. The vernacular revival persisted as part of the 'traditionalism' of the early twentieth century. The outstanding traditionalist was Edwin Lutyens, whose first country houses appeared in the last few years of the nineteenth century (Watkin 1990, 185–8). Perhaps his most outstanding country house, and one of his first major buildings in terms of sheer physical scale was Castle Drogo in Devon. It was with this commission, between 1910 and 1930, that he would achieve much of the drama that is associated with his greater structures. The building is recognised as one of the last great country houses in a period when circumstances had turned against their crafting (Aslet 1982, 182–9). Cook (1974, 238) concludes her survey of English country houses with this 'last baronial stronghold to be built in this country'. For Cook this final 'olden time masquerade' was a lesser exercise in castle building when compared to certain Victorian examples, and indeed Castle Drogo realised only a third of its intended size. Nonetheless, what it symbolises as the end of an art form and ideal is enduring. If the story of the country house in Britain can be told starting with Dartington, it can be finished at Drogo.

Conclusion

Hoskins was right in that the county does appear to lack the grandest of houses. However, it is argued here that adjustments can be made to his assessment, arrived in the late 1950s. Knowledge and appreciation has broadened and deepened since. First, there are two 'great' houses, even if their construction resides chronologically either side of the main phase of country-house building, from the sixteenth century to the nineteenth. Moreover, these houses, Dartington and Drogo, offer a fitting start and ending for a national chronicle of the history of the country house in Britain.

In addition, what Dartington and Drogo have in common with the other five houses discussed, are their levels of experimentation. This set of houses may not be great in terms of size and opulence, but they are all arguably seminal. The seven have much to contribute to general understandings of key shifts in architectural planning and design, and background cultural context. Moreover, a particular theme that their study helps to expound upon is the steady movement away from the medieval age, and an equally gradual attempt to contrive a return to it.

Finally, the very peripherality that meant that great houses are relatively rare in Devon also contributed to the development of this particular set of seven houses in the county. The distance from court may well have been a factor in the appeal of the locations chosen for Dartington Hall and Berry Pomeroy. At the other end of the period considered here, that peripherality would come to constitute a cultural ideal, with the qualities of the landscapes to be found therein forming an essential and integral ingredient in the creation of the remaining five.

Acknowledgements

This history of the Devon country house originates in research undertaken in preparation of a Leicester MA dissertation supervised by Harold Fox: 'The landed estate economy in decline, East Devon, 1870–1939' (Jackson, 1993; see also 1996, and Jackson, Higham and Stanes 2008, 2). Historical investigations in Devon continued following a successful application for ESRC funding for a PhD studentship in geography, encouraged and endorsed by Harold, on 'Rural property rights and the survival of historic landed estates in the late twentieth century' (Jackson, 1998). The accumulated body of research on the Devon country house, together with its central argument on the status of the county's buildings, formed the basis for a number of lecture series for the University of Exeter, the Workers Educational Association and Somerset County Council over a period of ten years. The author is also grateful for the help of Katherine Dunhill of the Westcountry Studies Library, Exeter, in selecting and obtaining the illustrations included.

Bibliography

Aslet, C. (1985) *The Last Great Country Houses*. New Haven: Yale.

Beacham, P. (1991) Rural building: 1400–1800, in B. Cherry and N. Pevsner (eds) *The Buildings of England: Devon,* 2nd edn, 62–78. Harmondsworth: Penguin.

Bonham-Carter, V. (1970) *Dartington Hall. The Formative Years: 1925–1957*. Dulverton: Exmoor Press.

Brown, S. (ed.) (1998) Berry Pomeroy Castle. *Devon Archeological Society Proceedings* 54.

Cherry, B. and Pevsner, N. (eds) (1991) *The Buildings of England: Devon,* reprinted 2nd edn. Harmondsworth: Penguin.

Child, P. (1977) Devon's greater buildings, in, *Doorway to Devon,* 68–75. Exeter: Devon County Council.

Clemenson, H. A. (1982) *English Country Houses and Landed Estates*. London: Croom Helm.

Cook, O. (1974) *The English Country House: an Art and a Way of Life*. London: Thames and Hudson.

Currie, C. (2003) Dartington Hall and Shilston Barton: archaeological excavation at two Devon gardens, 1991–2000, in R. Wilson-North (ed.) *The Lie of the Land: Aspects of the Archaeology and History of the Designed Landscape in the South West of England*, 51–65. Exeter: Mint Press and Devon Gardens Trust.

Delderfield, E. R. (196) *West Country Historic Houses and their Families*, Newton Abbot: David and Charles.

Emery, A. (1970) *Dartington Hall*. Oxford: Clarendon Press.

Faussett, R. (1994) Castle Hill: the formal and transitional garden, in S. Pugsley (ed.) *Devon Gardens: an Historical Survey*, 42–58. Stroud: Alan Sutton.

Gray, T. (ed.) (1997) *Travels in Georgian Devon: the Illustrated Journals of the Reverend John Swete, 1789–1800*, Vol. 1. Tiverton: Devon Books.

Girouard, M. (1978) *Life in the English Country House: a Social and Architectural History*. London and New Haven: Yale University Press.

Gray, T. (ed.) (2001) *Devon Country Houses and Gardens Engraved: A-La-Ronde to Lifton Park*. Exeter: The Mint Press.

Harris, J. (1979) *A Country House Index*, 2nd edn. London: Pinhorns.

Harris, J. (1985) *The Architect and the British Country House, 1620–1920*. Washington: American Institute of Architects.

Havinden, M. (1996) Improvement to the park of Castle Hill, Filleigh, and the conversion of an old lime kiln into a mock fort, 1769–70, in T. Gray (ed.) *Devon Documents in Honour of Mrs Margery Rowe*, 97–9. Tiverton: Devon and Cornwall Notes and Queries.

Heathcoat, J. (1999) The Heathcoat Amorys and their architects, in H. Meller (ed.) *Knightshayes Court*, 40–8. London: National Trust.

Heathcoat Amory, J. (1999) Living at Knightshayes, in H. Meller (ed.) *Knightshayes Court*, 4–5. London: National Trust.

Higham, R. (1987) Public and private defence in the medieval south west: town, castle and fort, in R. Higham(ed.) *Security and Defence in South-West England before 1800*, 27–50. Exeter: Department of History and Archaeology, University of Exeter.

Holmes, M. (1986) *The Country House Described: an Index to the Country Houses of Great Britain and Ireland*. Winchester: St Paul's Bibliographies.

Hoskins, W. G. (1952) The estates of the Caroline gentry, in W. G. Hoskins and H. P. R. Finberg (eds) *Devonshire Studies*, 334–65. London: Jonathan Cape.

Hoskins, W. G. (1954) *Devon*. London: Collins.

Hoskins, W. G. (1963) The rebuilding of rural England, 1570–1640, in W. G. Hoskins (ed.) *Provincial England: Essays in Social and Economic History*, 131–48. London: Macmillan.

Hunt, J. D. (1992) *Gardens and the Picturesque: Studies in the History of Landscape Architecture*. Cambridge, MA: Massachusetts Institute of Technology.

Hunt, P. (1984) *Devon's Age of Elegance: Described by the Diaries of the Reverend John Swete, Lady Paterson and Miss Mary Cornish*. Exeter: Devon Books.

Hunt, P. J. (1977) Devon's vernacular buildings, in *Open Door to Devon*, 76–93. Exeter: Devon County Council.

Jackson, A. J. H. (1993) The landed estate economy in decline, East Devon, 1870–1939. Unpublished MA dissertation, University of Leicester.

Jackson, A. J. H. (1996) Managing decline: the economy of the Powderham estate in Devon, 1870–1939. *Transactions Devonshire Association* 128, 197–215.

Jackson, A. J. H. (1998) Rural property rights and the survival of historic landed estates in the late twentieth century. Unpublished PhD thesis, University of London.

Jackson, A. J. H. (2004) Investigating the break-up of the great landed estates of Devon: the use of commercial directories, 1875–1939. *Transactions Devonshire Association* 136, 165–74.

Jackson, A. J. H., Higham, R. and Stanes, R. (2008) Harold Fox (1948–2007): Devon and Leicester; landscape and locality. *The Devon Historian* 76, 2–5.

Meller, H. (ed.) (1999) *Knightshayes Court*. London: The National Trust.

Morley, J. (1993) *Regency Design, 1790–1840: Gardens, Buildings, Interiors, Furniture*. London: Zwemmer.

Murray, J. (1859) *Murray's Handbook for Travellers in Devon and Cornwall*. London: John Murray.

Presswell, D. (2007) Charles Fowler: architect, 1792–1867. *The Devon Historian* 74, 11–24.

Prince, J. (1811) *The Worthies of Devon,* new edn. London: Rees and Curtis.

Pugsley, S., 1992. Landed society and the emergence of the country house in Tudor and early Stuart Devon, in T. Gray, M. Rowe and A. Erskine (eds) *Tudor and Stuart Devon: the Common Estate and Government; Essays Presented to Joyce Youings*, 96–118. Exeter: University of Exeter Press.

Risdon, T. (1811) *The Chorographical Description or Survey of the County of Devon,* reprinted and revised edn. London: Rees and Curtis.

Seymour D. and Hazzard, J. (1982) *Berry Pomeroy Castle.* Privately printed.

Smiles, S. (1995) Artists, tourists and the discovery of Devon, in S. Smiles and M. Pidgley (eds) *The Perfection of England: Artist Visitors to Devon, c.1750–1870,* 9–24. Plymouth: University of Plymouth.

Stephens, W. B. (1996) Theresa Parker of Saltram, in T. Gray (ed.) *Devon Documents in Honour of Mrs Margery Rowe,* 172–7. Tiverton: Devon and Cornwall Notes and Queries.

Stone, R. (1994) The creation of Endsleigh: a regency picturesque masterpiece, in S. Pugsley (ed.) *Devon Gardens: an Historical Survey,* 76–90. Stroud: Alan Sutton.

Summerson, J. (1989) *Architecture in Britain, 1530 to 1830,* Harmondsworth: Penguin.

Thompson, F. M. L. (1963) *English Landed Society in the Nineteenth Century.* London: Routledge.

Watkin, D. (1990) *English Architecture: a Concise History.* London: Thames and Hudson.

Williams, T. H. (1815–6) *Picturesque excursions in Devonshire: the environs of Exeter,* part 2, in Devon County Council (2010) 'Etched on Devon's memory'. Available: http://www.devon.gov.uk/localstudies (accessed 29 January 2010).

Wilson-North, R. (2003) Approaches to garden archaeology and designed landscapes in south west England, in R. Wilson-North, (ed.) *The Lie of the Land: Aspects of the Archaeology and History of the Designed Landscape in the South West of England,* 1–4. Exeter: The Mint Press and Devon Gardens Trust.

CHAPTER ELEVEN

Regional Differentiation in Farming Terminology, 1500–1720

Alan Fox

The aim of this chapter is to present an analysis of probate inventories from the East Midlands and to search for regional variations in the language used. For the purpose of this study, the East Midlands consist of the pre-1974 counties of Nottinghamshire, Leicestershire, Lincolnshire, Northamptonshire and Rutland; and the Soke of Peterborough (Fig. 11.1). The findings of the preliminary investigation were reported at the Harold Fox Memorial Conference at the University of Leicester on 19 July 2008. In response to the discussion at that meeting further investigation has led to the acquisition of supplementary data which have helped to clarify and slightly modify the initial conclusion.

Preliminary investigation: the sources

Between approximately 1500 and 1720 probate inventories were required as an adjunct to the proving of wills and the whole probate process was under the supervision of church courts, either at diocesan or archdeaconry level. The inventories consisted of lists, drawn up by neighbours, of the estimated value of the belongings of deceased persons. As many inventories were from rural areas it was decided, in this investigation, to concentrate on the regional variation of farming terminology.

Nottinghamshire was part of York Diocese and management of the probate process was largely organized by the three deaneries of Nottingham, Retford and Newark. Most of the county of Lincolnshire was in the Lincoln Diocese and was mainly treated as one area by the Lincoln Consistory Court. Leicestershire was also in Lincoln Diocese but much of the county was treated separately from Lincolnshire in the Leicester Archdeaconry Court. Peterborough Diocese was responsible for the Soke of Peterborough, Rutland and the northern part of Northamptonshire. The rest of Northamptonshire was largely supervised by the Northampton Archdeaconry Court. In addition there were a number of Peculiars such as that of the Dean and Chapter of Lincoln Cathedral and the one for Southwell in Nottinghamshire.

In each archive today, probate inventories are usually indexed and organized

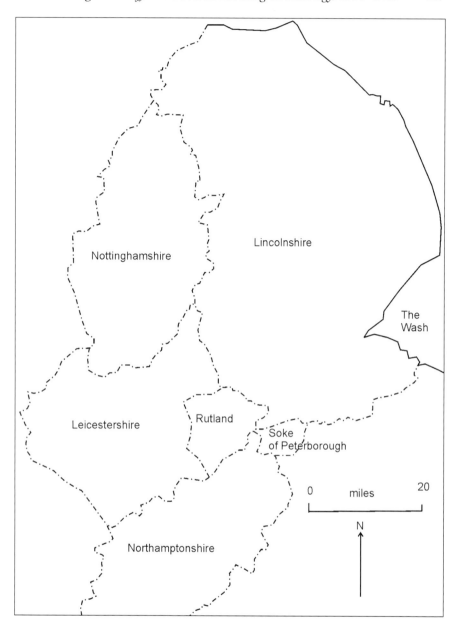

FIGURE 11.1. Counties of the East Midlands in this study

on a yearly basis and then placed in alphabetical order of the surname of the deceased person. The parishes of residence of the subjects and frequently their occupations are also listed. Ideally, it would be preferable to produce an even geographical spread of data but the organization of the sources makes this difficult, especially as each archive allows access to the sources on a different basis. Quite often, inventories have only short lists of items and thus do not provide useful information, but of course the value of a particular inventory is not evident until it is presented to the researcher. Fortunately at the Leicestershire, Leicester and Rutland Record Office the inventories for the whole of each year are bound together into volumes and, as three of these can be called at one time, it is easy to select suitable items. At Lincoln Archives and Northamptonshire Record Office each inventory is held as a separate item and only three can be ordered at one time under normal circumstances. However, in each case it has been possible to come to an arrangement whereby speedier access has been achieved. Nottinghamshire's records are on microfiche along with wills and administrations, so acquisition of the data there is a relatively quick process. All these primary sources are listed in the bibliography.

In addition, it was possible to supplement the information found in record offices with data from elsewhere. Two sources of actual inventories were available, firstly those from a project conducted by Dr Mike Thompson who provided eighteen documents with transcripts for the parish of Countesthorpe in Leicestershire. Secondly, the present writer's MA study of six Wreake Valley parishes provided fifty-four more inventories in the same county for Asfordby, Frisby-on-the-Wreake, Kirby Bellars, Hoby, Brooksby and Rotherby (Fox 1997).

There are also a few full transcripts of inventories from the East Midlands in books, which provide other useful material. In particular, they are to be found in Thirsk (1957), which gives further data for Lincolnshire. Transcripts for Winteringham, on the Humber estuary in the same county, appear in a booklet edited by Neave (1984). The Leicestershire parishes of Braunstone, Glenfield and Kirby Muxloe have published transcripts by J. Wilshere (1983 a, b, c). Twenty-five inventories, edited by Kennedy (1963), covering the twenty-three parishes of Southwell Peculiar in Nottinghamshire are also included. A further eleven are to be found in a book on Clayworth parish in Nottinghamshire, edited by Perkins (1979). The geographical distribution of all the parishes which provided inventories for the initial survey are shown in Figure 11.2. In some cases there is more than one document for a particular parish.

Initial findings

At first glance there does not appear to be a great deal of variation within the East Midlands in the actual words used. The most obvious example of different word usage is that of 'burling', as applied to year-old cattle, which in south Lincolnshire replaces the term 'yearling' employed elsewhere (Fig. 11.3). The term 'weaning calf' is largely missing from Lincolnshire, partly because it is replaced by 'spaining calf' or 'spainding' in the north of that county, appearing in four inventories at Winteringham on the south bank of the Humber.

The term 'hog' was employed to refer to either a young sheep (or a lamb not yet shorn), or to a pig reared for slaughter. In Leicestershire both usages were in place with inventories referring to 'lamb hogs' and 'swine hogs' (Fig. 11.4). Leicestershire people also used the term 'hogril' i.e. hoggerel in place of 'lamb hog', especially to the west of Leicester. The term 'hog' was altogether rare in Nottinghamshire and north Lincolnshire whereas in Northamptonshire, Rutland and the Soke of Peterborough the term appears quite frequently.

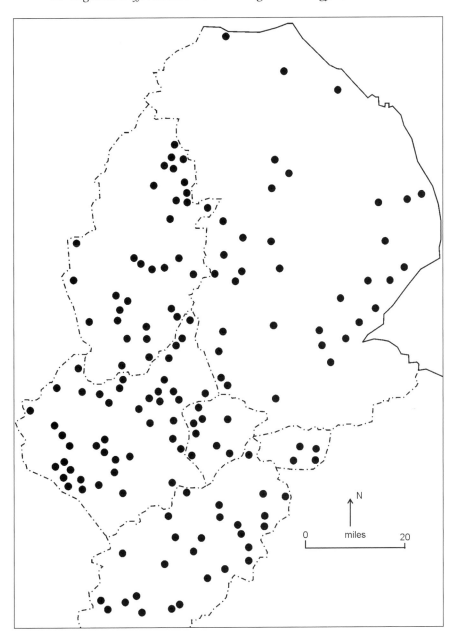

FIGURE 11.2. Preliminary study: distribution of parishes with at least one probate inventory

Examination of the lists of all farm animals seems to suggest it was used there to describe pigs only.

Vagaries of spelling in the early modern period make it difficult to identify different pronunciations of the same word. The most obvious case is the spelling of a 'flitch' of bacon which can be 'flick' or 'flyke', the last two probably variant spellings of the same pronunciation. In the linguistic atlas of Orton, Sanderson and Widdowson (1978), the authors refer to the pronunciation of this word in the early twentieth century, but they make no distinction within the East Midlands. However, the inventories of the initial study described

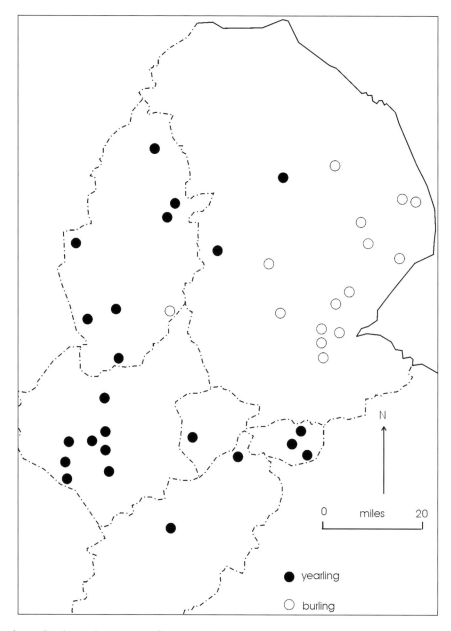

FIGURE 11.3. Distribution of 'yearling' and 'burling' in both preliminary and further studies

here do show the variant 'flick' or 'flyke' appearing in three west Leicestershire parishes, although in two of the parishes 'flitch' is also used in other inventories. The first variant also occurs once in north Nottinghamshire at Darlton, but generally neither appears in the inventories of that county, nor in Lincolnshire and Northamptonshire, with only one case in Rutland. The dropping of the 'l' in yearling appears in two Nottinghamshire inventories and in several inventories at Winteringham. In two inventories at Dogsthorpe in the Soke of Peterborough and in one at Whittlebury in south Northamptonshire 'heifers' is spelled 'herkfors'.

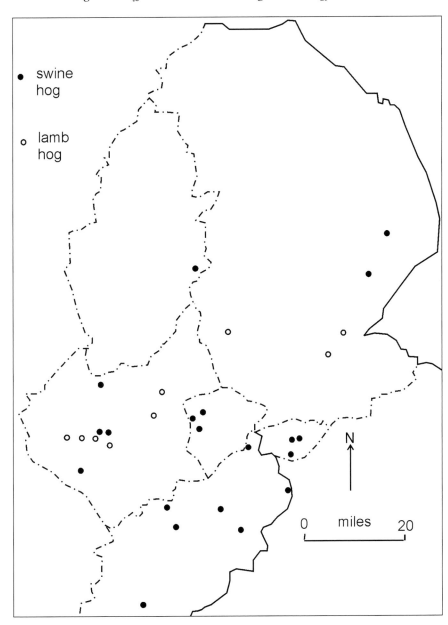

FIGURE 11.4. Preliminary study: distribution of 'hog'

Although there were some cases of regional differences in the use of words, the main distinctions in the initial survey appear to be the presence or absence of particular terms. A good example is the word 'quarter' which describes a quantity of grain, that is eight bushels. It is found throughout the western half of the study area but is largely missing from Lincolnshire (Fig. 11.5). The term 'steer' describes a beast used for draught purposes and the word is found only to the north of the Welland Valley and is therefore absent from Northamptonshire (Fig. 11.6). The probable reason was that the innovation that replaced steers with horses had already spread to that county from the south of England.

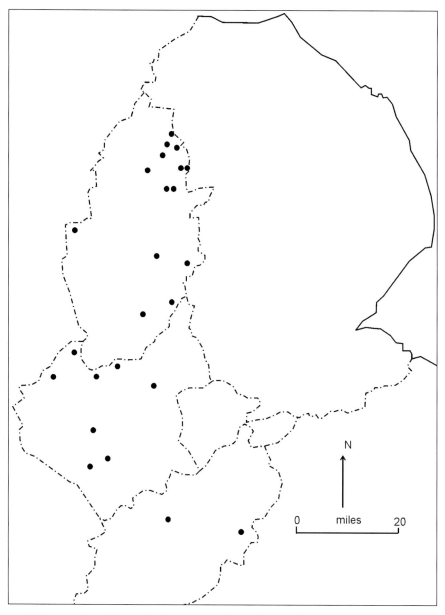

FIGURE 11.5. Preliminary
study: distribution of
'quarter'

With regard to farm vehicles, Nottinghamshire and Lincolnshire inventories refer variously to 'carts', 'wains' and 'waggons', but the use of 'wains' is absent from Northamptonshire, Rutland, the Fen area of Lincolnshire and east Leicestershire. According to Edwards (1991, 151), there was a gradual development from medieval times into the early modern period of the two-wheeled cart to the larger wain and finally to the four-wheeled waggon.

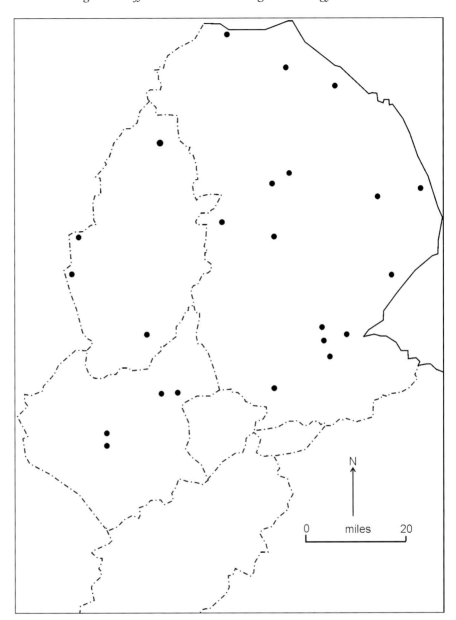

FIGURE 11.6. Preliminary study: distribution of 'steer'

Two boundaries proposed

The initial survey indicated that several words appeared in some parts of the East Midlands but not in others. Maps showing the distribution of each term were drawn and superimposed on each other. It is possible to postulate two major boundaries which separated areas where particular words were used from those without them (Fig. 11.7). In the first case, the area to the west of the Lincolnshire boundary and west of central Rutland has seven farming terms that appear in the observed inventories but do not appear in documents to the

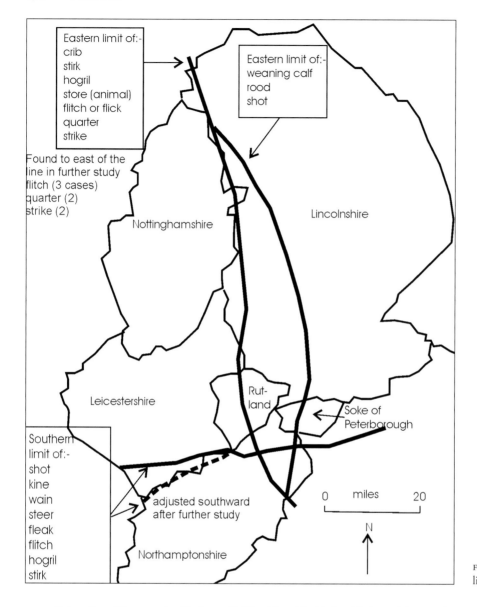

Eastern limit of:-
crib
stirk
hogril
store (animal)
flitch or flick
quarter
strike

Found to east of the
line in further study
flitch (3 cases)
quarter (2)
strike (2)

Eastern limit of:-
weaning calf
rood
shot

Lincolnshire

Nottinghamshire

Leicestershire

Rut-
land

Soke of
Peterborough

Southern
limit of:-
shot
kine
wain
steer
fleak
flitch
hogril
stirk

adjusted southward
after further study

Northamptonshire

0   miles   20

N

FIGURE 11.7. Proposed
linguistic boundaries

east of that line. They are 'crib', 'hogril', 'flitch' or 'flick', 'stirk', 'store' (animal), 'strike' and 'quarter' (though it will be seen below that examination of further data did produce two or three cases each of 'flitch', 'strike' and 'quarter'). In addition, there is only one case of the word 'fleak', meaning a hurdle, in all the Lincolnshire inventories. A further three words appear in west Lincolnshire inventories but not further east. They are 'rood', 'shot' or 'shote' (a young pig) and 'weaning calf'. There is also only one case of the term 'parcel', a quantity of grain, which is found in the Boston area.

Basically, the north-south variation is due to those terms which appear to the north of Northamptonshire but are absent in the county itself. They include 'shot', 'kine', 'wain', 'steer', 'fleak', 'flitch' or 'flick', 'hogril' and 'stirk'.

In addition, the word 'strike' is used quite frequently in Northamptonshire to describe an implement, but there are only two cases of its use as a measure of corn or malt in store. It must be emphasized that it is possible that these words were used in everyday conversation in Northamptonshire but for some reason do not appear in the initial sample of inventories.

Further data

There does seem to be a strong case for postulating regional variations in the use of farming terms in probate inventories within the East Midland counties, but how can this distinction be explained? The first possibility is that there are insufficient data and that the geographical spread of the parishes is uneven, owing to difficulties presented by the organisation of the sources. The 'negative areas' with the missing terms may simply have insufficient coverage. The problem of inadequate data in the initial survey has been addressed by the acquisition of further information, concentrating specifically on Lincolnshire and Northamptonshire, in order to search for examples of the missing terms (Fig. 11.8).

Examination of a further seventy-three Lincolnshire inventories has revealed very few cases of the missing terms. The most frequent were 'flitch' and 'strike', each of which appeared in three widely separated locations. 'Quarter' occurred twice, at Barton-on-Humber and near Horncastle in the Wolds. It is therefore not true to say that these words were completely absent east of the line on Figure 11.7, but even so, they are extremely scarce. Furthermore, the second boundary further east in Lincolnshire still holds good for none of the terms 'weaning calf', 'rood' and 'shot' appear, to the east of this line, and the use of the word 'parcel' near Boston still remains the only case.

In an analysis of another sixty-five Northamptonshire inventories not one of the missing terms appeared, so the case for this linguistic frontier close to the River Welland remains very strong. Originally, the linguistic boundary had been placed further north in the neighbourhood of Lutterworth, but the haphazard selection of data meant that the area to the south of that town was poorly represented. The study of more documents, concentrating on that particular area, had the effect of pushing the boundary southward to align with the Leicestershire/Northamptonshire boundary along the River Welland.

Explanations

Another explanation for the observed regional variation in terminology could be that instructions from the archdeaconry or diocesan (consistory) court differed. It is also possible that individuals in the Church of England hierarchy managed to put their own interpretation onto directives from above, as they passed them down the chain of command. This seems unlikely in the case of Leicestershire and Lincolnshire since both were in the same diocese (though the former was administered as an archdeaconry).

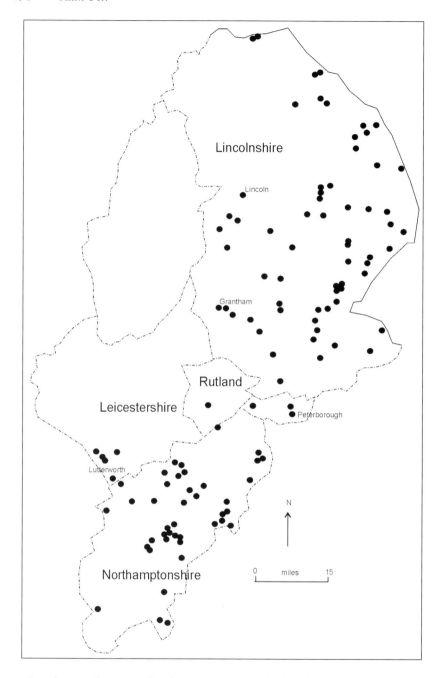

FIGURE 11.8. Further study: location of parishes of Lincolnshire, Northamptonshire, Rutland and Lutterworth area

Another explanation for the variation might be the presence of different cultural provinces or regional societies in the early modern period. The two boundaries on Figure 11.7 coincide almost exactly with the boundaries of regional societies (formerly called cultural provinces) proposed by Phythian-Adams (1993, xvii; 2007, 7). He includes Leicestershire and Nottinghamshire as two of the four sub-regions within the Trent region, whereas Lincolnshire and Rutland are combined into a Witham Region. Northamptonshire is part of the Wash/Ouse region. He also proposes the Welland Valley, whose river forms the boundary between Leicestershire and Northamptonshire, as one of three major 'frontier valleys' in England (Phythian-Adams 2000, 236–8). He bases his regional or sub-regional societies partly on combinations of economic factors (Phythian-Adams 2007, 8). The willingness of Leicestershire appraisers to differentiate between types of cattle and sheep may reflect the increasing importance of pastoral farming in that area. Early enclosure of the open fields was probably more widespread in Leicestershire than in Lincolnshire. In the former county, this process was usually accompanied by a change in land use from arable to pasture, but in the latter the land often remained in arable use (Stocker 2006, 85).

The present writer has specifically examined the boundary zone between Leicestershire and Lincolnshire and has concluded that there is a strong case for a frontier there between regional societies in the early modern period and probably at other times too (Fox 2009). The evidence for this assertion is based on low population density astride the county boundary, in former heathland which is underlain by Lincolnshire limestone. Even after the heath was transformed into arable land in the 1770s it remained sparsely populated with widely scattered farmsteads and it presents a rather empty landscape to this day. There was a reluctance to choose marriage partners from across the proposed frontier. Links to other parishes from border parishes, as revealed by persons and property mentioned in wills and probate administrations, were strongly biased to the home county. Furthermore, full family constitution of a group of border parishes indicates a low level of migration between the two counties. Analysis of the routes taken by carriers' carts in the nineteenth century also strongly supports the proposition that Leicestershire and Lincolnshire operated largely separate economic systems. Even the pre-brick vernacular architecture of the two counties is different, with cob or timber-frame of Leicestershire in contrast with the mud and stud of Lincolnshire. It is therefore not surprising to find a linguistic frontier spanning the same boundary.

Comparable research

An important text on traditional dialect is the linguistic atlas of Orton, Sanderson and Widdowson, based on research undertaken in the mid-twentieth century (1978). The investigators used key words and phrases through which they sought regional variation in pronunciation, word use, grammatical construction and syntax throughout the whole of England. The results are shown in a series of maps with lines called isoglosses separating different usages. In many cases in the East Midlands these align, wholly or partly, along Lincolnshire's western border and along the Welland Valley of the Leicestershire/Northamptonshire border. Out of the 406 usages that were tested, the dividing isogloss was placed along the Leicestershire/Lincolnshire border in seventeen per cent of cases (Fig. 11.9). The Nottinghamshire/Lincolnshire border is much longer, but even here the dividing line (for pronunciation only) was placed along it for eleven per cent

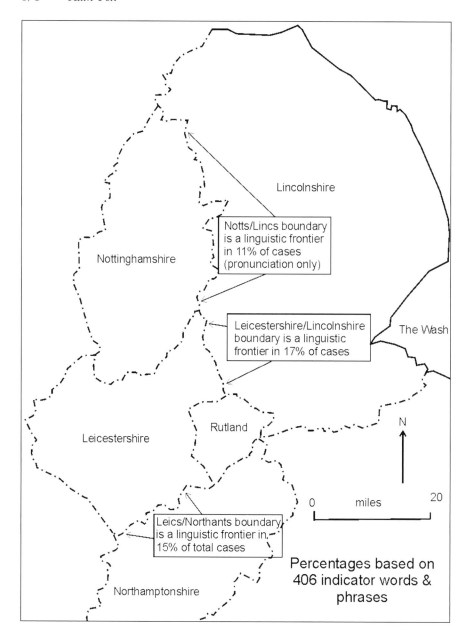

Notts/Lincs boundary is a linguistic frontier in 11% of cases (pronunciation only)

Leicestershire/Lincolnshire boundary is a linguistic frontier in 17% of cases

Leics/Northants boundary is a linguistic frontier in 15% of total cases

Percentages based on 406 indicator words & phrases

Lincolnshire

Nottinghamshire

The Wash

Rutland

N

Leicestershire

0   miles   20

Northamptonshire

FIGURE 11.9. Linguistic frontiers based on the *Linguistic Atlas* (Orton *et al.* 1978)

of cases. For the Leicestershire/Northamptonshire border the figure is fifteen per cent of the 406 indices. In all instances, there are further cases where the dividing isoglosses are close by although not exactly along the border.

Conclusion

The study of probate inventories in the East Midland counties suggests that there are a few variations in the actual words used, but more significant was the presence or absence of groups of terms. It is postulated that there was a north-south line along the western Lincolnshire boundary, which separated the use of several terms to the west from non-usage to the east. A little further east into Lincolnshire more words disappeared from the inventories. Another line along the Welland Valley separated the use of another group of terms to the north from non-usage to the south in Northamptonshire. An investigation into more inventories has confirmed the original conclusion for the Welland Valley linguistic divide. In the case of the Lincolnshire western boundary, so few cases of the missing words were discovered to the east of the line that the original conclusion is still maintained. The inclusion of further inventories probably answers any accusation of inadequate data. The fact that Leicestershire and Lincolnshire were in the same diocese suggests that the instructions given to inventory appraisers were unlikely to have been different.

It is postulated that the reason for the linguistic boundaries is that they coincide with the frontier areas of cultural provinces or regional societies as conceived by Phythian-Adams. He places one such frontier between Leicestershire and Nottinghamshire on the one hand and from Lincolnshire and Rutland on the other. Does the fact that Leicestershire documents are more likely to tell of weaning calves, yearlings, stirks and store cattle rather than just cattle and calves say something about the importance of pastoral farming there? There is evidence that Leicestershire, for example, had a much higher proportion of its area enclosed before the Parliamentary Enclosures compared with Lincolnshire (Stocker 2006, 84). Commercial pastoral farming may therefore have arrived early in Leicestershire and thus have more specialised terms to go with it. The north-south line along the Lincolnshire border coincides largely with the Jurassic limestone escarpment, a quite sparsely populated area, originally heathland. It may therefore have separated regional societies which used words differently from each other. Yet another major frontier, proposed by Phythian-Adams, aligns along the Welland Valley. Further support for these two linguistic boundaries is found in the linguistic evidence recorded by Orton, Sanderson and Widdowson (1978). Whatever the causes of these differences, they endured for over two centuries from 1500 to 1720.

Bibliography

Unpublished sources – probate inventories

Lincolnshire Archives
INV149 1–62, 1638–9; INV150, 101–133, 1640.
INV163 7, 26, 47, 51, 38, 83, 1663–4; INV199 17, 84, 225, 238, 1705; INV200 53, 70, 78, 91, 95, 100, 102, 110–112, 1706.
Northamptonshire Record Office
Northamptonshire Archdeaconry; 1661NS, selection of 62, 1660; 1660–99 Box 103–137, 1679–81.
Peterborough Diocese; Box 1 Bundle 1 selection of 41, 1683–9.
Nottinghamshire Archives
Nottingham & Bingham Deanery selection of 12, 1700.

Record Office of Leicestershire Leicester and Rutland
PR/1/70, 2–76 selection of 18, 1670; PR/I/106, 27–137 selection of 25, 1700; PR/1/105, 2–111 selection of 17, 1700.
Selection of 18 from Countesthorpe parish, 1634–1709.
Selection of 50 in Lutterworth area from occupational index on shelves, 1535–1705.
Selection of 67 from parishes of Asfordby, Brooksby, Hoby, Frisby on the Wreake, Kirby Bellars and Rotherby, 1540–1680.

Published Sources

Edwards, P. (1991) *Farming: Sources for Local Historians*. London: Batsford.

Fox, A. W. (1997) *The Agrarian Economy of Six Parishes in the Wreake Valley from 1540 to 1680*. Unpublished MA dissertation, University of Leicester.

Fox, A. W. (2009) *A Lost Frontier Revealed: Regional Separation in the East Midlands*. Hatfield: University of Hertfordshire Press.

Kennedy, P. A. (1963). Nottinghamshire household inventories. *Thoroton Record Series* 22, 1–151.

Neave, D. (1984) *Winteringham 1650–1760: the Life and Work in a North Lincolnshire Village Illustrated by Probate Inventories*. Winteringham: Winteringham WEA.

Orton, H., Sanderson, S. and Widdowson, J. (1978) *The Linguistic Atlas of England*. London: Croom Helm.

Perkins, E. R. (1979) *Village Life from Wills and Inventories: Clayworth Parish 1670–1710*. Nottingham: Centre for Local History, University of Nottingham.

Phythian-Adam, C. (1993) Introduction: an agenda for English local history, in C. Phythian-Adams (ed.), *Societies, Culture and Kinship: Cultural Provinces and English Local History*, 1–23. Leicester: Leicester University Press.

Phythian-Adams, C. (2000) Frontier valleys. in J. Thirsk (ed.), *Rural England: An Illustrated History of the Landscape*, 236–264. Oxford: Oxford University Press.

Phythian-Adams, C. (2007) Differentiating provincial societies in English history: spatial contexts and cultural processes, in B. Lancaster, D. Newton and N. Vall (eds) *An Agenda for Regional History*, 3–22. Newcastle upon Tyne: Northumbria University Press.

Stocker, D. (2006). *England's Landscape: The East Midlands*. London: Collins.

Thirsk, J. (1957). *English Peasant Farming: the Agrarian History of Lincolnshire from Tudor to Recent Times*. London: Routledge Kegan and Paul.

Wilshere, J. (1983a) *Braunstone Probate Inventories 1532–1778*, Leicester: Leicester Research Department of Chamberlain Music and Books.

Wilshere, J. (1983b) *Glenfield Probate Inventories 1542–1831*. Leicester: Leicester Research Department of Chamberlain Music and Books.

Wilshere, J. (1983c) *Kirby Muxloe Probate Inventories 1547–1783*. Leicester: Leicester Research Department of Chamberlain Music and Books.

CHAPTER TWELVE

The Smallholders of Southampton Water: the Peasant Land Market on a Hampshire Manor before the Black Death

Mark Page

Introduction

More than any other historian, Harold Fox introduced me to the ingenuity, resourcefulness and humanity of the medieval smallholder. I first met him in 1994 when I was working on the Winchester pipe rolls, the bishop of Winchester's estate accounts, and he was about to publish two important papers on servants, cottagers and the landless (Fox 1995; Fox 1996). Both papers helped to inform my understanding of tenant landholdings on the Winchester estate and alerted me to the likely significance of topography and landscape in explaining the patterns of social structure and settlement which can be reconstructed from medieval surveys and court rolls. Harold's depiction of the Devon manor of Sidbury's 'diversified economy with numerous opportunities for earning a livelihood' is particularly telling in its optimistic assessment of smallholders' strategies for survival. Woodland and common pasture provided grazing for cottagers' cows, horses and sheep, while a variety of resources were available which could be traded at the local market (Fox 1995, 134–6). Far more challenging were the conditions faced by the smallholders of the Somerset manor of Ditcheat, whom Harold judged to be 'condemned to hard and unremitting, relentless toil throughout the working year, and for small returns' (Fox 1996, 555). Nevertheless, his careful analysis of the social and economic circumstances of tenant households on the Glastonbury estate revealed the ways in which individual families adapted to their particular tenurial and working environments to make the most of their chances of improvement, and highlighted the importance of drawing distinctions between manors belonging to a single lord.

Such writings stand in marked contrast to some earlier studies of English rural society in the thirteenth and early fourteenth centuries, which are notable above all for their gloomy pessimism of the smallholder's lot. The historian of the bishop of Winchester's estate, in particular, has to confront an interpretation of tenant living standards which gives short shrift to the idea that smallholders may have eked out an adequate subsistence from trade, wage labour, and the natural resources they found around them, or that they may have been favoured

Manor	Percentage of tenants holding 10 acres or less	Percentage of tenants holding 10.1–20 acres	Percentage of tenants holding 20.1 acres or more
Bitterne	85.9	14.1	0.0
Twyford	61.0	25.5	13.5
Bishop's Waltham	58.2	26.3	15.5
Bishopstoke	53.7	32.6	13.7
Ecchinswell	51.0	28.6	20.4
Merdon	39.2	32.9	27.9
Crawley	38.9	33.3	27.8
Bishop's Sutton	37.8	37.8	24.4
Droxford	37.3	37.3	25.4
Cheriton	36.1	19.6	44.3
Alresford	35.4	20.8	43.8
North Waltham	23.8	11.9	64.3
Beauworth	23.5	17.7	58.8
All manors	44.7	25.8	29.5

TABLE 12.1. Size of tenant landholdings on some Hampshire manors belonging to the bishops of Winchester in the mid to late thirteenth century. Source: British Library, Egerton MS 2418; Titow 1962a, 108

by the opportunities available in particular localities (Titow 1969, though for a more nuanced account by the same author of the differences between manors and their effects on peasant prosperity, see Titow 1962b). Smallholdings were a common feature of the Winchester estate before the Black Death, but the social structure of individual manors varied considerably. In Hampshire, evidence from thirteen manors shows that in the mid to late thirteenth century the proportion of tenants holding ten acres or less ranged from less than a quarter to more than four-fifths (Table 12.1). The most extreme case of fragmentation of holdings, noted but not named by Titow (1969, 79), occurred at Bitterne near Southampton (Fig. 12.1). Around two-thirds of the 64 customary tenants recorded on this manor in *c.*1250 lived on eight-acre holdings (a quarter of a virgate), and only nine held half a virgate (sixteen acres) or more. To put this in perspective, many historians argue that the basic subsistence needs of a peasant family in medieval England could not be met from less than about ten acres, though debate on this subject is set to continue (Dyer 1989, 109–40; Kitsikopolous 2000; Stone 2005, 262–72; Bailey 2007, 39, 58–64).

Bitterne's social structure may have been distinctive in the context of the Winchester estate, but it was characteristic of other manors nearby. On Titchfield Abbey's estate before the Black Death, the smallholder with two to five acres was typical at Cadland (on the Solent south-east of Beaulieu) and at Portchester. In the large ancient parish of Titchfield, holdings of eight and sixteen acres were common at Funtley, Stubbington, and Swanwick, while the inhabitants of Titchfield itself, which served as a market town for the surrounding area, included a large proportion of cottagers (Watts 1958, 63–4). Another distinctive feature of the area around Southampton Water, in a county dominated by large and anciently established Church manors, was the unusually high proportion of small lay manors of low value, on which smallholders are again likely to have been common (Campbell and Bartley 2006, 81, 85). Seen in this context, Bitterne's social structure appears less remarkable and suggests that, as with farming practices, tenants' conditions on individual bishopric

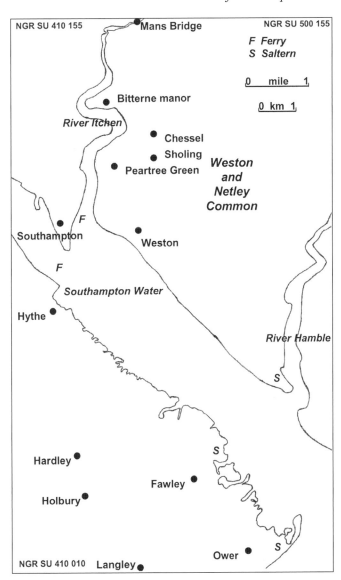

NGR SU 410 155

Mans Bridge

NGR SU 500 155

F *Ferry*
S *Saltern*

0 mile 1

0 km 1

Bitterne manor

River Itchen

Chessel

Sholing

Peartree Green

Weston and Netley Common

F

Southampton

Weston

F

Southampton Water

Hythe

River Hamble

S

Hardley

Fawley

Holbury

S

S

Ower

NGR SU 410 010   Langley

FIGURE 12.1. Bitterne manor and surrounding area (showing places mentioned in the text)

manors often conformed to those of the immediate locality. However, unlike some Winchester manors, and many small lay manors nearby, little mention has been found at Bitterne of free tenants or sub-tenants (British Library, Egerton MS 2418; Campbell 2005, 30; Page 2005, 331–2).

The aim of this paper is to explore the social and economic conditions of the bishop's customary tenants at Bitterne in the decades before the Black Death, and to explain how they survived (and even thrived) despite holding relatively small amounts of land. It is divided into three parts: the first outlines the main features of the manor's topography and land-use in the Middle Ages; the second examines in some detail the peasant land market at Bitterne and identifies different patterns of behaviour in different parts of the manor; finally, an attempt is made to explain those differences, focusing in particular on the opportunities for non-agricultural employment in an estuarine landscape on the edge of the New Forest. The paper suggests, first, that proximity to the town and the manor's varied landscape allowed smallholdings to proliferate. Secondly, it argues that there was no crisis in living standards on the manor in the early fourteenth century, although economic conditions may have deteriorated on the north side of the estuary from the 1320s. Thirdly, it points to the distinctive landscape, economy and society of the southern part of the manor as decisive factors in enabling smallholders to survive.

Topography and land-use

Present-day Bitterne forms part of the city of Southampton, lying on the eastern side of the river Itchen. The bishop's manor house lay only about two miles from the centre of the medieval town, although (before a bridge was built in the eighteenth century) the journey would have required the taking of a ferry across the Itchen or a lengthy diversion to the lowest crossing-point of the river at Mans Bridge. Nevertheless, the proximity of one of England's twenty wealthiest towns in 1334, with 1,152 recorded taxpayers in 1377, must have provided a ready market for the agricultural producers of Bitterne and other settlements within Southampton's rural hinterland (Palliser 2000, 124, 759). The bishop of Winchester probably sold much of Bitterne's demesne produce in the town. In 1301–2, for example, about half the wheat harvest was sold, fetching 6s a quarter, considerably more than the 'national' average for that year. More than four-fifths of the manor's dredge (a mixture of oats and barley) was also marketed, the bishop benefiting from rising prices over the course of the year. Dredge was a highly commercialized crop suitable for malting which was most likely bought by the town's brewers (Farmer 1988, 790; Page 1996, 243; Campbell 2000, 226).

Bitterne's tenants may also have had the opportunity to sell surplus grain at Southampton and a wide range of other resources which could be gathered (legally and illegally) across the manor's rich and varied landscape. Nuts were collected from surrounding woodland, while the manor's heaths produced a range of plants which could be sold as fuel, fodder, fencing, litter and thatch (Rackham 1986, 295; Page 1996, 243). Bitterne's coastal and freshwater marshland was probably especially valuable: in 1301–2 two tenants paid for permission to enter the marsh to dig up marl, a chalky clay which was commonly used as a fertilizer, and others may have harvested rushes, dug turves, caught fish and birds, and manufactured salt. Richard le Salter was named as one of the manor's tenants in that year, and salterns were marked along the estuary on eighteenth-century maps (Taylor 1759; Page 1996, 243; Page 1999, 203; Campbell 2000, 82). The bishop's fishery at Bitterne produced considerable numbers of salmon for sale, and tenants may have had the opportunity to fish both in the river and the sea. Cider was also produced on the manor: the orchard perhaps lay within the bishop's park, where tenants were able to feed their cattle and pigs in return for a small payment (Page 1996, 242–3, 245, 249). In short, the variety of resources at Bitterne was considerable, and their availability, together with the manor's proximity to a large urban market, provides prima facie evidence for suggesting that the marked fragmentation of customary holdings into ferlings (eight acres), evident at Bitterne from the mid-thirteenth century, was both a cause and a consequence of tenants diversifying into a range of productive activities other than agriculture.

Before discussing the tenants further, it is necessary briefly to characterize the manor in the Middle Ages. Bitterne's medieval boundaries are not precisely known, but it is clear that the manor was extensive and was not confined to a single parish. It included land on both sides of Southampton Water, in the parishes of South Stoneham and St Mary Extra on the north bank and in Fawley parish on the south side of the estuary (Page 1900–14, III, 292–3, 297–8, 481–2, 484). On both sides of the water the manor lay chiefly on the acidic sandy soils of the Barton, Bracklesham and Bagshot Beds that resulted in the extensive heaths and commons shown on eighteenth-century maps (Taylor 1759; Milne 1791; Short 2006, 24, 58). In places, however, a mixture of clay, sand, and gravel produced a fertile loam which allowed medieval and later farmers to raise considerable crops of wheat, barley and oats. In later centuries the area was also known for its market gardening and soft fruit (Page 1900–14, III, 481; Green 1940, 300, 331, 354, 363–4). Tenants' landholdings were dispersed across the manor in widely spaced villages and hamlets: on the north bank of Southampton Water settlements included Bitterne, Chessel, Sholing, Ridgway Heath (including the present Peartree Green), and Weston. On the south side of the estuary tenants held land at Ower, Fawley and Hythe (the name means 'landing place') where there was a ferry to Southampton. Although tenants on both sides of the estuary had access to a similar range of resources, clear contrasts can be drawn between the two groups of settlements, in particular with regard to tenants' landholdings.

The peasant land market

Further evidence of Bitterne's tenants and their landholdings can be found in the entry fines recorded in the Winchester pipe rolls. An entry fine was due to the bishop as lord of the manor every time a change in the tenancy of customary land occurred. At Bitterne more than 600 entry fines were paid in the eighty years before the outbreak of plague in 1348–9, an examination of which can shed much light on the ways in which the manor's tenants reacted to changing economic and social conditions (Table 12.2). For example, one particularly notable feature of this data is the relatively muted rise in the number of land transfers at the time of the Great Famine and associated agrarian crises (1315–22). Across the Winchester estate as a whole there was a sharp increase in the payment of entry fines at the height of the famine in 1316–17, which can be explained partly by a rise in mortality caused by disease and starvation

Years	Number of entry fines recorded	Number of relevant accounts surviving	Average number of entry fines paid per account
1263–69	24	5	4.8
1271–78	20	5	4.0
1283–89	27	7	3.9
1290–99	36	6	6.0
1300–09	38	9	4.2
1310–19	65	10	6.5
1321–29	52	7	7.4
1330–39	124	9	13.8
1340–48	146	9	16.2
1349	86	1	86.0
1263–1349	618	68	9.1

TABLE 12.2. Number of entry fines recorded at Bitterne, 1263–1349. Source: Hampshire Record Office, 11M59/B1/29–101

and partly by tenants selling land in order to raise money to buy food and settle debts (Page 2002, 19; Page 2003a, 167–8). That relatively few of Bitterne's smallholders entered the land market at that time, either as a result of death or exigency, suggests that the diverse range of resources which they were able to exploit shielded them from the famine's worst effects (cf. Campbell 1984, 106–7). By contrast, as elsewhere on the estate, the manor enjoyed little protection from the onslaught of the Black Death in 1348–9.

The rate at which entry fines were paid at Bitterne began to quicken in the 1320s and rose sharply after 1330. A closer examination of the types of land transfer recorded shows that the rise mostly was due to an increase in activity in the land market (Table 12.3). Until the 1310s around half the entry fines paid at Bitterne were for the inheritance of holdings by sons, widows or other family members, but thereafter the proportion fell to less than a fifth in 1340–8. During the same period the proportion of entry fines paid for the transfer of land between unrelated individuals (called here 'inter-vivos transfers outside the family') increased from around a fifth in 1290–9 to more than half in 1340–8. Thus, while the number of land transfers by inheritance custom remained about the same, averaging twenty-eight per decade in the period 1300–48, the number of land sales between non-kin rose from six in 1300–9 to eighty-two in 1340–8. Given that there was intense demand for land almost everywhere in early fourteenth-century England as the population remained close to its medieval peak, the most likely explanation for a sudden surge in land market activity as occurred at Bitterne is that the supply of land expanded. But what accounts for the change in supply and how were Bitterne's customary tenants affected?

On most manors in medieval England there were three main ways in which the supply of land available to customary tenants could increase. The first was that the lord of the manor leased out former demesne land. At Bitterne the demesne acreage under seed fell sharply following the death of Bishop John of Pontoise in 1304 and the election of his successor Henry Woodlock. However, there is little evidence to suggest that the manor's customary tenants subsequently obtained much of this land: rents were broadly stable after 1300 and the entry fines show that on the few occasions when the bishop granted

Years	Inter-vivos transfers within the family	Post-mortem transfers within the family	Inter-vivos transfers outside the family	Post-mortem transfers outside the family	Transfers outside the family by marriage	Record of incoming tenant only*	Total
1263–69	0	1	0	0	1	22	24
1271–78	1	5	1	1	6	6	20
1283–89	1	21	2	0	2	1	27
1290–99	4	19	8	0	4	1	36
1300–09	6	21	6	1	4	0	38
1310–19	6	32	11	4	11	1	65
1321–29	3	24	21	0	3	1	52
1330–39	12	36	60	0	11	5	124
1340–48	26	27	82	0	11	0	146
1349	3	57	7	8	11	0	86
1263–1349	62	243	198	14	64	37	618

TABLE 12.3. Number of land transfers recorded at Bitterne, 1263–1349. Source: Hampshire Record Office, 11M59/B1/29–101

* Either because of a lack of information about the outgoing tenant in the pipe rolls, or because the land was granted directly to the tenant by the lord.

land directly to his tenants it mostly comprised small plots (Titow 1962a, 25, table 1). The second way in which tenants could acquire additional acres was to encroach on the manor's common or waste and convert the land to more productive use. Although, as we have seen, heaths and commons were a distinctive feature of Bitterne's landscape, relatively little encroachment seems to have occurred, presumably because tenants were prevented from doing so by the bishop's officers or their own communities (see below). Plots of purpresture, the name given to former common or waste at Bitterne, rarely exceeded four acres in size and were held by only a small number of the manor's tenants. The final method of increasing the supply of land was for tenants themselves to break up their own landholdings and to sell (or give away to family members) the resulting fragments. This practice was widespread on the Winchester estate before the Black Death and Bitterne was no exception (Page 2003b).

In the absence of a mid fourteenth-century survey to compare with that of *c.*1250, the extent to which customary landholdings at Bitterne fragmented over the intervening 100 years can be estimated very roughly by looking at the size of those tenements transferred in 1348–9, when a large proportion of the population was killed by the Black Death, and a significant part of the contemporary landholding structure was thereby revealed (Table 12.4). Only around a third of entry fines paid in 1348–9 were for the transfer of standard-sized ferlings (eight acres), including those which had been enlarged by the addition of small amounts of other land or property. By contrast, nearly three-fifths of the landholdings recorded in that year comprised seven acres or less (including cottages with little or no land attached), of which a substantial number measured four acres (half a ferling) or six acres (three-quarters of a ferling), suggesting that they had probably been created by the fragmentation of ferlings or half-virgates. A number of tenants who held fractions of ferlings in the 1340s belonged to families whose members had occupied standard-sized

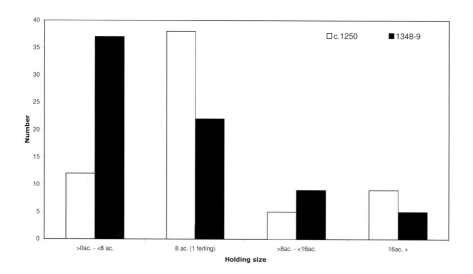

Year	Less than 8 acres (including 'land')	8 acres (ferling)	8 acres plus additions*	16 acres (½ virgate)	Total
*c.*1250	12 (19%)	38 (59%)	5 (8%)	9 (14%)	64 (100%)

Year	Cottage only	½-3 acres	4 acres (½ ferling)	4½-7 acres	8 acres (ferling)	8 acres plus additions*	16–32 acres (½-1 virgate)	Total
1348–9	13 (15%)	13 (15%)	12 (14%)	12 (14%)	22 (26%)	9 (10%)	5 (6%)	86 (100%)

* Additions include cottages, crofts, plots, purprestures, salterns, and other small pieces of land.

TABLE 12.4. Number and percentage of different sized tenant landholdings recorded at Bitterne, *c.*1250 and 1348–9. Source: British Library, Egerton MS 2418; Hampshire Record Office, 11M59/B1/101

holdings in the mid to late thirteenth century and who had later engaged in the buying and selling of small pieces of land. William Gott, for example, became tenant of a ferling in 1272 when he married an heiress, William Godwin inherited half a virgate from his father in 1289, and two members of the Norman family held ferlings in *c.*1250. In each of these cases, the family's landholdings became fragmented over time, small plots of land were regularly bought and sold by family members, particularly in the 1330s and 1340s, and fractured holdings were inherited by their descendants. Thus, in the plague year of 1348–9 different members of the Gott family inherited holdings of six acres and two acres from William and Richard Gott, their father and uncle respectively.

Further mention of the Gotts and their contemporaries is made below, but first it is necessary to demonstrate that the increase in land market activity after 1330 was the result of the buying and selling of small plots of land; in other words, that there was a correlation between rising numbers of entry fines paid to the bishop and an increased supply of land from the fragmentation of holdings (Table 12.5). This exercise is only possible from around 1310 when the Winchester pipe rolls begin to record consistently the exact size of the holding transferred; before that date a significant minority of tenements were given the indeterminate description

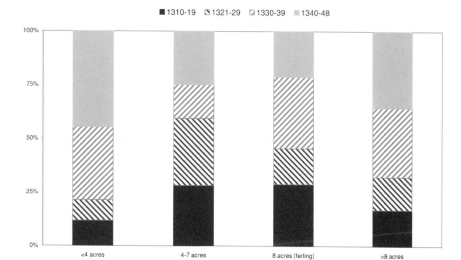

Years	Less than 4 acres	4–7 acres	8 acres (ferling)	More than 8 acres	Total
1310–19	27 (42%)	9 (14%)	19 (29%)	10 (15%)	65
1321–29	22 (42%)	10 (19%)	11 (21%)	9 (18%)	52
1330–39	78 (63%)	5 (4%)	22 (18%)	19 (15%)	124
1340–48	103 (71%)	8 (5%)	14 (10%)	21 (14%)	146
1310–48	230 (60%)	32 (8%)	66 (17%)	59 (15%)	387

TABLE 12.5. Number and percentage of entry fines paid for different sized landholdings at Bitterne, 1310–48. Source: Hampshire Record Office, 11M59/B1/65–100

of 'land'. The proportion of entry fines paid for the transfer of holdings measuring less than four acres rose from around two-fifths of the total in the 1310s and 1320s to nearly three-quarters in 1340–8, demonstrating beyond doubt that the land market was driven to an increasing extent by the sale and purchase of the smallest plots. Such activity was not uncommon on other English manors before the Black Death, where it has been variously interpreted, but before assessing its impact upon the customary tenants at Bitterne, another dimension of the manor's landholding structure must be explored.

From 1310 not only do the pipe rolls record the exact size of tenants' landholdings at Bitterne, but they also register its location. Analysis of this information reveals marked differences between the settlements on either side of Southampton Water (Table 12.6). In the period 1310–48 the overwhelming majority of land transfers involving undivided ferlings (eight acres) took place on the estuary's north bank in the 'Bitterne group' of settlements (including Bitterne, Chessel, Ridgway Heath, Sholing and Weston). By contrast, on the southern side of the water in the 'Fawley group' of places (including Fawley, Hythe and Ower) most entry fines were paid for the transfer of smaller plots of land. The fragmentation of standard-sized holdings and the circulation of the resulting pieces in an increasingly active land market thus happened to a much greater extent on the south side of the estuary than on the north bank, where the transfer of small plots (though still apparent) was not so pronounced. Having thus established, at some length, the character of

Places	Less than 8 acres	8 acres (ferling)	More than 8 acres	Total
'Bitterne group'	**63**	62	29	154
'Fawley group'	186	3	29	218
All places (including unidentified)	262	66	59	387

the customary land market at Bitterne in the decades prior to the Black Death, it is time to draw on this and other evidence to reveal something of the lives of the manor's tenants on either side of Southampton Water and to explain some of the contrasts between them.

TABLE 12.6. Number of entry fines paid in different parts of Bitterne manor, 1310–48. Source: Hampshire Record Office, 11M59/B1/65–100

Contrasting communities: Bitterne and Fawley

The repeated inheritance of a tenant family's customary landholding and its continuous occupation by successive generations (sometimes called the 'family-land bond') has been widely observed by historians on many manors in pre-Black Death England (Schofield 2003, 53). At Bitterne, particularly in the 'Bitterne group' of settlements on the north side of Southampton Water, a number of families retained possession of an undivided ferling (eight acres) for a century or more, neither accumulating additional plots of land nor fragmenting the main holding in response to changing social and economic circumstances. The ferling held by Augustine Fry c.1250 in Weston, for example, was inherited intact by John son of William Fry, probably his grandson, in 1349; in the intervening period the family made no recorded intervention in the land market, either as buyers or sellers. Also at Weston, the ferling held by Augustine Child c.1250 was probably inherited in 1326 by his grandson William son of Walter Child, whose widow Matilda remarried in 1337, taking the family holding with her. The significance of these examples, in the context of the earlier discussion of tenant living standards, is that at Bitterne eight acres was evidently sufficient for a family to survive without recourse to the land market, even during periods of crisis such as the Great Famine. The ways in which such families made their living, beyond the generalized description given above of the range of resources available locally, is not known, but an attempt to gauge their prosperity can be made by examining the size of entry fines paid to the bishop for the inheritance of customary holdings.

The entry fine was a variable payment, the rate of which was influenced by a range of different factors, although it is generally agreed that the cost must broadly reflect the demand for land and the ability of tenants to pay (Dyer 2005a, 223–6; Page 2005, 338–40). In the 'Bitterne group' of settlements between 1310 and 1349 more than fifty entry fines were paid for the inheritance of undivided ferlings, most of which fell within a band ranging from 3s. 4d. to 13s. 4d. (that is, from 5d. to 20d. an acre). That level of payment was relatively low by national standards, though it was perhaps more typical of the bishop of Winchester's estate in general, and of his Hampshire manors in particular (Dyer 2005a, 228–30). However, the point that needs to be emphasized here is that the trend in the level of payment was emphatically downwards: the average fine per acre for the inheritance of a

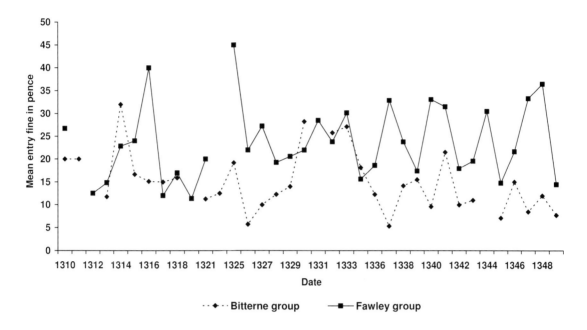

FIGURE 12.2. Annual averages of entry fines at Bitterne, 1310–49 (pence per acre)

ferling was 18.2*d* in the decade 1310–19, or 14*d* if an unusually large entry fine of £2 is excluded; it fell to 11.4*d* in 1321–9, and to 10.9*d* in 1330–9, falling still further to 9.3*d* in 1340–8, and to 7.4*d*. in the plague year of 1348–9. This evidence suggests that although Bitterne's tenants were largely successful in preserving their customary holdings intact, they found the economic conditions of the early fourteenth century increasingly difficult, with the result that the bishop was compelled to moderate his demands for entry fines. For example, the fines paid for the Child family's ferling, mentioned above, fell from 6*s* 8*d* in 1326, to 3*s* 4*d* in 1330, and to 2*s* in 1337. Moreover, the absence of men such as William Child and William Fry from the lay subsidy roll of 1327 provides another indication that Bitterne's eight-acre tenants were not among the wealthiest members of the local community (TNA: PRO, E 179/173/4, m.13).

The trend in the level of all entry fines paid in the 'Bitterne group' of settlements (not just those given for the inheritance of a ferling) was also generally downwards in the period 1310–48, though the average was around 15*d*. per acre (Fig. 12.2). By contrast, in the 'Fawley group' of settlements, the cost of transferring property was much higher and may even have been rising. The average fine per acre on the southern side of Southampton Water was about 24*d* (2*s*) between 1310 and 1348, with relatively little variation from one decade to the next (though individual payments could be volatile). In this part of the manor the bishop was able to charge considerably larger sums, particularly for the conveyance between unrelated individuals of small plots or fragments of holdings. At Ower, for example, fines of 48*d* (4*s*) per acre or more were not uncommon in the 1330s and 1340s, such as that given by John Langford in 1340 who paid 2*s* for the surrender of half an acre by Agnes Gott. What observations can be made about the buyers and sellers in the 'Fawley group' of settlements in the 30 years or so before the Black Death, and about the character and timing of the conveyances registered in the manor court? The following remarks focus upon the case histories of particular individuals and families, and cannot necessarily be regarded as typical; nevertheless, they are based on a wider examination of around fifty tenants of the manor.

The number of tenants who bought land (but did not sell it) was about the same as the number who sold land (but did not buy it); a significant minority of tenants both bought and sold land, usually in that order. Many of those buying land made their first recorded appearance at Fawley and Ower in the 1320s and 1330s, suggesting that they were probably newcomers. John Langford, for example, may have been a member of a long-standing New Forest family, one of whom was accused of hunting the king's deer in 1270 (Stagg 1979, 98–9). Langford was first mentioned in 1327 acquiring half an acre in Ower from Richard Harding; in the same year he was assessed for taxation on the relatively modest sum of £1 (the average for Fawley township was £1 18s 4d) (TNA: PRO, E 179/173/4, m.13). In the following years Langford made several more purchases of small plots of land in Ower as well as the considerably larger acquisition of half a virgate in Fawley from Cecilia Spillman. In 1339 he married a local heiress Cecilia Harvey who brought with her a further 12 acres, and in 1348 the two of them paid the large fine of £6 13s 4d for a house and ferling with a dovecot, watermill, and 10 acres of moor and marsh.

Those who sold land to Langford, including the Gotts, Hardings, Normans and Spillmans, were mostly from well-established tenant families, many of whom still lived on the manor in 1349 and beyond. Their intentions in selling part or all of their holdings cannot easily be discerned, but they were not necessarily driven to do so by hardship. Although there were years of high grain prices during the 1330s and 1340s, which may have encouraged the sale of small plots of land, the correlation between periods of dearth and an increase in transfers of land outside the family is not entirely convincing (Table 12.7). Certainly in the 1330s activity in the land market shows a rough correspondence with fluctuating grain prices, but thereafter the relationship is less clear and more difficult to interpret. Even as a lagging indicator of distress, changes in the land market at Bitterne are more equivocal of explanation than those observed elsewhere (Campbell 1984, 107–20; Schofield 1997, 5–15). Tenants may instead have sought to profit from a growing demand for land from outsiders such as John Langford. A possible indication of the increasing pressure on local resources at this time, and thus of their potential value, is provided by a case heard by the justices of the forest in 1330. Several men from Fawley and the neighbouring settlements of Hardley and Langley were accused of entering the New Forest 'in arms', where they 'broke down the hedges and ditches about the purprestures rented to various men by the king's writ, to the damage of £10' (Stagg 1979, 184). Disputes over purprestures were often fought when land was in short supply between established tenants concerned to protect their common rights and newcomers seeking to increase the area of productive arable and pasture (Dyer 2006).

Among those who attacked the forest purprestures were several men of

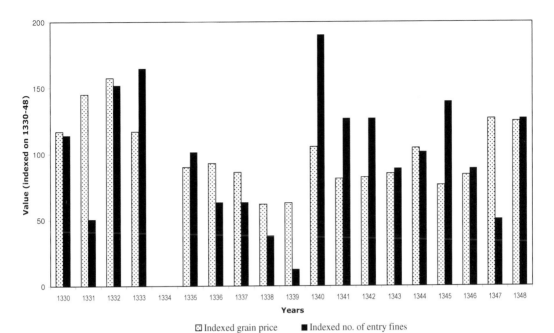

	1330	*1331*	*1332*	*1333*	*1335*	*1336*	*1337*	*1338*	*1339*
Grain price index	121	150	163	121	93	96	89	64	65
No. of entry fines	9	4	12	13	8	5	5	3	1

	1340	*1341*	*1342*	*1343*	*1344*	*1345*	*1346*	*1347*	*1348*
Grain price index	109	84	85	88	108	79	87	131	129
No. of entry fines	15	10	10	7	8	11	7	4	10

TABLE 12.7. Mean grain price index (base=100) and number of *inter-vivos* land transfers outside the family recorded at Bitterne, 1330–48. Source: Hampshire Record Office, 11M59/B1/83–100; Farmer 1988, 791

substance from Fawley, including the rector of the parish church, John of Fawley, and Ralph de Munselewe. The Fawleys were long-standing tenants of the manor: Robert of Fawley inherited land from his father in 1269, which his own son John inherited 20 years later. As with several of his contemporaries in the 'Bitterne group' of settlements, John of Fawley did not engage in the land market. He was assessed on goods worth £3 in 1327 and died in 1349, when his son John inherited a house and 30 acres. Ralph de Munselewe was also a substantial landholder, whose son John surrendered property, including a dovecot, watermill, moor and marsh, to John Langford in 1348. Although most tenants of the manor were smallholders, Fawley was evidently a place where those with spare capital were able to invest in land and build up significant portfolios of property. In 1317, for example, Roger Hurn entered the manor by marrying the widow of Robert Spillman who brought with her a ferling of land in Ower. In the following years Roger made nine further purchases of property and in 1327 was the wealthiest taxpayer in the vill, assessed on £5 worth of goods. He died in 1339 leaving his brother Geoffrey a house, 15 acres, and the moiety of a windmill.

The demand for land from outsiders may help to explain both the high level of entry fines levied at Fawley and the willingness of tenants to fragment or sell their holdings. In contrast to the settlements at Bitterne, those on the south side of Southampton Water were marked by a more fluid, and probably more polarized, social structure. Tenants at Bitterne seem to have considered a ferling (8 acres) as the minimum necessary to support their families; those at Fawley were apparently able to survive on even smaller holdings, possibly because there were more opportunities to engage in non-agricultural activities. Proximity to the New Forest may have encouraged poaching and the creation of purprestures: such activities certainly occurred at neighbouring Hardley, Holbury and Langley (Stagg 1979, 109–10, 153, 200, 203–4). Tenant mills, salterns and marsh were more prominent on the south bank of the estuary than on the north side. In 1319, for example, Edward Gott acquired a salt-works at Fawley which formerly belonged to Robert of Langley, while in 1343 Robert de Hazelden surrendered his share of a salt-pan and 10 acres of marsh in Fawley to his son William. Salt was a valuable commodity, and much in demand in towns such as Southampton, from where it was traded (Coleman 1960, xxv). In the late thirteenth century the keeper of the New Forest accounted for an annual render of 30 quarters of salt from Hardley worth £1 10s (Stagg 1979, 136, 140). It is probably no coincidence that two tenant families mentioned in 1349 owning salt-pans at Fawley also held half-shares in the ferry from Hythe to Southampton, a vital link for local trade.

The 'Fawley group' of settlements was thus characterized by an active market in small plots of land, which was probably stimulated by an increasing demand for local resources; lying on the edge of the New Forest, the manor's land market intensified at the same time as the conversion of woodland and waste into arable and pasture was conspicuous enough to create tension within the local community. The bishop's customary tenants engaged not only in arable farming but also in the exploitation of other resources, including marsh, moor (probably grazing for livestock) and salt-works. This was a diversified economy in which even smallholders were able to generate sufficient surpluses to be taxed. In 1327, for example, Robert Austen and John Norman, who held no more than a ferling each, were assessed on goods worth £1 and 11s 8d respectively (TNA: PRO, E 179/173/4, m.13). In the 'Bitterne group', by contrast, the land market was less intense, holdings were less likely to be fragmented, and they tended to be inherited by successive generations. Despite the appearance of stability, however, prosperity may have been more fragile and was perhaps dependent on a narrower range of resources than on the south side of the estuary. Entry fines were lower at Bitterne and its tenants paid less in tax (the average assessment for the lay subsidy of 1327 was £1 4d). On both sides of Southampton Water, proximity to a major town and access to non-agricultural resources may have encouraged the fragmenting of virgates into ferlings in the thirteenth century, but only at Fawley did the process of fragmentation continue as a result of particular social and economic forces.

Conclusion

Harold Fox excelled at the local historian's art of generalizing from the particular. The following brief remarks suggest some of the implications of the findings from Bitterne. Three themes emerge: the question of peasant welfare before the plague; the relationship of town and countryside; and the distinctive landscape and economy of estuary and coast.

The long-established pessimistic view that a large part of the pre-Black Death peasantry was made up of smallholders enduring a 'wretched existence on an inadequate number of acres' (Titow 1969, 93) has not been overturned, and indeed has been powerfully and eloquently restated (Bailey 1998; Campbell 2005, 60–70; Bailey 2007, 63–4; Schofield 2008). Nevertheless, there is a growing recognition that medieval peasants were resilient, adaptive and had the ability to overcome their problems in a flexible and innovative way (Dyer 2005b, 7–45; Stone 2005, 262–72; Langdon and Masschaele 2006; Dodds 2008; Briggs 2009, 173–5, 214–23). The evidence of early fourteenth-century Bitterne presented here offers a broadly optimistic picture of peasant welfare: most of the manor's eight-acre tenants survived the shock of famine and agrarian crisis without apparent difficulty, though on the north side of Southampton Water falling entry fines suggest increasing economic hardship from the 1320s. On the south side of the estuary competition for resources no doubt produced winners and losers, but many smallholders seem to have led a successful 'hybrid existence as farmers who also engaged in by-employment', most notably in Fawley's marshes and salterns (Harvey 2001, 4).

The influence of medieval towns on their rural hinterlands is a subject of enduring interest to historians (for recent collections of essays, see Galloway 2000; Giles and Dyer 2005). Employment and trading opportunities, in particular, are often emphasized, and it is no surprise to find large numbers of smallholders living in close proximity to a wealthy town such as Southampton. Similar patterns have been found elsewhere, including on manors surrounding Gloucester and Worcester (Dyer 1980, 90, 107–8). However, at Bitterne the differences between the settlements on either side of Southampton Water suggest that the town was not the only factor in determining the size of tenant landholdings and the level of peasant prosperity. The role of the New Forest and the availability of salt-works and marshland must also be taken into consideration when discussing the smallholders of Fawley. Indeed, Fawley's location, on the edge of forest, estuary, and coast, is perhaps its most distinctive characteristic, and would doubtless have been emphasized by Harold Fox. One of Harold's major contributions to the historiography of medieval England was to demonstrate the significance of estuary and coast in the development of settlements (and their economies, societies and landscapes) which had links to the shore (Fox 2001; Fox 2007). My interpretation of Fawley and Bitterne owes much to his pioneering work.

Bibliography

Bailey, M. (1998) Peasant welfare in England, 1290–1348. *Economic History Review* 51, 223–51.

Bailey, M. (2007) *Medieval Suffolk: An Economic and Social History 1200–1500.* Woodbridge: Boydell.

Briggs, C. (2009) *Credit and Village Society in Fourteenth-Century England.* Oxford: Oxford University Press.

Campbell, B. M. S. (1984) Population pressure, inheritance and the land market in a fourteenth-century peasant community, in R. M. Smith (eds), *Land, Kinship and Life-Cycle,* 87–134. Cambridge: Cambridge University Press.

Campbell, B. M. S. (2000) *English Seigniorial Agriculture 1250–1450,* Cambridge: Cambridge University Press.

Campbell, B. M. S. (2005) The agrarian problem in the early fourteenth century, *Past and Present* 188, 3–70.

Campbell, B. M. S. and Bartley, K. (2006) *England on the Eve of the Black Death: An Atlas of Lay Lordship, Land and Wealth, 1300–49.* Manchester: Manchester University Press.

Coleman, O. (ed.) (1960) *The Brokage Book of Southampton 1443–4,* Vol. I. Southampton Records Series 4.

Dodds, B. (2008) Demesne and tithe: peasant agriculture in the late middle ages. *Agricultural History Review* 56, 123–41.

Dyer, C. (1980) *Lords and Peasants in a Changing Society.* Cambridge: Cambridge University Press.

Dyer, C. (1989) *Standards of Living in the Later Middle Ages.* Cambridge: Cambridge University Press.

Dyer, C. (2005a) Seigniorial profits on the landmarket in late medieval England, in L. Feller and C. Wickham (eds) *Le Marché de la Terre au Moyen Âge,* 219–36. Rome: École française de Rome.

Dyer, C. (2005b) *An Age of Transition? Economy and Society in England in the Later Middle Ages.* Oxford: Oxford University Press.

Dyer, C. (2006) Conflict in the landscape: the enclosure movement in England, 1220–1349. *Landscape History* 28, 21–33.

Farmer, D. (1988) Prices and wages, in H. E. Hallam (ed.), *The Agrarian History of England and Wales, Vol. II, 1042–1350,* 715–817. Cambridge: Cambridge University Press.

Fox, H. S. A. (1995) Servants, cottagers and tied cottages during the later middle ages: towards a regional dimension. *Rural History* 6, 125–54.

Fox, H. S. A. (1996) Exploitation of the landless by lords and tenants in early medieval England, in Z. Razi and R. Smith (eds), *Medieval Society and the Manor Court,* 518–68. Oxford: Clarendon Press.

Fox, H. S. A. (2001) *The Evolution of the Fishing Village: Landscape and Society along the South Devon Coast, 1086–1550,* Leicester Explorations in Local History, 1. Oxford: Leopard's Head Press.

Fox, H. S. A. (2007) Two Devon estuaries in the middle ages: fisheries, ports, fortifications and places of worship. *Landscapes* 8.1, 39–68.

Galloway, J. A. (ed.) (2000) *Trade, Urban Hinterlands and Market Integration c.1300–1600,* Centre for Metropolitan History Working Paper Series 3. London: Institute of Historical Research.

Giles, K. and Dyer, C. (eds) (2005) *Town and Country in the Middle Ages: Contrasts, Contacts and Interconnections, 1100–1500.* Leeds: Society for Medieval Archaeology Monograph 22.

Green, F. H. W. (1940) *The Land of Britain: The Report of the Land Utilisation Survey of Britain*, Part 89, *Hampshire*, ed. L. Dudley Stamp. London: Geographical Publications.

Harvey, B. (ed.) (2001) *The Twelfth and Thirteenth Centuries*. Oxford: Oxford University Press.

Kitsikopolous, H. (2000) Standards of living and capital formation in pre-plague England: a peasant budget model. *Economic History Review* 53, 237–61.

Langdon, J. and Masschaele, J. 2006) Commercial activity and population growth in medieval England. *Past and Present* 190, 35–81.

Milne, T. (1791) Hampshire map, 1 inch to 1 mile, (http://www.geog.port.ac.uk/webmap/hantsmap/hantsmap/milne1/mln43f.htm, accessed 20 July 2009).

Page, M. (ed.) (1996) *The Pipe Roll of the Bishopric of Winchester 1301–2*, Hampshire Record Series, 14. Winchester: Hampshire County Council.

Page, M. (ed.) (1999) *The Pipe Roll of the Bishopric of Winchester 1409–10*, Hampshire Record Series, 16. Winchester: Hampshire County Council.

Page, M. (2002) *The Medieval Bishops of Winchester: Estate, Archive and Administration*, Hampshire Papers, 24. Winchester: Hampshire County Council.

Page, M. (2003a) The peasant land market on the bishop of Winchester's manor of Farnham, 1263–1349. *Surrey Archaeological Collections* 90, 163–79.

Page, M. (2003b) The peasant land market on the estate of the bishopric of Winchester before the Black Death, in R. Britnell (ed.), *The Winchester Pipe Rolls and Medieval English Society*, 61–80. Woodbridge: Boydell.

Page, M. (2005) The peasant land market in southern England: the estate of the bishops of Winchester, 1260–1350, in L. Feller and C. Wickham (eds), *Le Marché de la Terre au Moyen Âge*, 315–40. Rome: École française de Rome.

Page. W. (ed.) (1900–14) *Victoria County History of Hampshire and the Isle of Wight*, 5 vols in 6. London: Constable.

Palliser, D. (ed.) (2000) *The Cambridge Urban History of Britain*, Vol. I, *c.600–1540*. Cambridge: Cambridge University Press.

Rackham, O. (1986) *The History of the Countryside*. London: Dent.

Schofield, P. R. (1997) Dearth, debt and the local land market in a late thirteenth-century village community. *Agricultural History Review* 45, 1–17.

Schofield, P. R. (2003) *Peasant and Community in Medieval England 1200–1500*. Basingstoke: Palgrave Macmillan.

Schofield, P. R. (2008) The social economy of the medieval village in the early fourteenth century. *Economic History Review* 61, 38–63.

Short, B. (2006) *England's Landscape: The South East*. London: Harper Collins.

Stagg, D. (ed.) (1979) *A Calendar of New Forest Documents 1244–1334*, Hampshire Record Series, 3. Winchester: Hampshire County Council.

Stone, D. (2005) *Decision-Making in Medieval Agriculture*. Oxford: Oxford University Press.

Taylor, I. (1759) Hampshire map, 1 inch to 1 mile, (http://www.geog.port.ac.uk/webmap/hantsmap/taylor4/ty43.htm, accessed 20 July 2009).

Titow, J. Z. (1962a) Land and population on the bishop of Winchester's estates 1209–1350. Unpublished PhD thesis, University of Cambridge.

Titow, J. Z. (1962b) Some differences between manors and their effects on the condition of the peasant in the thirteenth century. *Agricultural History Review* 10, 1–13.

Titow, J. Z. (1969) *English Rural Society 1200–1350*. London: Allen and Unwin.

Watts, D. G. (1958) The estates of Titchfield abbey, 1245–1381. Unpublished BLitt thesis, University of Oxford.

CHAPTER THIRTEEN

Peasant Names on Glastonbury Abbey's Polden Hill Manors (1189–1352): Some Straws in a Wind of Change

Mike Thompson

This essay draws upon personal names given to the peasantry of Glastonbury Abbey's Polden Hill manors from the mid-twelfth to the mid-fourteenth centuries. These manors – Street, Walton, Ashcott, Greinton, Moorlinch and Shapwick – lie immediately south and east of the town of Glastonbury and look over King's Sedgemoor to the south from the Polden ridge, which rises to a little over 300 feet at its highest points in this vicinity. The transition from insular (usually Old English) names to those of Continental, biblical or classical origin is addressed and this casts light on different rates of change as between males and females. The evolution of hereditary surnames from ephemeral by-names is considered and there are discursions upon what locative and occupational names tell us about the origins and workaday lives of Polden peasants.

Names are a reflection of cultural identity. A well-known change of naming practice occurred after the Norman Conquest, when Continental personal names replaced Old English ones. This paper investigates that change on Glastonbury Abbey's estate in Somerset and argues that it happened more quickly among customary tenants living closer to the monastery than among those who lived further away. The Norman monks were the most likely source of influence, which affected both male and female naming patterns. The paper draws upon five estate surveys dating from 1189 to 1325 and a series of account and court rolls from 1256 to 1352, and reveals that bynames (which often evolved into surnames) preserved some traces of Old English naming traditions. Other influences on bynames included community ceremonies and pageants. Locative names indicate migration to Glastonbury's manors from other parts of England and a few from overseas, while the distribution of occupational names (in general wholly unexceptional) may suggest some specialization.

That the generation immediately preceding that of 1189 was subject to marked change in naming fashions there can be little doubt. In 1189 while fifty-nine tenants of the abbey were only identified by a single baptismal name, thirty-eight had identifiers of the *x filius y* type and twenty of these illustrate how parents bearing insular names had sons to whom they gave names of continental origin (Table 13.1). The indicated chronology of change appears to be broadly consistent with that of Ramsey Abbey (*c.*1166–1171) where 45.6% of peasant tenants whose fathers had insular names themselves held new names (Postles 1997, 36).

The whole stock of personal names held by tenants of the Polden manorial bloc as recorded in the manorial surveys of 1189, *c.*1239, 1260, 1317 and 1325 (Jackson 1882; BL Add MS 17,450; Egerton MS 3321) is listed in Tables 13.2 and 13.3. Old English insular names including one pre-Conquest name of possible Anglo-Saxon origin, *Turstin* (Insley 1987, 189, 191) are italicized; ambiguous names exhibiting OE elements but which were probably introduced or reintroduced from the Continent after the Conquest are indicated by an asterisk, and names of uncertain provenance are underlined.

The top ten names in 1189, shared by over two-thirds of all men, were 'new' names of Continental Germanic (hereinafter C-G) origin as identified by Forssner (1916). Amongst the second tranche of twelve names which were ascribed to more than one individual we find another three C-G names and seven scriptural or saints' names. There is only one name of insular origin in this second group – Alfred – with a further possible survivor to be found in Hemus, just possibly from OE *eam*, 'uncle'. It is clear therefore that whatever the Anglo-Saxon name stock had been, the OE heritage was fast disappearing by 1189 as far as men's names were concerned, with only eleven certain individual survivals and a further four ambiguously named men making a bare 10.5% of the total.

Women's names of 1189 reflect a higher insular survival rate with seven, or possibly eight, out of ten names perpetuating the OE stock. This higher incidence may, as Cecily Clark suggested, have been due to the small numbers of Norman women settling in twelfth-century England and the consequential inter-marriage of Norman men and native women, with their female children being named after parents or godparents (Clark 1978, 223–51). However, the subsequent records show that even in the case of women, diffusion of continental forms of baptismal name, including many specifically Christian or scriptural names, soon brought about the almost complete extinction of the island stock. The main exceptions to this were the continuing popularity of Edith and, perhaps, the ambiguous Alice. Very few Polden peasant women were given names of a more exotic kind which in the upper reaches of society owed their popularity to the revival of classical learning, or to the cult of courtly love (Bennett 1989, 69).

Taking the 1189 corpus of male and female tenant names

TABLE 13.1. *x filius y* type names showing insular names of parents. Sources: Jackson 1882; BL. Add. MS 17,450. *c.*1239 and 1260 *Rentalia et Custumaria Monasterii Glastoniae Michaelis de Ambresbury* 1235–1252 *Rogeri de Ford* 1252–1261; Egerton MS 3321. 1317 and 1325. Manorial surveys of Street, Shapwick, Ashcott, Greinton and Moorlinch

Year	Names	OE etyma
1189	*Galfridus f. Aelfrici*	*Ælfric*
	Henricus f. Ailfrici	*Ælfric*
	Johannes f. Gode	*Gode*
	Radulfus f. Liveve	*Leofgifu*
	Ricardus f. Edmund	*Eadmund*
	Ricardus f. Edmeri	*Eadmær*
	Ricardus f. Algari	*Ælfgar*
	Robertus f. Eilfrici	*Ælfric*
	Robertus f. Eltorie	*Ælf*
	Robertus f. Alstones	*Ealhstan or Ælfstan*
	Walterus f. Algari	*Ælfgar*
	Walterus f. Alveve	*Ælgifu*
	Willelmus f. Ledfrici	*Leofric*
	Willelmus f. Elmeri	*Ælmær*
	Willelmus f. Briod	*Beorht*
	Willelmus f. Seive	*Sægifu, or Sæwig*
	Willelmus f. Ulfi	*Wulf.*
	Willelmus f. Ethele	*Æðel*
	Willelmus f. Edrici	*Eadric*
	Willelmus f. Sewi	*Sægifu or Sæwig*
1239	*Galfridus f. Aldetha*	*Ealdgyð*
	Johannes f. Aldetha	*Ealdgyð*
1260	none	
1317/25	none	

1189	Number	1239	Number	1260	Number	1317/25	Number
Robert	20	Robert	22	William	32	John	66
William	19	William	22	Robert	26	William	55
Richard	17	Walter	17	Walter	23	Robert	30
Walter	15	John	17	John	17	Walter	26
Ralph	8	Richard	10	Reginald	9	Richard	20
Hugh	8	Thomas	10	Henry	9	Thomas	14
Geoffrey	6	Roger	6	Adam	8	Henry	6
Reginald	5	Hugh	5	Richard	4	Adam	6
Roger	4	Henry	5	Martin	4	Roger	4
Henry	4	Martin	5	Geoffrey	3	Nicholas	4
Humphrey	4	Adam	5	Thomas	3	Stephen	4
John	3	Geoffrey	4	Ralph	2	Hugh	3
Thomas	3	Ralph	2	Hugh	2	Geoffrey	3
Alfred	3	Gilbert	2	Roger	2	Reginald	3
Martin	3	Constantine	2	Peter	2	Phillip	3
Adam	2	Andrew	2	Humphrey	1	Martin	2
Bernard	2	Humphrey	1	Gilbert	1	Peter	2
Nicholas	2	*Alfred*	1	Andrew	1	*Edward*	1
Peter	2	Nicholas	1	Absolon	1	Goscelyn	1
Tancred	2	Peter	1	*Selewi*	1	Michael	1
Denisel	2	Tancred	1	Walkelyn	1	Alexander	1
*Hemus**	2	Durand	1	Costin	1	Bathin	1
Durand	2	Gervase	1	Goscelyn	1	Julian	1
Phillip	1	*Aylward*	1	Jordan	1		
Edward	1	Absolon	1	Michael	1		
Baldwin	1	Lebelin	1	Sampson	1		
Gilbert	1	David	1				
Acerre	1	Savericlif	1				
Ælric	1	Scarlet	1				
Alan	1	*Selewi*	1				
Algar	1	Walkelyn	1				
Basil	1						
Constantine	1						
Custenge	1						
Eldwin	1						
Foliot	1						
Garmund	1						
Gervase	1						
Headulf	1						
Knightwin	1						
Lewin	1						
Odo	1						
*Osbert**	1						
*Osmund**	1						
Seolf	1						
Sternold	1						
Turstin	1						
47 names	162 men	31 names	151 men	26 names	157 men	23 names	257 men

Old English insular names including one pre-Conquest name of possible Anglo-Saxon origin, *Turstin* (Insley 1987, 189, 191) are italicized; ambiguous names exhibiting OE elements but which were probably introduced or reintroduced from the Continent after the Conquest are indicated by an asterisk, and names of uncertain provenance are underlined.

TABLE 13.2. Male baptismal names from surveys: 1189 to 1325

1189	Number	1239	Number	1260	Number	1317/25	Number
Edith	2	Albretha	2	Cecilia	3	*Alice/Alison*	5
Matilda	2	Isabel	2	*Alice/Alison*	2	Cecilia	4
*Alice/Alison**	1	Matilda	1	Isabel	2	Margaret	3
Aileva	1	*Alice/Alison*	1	Matilda	2	Christine	3
Alditha	1	Christine	1	Christine	2	Agnes	3
Alveva	1	Eva	1	*Edith*	1	*Edith*	2
Athela	1	*Gilla*	1	Annora	1	Matilda	2
Enitha	1	*Hereburgtha*	1	Lucy	1	Emma/Emmote	2
Hoda	1	Mariota	1	Margaret	1	Sabina	2
Luviva	1	Scarlet	1	Milesanda	1	Annora	1
				Juliana	1	Juliana	1
						Avicia	1
						Felicia	1
						Joanna/Joan	1
						Hawisia	1
10 names	12 women	10 names	12 women	11 names	17 women	15 names	32 women

TABLE 13.3. Women's baptismal names from surveys: 1189 to 1325. The sources for Tables 13.2 and 13.3 are as indicated for Table 13.1

Gilla can be a man's name, here it is undoubtedly female as it was applied to a widow of Walton holding a half-virgate in 1239.

together there was a maximum insular survival level of some 15% compared with the 25 to 30% that Cecily Clark referred to as the total Glastonbury estate stock of insular names found in the 1189 survey of some 30 manors (Clark 1992, 559). The reason for this disparity may be found in the especially close proximity of the Polden manors to the abbey which saw an unbroken succession of Norman rule from the time of Abbot Thurstan (*c*.1077–1096) to that of Henry de Soliaco (1189–1193). The Polden tenantry were, therefore, more likely to have been conditioned by these agents of changing fashion than those in communities more remote from such influences. It is also possible that the Abbey's clerks may have had a hand in hastening change by ascribing, or modifying, names as they wrote down the verbal testimony of the peasants themselves.

The momentum for change continued and by 1239 we find that only Alfred (*Alured*), Aylward and *Selewi* reflect the OE heritage as far as masculine names are concerned. There had also been a collapse of the insular in feminine names with none of the names of 1189 being repeated, although the widows *Hereburgtha*, and possibly *Gilla*, both tenants of half-virgates, kept island tradition alive (Feilitzen 1937, 261) . After 1239 we find only the merest traces of the insular, masculine, personal-name stock remaining. The biggest surprise is the disappearance of Alfred, a name which continued to be the fourth most popular name of OE origin in Norfolk – far distant from the Wessex homeland of the hero-king – between 1100 and 1349 (Seltén 1972, 28). Amongst the few women's names Edith, and possibly the ambivalent, and increasingly popular Alice, recalled the OE past.

Masculine names of 1239 show a shift towards scriptural and saints' names with John moving from eleventh place in 1189 to third in order of popularity. The subsequent listings of 1260 and 1317/25 show that this was a continuing process such that by the third decade of the fourteenth century John was the most popular name and four other 'Christian' names (including Stephen not found in the earlier surveys) had found their way into the top ten. Meanwhile the total stock of male names had shrunk to less than half that of 1189 and the top ten names accounted for 91.4% of the total stock. Only Edward carried forward the OE heritage while Alexander heralded the renascence of classicism.

Although the number of women's names increased in the fourteenth-century surveys, this probably is due to the increase in the number of female tenants listed. There is no evidence of any greater preparedness to go beyond the Continental Germanic or Christian *corpora*. This in spite of names such as Milesanda, Felicia and Sabina which may sound exotic but which are as firmly rooted in these stocks as the increasingly popular Cecilia. While an impression of greater variety and imagination in the naming of women as compared with men may be gained from the lists garnered from account and court rolls (Table 4), it is difficult to attach much weight to the evidence, which is made more problematical by the incidence of cross-gender forms such as Basilia.

Although the evidence of names found in manorial account and court rolls is not amenable to reliable statistical analysis because of the unquantifiable extent of individual name repetition, these records add twenty-one women's and twenty-three men's names to those found in the surveys. In spite of the caveat about analysis it is notable that the 6,998 separate records of names from these sources (*e.g.* of payers of various fines, trespassers, *etc.*) between 1258 and 1352 reveal the same rank order amongst the top five male names as in the fourteenth-century surveys (*i.e.* John, William, Robert, Walter, Richard). Some reliance may therefore be placed on the ranking of 676 records of women's names which produce the following top rank order: Alice, Christine, Edith, Margaret/Margery and Joan/Johanna. It is of interest to note that whereas in this corpus the top five men's names account for 71% of the total and the top five women's 63%, if the top ten names in each group are aggregated the comparative figures are 87.6% male and 92.8% female, a statistic that runs somewhat counter to the view that the naming of women was more imaginative and less constrained by custom than that of men. The list of additional names from account and court rolls, many of which were of customary tenants of the abbey, but also belonged to casual visitors to, or trespassers upon, the Polden manors, is given in Table 13.4.

Of the male names in this table only four would certainly have been known in peasant communities before the Conquest – *Sely, Golde, Aluerd* and *Edmund* – while *Sturmci* is of uncertain provenance although Reaney instances the Old Germanic personal name *Sturmi*, possibly transmuted via a postulated Old French *Estourmi,* as one possible origin of the surname Sturmey (Reaney 1976, 337–8). Surprisingly perhaps we find even fewer female names redolent of the Old English past in this collection, with only *Selyeth* as a fairly obvious patronymic from *Sely (Sælwig), Lovote,* perhaps owing something to the OE *Lufufe/Leofgifu,* and *Gunild,* of Anglo-Scandinavian origin, as the only other pre-Conquest representative.

TABLE 13.4. Additions to baptismal name stocks from account and court-roll records 1265 to 1352. Sources: all extant (Longleat House archive and Chivers Microfilm Record) manor court rolls for Ashcott, Walton, Street, Shapwick and Greinton between1265 and 1352. A total of 15 single (*i.e.* specific to one manor) and 15 multiple rolls (*i.e.* those covering between three and five of these manors); all extant (Longleat House archive and Chivers Microfilm Record) Account rolls for the same group of manors between 1258 and 1352 a total of 29 single rolls and 12 multiple rolls

Male	First record	Female	First record
Simon	1265	*Selyeth*	1275
Eustace	1275	Isote	1275
Elias	1283	Edelina	1284
Selcock/Sely	1284	Muriel	1284
Abraham	1284	Clemencie	1301
Clemens	1284	Constancia	1301
Colin	128	Evelote	1301
Wylemot	1284	Elisabet	1305
Golde	1284	Ascelina	1307
Kyngman	1284	Claricia	1308
Aluerd	1284	Elena	1312
Antony	1301	Amfilis	1313
Luke	1301	*Gunild*	1314
Eliot	1301	Hillary	1321
Lovekyne	1308	Dyonisia	1321
Marcus	1308	*Lovote*	1334
<u>Sturmci</u>	1312	Basilia	1343
Gregory	1315	Helewys	1344
Laurence	1334	Katerina	1344
Amyas	1344	Mabilia	1347
Benedict	1345	Sibilla	1348
Jacob	1345		
Godfrey	1347		
Edmund	1352		

Bynames – continuity and change

The suggestion that secondary identifiers or bynames did more to perpetuate the insular tradition seems to have some validity. There are five dithematic name forms which exhibit OE ancestry to be found in the post-1189 surveys and a number of monothematic names which are well-attested OE *nomina*. Table 13.5 lists the first of these categories and gives some examples of the second.

The table might have included many more monothematic names which had their counterparts in pre-Conquest England *e.g* . Brun/*Bran*, Child/*Cild*, Snel/*Snel*; but these were omitted because they are inseparable from the Middle English lexis and vernacular. Apart from the instances given and noting that *Wigburg* is a doubtful case (more probably from a Continental Germanic etymon, see Seltén 1979, 164–5), there is little other evidence to suggest that family names of bondmen were generally fixed before 1239 by which time some seventy new bynames had been introduced on the Polden manors. For similar views about the period of fixation of villein surnames in certain regions see Reaney (1976, xl–xlv) and McKinley (1988, 53–7).

In 1189 some fifty bynames were shared between seventy-four tenants possessing such identifiers. There was therefore considerable, potentially confusing, overlap with the commoner occupational bynames, such as *faber,* applying to tenants on several of the manors. Clearly such occupational forms, as well as locative and topographical types, occurring in the twelfth and repeated in the thirteenth and fourteenth centuries are not reliable indicators

Survey year	Byname	OE etyma	Authority
Dithematic			
1239	Cuitwine	*Cuthwine*	S
1239	Lufufe	*Leofgifu*	E F
1260/1325	Seweol	*Sæweald*	E S
1260/1325	Wyberi/Wybery	*Wigburg*	S
	Wibard/Wyberd/Weyberd	*Wigbeorht*	E S
Monothematic			
1189/1239/60	Bac(t)	*Bacca/Bat*	T R F
1260/1317/1325	Cres/Crese	*Creas*	T
1239/1260/l3l7	Swein/Sweij/ Sweyn	*Sveinn* (ON)	T
1189/1260	Scote	*Scott*	T F
1260/1325	Hulf/Oulfi	*Wulf*	T R
1317/25	Golde	*Golda(e)*	T R F
1325	Gode	*Gode(a)*	T R F
1325	Harde	*Heard*	R

TABLE 13.5. Bynames of insular origin on Polden manors 1189–1325. The following authorities are instanced in the fourth column of the table: (F) Feilitzen 1937; (T) Tengvik 1938; (R) Redin 1919; (S) Seltén 1972 and 1979; (E) Ekwall 1947. Sources: as for Table 13.1

of family continuity, because of the ubiquity of the trades, the proximity of many locations, and the common occurrence of landscape features that served the abbey's purposes in distinguishing one tenant from another. It is fairly clear, however, that many such names were becoming fixed as family-names between 1239 and the end of the thirteenth century. This was the case, not only with some of the families of smiths and hoopers, but also in such cases as the Burimans and Harepaths (this last being a topographical name pertaining to the 'army path' that ran along the Polden ridge) of Shapwick, the Burinexts of Ashcott and Street, and the Bickenhams of Street, all of whose names are to be found on these manors in 1239, 1260, and 1317 or 1325. It is of interest to note that Vinogradoff (1892, 145) refers to 'buriman' as a relic form of the Saxon *gebur* and suggests that it was used in two distinct ways '[as applied] ... to the chief villains of the township in some places, and to the smaller tenantry, apparently in confusion with the Norman *bordarius* in some other'. (On the other hand, Reaney suggests 'servant at the manor-house' (1976, 32)).

Reaney (1976, xlii–xlv) argued that bynames may have become hereditary surnames when they were based on nicknames and personal names that had disappeared from the personal name corpus, and were either held by several people in the same village at the same time, or were repeated in surveys separated by more than a generation. On the Polden Hills it is clear that some of the names which perpetuated the OE heritage, along with many that did not contain insular elements, had clearly acquired the character of inherited family names by the end of the thirteenth century. This is evidenced by the Swein (*Sveinn*) family whose members held customary five/acre (ferdellar) tenancies at Walton in 1239, 1260, and 1317; the Wibards (*Wigbeorht*) who held at Ashcott in 1260 and 1325; and possibly the Wyberys (*Wigburg*), tenants at Shapwick over the same period.

The recurrent names of the exemplars for the various tenant classes (that is the first names listed in any discrete group of tenants in the surveys whose rents and services were the only ones spelt out in full) provide further evidence for family name inheritance. Thus at Street the Leighs (*de Lega/de Legh*) were virgater exemplars in each of the four surveys, while John *le Hert* of 1317 succeeded Geoffrey *le Hert* of 1260. At Shapwick, we find that Richard Hiris was the five-acre *gavelman* exemplar in 1189, as was Thomas Iris in 1239 and we find John le Irissche occupying that role, as a *gavelman* ferdellar, in 1325. This family is of particular interest – in 1344 at Shapwick's Michaelmas hallmoot Walter, son of Walter *le lryssh*, having paid chevage (*capitagium*) for his *consanguinei*, probably his nephews, then paid two shillings for an enquiry into their status, claiming that they should be free of the impost because his grandfather (*avus*) Thomas de Hibernia was an *adventicius*, born in Ireland but settled in Shapwick where he had married Sabina, Walter's grandmother. (On the presumed freedom of immigrants to a manor see Hyams 1980, 209). Also at Shapwick, William, Roger and Alice Spede were the half-virgater exemplars in 1239, 1260 and 1325 respectively, a position held over the same period by Walter (1239 and 1260) and William Pyperwyht (1325) of Ashcott.

It is also possible that what at first appears to be an unlikely early instance of family name inheritance may be found in the epithet of *juvenis* (later *le Yonge*). This identifier was used in 1189 to distinguish two half-virgaters and one five-acre man at Shapwick; in 1239 the term was used again to identify Adam a virgater and another five-acre man. At some time after 1260, when he was the exemplar for the class, we find Adam succeeded by Reginald *Juvenis* until in 1325 Walter *le Yonge* is, like Adam before him, the virgater exemplar.

As family names became fixed they evolved in the ways illustrated and showed greater variety. From the late thirteenth century, references to families of 'Kings' and 'Bishops' are to be found in the records, and one William Kyng rose from being a young *garcio* in 1299 to be the ferdellar exemplar at Shapwick by 1325. William started out as one of the numerous young landless men (*garciones*) listed in successive court rolls of these and other manors, in which Harold Fox found a store of social and demographic evidence (Fox 1986, 1996). Such names may have been the kind of ironic or reflective nicknames, or pageant names, of the kind found in many contemporary communities (Reaney 1976; Hutton 1996, 8–12). Certainly, when put alongside the 'Pyperwhyts' and such as '*le Harpere*', they do suggest peasant communities more than usually exposed to pomp and ceremony attendant upon the many illustrious personages who visited the abbey on business or pilgrimage. 'Pyperwhyt' is particularly interesting. The name is not to be found in Reaney's *Dictionary*, but it probably related to pipe playing. It is of interest to note that there is still a 'Pipers Inn' public house situated on the line of the ancient ridgeway (the aforementioned harepath – today the A39) in Ashcott parish. Such travellers would have added to the numerous abbey officials visiting their rich marshland manors of Sowy in Sedgemoor, as the ridge provided the easiest access, especially after the construction of the Greylake Fosse causeway south of Greinton around 1300. Certainly the Chapmans and Hucksters would have profited from the wayside trade that such luminaries brought in their wake.

The 1260 survey adds sixty new bynames to the earlier Polden corpus of which thirty (in addition to fifteen from 1189 and twenty-three from 1239) are to be found in the fourteenth-century surveys. Up to 54% of names found in the 1260 survey survived to the Black Death and 34.2% are to be found in the surviving court rolls of 1349/50 and 1351/52, although some of these were of deceased tenants. By 1348 therefore, new family names occurring after 1260 amounted to almost half of the stock – a proportion which, given the probable continuing instability of many bynames during the period of family-name fixation, should neither surprise, nor necessarily suggest significant inward migration to the Polden manors.

Locative names

That some immigration did take place is illustrated by the incidence of locative names. Most of these, particularly in the three earlier surveys, were derived from the home or neighbouring manors, and it was not until the fourteenth century that many indicated origins from further afield. Thus, in 1189, amongst *de Greintona*, *de Lega* (Legh in Street), *de Hamme* (High Ham, due south of Ashcott) and other such local places, only the knight Geoffrey *de Meisi* (probably from Maisy in Normandy) and the five-acre man Richard Hiris held locative names from afar, and by 1260 just another four or five probable immigrants can be identified. These included the man called *Cornubiensis* and Walter *de Clopton*. Both of these men were customary cottars (*lundinarii* or Monday men) at Street in 1239. Clopton appears as a place-name in several counties of England. Nearest of these to Somerset are Northamptonshire and Suffolk, so wherever the humble Mondayman got his name it seems he was far from his native heath. Other incomers included the free virgater of Shapwick – Saveric *de Cinnoc* (East or West Chinnock near Crewkerne in South Somerset) also in 1239, John *de Kent* the miller of Shapwick in 1260 and Hugh *le Waleys*, a free tenant who held five acres at Walton in 1260.

There was a longer list of immigrants from some distance in the later surveys. These contain locative names from Brittany (*le Bret*), Worcestershire (Malverne), Wiltshire (*de Salesbury*) and Devon, as well as from several other places in Somerset itself. We also find two names in the account rolls of men who were probably landless *garciones*. These were John *de Lym*, probably from the Abbey's manor at Uplyme in south-east Devon, who was recorded at Shapwick in 1313 and 1315, and John *de Mulverton* from Milverton in the Taunton area of Somerset, who was at Greinton in 1331 and 1334. They paid chevage (*capitagium*) in wax as opposed to the usual pence, but as neither of them appears in the court roll lists of *garciones*, and as no recorded tenants held the same byname, it may be that they were treated differently as extraneous temporary workers on the manors concerned. In 1330 the October court roll for Walton records a fine for trespass of John *le Devenyssh*, described as the servant of John Piperwit, and he too was probably a *garcio* following in the footsteps of John from Uplyme.

Occupational names

Most occupational names found in the surveys are unexceptional (Table 13.6). If those occupations associated primarily with manorial administration or the church, are put to one side – that is the reeves, clerks and chaplains – we are left with a relatively small number of craftsmen's names amongst which 'smiths' predominate. Carpenters, known to exist in some numbers because of the numerous references in the account rolls to the wages or rent remissions that were their due, are notably almost absent from the later surveys, although in the 1317 survey of Street one was said to be quit of churchscot and hearthpenny and in receipt of one bushel of wheat yearly. Namewise they are far outnumbered by 'hoopers', a name often associated with coopers or barrel makers, but more likely in these cases to relate to wheelwrights whose skills were needed to maintain both demesne and peasant carts. There is no doubt about the general woodworking skills of those so named – Geoffrey Hopere of Ashcott in 1239 was to be quit of 7.5 pence rent *si facit carucam domini*, and John le Hopere of Street in 1317, a plough- and cartwright, was also to be quit of rents in return for making and repairing the lord's ploughs, ox-yokes and wains (*plaustura*) as well as such 'draggs' and harrows as were required.

Recourse to the account and court rolls of the period reveals other names indicative of involvement in baking (*Pistor*, Bakere); butchery (*Bouchere*); merchandising (Cornmonger, Chepman and Huckstere); laundry (*Le Lavender*, possibly connected with retting or fulling of locally made cloth, as was the tenant Tukar of 1189); entertainment (*le Harpere*); gardening (*le Gardinier/ Gardinarius*); gamekeeping (*le Parkere de Compton*). Given the existence of many small quarries on Polden, and the known deployment of the craft, it seems surprising that stonemasonry (*le Mason*) does not appear until after the Black Death. Leather crafts of which the Cheverels (makers or sellers of kid-leather goods; Reaney 1976, 72) and Isabel Bulger (from Old French *Boulgier*, 'a maker of leather wallets or bags'; Reaney 1976, 46) were the only apparent tenant representatives, were the concern of Thomas Glover of Glastonbury who bought seven sheepskins at Ashcott in 1344, and also perhaps of Martin Souter (*i.e.* a shoemaker; Reaney 1976, 327) alias Cornmanger, who rented an acre of land at Ashcott around 1350. Like Martin many of these people were smallholders of arable or pasture rather than customary tenants and it is probable that some had a town base in Glastonbury. Such was Thomas Chauntrel (that is a bellman or cantor) who paid one shilling to have seisin of a vacant plot in Street in 1331.

Another family putting down deeper roots in the area were the Chapmans who were acquiring land in Street and Walton on a piecemeal basis from 1305 onwards, but who did not become customary tenants until 1331 when John and his wife Cristina obtained a ferdel at Walton. Sometimes they came from further afield as did Hugh *le Barber de Welles* who in 1345 was alleged to have leased a ferdel in Walton from Robert *le Bouchere* without the abbey's permission.

Although 'Hurde' does not occur (except as Schephurde) as a tenant

Byname	1189	1239	1260	1317/25	Totals
Faber/Mareschal/ le Ferour / le Smyth	3	4	7	7	21
Prepositus/ vetus prepositus/ Oldreve	2	2	8	3	15
Le Hopere	0	1	2	6	9
Capellanus/ Chapeleyn	1	3	2	2	8
Molendinarius	0	3	2	2	7
Clericus/ le Clerk	2	0	2	2	6
Carpentarius/ Carpenter	3	1	1	0	5
Tixtor/Textor/ Webbe	2	2	1	0	5
Cocus/ Cok	1	0	2	1	4
Helierus/ Thechere	0	0	0	3	3
Bedellus	1	2	0	0	3
Buriman	0	1	1	1	3
Cheverel	0	1	1	1	3
Beleclerk	0	0	1	1	2
Schephurde/Shepman	0	0	1	1	2
Wodeward	0	0	0	2	2
le Daber	0	1	1	0	2
le Hurter	0	1	1	0	2
Person	0	0	0	2	2
Sapurus/ le Sapere	1	0	0	1	2
Bubulcus	1	0	0	0	1
Bulge[r]	0	1	0	0	1
Colihod	1	0	0	0	1
Hayward	0	0	1	0	1
Horn	0	0	0	1	1
le Leche	0	1	0	0	1
Marener	0	0	0	1	1
Mercator	1	0	0	0	1
Palmarius	1	0	0	0	1
Piscis	1	0	0	0	1
Le Schetere	0	0	0	1	1
Taillour	0	0	0	1	1
Tukar	1	0	0	0	1
Totals	22	23	34	39	118

TABLE 13.6. Occupational bynames from the Polden manorial surveys. Sources: as for Table 13.1

name, eight men so described between them accounted for twenty-five court appearances for trespass between 1284 and 1352. Three of these were landless *garciones*, no doubt following an occupation typically filled by precursors of 'little boy blue'. One of them, Thomas le Hurde, was recorded at Walton, Street and Ashcott between 1330 and 1352 and is described as *le hurde de Walton* in the October court roll for Ashcott in 1347. Similarly Walter the herd of Pedwell had an ox impounded at Greinton in 1339 and Laurence of Shapwick a steer at Ashcott in 1347.

Although there are few 'carpenters' in the record (the 'carpenter' name is not found in any record after 1315 when Reginald, a ferdellar of Ashcott, was for the second consecutive year excused payment of churchscot because of his poverty), smiths, hoopers, clerks, chaplains, shepherds, tailors, roofers and mariners, are well represented and, when added to the survey stock, their distribution suggests some small degree of specialisation between the manors.   Making allowance for the small differences in the numbers of surviving rolls a crude appreciation of this can be obtained by totalling the number of times a particular name appears in the court rolls of each manor. This, for instance, shows that smiths were the subject of 116 entries of which 36 occur at Shapwick between 1265 and 1346, 16 at Moorlinch from 1284 to 1315, 32 at Walton from 1265 to 1350, 16 at Street from 1307 to 1352, and 11 at Greinton from 1284 to 1340. This general ubiquity is dented by the continuing almost complete absence of the name at Ashcott which, although having two out of three records relating to farriers (*le ferrour*), only records 'smiths' on four occasions – as trespassers in 1308, 1313 and 1314. Although the inference is crude there is little doubt that the incidence of the 'mariner' name at Greinton was linked to an inland trade on the River Cary. Greinton accounts for all but one of the thirty-nine records occurring between 1304 and 1352, where the river formed the southern boundary of the manor and linked Bridgwater with Langport.

Conclusion

With regard to the displacement of insular baptismal names amongst peasants by 'new' names of Continental or Christian origin we have found that by 1189 two-thirds of Polden male tenants bore new names of Continental Germanic origin, while only some 10% had names in use before the Conquest, the balance being made up by scriptural or saints' names. At the same time the small number of names in the corpus does no more than hint at a more prolonged survival of insular forms of women's names, and even if there was a greater degree of survival at this time then the period of perpetuation appears to have been short-lived. It is clear that the generation prior to that of 1189, when 20% of tenants had parents with Anglo-Saxon names, was the last to have remained true to the island names of centuries past in any significant degree. A bare 15% insular survival level in 1189 (male and female) amongst Polden tenants as compared with the 30% of the Glastonbury estate as a whole suggests that the degree of proximity and exposure to the agents of change in and around the abbey itself was a factor.

By 1239 the increasing application of 'Christian' names *per se* meant that the traditional culture in respect of both male and female names had been overwhelmed by the new. By 1317 to 1325 the total stock of men's names had shrunk to less than half that of 1189 and the top ten names accounted for over 90% of the corpus. Thus as secondary identifiers, many now becoming fixed as family names, grew in number and variety, the range of personal names of choice reduced. Only Edward perpetuated the OE heritage and Alexander was the sole example of the classical exotic type. Also, and in contrast with women of higher birth, although the recorded stock of women tenants' names increased from ten to fifteen between 1189 and 1325, peasant women rarely bore exotic names and indeed with the top ten female names occurring within the account and court rolls amounting to over 93% of that total stock, there is little to indicate that by the early fourteenth century their parents were any more inclined to be fanciful, or mindful of the insular tradition, than they were when naming their male offspring.

As far as the development of family-names from earlier bynames is concerned, evidence has been adduced to show that OE personal names were preserved in the bynames that were fast becoming inherited surnames during the course of the thirteenth century. New bynames in the surveys of 1317 and 1325 accounted for around 60% of the tenant stock of 160 names of which only 10% were recorded in 1189 and even then only five (3.1%) are likely to represent continuity of family as revealed by inherited family-name. It is, however, probable that the real extent of family continuity was far greater than this. It seems likely that at least a third of fourteenth-century Polden families had roots stretching back for more than 60 and for up to 130 years, although they may have been outnumbered by the estimated two-fifths of tenants who had probably settled within the first quarter of the century – an inference from the data which broadly coincides with well-based estimates of local population trends (Thompson 1997; 1998).

Locative bynames tell us a little about the origins of a few of the Polden population and reveal that even those of lowly peasant status were increasingly often to be found, sometimes as a direct consequence of lordly influence, far from their native vill. A little more is learned from occupational names but in the main these are unexceptional. They are representative of expected trades and crafts – smithing, carpentry and roofing, the skills of wheelwrights, weavers and leather workers – and there is just a hint of a degree of specialisation of occupation as between the manors concerned.

As a footnote it is of interest to record the persistence of certain names down the centuries, particularly for males. In the Office of National Statistics listing of the ten most popular boys' names of 2008 in England and Wales, we find that of over 362,963 names, Jack (the diminutive of John) was the first in the list just as it was in 1325; Harry was fourth (Henry was seventh in 1325). William had declined from second to tenth, but Thomas had risen from tenth to third. Perhaps most cheering of all is the resurgence of Alfred – albeit in a form he may not have answered to – for Alfie emerges as the sixth most popular name in 2008. Given the longevity of male names it seems strange that for girls only one name – Evie at tenth in the list – harks back to Eva of 1239; and of the names of 1317 and 1325 only Isabelle (17th) and Emma (31st) remain widely popular.

Acknowledgements

I was very grateful to David Postles for reading an early draft of this paper. His work inspired me in the first place and his subsequent kindly advice and comment saved me from much error. I also received early encouragement from Margery Tranter as well as from my much admired erstwhile supervisor and friend, Harold, to whose influence this whole volume bears witness. My friend and fellow student of Glastonbury's manors, Jem Harrison, read and commented on a late draft and I am grateful for his helpful and constructive criticism. Finally I should like to thank the unknown (to me) reader of this essay for his, or her, helpful contribution and suggestions.

Bibliography

Manuscript sources

BL. Add. MS 17,450. *c.*1239 and 1260 *Rentalia et Custumaria Monasterii Glastoniae Michaelis de Ambresbury 1235–1252 Rogeri de Ford 1252–1261.*

Egerton MS 3321. 1317 and 1325. Manorial surveys of Street, Shapwick, Ashcott, Greinton and Moorlinch.

All extant (Longleat House archive and Chivers Microfilm Record) manor court rolls for Ashcott, Walton, Street, Shapwick and Greinton between1265 and 1352. A total of 15 single (*i.e.* specific to one manor) and 15 multiple rolls (*i.e.* those covering between three and five of these manors).

All extant (Longleat House archive and Chivers Microfilm Record) Account rolls for the same group of manors between 1258 and 1352 a total of 29 single rolls and 12 multiple rolls.

(For further details of the Court and Account roll records see Harris, K. 1991. *Glastonbury Abbey Records at Longleat House: a Summary List.* Taunton: Somerset Record Society.)

References

Bennett, J. M. (1989) *Women in the Medieval English Countryside. Gender and Household in Brigstock Before the Plague.* Oxford: Oxford University Press.

Clark, C. (1978) Women's names in post Conquest England: observations and speculations. *Speculum* 53, 223–51.

Clark, C. (1992) Onomastics, in N. Blake (ed.), *The Cambridge History of the English Language Volume II 1066–1476*, 542–606. Cambridge: Cambridge University Press.

Ekwall, E. (1947) *Early London Personal Names.* Lund: C. W. K. Gleerup.

Feilitzen, O. V. (1937) *The Pre-Conquest Personal Names of Domesday Book.* Uppsala: Almqvist and Wiksells boktryckeri.

Forssner, T. (1916) *Continental-Germanic Personal Names in England in Old and Middle English Times.* Uppsala: K. W. Appelbergs boktryckeri.

Fox, H. S. A. (1986) The alleged transformation from two-field to three-field systems in medieval England. *Economic History Review* 39(4), 526–48.

Fox, H. S. A. (1996) Exploitation of the landless by lords and tenants in early medieval England, in Z. Razi and R. M. Smith (eds), *Medieval Society and the Manor Court*, 518–68. Oxford, Oxford University Press.

Hutton, R. (1996) *The Rise and Fall of Merry England. The Ritual Year 1400–1700.* Oxford: Oxford University Press.

Hyams, P. R. (1980) *King, Lords and Peasants in Medieval England: The Common Law of Villeinage in the Twelfth and Thirteenth Centuries.* Oxford: Oxford University Press.

Insley, J. (1987) Some aspects of regional variation in early Middle English personal nomenclature. *Leeds Studies in English* n.s. 18, 183–99.

Jackson, J. E. (ed.) (1882) *Liber Henrici de Soliaco Abbatis Glaston: An Inquisition of the Manors of Glastonbury Abbey of the year 1189.* London: Roxburghe Club.

McKinley, R. (1988) *The Surnames of Sussex.* Oxford: Leopard's Head Press.

Postles, D. (1997) Cultures of peasant naming in twelfth-century England. *Medieval Prosopography* 18, 25–54.

Reaney, P. H. (1976) *A Dictionary of British Surnames.* 2nd edn, revised by R. M. Wilson. London: Routledge.

Redin, M. (1919) *Studies on Uncompounded Personal Names in Old English*. Uppsala: Akademiska bokhandeln.

Seltén, B. (1972–79) *The Anglo-Saxon Heritage in Middle English Personal Names: East Anglia 1100–1399*. 2 Vols. Acta Regiae Societatis Humaniorum Litterarum Lundensis 73. Lund: Gleerup.

Tengvik, G. (1938) *Old English Bynames*, Uppsala: Almqvist and Wiksells boktryckeri.

Thompson, M. G. (1997) The Polden Hill manors of Glastonbury Abbey: land and people *circa* 1260 to 1351. Unpublished PhD thesis, University of Leicester.

Thompson, M. G. (1998) Demographic aspects of thirteenth- and fourteenth-century Shapwick with Moorlinch, in M. Aston, T. Hall and C. Gerrard (eds) *The Shapwick Project: an Archaeological, Historical and Topographical Study: the Eighth Report*, 171–80. Bristol: University of Bristol.

Vinogradoff, P. (1892) *Villainage in England*. Oxford: Oxford University Press.

CHAPTER FOURTEEN

Lord's Man or Community Servant? The Role, Status and Allegiance of Village Haywards in Fifteenth-Century Northamptonshire

Mike Thornton

The role of the village hayward has been described as 'particularly prominent' by Bailey (2000, 171) in his study of the medieval manor and its court. On the other hand, a number of other recent, valuable and scholarly works which examine rural life, peasant society and the manor in late medieval England (see, for example, McIntosh 1986; Razi and Smith 1996; Dyer 2000; Schofield 2003) contain few references to the office and those are often of a summary nature. Moreover, modern references tend to differ in the emphasis put upon the hayward's responsibilities. Bailey says he was 'responsible primarily for overseeing the harvest', but a compendium for family and local historians (Hey 1996, 213) identifies his responsibility as being for hedges and fences and preventing cattle from straying.

Earlier historians offered fuller, descriptive accounts of the hayward and his role. Bennett's investigation of peasant life on the English manor (1937, 179–180), Homans' study of thirteenth-century villagers (1942, 292–7) and Ault's investigations of village by-laws (1965, 49; 1972, 63) all offered some account of the hayward at work and of his relationship to the lord of the manor and the community of the vill. Bennett emphasized supervision of the harvest: measuring the sheaves, ensuring at the end of each day that no unauthorized person carried away the lord's corn and, at the end of the year, tallying with the reeve. During the harvest he ate with other manorial officials at the lord's expense, and his rewards might include perquisites such as a measure of seed-corn, an area of meadow or a number of sheaves, or having his rent reduced or excused. This is clearly a picture of the hayward as the lord's man. Ault described him similarly, particularly as warden of the fences, and also took the view that he was a manorial officer, emphasizing his presentment of trespassers at the manor court; the fact that he was found being elected there, he argued, simply made his fellow tenants responsible to the lord for ensuring that the hayward carried out his duties satisfactorily. He further emphasized his view by contrasting the hayward who, he said, was paid, with the unpaid wardens of Autumn whom he had identified in a number of by-laws and were, by implication, more akin to community servants.

Homans saw him as warden of the hedges which in an open-field village would have surrounded those fields under crop. He insisted, however, that he was an officer of village government as well as of the lord, and commented that 'many [contemporary] sources speak as if the hayward protected only the lord's crops; in fact he was chosen to protect the crops of all the villagers. His duty to his lord was only part of his duty, though it was the most important part' (1942, 294).

Ault, Bennett and Homans all drew heavily on evidence from the late thirteenth and earlier fourteenth centuries. In contrast, the evidence used here is taken from the manorial documentation surviving for Northamptonshire from between about 1350 and 1520. It is drawn from different regions of the pre-1974 county, including the soke of Peterborough, and reflects different types of lordship: crown, aristocratic, gentry and conventual.[1] On the basis of it, this essay considers not only the role of the hayward but also his social status, as well as the different emphases given to his allegiance by Ault and Bennett on the one hand and Homans on the other.

Rice (1996, 1) has described Northamptonshire as 'a fairly cohesive unit … [where] … there is no division into distinctive regions…' This is to understate the subtle variations to be found between Rockingham Forest in the north-east, the Northamptonshire heights on the western boundary, the Nene Valley on the east and the Whittlewood-Salcey region to the south-east. Throughout the county, however, in the late Middle Ages the landscape was one of open fields and nucleated village settlements. As Lewis, Mitchell-Fox and Dyer (1997, 70) have pointed out the pattern predominated even in the Rockingham Forest region. Jones and Page (2006) have recently pointed to the dispersed settlements, considered in the course of the Whittlewood project, on the Buckinghamshire-Northamptonshire border, but even there open-field agriculture prevailed in the fifteenth century. Ever since Maitland distinguished between a 'land of hamlets' and a 'land of villages', successive scholars have acknowledged the existence of an extensive zone of nucleated settlement and adjacent common fields in the English midlands, and the Northamptonshire villages with their haywards, considered here, were firmly in that zone.

The descriptions of the hayward's activities cited above are not entirely reflected in surviving Northamptonshire court rolls. For instance the only hint of a specific harvest responsibility is at Brigstock in 1440 with the description of Nicholas Count as *messor ad garbas*.[2] The title attached to the office by manorial clerks varied through time. From about 1350 to about 1450 the terms used were hayward or, more commonly, *messor*, but later the appellation *agellarius* was normally used. At Barby, at a court held in 1518, the clerk even confirmed that the official concerned was William Catall, *agellarius vocatur le hayward*.[3] Other terms, such as *inclusarius*, which appeared at Broughton and Geddington during the first decade of the fifteenth century, were also sometimes used, but the job-title does not appear to have indicated any change or difference in responsibilities. The most frequently recorded of his activities throughout the period in all manors where these were recorded was, as Homans and Ault noted, the presentment of tenants and sometimes outsiders, who had trespassed with their animals or carts in the sown fields, growing crops, meadows or pasture of the manor. He was also to be found, at the royal manor of Brigstock for example, presenting tenants for damage to or failure to repair hedges; and for breaking into the pinfold where their distrained animals were held, in order to retrieve them; he also had custody of strays.[4] At Buckby (now Long Buckby), a manor of the duchy of Lancaster, Thomas Chater the *agellarius*, presented three men in July 1454 for failure to repair their fences, another three for trespassing with various of their animals and a further two for having failed to contribute to the repair of the common pinfold, an issue which developed into a long-running dispute.[5]

The requirement to protect hedges and deter animal-trespass will have been important in all open-field midland villages, but it is unclear whether a named hayward was invariably elected or, indeed, existed. Evans (1996, 222) found at Thorncroft in Surrey, a manor of Merton College, that references in the rolls to a hayward in the first half of the fourteenth century were extremely rare. He took the view that the beadle, or possibly the reeve, had undertaken the hayward's duties or that the duties of hayward and beadle were combined in a single official. For Northamptonshire, twenty-nine villages have been examined for which sufficient manorial documentation has survived for it to be a reasonable expectation that the activities of a hayward would have been recorded had such an official been elected or appointed.

From this evidence it can be shown that only seven – Clipston, Cranford, Lowick, Morton Pinkney, Northborough, Weekley and Weston – may not have had a hayward, although Hall (1995) has demonstrated the existence of late medieval open-field agriculture in each of these settlements except Northborough. At Cranford, Lowick and Weekley there are recorded instances in each vill of animals damaging crops and their owners being penalized in consequence. At Cranford, John Adam was amerced following destruction of the lord's peas at *croftfurlong* and at Lowick similarly when John Godestopwe pastured his cattle in the tenants' meadow contrary to a local ordinance. At Weekley there was only one presentment for trespass but, on another occasion, the sworn men of the jury in considering petty litigation, judged that the beasts of Alan Swaledale had destroyed the barley on a rod of Thomas Joyle's land.[6] Similarly, at Clipston the tithingmen presented five tenants who had trespassed with their sheep against the ancient custom of the vill and contrary to the *pena* laid down by the steward and the whole vill; at Morton Pinkney the homage said that William Selesby and William Webbe had illicitly taken herbage from a headland and, at Weston, that John Tewe had not repaired a broken hedge.[7] The broken series of court rolls for Northborough is generally uninformative, but there seems to have been some association, certainly of lordship, with Etton and Woodcroft (now lost) which may have involved a field system policed by the haywards who are regularly recorded as having presented at the Etton and Woodcroft courts.

In contrast, it can be seen in the rolls of the manors of which they were part that twenty-two villages enjoyed the services of a hayward for at least some part of the period between the later fourteenth and early sixteenth centuries. They were Adstone, Barby, Boddington, Boughton, Brigstock, Long Buckby, Canons Ashby, Castor, Catesby, Draughton, Etton, Geddington, Helpston, Islip, Kelmarsh, Loddington, Maidwell, Marholm, Onley, Sudborough, Woodcroft and Woodnewton. In addition, on the estates of the duchy of Lancaster, the small town of Daventry elected a hayward and a view of frankpledge held at Irchester refers to a hayward in the nearby village of Knuston. It seems clear that over much of rural Northamptonshire the village hayward was important in the supervision and regulation of farming practice. There were also custodians – sometimes common custodians – of various flocks and herds, warreners, and keepers of parks and woods, but their court appearances are relatively few. The hayward was certainly the most frequently mentioned of agricultural officials in the court rolls.

It is less clear that this reflected a particularly high socio-political status in village society. A coroner's jury in 1321 found that Thomas Jordan of Marston had died as a result of being struck on the head with a *kentischestaf* by John of Cornwall, with whom he had quarrelled (see Gross, 1896, 76). John, they said, was the hayward of Chacombe but he had fled, they knew not where, and had no chattels. The impression is of an outsider with no material stake in the community who was, therefore, likely to have followed a low-status occupation. Another possible outsider, Davit Walshman, was the *inclusarius* at Broughton in 1409. Six years previously a man of that name, accompanied by Ralph Walsheman, had come to the village in a warlike manner, armed with a sword and buckler, a bow and a poleaxe and broken into the rectory. They were held in custody and amerced, but the record is silent on their subsequent fate until Davit reappears as the hayward in 1409.[8]

The impression of low status is reinforced on those manors where it is possible to compare the names of haywards with those of villagers who undertook such high-status offices as bailiff, tithingman and juror. The records of Brigstock, a royal manor with a form of socage tenure almost indistinguishable from free tenure, are particularly informative.

Dyer (1980, 157–8) has shown that on the estates of the bishop of Worcester between 1400 and 1540 bailiffs were drawn from the ranks of the peasant elite, and there was a rise in the social status of manorial officials. There is some evidence of this tendency in the manor of Brigstock; in its dependency of Stanion in 1413, John Tyndale was elected and was sufficiently prosperous to appoint Robert Carder, his tenant, to do the work. Thomas Mulso, a member of an influential local gentry family, was bailiff there in 1430 and Thomas Wawton, *chevalier*, in 1436. At Brigstock itself, in 1503, Robert Wawton, *armiger*, was one of the two bailiffs who presented their accounts. Although the presence of the bailiff was often noted in the court rolls only by an abbreviated version of his title, fifty-eight names have survived from the period 1408–1504, and of these only three – John Brandon, Henry Bukmynster and John Grubbe – are also among the twenty-seven haywards whose names are known.

A comparable picture emerges from comparison with the tithingmen. Although Crowley (1975, 1–15) and Schofield (1996, 408–450) have demonstrated the decay of the tithing as a unit, Hilton (1975, 54–8) argued that as late as the middle of the fifteenth century the chief tithingmen, as individuals or a group, were among those having *de facto* control of village affairs. Five Brigstock tithingmen normally presented to the view of frankpledge there during the fifteenth century; forty-seven of their names survive from between 1403 and 1450 and a further eighty-six from the second half of the century. They include only six haywards: William Tukke, William Werketon, Richard Hencok, John Brandon, John Marcaunt and Richard Yoman. A seventh man, Thomas Laverok, may be an addition to the list, but the thirty years which elapsed between his being a tithingman in 1468 and hayward in 1498 make it likely that there were two different individuals with the same name.

Olson (1991, 241–5) has argued that only men of good reputation and fully engaged with the community became jurors. This is reflected at Brigstock in an order to the bailiff to summon a jury to enquire into possible encroachment on demesne land, which should comprise twelve free and legal men of the better and discreet kind. A particularly reliable indicative measure of the socio-political status of the hayward is, then, the frequency with which they served as jurors at the manor court or the view of frankpledge. At Brigstock between 1412 and 1449 nine named individuals can be identified as hayward and four appear on at least one of the five surviving lists of jurors. A fifth individual, suggestively named John Hayward, appears on the jury lists of 1422 and 1427, but no one of that name is recorded as hayward until much later, in 1455. Also, Nicholas Counte was hayward in 1440, and much later in 1469 a juror bore the same name.

Between 1452 and 1504 the evidence is clearer. It is possible to identify eighteen named haywards and there are forty-six surviving jury lists. Only six of the named haywards served as jurors. A seventh individual, John Hayward (see above), was hayward in 1455 but may or may not have been the same man who served as juror in the 1420s.

Comparisons at Broughton and Barby with Onley produce similar results. At Broughton between 1405 and 1487 the clerk normally recorded the hayward only by his title, but twelve are named and there are sixty-one jury lists, albeit not all are complete. Of the named haywards only William Pightesley appeared as a juror, twice in the 1470s when he was also the hayward. Similarly, some seventy-four tithingmen presented between 1354 and 1487 but none of the named haywards appears in that role.

At Barby, fifteen views of frankpledge with small court, of Sir John Zouche, were held between 1517 and 1525. Tenants owing suit to Sir John's court from nearby Onley also attended. Each roll lists a jury of twelve or thirteen men of whom the majority were Barby tenants; on the two occasions when the clerk recorded the distinction the proportions were 9:4 and 8:4. Four haywards are named at Barby, but none served as either juror or tithingman. At Onley, there were three named haywards. None served as a tithingman, but John Abbot who was a regular juror also appeared once as the hayward there, although he made no presentments. It is likely that Onley (now the site only of a prison) already had a declining population and in the circumstances perhaps a man of some standing there briefly held an office of low socio-political status.

Scattered through the court rolls are cases of hostility and sometimes violence towards various officials and a disregard for their authority. Occasionally even the steward, normally a man of gentry status, found his instructions being flouted. It is possible, however, that the recorded instances of aggression towards the hayward are further evidence of the lack of esteem in which an official perceived to be of low status may have been held. One example of a not uncommon type of presentment was recorded at Long Buckby in 1444 when the hayward, John Parterych, presented that John Weston had trespassed in the grain with a horse, for which he had put the horse in the common pound, but John Weston had broken the pound and taken the horse without licence and against his will. In 1485 Alice Baret hurled abuse at Thomas Laverok in the execution of his office; earlier, at the same court, Thomas Baret had been presented as having trespassed with his beasts at *starforth* which was presumably the circumstance which had provoked Alice, although the record does not make that connection. More seriously, at Geddington in 1386, John Busshe and John Baskervill were presented for breaking into the house of the (unnamed) hayward and beating him. The unusually high level of amercement levied, 46d on each man, reflects, perhaps, the severity of the attack. On occasion the fact of being related to the hayward attracted hostility and at Brigstock in 1421 Stephen Chamberlyn, a member of a well-established local family, trespassed with his beasts in the meadow and insulted and beat Agnes the wife of William Rubery the hayward.[9]

It remains to consider the extent to which the hayward was the lord's man and how far he was the servant of the community. This assessment takes into account any indicative descriptions of the hayward at work, together with terms in which the clerk referred to him; his election; evidence of how and by whom he was paid; and finally the terms in which certain of his presentments were recorded.

At Helpston in 1387, Nicholas Hayward, described as the *messor*, presented William Graunt for rescuing from him a boar which Nicholas had seized in the lord's grain, but three years later Nicholas was himself amerced for failure to attach John Raulynesson, a weaver, to pay fealty to the lord for the half-messuage he had bought. Overall this suggests that Nicholas was deployed, as required, as a servant of the lord.[10]

Early fifteenth-century presentments at Catesby, a manor held by a small Cistercian priory, are more specific. At a court held shortly before Christmas in 1401 John Heyward made fourteen presentments for trespass with animals and the taking of wood from fences and hedges. He appears in the roll as the *messor* of the lady prioress, which puts him in the same category as Thomas Astnell, described at the same court as the bailiff of the said lady.[11] Both John and Thomas were the lady's men and John's status as such supports Ault's perception of the allegiance of the hayward.

Such a description contrasts with what is found at the royal manor of Geddington in Rockingham Forest. Here, lordship was remote, the crown having long since abandoned the forest as a hunting ground. At a view of frankpledge in 1380, John in ye Schoppe and Roger his son are recorded as having been elected and sworn as common *messores*, suggesting a direct responsibility to the community. This appears to have been part of a more complicated set of arrangements for policing the fields and hedges, since at a small court earlier on the same day John Bell had been elected and sworn as *messor* of the west field. On two further occasions in the 1380s at Geddington, the clerk recorded presentments as having been made by the common *messor*. A quarter of a century later in the same manor, Henry Wryght presented John Warde and his wife Isabelle for having unlawfully rescued from him certain animals which he had distrained; and again, he is described as being the common *inclusarius*.[12]

Perhaps this is a contrast between a conservative conventual manor with a resident lady and a royal manor. The Catesby rolls certainly reflect the well-attested concerns of many late medieval lords: unfree tenants leaving their holdings without permission, farmsteads and cottages falling into disrepair, *heriots* being exacted only with difficulty when tenants died, and so on. Geddington, in contrast, had a form of tenure close to although not identical with freehold, ruinous buildings are never mentioned despite indirect evidence that there must have been such and it is likely, as McIntosh (1986) has shown for the royal manor of Havering, that the tenants managed the manor in their own interests, subject to little more than annual payments to the crown or its nominees.

However, the contrast between conservative resident lordship and distant royal lordship was not invariably an explanation of the hayward's allegiance. The manor and vill of Buckby was for much of the period between 1430 and 1470 held by the earls of Warwick. It was effectively managed by stewards probably drawn from the Northamptonshire gentry, men like William Catesby who were not entirely unsuccessful in regulating social and economic change in the lord's interests. *Nativi domini de sanguine*, hereditary serfs of the blood, continued to be identified and payment exacted from them for living outside the manor and, in the case of women, for approval to marry. Other servile dues such as *heriot* were exacted and the building stock kept in some degree of repair by a shrewd mixture of firmness and acknowledgement of the custom of the manor. It was clearly the lord's manor.[13]

Despite the effective seigneurial authority exercised at Buckby, however, the rolls include a notably emphatic statement of the hayward's responsibility to the wider community. The clerk recorded in 1442 that 'to this court came John Parterych and in open court was elected to the office of *agellarius* and burdened and sworn in the said office *ad serviend communitam villae bene et fideliter* (to serve the community of the vill well and faithfully) in the aforesaid office'.[14] That is an unequivocal statement of Homans' perception of the role of the hayward; indeed it is more decisive in that there is no reference at all to the lord. This is in marked contrast to the regular election at Buckby of the court-reeve, who combined the collection of amercements and other payments arising from the business of the court, with the function of ale-taster. It was clearly recorded at each election to this office that the homage had elected two named men from whom the steward, acting on behalf of the lord, would select one.[15] John Parterych, however, may have been elected as hayward solely by his fellow villagers.

Five years later at Buckby, John Derby was described as the sub-bailiff of the lord and the *agellarius* there, but the statement does not invalidate the terms of John Parterych's election. For one man to hold those particular two offices simultaneously appears not to have been unusual. Evans noted it at Thorncroft in Surrey (see above) and it was well documented in Northamptonshire at Brigstock (see below).

Despite the number of other villages having a hayward no other descriptions of his role or indicative of his allegiance have been found, but indications of how and by whom he was paid throw further light on his situation. There is no hint of the kind of arrangement that Whittle (2000, 51–2) found at Hevingham Bishops in Norfolk in the mid-fifteenth century, where a group of six tenements, of five to ten acres in size, was responsible for providing a reeve and hayward. Moreover, the only reference in surviving Northamptonshire account rolls of estates with a hayward is at Raunds where the *compotus* of Ralph, son of Henry, *praepositus* of Henry, duke of Lancaster, includes in the list of stipends paid to *famuli*, demesne or household servants, the sum of 12d for a *messor* for one year.[16] Given that this approximates to the wages of a skilled building worker for only three days at that time, it seems unlikely that anything like continuous service was expected of the hayward who presumably had a holding of his own or worked as a day labourer or both. Possibly, however, his income as hayward was supplemented by payments from the community.

At Geddington and Brigstock the hayward was undoubtedly paid by a charge levied directly on the tenants through arrangements apparently agreed between them, and legitimized in the manor court. At Geddington in 1414, John Dalby and Richard Gryndell were elected as haywards; their topographical areas of responsibility were roughly defined with reference to the river Ise and it was ordered 'with the assent and consent of the whole vill' that Richard Thorn and John Pykeryng would collect the stipend from the area served by John Dalby, and Henry Lambert and Nicholas Bocher from that served by Richard Gryndell.[17] No comparable court order survives from Brigstock but it is probably indicative that in 1453, John Brandon, a particularly well-documented member of the community there, in his capacity as *messor*, impleaded John Weldon in court for his *salaria* and the defendant acknowledged a debt of 7½d, presumably his share of the official's stipend; two years later John was equally successful in a similar plea of debt against John Coldewe for 6d.[18]

A complicating factor at Brigstock as at Buckby was the association of the post of hayward with that of beadle. Only three of the sixteen fifteenth-century

1	2	3	4	5	6	7	8
Monastic							
Castor	1363–1546	36	61				61
Catesby	1350–1431	150	345			381	726
Gentry							
Loddington	1353–1502	81	213			94	307
Broughton	1354–1489	98	41		11	44	96
Royal							
Geddington	1360–1425	488	4		2	42	48
Brigstock	1403–1504	626		20	36	573	629

TABLE 14.1. Presentments by Haywards for Trespass with Animals, 1350–1504

Key: 1. Manor; 2. Timespan; 3. Number of courts/views of frankpledge; 4. Number of presentments referring to the lord's land or crops; 5. Number of presentments referring land or crops of both lord and tenants; 6. Number of presentments referring to tenants' or common land; 7. Presentments without specific reference to either lord's, tenants' or common land; 8. Total presentments.

beadles whose names have survived there cannot be shown to have held both posts simultaneously. In several cases they are recorded as being elected to both at the same time and in others the presentments they made indicate that they carried out both jobs. Moreover, at Brigstock in contrast to Geddington, the beadle's responsibilities appear to have been linked to the agricultural economy of the manor. Between July 1438 and June 1468 the Brigstock beadles made only twenty presentments: apart from one for selling on a non-market day and another for illicit fishing, all were for trespass with animals, or damage to or neglect of hedges. The post was undoubtedly tied to the manor rather than the community and the half-year accounts recorded on the roll of the view of frankpledge regularly recorded an allowance of twelve shillings for the two bailiffs and the beadle, although how that sum may have been divided between the recipients is unclear. Overall, the evidence indicates that at Brigstock the hayward, in effect, received a stipend from the manor as well as income paid to him by his fellow villagers.

The final body of evidence indicative of the balance of allegiance of the hayward between lord and fellow villagers is set out in Table 14.1 above. It comprises the presentments made by the hayward for trespass with animals in the crops, meadow or pasture in six manors from each of which a reasonable body of such presentments survives; two were monastic, two held by local gentry and two were royal. Presentments made by other officials or groups of villagers – the bailiff, the warrener, the homage, the *nativi* and so on – have been excluded. Also excluded are certain categories of presentment made by the hayward, notably relating to hedges, the pinfold and the unlawful recapture of animals, as well as the occasional oddity such as the presentment in Brigstock of a group of women for washing clothes in a certain brook. The presentments incorporated into Table 14.1 have been categorized by tenurial location, and distinctions made between trespass said to have taken place on the lord's land, on the land of both lord and tenants, on tenanted or common land, or none of those in cases where the clerk did not record such information.

At Castor, a manor of Peterborough Abbey, relatively few rolls survive and the presentments of the *messor* are concentrated between 1364 and 1411.[19] They appear to have been wholly concerned with the lord's land and, indeed, the *nativi* there sometimes made separate presentments in their own interests, particularly of men unlawfully grazing animals on the common pasture.

At Catesby there is significantly more evidence and the situation is less clear-cut. A typical set of presentments was made in July 1380.[20] The first three instances of trespass had taken place in the lady's grain; the next two, with flocks of sheep in *le mere*, the location of which is unrecorded; the next two were in the lady's peas followed by four in *le coseleye*; four were then identified as having taken place in *le Byggyng*, a close belonging to the prioress, although the frequency with which trespass took place there suggests it was not well fenced; finally, two men trespassed with their mares in the lady's meadow. The sequence suggests that the clerk tried to distinguish in his record between demesne and tenanted or common land specifying the demesne where that was appropriate. If that is so it is apparent that the hayward was concerned to watch over the prioress' land, but over a well-recorded period of eighty years more than half of his presentments for trespass with animals took place on land or in crops which were not said specifically to be those of the lady prioress, which suggests that his vigilance was exercised to a significant degree on behalf of his fellow villagers.

On the two gentry manors of Broughton and Lodddington, little more than two miles apart, a similar situation is indicated. At Loddington, held by the Kynnesman family, the evidence from a reasonably spread, broken series of rolls indicates clearly that the hayward was primarily the lord's man, but on the Germayn family's manor of Broughton, with evidence comparable in scope to Loddington, the presentments are almost evenly balanced.

The striking contrast is between the monastic and gentry manors already considered on the one hand and, on the other, the two royal manors, particularly Brigstock. At Geddington presentments for trespass were rare, in marked contrast to Catesby during much the same period. However, they were numerous at Brigstock and, although this is not shown in Table 14.1, became increasingly so during the half-century after 1450. Moreover, after 1493 the clerk adopted an abbreviated form of record in which only the first name on the hayward's list and the total sum due in amercements from all trespassers were noted. This data is not incorporated into the table but if a typical individual amercement of only a few pence is assumed for it the total presentments for trespass during the fifteenth century were approximately one thousand. Amid all this activity there is only one reference to crown land (which does not qualify for inclusion in Table 14.1) when, in 1449, the servant of William Harueby cut the meadow of the lord king. There were no presentments of trespassers in the lord's land or grain. In contrast, the references are of a general nature: in the grain and meadow of various tenants, in the grain to great nuisance, in the sown fields, in divers places in the sown fields and so on. All the indications are that throughout the fifteenth century the Brigstock hayward was pre-eminently a servant of the community.

Overall, the figures suggest some degree of correlation between lordship and the allegiance of the hayward. Monastic and gentry manors, particularly where the lord or lady was resident, as in three of the examples given here, were settings in which service was due primarily to the lord. This contrasts with crown manors where lordship was remote: late-medieval English monarchs were preoccupied with issues other than what was happening in Brigstock and Geddington, but the existing framework of manorial courts, officials and discipline could be used, quite legitimately, by the local peasant elite, in the interests of the tenants. However, as always generalizations about rural life in medieval England are fraught with difficulties; lordship at Buckby was not remote in the sense that it was at Brigstock and one should not overlook John Parterych, an obscure Northamptonshire peasant who, when he became hayward, swore in the presence of the steward of the powerful earl of Warwick to serve well and faithfully the community of the vill.

Bibliography

Ault, W. (1965) *Open Field Husbandry and the Village Community: a Study of Agrarian By-laws in Medieval England*, American Philosophical Society Transactions, new series, vol. 55, pt 7. Philadelphia: American Philosophical Society.

Ault, W. (1972) *Open Field Farming in Medieval England. A Study of Village By-Laws*. London: Allen and Unwin.

Bailey, M. (2000) *The English Manor, c.1200–c.1500*. Manchester: Manchester University Press.

Bennett, H. (1937) *Life on the English Manor. A Study of Peasant Conditions, 1150–400*. Cambridge: Cambridge University Press.

Crowley, D. (1975) The later history of frankpledge. *Bulletin Institute Historical Research* 48, 1–15.

Dyer, C. (1980) *Lords and Peasants in a Changing Society. The Estates of the Bishopric of Worcester, 680–1540*. Cambridge: Cambridge University Press.

Dyer, C. (2000) *Everyday Life in Medieval England*. London: Hambledon Press.

Evans, R. (1996) Merton College's control of its tenants at Thorncroft, 1270–1349, in Z. Razi and R. Smith (eds) *Medieval Society and the Manor Court, 199–260*. Oxford: Oxford University Press.

Gross, C. (1896) *Select Cases from the Coroners' Rolls, 1265–1413, with a Brief Account of the History of the Office of Coroner*, Selden Society 9. London: B. Quaritch.

Hall, D. (1995) *The Open Fields of Northamptonshire*. Northampton: Northamptonshire Record Society 38.

Hey, D. (ed.) (1996) *The Oxford Companion to Local and Family History*. Oxford: Oxford University Press.

Hilton, R. (1975) *The English Peasantry in the Later Middle Ages*. Oxford: Oxford University Press.

Homans, G. (1942) *English Villagers of the Thirteenth Century*. Harvard: Harvard University Press.

Jones, R., and Page, M. (2006) *Medieval Villages in an English Landscape*. Oxford: Windgather Press.

Lewis, C., Mitchell-Fox, P. and Dyer, C. (1997) *Village, Hamlet and Field. Changing Medieval Settlements in Central England*. Oxford: Windgather Press.

McIntosh, M. (1986) *Autonomy and Community. The Royal Manor of Havering, 1200–1500*. Cambridge: Cambridge University Press.

Olson, S. (1991) Jurors of the village court: local leadership before and after the plague in Ellington, Huntingdonshire. *Journal of British Studies* 30, 241–5.

Razi, Z. and Smith, R. (eds) (1996) *Medieval Society and the Manor Court*. Oxford: Oxford University Press.

Rice, D. (1996) Patterns of progress and mobility in some Northamptonshire families, *c.*1460 to 1560. Unpublished PhD thesis, University of Leicester.

Schofield, P. (1996) The late medieval view of frankpledge and the tithing system: and Essex case study, in Z. Razi and R. Smith (eds) *Medieval Society and the Manor Court*, 408–450. Oxford: Oxford University Press.

Schofield, P. (2003) *Peasant and Community in Medieval England, 1200–1500*. Basingstoke: Palgrave Macmillan.

Whittle, J. (2000) *The Development of Agrarian Capitalism. Land and Labour in Norfolk, 1440–1580*. Oxford: Oxford University Press.

Notes

1. Documentary sources cited are from certain family collections in the Northamptonshire Record Office (hereafter NRO) including the Fitzwilliam (hereafter FW), Lionel Brassey (hereafter LB), Montagu (Boughton) (hereafter M(B)), and Stopford Sackville (hereafter SS) collections; also in NRO the rolls of the Dean and Chapter of Peterborough Cathedral (hereafter PDC); and in The National Archives, Special Collections 2 (hereafter TNA SC2) and the accounts of the duchy of Lancaster (hereafter DL29).

2. NRO M(B) Box X366, View Michaelmas 19 Hen. VI.

3. TNA SC2/183/116 m5, View 27th October 10 Hen. VIII.

4. NRO M(B) Box X366, Court Scholastica 32 Hen. VI; Box X367, Views Michaelmas 2 Edw. IV and 30th April 21 Edw. IV.

5. TNA SC2/194/103 m5d., Court 31st July 32 Hen. VI.

6. NRO M(B) Box X363, Court All Souls 9 Hen. VI; SS 3465, Court 21st October 11 Edw. IV; M(B) Box X340 Folder 2 m3, Court Mark 8 Ric. II.

7. NRO LB 59, View Thomas 21 Hen. VI; TNA SC2/194/39 m3d., Court 20th October 6 Hen. V; SC2/194/43 m1, Court 21st April 3 Hen. VIII.

8. NRO M(B) Box X386, Court 23rd October 5 Hen. IV and View Martin 11 Hen. IV.

9. TNA SC2/194/100 m4, View George 2 Hen. VI and 194/71 m3, View Easter 2 Ric. II; NRO M(B) Box X351B, Court 14th May 9 Ric. II; Box X366, Court Martin 9 Hen. V.

10. NRO FW 53, Court 3rd July 11 Ric. II; FW 54 m2, Court Michaelmas 14 Ric. II.

11. TNA SC2/195/6 m2, Court Christmas 2 Hen. IV.

12. NRO M(B) Box X351A, View Ambrose 3 Ric. II; X351B, Courts Ambrose 5 Ric. II, Matthias 6 Ric. II and Trinity 7 Hen. IV.

13. TNA SC2/194/99–194/108, Views and Courts 35 Hen. VI–11 Edw. IV.

14. TNA SC2/194/100 m1, View Dionysius 21 Hen. VI; my translation.

15. TNA SC2/194/105 m5, View Luke 39 Hen. VI includes an example.

16. TNA DL29/324/5292 m1, Accounts Michaelmas 30 Edw. III.

17. NRO M(B) Box X351B, View Pentecost 2 Hen. V.

18. NRO M(B) Box X366, Courts Bartholomew 31 Hen. VI and Egidius 34 Hen. VI.

19. NRO PDC: Court Rolls Bundle A, nos 3, 4 and 6; and Bundle B no. 9.

20. TNA SC2/195/4 m3, Court Translation Thomas Martyr 3 Ric. II.

CHAPTER FIFTEEN

Counting Houses: Using the Housing Structure of a Late Medieval Manor to Illuminate Population, Landholding and Occupational Structure

Matthew Tompkins

In 1995 and 2003 Harold Fox published two articles on late medieval farmworkers' accommodation, in which he analysed the numbers of cottages recorded in fourteenth- and fifteenth-century surveys and rentals from three Devon manors (Fox 1995; 2003). This paper describes a similar investigation into a Midlands manor, Great Horwood in Buckinghamshire, over the three centuries between 1320 and 1610.[1] It too uses surveys and rentals, but adds further statistical data derived from the manor court rolls to produce a more detailed picture of the manor's housing structure (by which is meant the numbers and types of dwellings and their distribution among the tenants and residents). Two things will, it is hoped, be demonstrated; first, that counting houses, at first sight perhaps not an obviously profitable activity, can illuminate other aspects of rural social history, in particular population size, landholding and occupational structure, and second, that manorial records of landholding, such as surveys, rentals and the tenancy transfer entries in court rolls, cannot always be taken at face value.

Great Horwood was a compact nucleated village in the middle of north Buckinghamshire, between Aylesbury and Buckingham, its township and manor containing an area of some 2,400 acres of heavy clays.[2] In 1320 its agriculture was heavily biased towards arable farming – its three open fields extended right up to the township's western, southern and eastern boundaries, though in the north there was an extensive common incorporating several large coppices, which gave it rather more pasture and woodland than many other Midland communities enjoyed. In the fifteenth century the township began a long and gradual conversion to pastoral farming, and by about 1600 perhaps a quarter of the former open fields lay under grass, either in small closes or in unenclosed strips called leys (Tompkins 2006, 29). The manor had belonged to the Priory of St Faith in Longueville in Normandy since shortly after the Conquest, but from 1367 was confiscated by the Crown as belonging to an alien priory and leased out to a succession of royal favourites and creditors. In 1441 it was granted to New College, Oxford, which has held it ever since. New College Archives contain voluminous records relating to the manor, including extraordinarily complete runs of court rolls from 1302 right through to the twentieth century.

New College also holds three documents which appear to provide full inventories of the housing stock. These are a manorial extent from 1320, an update of the extent made in about 1390, and a detailed rental of 1610, all of which mention the messuages and cottages included in the landholdings they list (NCA 4503; 9744, ff. 37–40; 3946).[3] Unfortunately, while informative for the points in time to which they relate, these three documents leave a large gap extending across the entire fifteenth and sixteenth centuries. This was plugged with data derived from the large number of landholding-related entries in the court rolls between 1390 and 1600. These entries, typically transfers of tenancies in the course of inheritance, sale or gift, nearly always mention whether the tenancy included a messuage, cottage, tenement, house or toft. By extracting them all and stringing them together ownership histories were created for every holding, connecting the relevant entries in the 1390 extent and the 1610 rental.[4] This made it possible to track changes in the status of individual dwelling-sites over time; for example, when a site always previously referred to as a messuage began to be described consistently as a toft it was clear that it was no longer inhabited.[5] Cross-sections were then taken across these 230-year-long tenurial histories to produce lists of tenants, landholdings and dwellings in any chosen year – the kind of data which otherwise would only be obtainable for those rare years when, and if, a survey of some sort happened to be produced, and to survive to the present day.

The results can be seen in Figure 15.1, which shows the numbers of dwellings held directly from the manor of Great Horwood in 1320 and at twenty- or thirty-yearly intervals from 1390 to 1610.

It is immediately noticeable that the total number of dwellings fluctuated very little during this period, notwithstanding the population loss caused by the Black Death. In 1320 the manor had contained sixty-one dwellings: three centuries later the 1610 rental recorded sixty nine. In between there had been very little change; by 1390, just forty years after the plague's first visitation, the number had only fallen to fifty-five, a decline of just 10%, and at the nadir in the mid-fifteenth century there were still fifty-three dwellings (a 13% decline over the previous century).[6] Between 1390 and 1590 the total never fell below fifty-three or rose above fifty-nine. The effect of the Black Death on house numbers has been less often researched than its effect on population, but what data is available suggest that most villages lost larger proportions of their dwellings than 10–13%. Cecily Howell (1983, 116–7) described the fall in dwelling numbers in Kibworth Harcourt, but did not quantify it; however comparison of the houses depicted on her conjectural village maps for 1384 and 1484 suggests a 24% drop, from sixty-eight to fifty-two houses. In the fifteenth century 20–40% of the tenements in several of the bishop of Worcester's manors studied by Chris Dyer (1980, 242) were tofts. Frances Davenport (1906, 105) tracked the

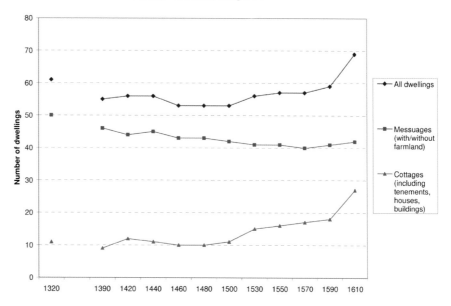

Dwellings - numbers, categories

FIGURE 15.1. Great Horwood's dwellings – numbers and types

Notes: The dwellings have been categorised as messuages or cottages according to their designations in the sources. The data exclude an uncertain number of cottages created within the curtilages of other tenements.

changing status of tenements at Forncett in Norfolk from messuages to tofts (and sometimes back again) in order to make deductions on population loss; she found that of 135 ancient customary tenements some sixty-eight (50%) were abandoned before 1420 (mostly before 1376, she thought). In Whittlewood, a few miles from Great Horwood, some villages lost a half or three-quarters of their dwellings (Jones and Page 2006, 204–7).

Great Horwood's 13% loss might be taken for evidence that it did not suffer greatly from the Black Death, but in fact as much as three-quarters of its population may have died in 1348–9 (the court rolls recorded the deaths of approximately 74% of the tenants and a 78% fall in the tithingpenny receipts, from 134d. in 1348 to 30d. in 1349) (Tompkins 2006, 182).[7] The discrepancy between the housing and population losses can be partly explained by the known fact that household sizes shrank in the post-plague period, as extended families previously squeezed into one tenement were able to disperse into others (Razi 1993, 9, 23), so that dwelling loss was usually less severe than the fall in population. Nevertheless many villages whose populations fell by less than Great Horwood's did seem to lose larger proportions of their dwellings. Great Horwood's small dwelling loss is therefore probably evidence that its population recovered unusually quickly. This is likely to have been at least in part a consequence of inward migration. During the two centuries following the Black Death many Midland villages shrank slowly to hamlet size or even disappeared entirely (Beresford 1954, 224, 230, 340; Reed 1979, 148), but this was more the result of outward migration than mortality. The migrants had to go somewhere, and many must have gone to other villages, such as Whittlebury, nine miles to the north of Great Horwood, which may 'have been able to attract migrants to take up vacant holdings' in the late fourteenth and fifteenth centuries (Jones and Page 2006, 208–9), and Sherington, twelve miles to the north-east, where a sixteenth- and seventeenth-century 'expansion in the ranks of the poorer people … must have been due to an influx of strangers from the vicinity' (Chibnall 1965, 200–2).[8] Great Horwood seems to have been another such village; of the forty-nine surnames borne by the tenants in the 1320 extent only ten were still present in 1390 – the remaining 80% had disappeared and been replaced by new surnames. It continued to be an attractive place to live throughout the two subsequent centuries, becoming in effect a kind of late medieval open village. It was almost unknown for its holdings to be abandoned into the lord's hands or remain in them for lack of a tenant, as was common elsewhere during this period, and instead a sizeable population of subtenants emerged. It is not entirely clear why Great Horwood was so successful in attracting and retaining population, but the explanation probably lay in its beneficial customary tenures, relatively unoppressive manorial regime and extensive common pasture (Tompkins 2006, 55–6, 176–7).

Dwelling numbers can also be used as a check on, and sometimes a corrective to, other sources commonly used to estimate late medieval population. For example, the Great Horwood court rolls provide a good series of tithingpenny data, running nearly continuously from 1307 to 1577, which appear to show the manor's population recovering slightly during the third quarter of the fourteenth century but declining steadily thereafter (much the same trends were revealed by many of the tithingpenny series used to such great effect by Poos in his study of late medieval Essex) (1985; 1991, ch. 5). A similar, though not quite so severe, picture of declining population in Great Horwood is provided by the numbers of manorial tenants. Before the Black Death the tithingpenny, tenant number and dwelling number data are all consistent with each other, but in the fifteenth and sixteenth centuries the two former sources are contradicted starkly by the dwelling numbers. Between about 1470 and 1570 there were only thirty to forty tenants (not all resident in Great Horwood) and, according to the tithingpenny data, fewer than twenty resident males over the age of twelve – yet as Figure 15.1 shows, there were fifty-three to fifty-seven dwellings. Clearly there were many more households than there were tenants, and equally clearly during the fifteenth- and sixteenth-centuries tithingpenny was paid in Great Horwood on a non-standard, but unknown, basis – which leaves it useless for population estimation.[9]

Concerns that it might be the house number data which are at fault can be allayed by comparison with other commonly used sources for population estimates. For example, the numbers of dwellings in 1522, 1524–5, 1563 and 1603 are not greatly discordant with the numbers of residents, taxpayers, households and communicants recorded in the military survey, lay subsidy and returns of households and communicants made in those years (Chibnall 1973, 178–80;

1950, 51; Dyer and Palliser 2005, 237, 362).[10] The closest correlation, reassuringly, is with the 1563 diocesan return, which reported fifty-eight households in the township of Great Horwood; Figure 15.1 shows fifty-eight dwellings in the manor in 1550 and fifty-seven in 1570 (though there are reasons to think the true number was slightly higher).

In addition, dwelling numbers can also be used directly as evidence for population size (except, perhaps, in the immediate aftermath of the first visitation of the Black Death), by application of the appropriate multipliers to convert households into people.

More can be done with the dwelling number data if we look beyond the total numbers and consider the *types* of dwelling, especially the changing ratio of farmsteads to cottages. Harold Fox used farm:cottage ratios in the two articles mentioned above, in which he analysed the numbers of cottages in three Devon manors in contrasting agrarian regions, as recorded in manorial surveys and rentals (Fox 1995; 2003). He showed that the ratio of cottages to farms, which he called the 'Cottage Index' (see Table 15.1), reflected the local agrarian type and enabled deductions to be made about the nature of farm labour in the region, in particular whether it was predominantly provided by servants in husbandry, employed by the year and living in the employer's own home, or by labourers, living independently in a cottage and employed by the day or week or task. In pastoral Ashwater, where large cattle-rearing farms needed more labour than the tenant's family could provide, but needed it at all hours and in all seasons, the dispersed settlement pattern made live-in servants essential, and so the few cottages recorded just before the Black Death, clustered centrally around the church, had disappeared completely shortly after it. The manor of Sidbury was also pastoral and dispersed, but its smaller family-run landholdings did not need extra labour. However, its abundant commons and plentiful opportunities for by-employment preserved the numerous cottagers who lived clustered in a central settlement, independent of the landholding tenants. In arable Stokenham both commons and by-employment were lacking but cottages were still found because, although the farms were large, they only needed extra labour at times of peak activity, which could most economically be supplied by day-labourers. After the Black Death many of Stokenham's tenant farmers acquired nearby cottages when they fell vacant, possibly as tied cottages for labourers, to ensure their occupants' availability when required.

Can this approach be applied to Great Horwood? Comparable indices, derived from the 1320 extent, its *c.*1390 update and the 1610 rental, have been added to Table 15.1, and Table 15.2 uses the court roll data to calculate indices at twenty- or thirty-year intervals between 1390 and 1610. Great Horwood's nucleated settlement and predominantly arable farming ought theoretically to result in a reliance on cottage-dwelling labourers and a high Cottage Index in the fourteenth and fifteenth centuries, falling to a lower Index by 1610 as the manor began to switch over to pasture. However, as can be seen, in the fourteenth century Great Horwood's Cottage Index was lower than those of both Stokenham and Sidbury and in the fifteenth century fell lower still, nearly

Manor	No. of farm holdings (a)	Mean size of farm holdings	No. of cottage holdings (b)	Cottage Index (c)	No. of tied cottages (d)
Ashwater 1464	38	38 acres	0	0%	-
Sidbury 1394	46	24 acres	31	40%	-
Stokenham 1347	147	31 acres	89	38%	-
Stokenham 1390	120	45 acres	25	17%	36
Great Horwood 1320	50	25 acres	7	12%	5
Great Horwood 1390	44	29 acres	7	14%	2
Great Horwood 1610	47	27 acres	18	28%	6

Notes:

TABLE 15.1. The Cottage Index.

a. Holdings of more than one acre (multiple tenancies held by one tenant treated as one holding).
b. Dwellings, however described, whose tenant held no land other than the dwelling's curtilage.
c. Cottage holdings as a percentage of all holdings (farms and cottages).
d. Cottages held by tenants of farm holdings (not included in the Cottage Index).

Sources: Ashwater, Sidbury, Stokenham; Fox 1995; Great Horwood; N.C.A. 4503, 3946.

	1320	1390	1420	1440	1460	1480	1500	1530	1550	1570	1590	1610
All Cottages	11	11	15	15	14	14	17	17	19	20	24	34
Landless Cottagers	6	7	7	7	4	2	1	4	6	7	10	17*
as % of all cottages	*55*	*64*	*47*	*47*	*29*	*14*	*6*	*24*	*32*	*35*	*42*	*50**
as % of all tenants (Cottage Index)	*11*	*15*	*18*	*16*	*10*	*6*	*3*	*13*	*17*	*18*	*18*	*23*

'Cottage' means any dwelling, whether described as cottage, tenement, house, building or messuage (and whether customary/copyhold or freehold), held from the manor by a tenancy which did not include farmland.

A few second tenancies of a single toft (probably ¼ acre) have been ignored. Three individuals who each held two cottage tenancies, but no farmland, have been counted as landless cottagers.

Some apparently landless cottagers may in fact have held farmland by subtenancy.

* A further seven cottagers held small amounts of land, all under 4 acres and most under 2 acres. If included in the count of landless cottagers their proportion would rise to two-thirds (67%).

TABLE 15.2. Landless Cottagers: tenants of cottages who did not hold farmland by other tenancies

reaching Ashwater's level, though by 1610 it had risen again. The explanation may lie in Great Horwood's average farm size which was smaller than at Stokenham, presumably reducing the need for extra-familial labour of either sort.[11] There was a large common, however, and artisans and tradesmen began to appear in the records in increasing numbers from the late fifteenth century onwards (Tompkins 2006, chs 4 and 6), so it seems likely that they are the explanation for the increased numbers of cottages in 1610. This is born out in the case of those few cottage tenants whose occupation is known; for example, in 1590 these were two weavers, a carpenter, a butcher and an alehouse keeper.

However, there is a methodological problem with the Cottage Index, at least so far as Great Horwood is concerned; there are several reasons for thinking that Great Horwood contained rather more cottages than were recorded in the manorial sources on which Tables 15.1 and 15.2 are based. This is a subject worth investigating in some depth, as it reveals some of the limitations of manorial records as sources for rural social structure.

Initially, a brief consideration of the terminological distinction between messuages and cottages is necessary. In general medieval usage a messuage was more than just a dwelling; the word also comprehended the complex of subsidiary structures surrounding the dwelling – barns, byres, kitchens, dairies, malthouses, yards *etc.* – and thus meant not a farm*house* but a farm*stead* (Dyer 1994, 141). Confusingly the same was sometimes also true of cottages. In modern usage a cottage is not only a smaller structure than a farmhouse but also has a different function – it is purely residential, is not the centre of a farm and has no surrounding farmstead. Medieval English cottage holdings, on the other hand, often included farmland (though usually just a few acres) and comprised a complex of buildings, in which case they were distinguishable from messuages only by their smaller associated landholdings, and perhaps fewer or less substantial structures (Dyer 1994, 141–2; 1997a, 2). Landless, purely residential cottages did exist, however, perhaps more commonly in woodland regions or areas of cottage industry, such as mining or clothworking (Fox 1995; Dyer 1997b, 70–1).

In Great Horwood's court rolls the habitational part of each landholding was normally referred to as either a messuage or a cottage (Latin *mesuagium, cotagium*) and individual properties were consistently described as either one or the other. What distinguished the two groups is not apparent, but from the consistency with which the two terms were applied it seems clear that they had mutually exclusive meanings and that the distinction was important (though less formal English-language documents, especially wills, tended to call everything a 'house', regardless of how it was categorised in the Latin court rolls). The difference does not seem to have been tenurial; although there were no freehold cottages, the customary/copyhold tenure by which the cottages were held was the same as that by which most of the messuages were held (there were minor differences between them, but there were also differences between the messuage holdings with full virgates and those with half virgates). The distinction may originally have been that cottage tenancies were those which did not include any farmland, and certainly some messuages which became detached from their farmland were thereafter always referred to as cottages – however others, though similarly detached, continued to be called messuages.

But if Great Horwood's cottage tenancies never included farmland, at least one cottage did have outbuildings and seems to have formed a farmstead; in 1400 Alice Gobyon surrendered a cottage (*cotagium*) with appurtenances to William Hogges, who granted it back to her for her life, retaining a barn (*grangia*) to which he reserved a right of access through the gate (*porta*) of the cottage. A proviso added that Alice's right to remain would end if she ceased to occupy the house (*domus*) of the cottage. The farmland whose produce filled the barn was no doubt the ten acres of arable and two perches of meadow which

Alice held by a separate tenancy (NCA 3916/7v). Some other cottage tenants also held farmland by separate tenancies (some as much as three-quarters of a virgate), and others may have held it by subtenancies from the manor's direct tenants[12] – their cottages may similarly have been farmsteads.

During the sixteenth century this ambiguity in the meaning of cottage faded, both in the English language generally and in Great Horwood's records. For a time in the middle of the century newly built dwellings in Great Horwood, almost certainly lacking farm buildings, were occasionally referred to as tenements or houses, suggesting that cottage may still have meant something different, but by 1600 cottage had become the term normally applied to dwellings which clearly lacked farm buildings. For example, in 1594 James Hobbes, George King and Robert Couper were each presented for having 'converted his barn to a dwelling house and so set up a cottage contrary to statute' (NCA 3705/5v; 16, f. 42).[13]

Whatever the precise meaning of cottage may have been, it is clear that cottages (in the modern sense of the word) are under-recorded in the manorial records. One reason is that these records tended to be concerned only with the principal dwelling in each tenancy and seldom mentioned the additional cottages which often stood within their curtilages. Such subsidiary cottages began to appear in the mid-fifteenth century, either purpose-built or, perhaps more commonly, converted from outbuildings (especially barns – which may reflect the shift of emphasis away from arable farming known to be beginning at this time) (Tompkins 2006, ch. 2). They were occasionally given a separate tenancy of their own, but most remained part of the principal tenancy and were usually ignored by the manorial records. We know of them only from occasional passing references, for example in presentments for illegal subletting of dwellings and creation of cottages (with which the court rolls became increasingly preoccupied during the sixteenth century). Thus in 1558 the widow Joan Varney, tenant of a messuage detached from its farmland, was ordered to have only one tenant in her house (*domus*) and additionally to remove the subtenant who was in the *domus* beside *le gate howse* (NCA 3921/12r, /13r,v, /15v). Because their number is unknown these tenurially invisible cottages could not be included in Figure 15.1 (or the other figures and tables).[14] There is little evidence for their presence between 1390 and the mid-fifteenth century, but it seems likely that they would also have been prevalent during the period of high population pressure before the Black Death – if so Figure 15.1 would show a steeper, more V-shaped decline and recovery.

A further reason for suspecting that Figure 15.1 under-represents the proportion of cottages is that many messuages may have been actually occupied not as farmsteads but as landless cottages. Occasionally messuages were severed tenurially from their associated virgate or half-virgate of farmland, yet continued to be described as messuages (by 1480 seven had been detached in this way).[15] Unless their tenants were farming land held by other tenancies, or by subtenancy, these messuages must have become *de facto* cottages. Other messuages may have been severed from their associated farmland informally, by

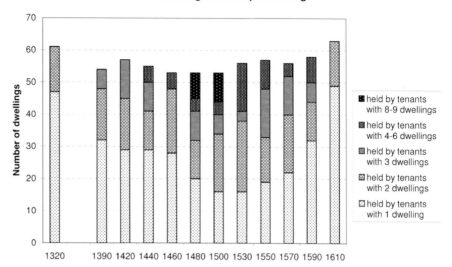

Accumulation of dwellings in multiple holdings

held by tenants with 8-9 dwellings
held by tenants with 4-6 dwellings
held by tenants with 3 dwellings
held by tenants with 2 dwellings
held by tenants with 1 dwelling

FIGURE 15.2.
Accumulation of dwellings: the proportion of the housing stock held in multiple holdings

tenants who held more than one messuage-plus-farmland tenancy. They might have been able to combine the farmland elements of their tenancies into one large farm, but could only live in one of their messuages. Before about 1450 this problem was often solved by converting the surplus dwellings into tofts, but thereafter this did not happen. Some at least of these surplus messuages must also have become *de facto* cottages.

Another factor which skews the landholding and housing structures revealed by the manorial records is the presence of non-resident tenants. During the fifteenth and sixteenth centuries a substantial number of tenants, usually around one quarter of them, lived outside Great Horwood, though between about 1450 and 1530 the proportion sometimes rose as high as 40% or more. These non-resident tenants held similarly substantial proportions of the dwellings; a peak was reached in 1530 when one third of the dwellings were held by just seven non-residents (who also held a little over a quarter of the farmland) (Tompkins 2006, 87–97, especially tables 4.5, 4.6). Clearly *every* dwelling held by a non-resident tenant was surplus to his needs and available for subletting, even those of tenants who held just a single cottage.

Figure 15.2 analyses the accumulation of multiple dwellings by Great Horwood tenants. In 1320 nearly all (81%) of the tenants had held just a single dwelling, but by the end of the fifteenth century only half did. Most of the rest had only two dwellings, but some larger accumulations did exist – the largest was the ten dwellings, seven of them cottages or landless messuages, accumulated by the Colyer family in the second half of the fifteenth century.[16] Taking non-residence into account, this meant that throughout most of the fifteenth and sixteenth centuries at least a quarter, sometimes more than a half, of the dwellings in Great Horwood were surplus, and may have been used as cottages. The extra dwellings which appeared within tenement curtilages from the mid-fifteenth century onwards would have increased the numbers still further.

	1320	*1390*	*1420*	*1440*	*1460*	*1480*	*1500*	*1530*	*1550*	*1570*	*1590*	*1610*
Total dwellings	60	55	54	57	53	53	53	56	58	57	58	65
Resident tenants	53	41	35	33	23	21	22	22	25	31	44	55
Surplus dwellings	7	14	21	24	30	32	31	34	33	26	14	10
Surplus dwellings as % of all	*12*	*26*	*35*	*42*	*57*	*60*	*59*	*61*	*57*	*46*	*24*	*15*

TABLE 15.3. Surplus dwellings: dwellings notionally available for occupation as landless cottages

'Surplus dwellings' are all dwellings less one for each resident tenant, on the assumption that each resident tenant and his household occupied just one dwelling. Thus the surplus dwellings consist of (i) all dwellings of non-resident tenants and (ii) all dwellings more than one held by resident tenants, but less (iii) a few dwellings for resident tenants who held land only and must have lived in a subtenanted dwelling. Some surplus dwellings in the second category may have been occupied by the tenant's adult children or hired labour, but many must have been sublet, either with farmland or as landless cottages.

Note: the number of surplus dwellings may have been underestimated, for the following reasons:

1. non-residents were identified cautiously and their number may have been underestimated. If so, the number of surplus landless dwellings might be greater. In particular, no 1320 tenants were identified as non-resident, due to lack of evidence as to place of residence.
2. from about 1450 onwards extra dwellings began to be created within the curtilages of other dwellings, but were not treated as distinct units tenurially, and so are effectively invisible in the manorial records.

Table 15.3 shows the number of surplus dwellings (other than the extra ones within curtilages) throughout the fifteenth and sixteenth centuries. After a steep increase in the first half of the fifteenth century, they became so large a proportion of the housing stock that less than half the known dwellings were sufficient to house the resident tenants of the manor, leaving at least thirty for occupation by someone else. Some may have been occupied by members of the tenant's extended family, but others could have been tied cottages for his hired labour, and many must have been sublet, some to subtenant farmers as farmsteads, but others as cottages to tradesmen, artisans or independent labourers. Towards the end of the sixteenth century, as a class of cottagers holding a single dwelling and a little farmland appeared for the first time, so the numbers of surplus dwellings fell (though there were still the additional dwellings within curtilages).[17] Some of this new cottager class occupied recently built cottages, but others no doubt now held as direct tenants of the manor formerly surplus dwellings which they had previously occupied as subtenants.

However, these figures for surplus dwellings cannot be a proxy for the number of cottages. On the one hand, they exclude the extra cottages within curtilages. On the other, they include dwellings used as farmsteads as well as landless *de facto* cottages, but just how many cannot be determined. Most of the surplus dwellings were part of a messuage-plus-farmland tenancy, and not all of them would have been detached from their associated farmland – there is evidence that some were retained as a unit, messuage and land together (either occupied by family members, typically sons or sons-in-law, or sublet to subtenant farmers). Even a dwelling whose tenancy did not include farmland might be combined by its subtenant with farmland held by a separate tenancy, or subtenancy.

Table 15.2 showed the proportion of cottages held directly from the manor whose tenants did not hold farmland by another tenancy (some may have held farmland by subtenancy, of course, but the sources never reveal this). It can be seen that from 1420 to 1590 less than half the cottages were held by such tenants, and around 1500 only one of them. If it is considered that the table excludes the extra cottages within curtilages and surplus dwellings occupied as cottages, both categories whose occupiers could not, by definition, have held directly from the manor, it will be realised that in Great Horwood the cottagers who occupied by subtenancy must often have been much more numerous than the cottagers holding directly from the manor, and a Cottage Index based only on the latter has little meaning.

It is, in fact, impossible to quantify the numbers of cottages in Great Horwood, because the manorial records available to us are blind to several categories of them. The extra cottages in curtilages are ignored, as are the subtenancies and other arrangements by which some of the surplus dwellings must have been occupied as landless cottages. Harold Fox drew a distinction between cottages held by landless tenants and cottages held by farmers, calling the latter 'tied cottages' and excluding them from the Cottage Index. This is not a distinction which could be justified in Great Horwood, where the vast majority of the recorded cottages were held by tenants of farmland. Some may indeed have been used as tied cottages, in the sense of accommodation for hired labour, but others were probably sublet for rent, to craftsmen, independent labourers, smallholders and the like, and there is no real reason to distinguish these subtenant cottagers from cottagers who were direct tenants of the manor.

It is hoped that this paper has demonstrated how productive an investigation into a late medieval community's housing structure can be, though the deficiencies of the manorial records from which the data come must always be borne in mind – landholding information from manorial records depicts a *pays légal*, not a *pays réel*, in Postan's terminology (1973, 145; see also Whittle and Yates 2000, 2). If they are available, surveys, extents and rentals provide the most easily accessible data on housing structure, but usually from only one or two dates, making it difficult to study change over time, whereas the less accessible court rolls provide coverage of whole periods rather than single points in time. The same caveat applies, however, and ideally the purely tenurial information from the tenancy transfer entries should be amplified by a close analysis of all the other entries, and all other available sources. At Great Horwood this approach reveals the existence of a populous substratum of subtenant farmers, tradesmen and artisans whose existence would otherwise be concealed by the manorial records' focus on tenancies held from the manor.

Bibliography

Ault, W. O. (1972) *Open Field Farming in Medieval England*. London: Allen and Unwin.

Benedictow, O. J. (2004) *The Black Death, 1346–1353: The Complete History*. Woodbridge: Boydell.

Beresford, M. W. (1954) *The Lost Villages of England*. London: Lutterworth Press.

Bolton, J. (1996) 'The world upside down'. Plague as an agent of economic and social change, in M. Ormerod and P. Lindley (eds) *The Black Death in England*, 17–78. Donington: Paul Watkins.

Chibnall, A. C. and A. Vere Woodman (eds) (1950) *Subsidy Roll for the County of Buckingham, anno 1524*. Bedford: Buckinghamshire Record Society 8.

Chibnall, A. C. (1965) *Sherington: Fiefs and Fields of a Buckinghamshire Village*. Cambridge: Cambridge University Press.

Chibnall, A. C. (ed.) (1973) *The Certificate of Musters for Buckinghamshire in 1522*. Buckinghamshire Record Society 17. London: HMSO.

Davenport, F. G. (1906) *The Economic Development of a Norfolk Manor, 1086–1565*. Cambridge, Cambridge University Press.

Dyer, A. and Palliser, D. M. (eds) (2005) *The Diocesan Population Returns for 1563 and 1603*. Records of Social and Economic History, New Series 31. Oxford: Oxford University Press/British Academy.

Dyer, C. (1980) *Lords and Peasants in a Changing Society; the Estates of the Bishopric of Worcester, 680–1540*. Cambridge: Cambridge University Press.

Dyer, C. (1994) *Everyday Life in Medieval England,*. London: Hambledon.

Dyer, C. (1997a) History and vernacular architecture. *Vernacular Architecture* 28, 1–8.

Dyer, C. (1997b) Peasant farmers: rural settlements and landscapes in an age of transition, in D. Gaimster and P. Stamper (eds), *The Age of Transition: the Archaeology of English Culture 1400–1600*, 61–76. Oxford: Oxbow.

Fox, H. S. A. (1995) Servants, cottagers and tied cottages during the later Middle Ages: towards a regional dimension, *Rural History* 6 2, 125–154.

Fox, H. S. A. (2003) Farmworkers' accommodation in later medieval England: three case studies from Devon, in D. Hooke and D. Postles (eds) *Names, Time and Place: Essays in Memory of Richard McKinley*, 129–64. Oxford: Leopard's Head.

Howell, C. (1983) *Land, Family and Inheritance in Transition: Kibworth Harcourt 1280–1700*, Cambridge: Cambridge University Press.

Jones, R. and Page, M. (2006) *Medieval Villages in the Landscape: Beginnings and Ends*. Oxford: Windgather Press.

Poos, L. R. (1985) The rural population of Essex in the later Middle Ages. *Economic History Review* 2nd ser. 38.4, 515–30.

Poos, L. R. (1991) *A Rural Society after the Black Death: Essex 1350–1525*. Cambridge: Cambridge University Press.

Postan, M. M. (ed.) (1973) *Essays on Medieval Agriculture and General Problems of the Medieval Economy*. Cambridge: Cambridge University Press.

Razi, Z. (1993) The myth of the immutable English family. *Past and Present* 140, 3–43.

Reed, M. (1979) *The Buckinghamshire Landscape*. London: Hodder and Stoughton.

Tompkins, M. (2006) *Peasant Society in a Midlands Manor: Great Horwood 1400–1600*. Unpublished PhD thesis, University of Leicester.

Whittle, J. and Yates, M. (2000) *Pays réel* or *pays légal* ? Contrasting patterns of land tenure and social structure in eastern Norfolk and western Berkshire, 1450–1600. *Agricultural History Review* 48.1, 1–26.

Abbreviations

NCA   New College Archives.
RH   *Rotuli Hundredorum* (1812). London: Record Commission.

Notes

1. This paper is based on a PhD thesis for which Harold Fox was the internal examiner (Tompkins 2006). I should like to record the debts I owe to Harold, and to my supervisor, Christopher Dyer, the external examiner, Richard Smith, and Caroline Dalton, quondam archivist at New College Oxford, for their advice, assistance and encouragement.

2. The parish of Great Horwood also contained the hamlet of Singleborough, a separate township and manor with its own field system. A small number of tenements in Great Horwood township – eight or fewer – and about 70 acres of arable belonged to the Singleborough manor and were excluded from the study.

3. NCA 3946 is an early seventeenth-century bundle of copies of extents and rentals, including the 1390 update of the 1320 Extent and ending with the 1610 Rental. The updated Extent has been printed, though with some inaccuracies of transcription, and mis-dated to 1320, by Ault (1972, 204). The 1279 Hundred Rolls contain an extent listing the tenants and their landholdings, but unfortunately without mentioning their messuages, cottages or other dwellings (*RH*, 336).

4. That was the theory, but of course the practice was not quite so simple. The methodological difficulties which were encountered are discussed in Tompkins (2006, 45–6).

5. A toft was a disused house-plot. In some regions the word meant a currently inhabited plot as well as an abandoned one, but in the Midlands it described only sites which no longer contained a dwelling (Dyer 1994, 139). The rolls occasionally provide explicit references to the abandonment of a plot, but in most cases it has to be inferred from the description.

6. Cross-referencing of the 1390 version of the Extent with the court rolls from the 1380s and 1390s revealed that the 1390 version had updated the tenants' names but not the descriptions of their dwellings – some dwelling-sites described in 1320 as messuages and cottages appeared in the 1390 version with that description unchanged, yet were referred to in the contemporary court rolls as tofts or crofts. The 1390 data in Table 15.1 reflects the court roll descriptions, not those in the incompletely updated extent.

7. The loss of life nationally is usually reckoned to have been something like 50% (Bolton 1996, 23; Benedictow 2004, 360–79).

8. On the bishop of Worcester's estates economically successful manors experienced similar recoveries in tenant numbers but less favoured ones did not (Dyer 1980, 240).

9. There is not space here to give this problem the fuller treatment it requires, but more can be found in Tompkins (2006, 179–86).

10. Again, for a fuller discussion, see Tompkins (2006, 187–91).

11. Both servants and labourers are mentioned in the court rolls, but only occasionally and not often enough to enable conclusions to be drawn.

12. Though subtenancy is difficult to identify in the manorial records, it can be demonstrated that it was an important feature of the landholding structure in Great Horwood. At times a half or more of the manor's farmland may have been sublet (Tompkins 2006, 97–113).

13. The statute was 31. Eliz., cap. 7, which laid down that 'no man may at this day build such a Cottage for habitation, unlesse hee lay unto it foure acres of freehold land, except in Market-townes, or Cities, or within a mile of the sea, or for habitation of labourers in Mines, Saylers, Foresters, Sheepeheards, &c;'.

14. Zvi Razi found that in pre-Black Death Halesowen occupation of tenements by more than one conjugal family was a permanent phenomenon, each tenement often containing a main house surrounded by cottages (Razi 1993, 8).

15. For this reason the totals of Great Horwood cottages differ in Figure 15.1 and Tables 15.1 and 15.2: in the tables landless messuages are treated as cottages, but not in Figure 15.1.

16. William Colyer, husbandman of Great Horwood, built up an estate of 1½ virgates and six dwellings between 1433 and his death in 1477. His son Henry, a lawyer living in Buckingham, added to the estate, which was inherited by his sons in 1502 and sold in the 1520s.

17. Aggregation of holdings was widespread at this time, of course, but in Great Horwood something unusual happened in the mid-sixteenth century; the process reversed itself and the accumulations began to break up, so that by 1610 no tenant held more than two dwellings or two virgates, and the vast majority had only one dwelling and either a virgate or a fraction of one, often just an acre or two, or were landless cottagers. For a detailed discussion of the breakup, see Tompkins (2006, 53–5).

CHAPTER SIXTEEN

The Demesne and its Labour Force in the Early Middle Ages: a Warwickshire Case Study

Penelope Upton

Introduction

For nearly forty years Harold Fox devoted his life to rural and agrarian history. He produced a wide range of articles in which he frequently developed new lines of approach with exceptional originality. One of his most notable contributions comprised a pioneering investigation of labour forms and labour usages in medieval communities (Fox 1996, 518–68). He examined in detail in a new way the lists of landless men (*chevagium garcionum*) which appeared at the beginning of the court rolls of the manors of Glastonbury Abbey. He further analysed the ways in which the landless were exploited, not only by the lord but also more particularly by their neighbours as servants. It seemed economically more advantageous for families with sons of their own to send them out in service and employ another family's sons.

This chapter is a broad tribute to Fox's research into the use of peasant labour. It encompasses an analysis of different types of demesne labour in the context of a localised case study, namely the four manors held by the bishop of Coventry and Lichfield in Warwickshire. The focus is placed on those demesnes in the late thirteenth and early fourteenth century and includes an examination of the unfree tenantry, their customary obligations, the regular labour force (*famuli*) and casual labourers. The main sources include an extent of the bishopric drawn up in 1298 and a handful of fourteenth-century account rolls, as well as evidence from other parts of the bishopric (for all the primary sources see the Bibliography at the end of this chapter).

In the early middle ages the bishop of Coventry and Lichfield was an influential landowner in the midlands, holding manors dispersed across five counties. In Warwickshire by the twelfth century these included (Bishops) Tachbrook, (Bishops) Itchington, Chadshunt and Gaydon (as well as Stivichall, now a suburb of Coventry, which will not be included in this study). Successive bishops of Coventry and Lichfield held these manors until 1547 when they were surrendered for political reasons (Upton 2002).

In surviving account rolls there is a wealth of detail about grain and livestock on the demesnes at Itchington and Chadshunt but a comprehensive analysis must await another publication. Here it is sufficient to note that cereal production for the market was evidently unimportant. In the early fourteenth century much of the wheat harvest was consumed in the form of liveries to the *famuli*, leaving only a small proportion to be sold. Any surplus was sent to Lichfield to the lord's larder which in general terms (according to Nellie Neilson) was supplied with food rents including grain, ale and dairy, as well as meat (Neilson 1910, 15, 20–21).

Dredge (a mixture of barley and oats) was made into malt, or sent to the lord's larder, and the surplus sold. There was also a ready market in the demands of commercial maltsters and brewers (Campbell 2000, 226) who very likely purchased the 172 quarters 1 bushel produced at Chadshunt in 1307 (about 70% of the yield), one-third of it in the form of malt. The same year about 65% of the yield from Itchington was sold. By contrast, in 1311 fifty-four quarters of dredge yielded at Itchington was supplemented by fifty-two quarters from Tachbrook and thirty-one quarters from Chadshunt. Eighty quarters two bushels were malted and carted by customary labour to Alex Janitor, an estate official at Lichfield, almost all the remainder being reserved for seed. Oats were used for fodder and a small percentage was made into potage for the *famuli*. Peas had a lowly use as they were distributed to the *famuli*, cattle and pigs. And yet in 1307 at Chadshunt thirty-seven acres of peas were sown in the fallow field and on fifty-six acres in *le Inheth* at Itchington, in both cases in addition to the total amount of arable normally sown. Here we have an example of *inhok* where a portion of the fallow was used for cropping as a short-term expedient (Fox 1981, 106 n.19).

Livestock typically included oxen which were used as plough beasts, and three or four horses used for hauling. In 1307 both Itchington and Chadshunt had a flock of sheep, adequate for the needs of the demesne. Because of the arrest and imprisonment for more than a year of the lord of the manor, Bishop Walter Langton, the entire flock was sequestered and delivered to the King, never to be returned. The oxen and horses were left behind so that arable cultivation could continue. In 1311 the account roll for Itchington records a net drop in the number of oxen from forty to thirty-two and one less plough team to cultivate 218 acres. This reduction may be related to the death, sometime during the accounting year, of Felicia widow of Richard Milot who held her half-virgate in return for full-time ploughing services (provided by a son or a servant: see below).

Customary tenants and their obligations

In the early middle ages there were three main types of demesne labour: customary, *famuli* and hired. Both Kosminsky and Hilton in their respective analyses of the Warwickshire Hundred Rolls of 1279 noticed in particular the high proportion of unfree tenants on the manors belonging to the bishop of Coventry and Lichfield. The figures were much higher than Hilton's average of 47% for Kineton Hundred: Tachbrook 54%, Itchington 66%, Chadshunt 74%, and Gaydon 88% (Kosminsky 1956, 170–171; Hilton 1950, 13, 16; Hilton 1967, 126; John 1992, 100–102, 184–7. Hilton included Itchington in Kineton Hundred for practical reasons). These unfree tenants (who do not include sub-tenants) formed an essential part of the demesne labour force. This accords with David Stone's observation that 'in the early fourteenth century customary labour was still a significant resource in many parts of England, especially in eastern, southern, and midland counties' (Stone 1997, 641). This may be demonstrated by exploring the obligations of the unfree by taking a sample tenant from each manor: Henry in the Lane, a half-virgater (16 acres) of Tachbrook; Emma la Smekere *alias* Senekere, a half-virgater (20 acres) of Itchington; Richard son of Reginald *alias* Reignald, a half-virgater (16 acres) of Chadshunt and Robert Morice, a virgater (20 acres) of Gaydon.

It is worth noting that in the 1279 Hundred Rolls the unfree half-virgaters at Tachbrook and Chadshunt were listed in pairs, virgate by virgate. Likewise, in the early fourteenth-century account rolls of Itchington, villein dues were also calculated by the virgate even though the majority of the unfree were also half-virgaters. When the reeve drew up his 'works' accounts, he did so on the basis of there being twenty-one customary 'virgaters' on the manor, where there were in fact nine virgaters and twenty-four half-virgaters (9 + (24 ÷ 2) = 21). Half-virgaters appear occasionally in the Hundred Rolls (19% of entries according to Kosminsky 1956, 223) but are listed in pairs in only two other vills: Wasperton and Wormleighton (John 1992, 78–9, 169, 171, 178–9, 196–7, 213–4). Does this indicate that in an earlier age the virgate was the standard holding? If unfree virgate holdings were at some time divided into half-virgate holdings, perhaps it was done as a response to demographic pressure in the post-Domesday era.

All four of our sample tenants appear in both the 1279 Hundred Rolls and the 1298 extent of the bishopric. All owed week-work, like the unfree of only four other vills out of forty-eight in Kineton Hundred at this time (Hilton 1950, 17). Week-works for Richard and Robert entailed three days every week on the demesne at Chadshunt (there was no arable demesne at Gaydon), even though the former was a half-virgater, whereas Emma and Henry as half-virgaters owed three such works every fortnight. Other obligations included ploughing, reaping, mowing and carrying. Incidental dues were paid for brewing ale, pasturing pigs and selling foals. Merchet was due when their daughters wished to be married. Ultimately, a heriot had to be surrendered at death.

Up to ten days' customary ploughing a year was demanded and each tenant had to bring his own beasts, in addition to which Henry at Tachbrook had to bring his own plough if he possessed one. Much of this ploughing at Itchington was performed in exchange for pasture rights (*gresherthe*) and full advantage was taken of it according to account roll evidence. At Chadshunt, in return for a cock and three hens at Martinmas, unfree tenants were permitted to enter the demesne pasture before the last sheaf had been lifted, another option which proved universally popular in 1306/7 when all the customary tenants rendered their full quota of poultry in exchange for this benefit.

For reaping there was an initial three-day period, when tenants were allowed to reap their own holdings and to send a substitute for the demesne reaping. It was understood that tenants would be extremely reluctant to be taken away from cutting their own corn. Therefore, Henry was permitted to send a man to reap on the demesne, Richard and Robert had to send two, whereas Emma could use members of her *familia*. In return she was allowed as much grass as she could lift up with her scythe. At hay-making lords 'felt the need to soften the burden of labour services by giving the peasants reciprocal benefits.' Thus Emma was able to take away as much grass as she could lift, ending 'a hard day's forced labour with a note of collective festivity as [she and her fellow peasants] gathered to compete in this trial of strength and skill' (Dyer 2000a, 82; Dyer 2000b, 23).

Subsequent reaping during the so-called love-boon (*Bondmansbedrepe*) was performed by virtually every tenant in the manor, free and unfree alike, the definition and practice of which varied considerably. Whereas Richard (with food) and Emma (with two men – clearly signifying a large demand for labour – and without food) had to perform an extra day's reaping for the 'love of the lord', Henry and Robert's three-day stint just mentioned was counted as love-boon with no other reaping demanded according to the 1298 extent. But the 1307 account roll for Chadshunt gives a different picture as the customary tenants (or possibly their substitutes) not only assisted in reaping 153 acres of corn but also performed six boon-works each when a further sixty-nine acres were reaped.

The obligation to cart firewood (*busce*) for use in the ovens and fires of the lord's *curia* was consistently commuted – and not even the reeves were exempted from payment. More onerous were the remaining carting services. Henry, Emma and Robert had to cart three bushels of wheat or four bushels of dredge, malt or oats to Lichfield (more than forty miles away) at the lord's will, whereas Richard had to cart a variety of poultry and game. That such carting services were still part of these villeins' dues as late as the early fourteenth century gives weight to David Postles' view that customary carrying services were not in decline by 1250, as had been argued by Gras (Postles 1984, 1–2). In 1307 customary labour was used at Itchington to cart twenty-eight quarters of dredge to Lichfield which accounted for about three summer works each for the eight virgaters worth 3s 6d and about twelve bushels each (half those amounts for the twenty-three half-virgaters like Emma). In 1311 they carted great quantities of wheat (nineteen quarters five bushels) and malt (93 quarters) to Lichfield, using up 714 winter works at about thirty-six per virgater and worth a total of 29s 9d (see also below). Given the sheer number of journeys involved, this use of customary labour must have been infinitely cheaper than hired labour, particularly as all the expenses were incurred by the customary tenants.

Holy-days must have been welcomed with much relief. These were occasions 'when laymen should rest from labour and go to church' (Cheney 1961, 117). Henry and Emma were allowed a week's holiday at Christmas, Easter and Pentecost and if any festival or its vigil occurred on a work day, a work was to be allowed. In reality according to the account rolls, holidays were granted at Christmas, Easter and Pentecost and mostly on the feast days of the Apostles if they fell on a Monday, Wednesday or Friday. The most complete works account appears in the 1311 account roll and apart from the said festivals, holidays were also granted for the feasts of St John *ante portam latinam* (Thursday), St Barnabas (Friday) and the Discovery of the Holy Cross (Monday). Holidays were not mentioned in either Richard's or Robert's entry in the 1298 extent.

How did the reeve make use of this vast reserve of customary labour? At Itchington he had thirty customary tenants from which to draw labour. Between 29 September 1306 and 25 March 1307, 521 out of 1,575 customary works were sold. Other works were either commuted or relaxed because of holidays, so that the villeins only actually performed 40% of their obligations. The situation was different between 25 March and 29 September 1307 when no works were either commuted or sold and the villeins were engaged in weeding, mowing and reaping as well as boon-work and customary ploughing. Throughout the year the reeve was exempt from all customary labour.

Four years later there was far less commutation or selling of works. From 29 September 1310 to 25 March 1311 only the carting of firewood was commuted. As mentioned above, during that period 714 carting services were rendered (56% of total works), all involving carting wheat and malt to Lichfield. The next most onerous demand was harrowing, totalling 231 works (30% of the total). There is no evidence that the reeve hired extra labour to fill in any gaps while the customary tenants were carting away from the manor. Between 25 March and 24 June 1311 the pressure eased somewhat and week-works were demanded for only about half the period, not least because of holidays at Easter and Whitsun. But from 24 June to 29 September there was virtually no relief as the villeins mowed and reaped and cut the stubble on the demesne.

A further glimpse into the varied policy of commutation is evident in a partial account drawn up for the period between 13 November 1321, four days after Bishop Langton's death, and 12 April 1322, which was Easter Monday. According to that account roll all the villeins at Chadshunt and Gaydon had already paid a commutation of 2*s* and 4*s* respectively in lieu of doing any work-weeks on the demesne for the whole year. The villeins at Itchington also had the 'option' of paying 4*s* per virgate for commutation but this had not been implemented. Rather, their week-works were being commuted piecemeal at a rate of ½*d* per winter work per virgater and ¾*d* per summer work per virgater. Such an arrangement indicates that the reeve still had the option of enforcing week-works on the demesne if needed.

By the end of the lengthy episcopal vacancy which lasted from 1358 to 1360, commutation had become universal. In 1360 the demesnes all lay uncultivated (*frisc*) and there was no need for any customary labour. In any event there may have been a scarcity of labour as many customary holdings were vacant. It was recorded in 1360 that at Tachbrook ten out of nineteen half-virgate holdings remained unoccupied. At the same time nine half-virgate holdings at Itchington and four virgate-holdings at Gaydon remained vacant, whereas at

Chadshunt full tenurial capacity continued to be maintained. The reason for the vacant holdings was said to be that no-one wanted to perform customary services as before the pestilence (*pro dictis operibus faciendis, prout custumarii, qui terram illam ante pestilenciam tenuerunt, prius facere consueverunt*). This clearly epitomises the recalcitrance of the peasantry in the aftermath of the Black Death. Some villeins decided to seek their fortunes elsewhere. In October 1360 it was reported that Thomas de Welneford had fled from Tachbrook to Staffordshire, and that of the three Adams brothers of Itchington, one had gone to Banbury (Oxon.), one to Coombe Abbey near Coventry, and the third had fled. The following year nine villeins were reported to be living away from Itchington including three members of the Toly family – Lucy at Willoughby (Warws.), Margery at Leicester (Leics.) and Henry at Haywood (Staffs.). Nevertheless, in one court alone in March 1361 newly surrendered customary holdings were immediately taken up. Adam de la Hale, vicar of the parish since the early 1320s, surrendered his family's half-virgate holding (in his family since at least the 1270s) to William Bedel. Four men took up a total of three half-virgate holdings, whilst Adam Knyght and John Haukyns undertook the joint tenancy of a virgate holding late of Henry Don.

The demesne labour force

Although the contribution of customary labour was important, perhaps more essential and more effective was the input of the stipendiary labour force, namely the ploughmen, the carters, *garciones* and casual labourers, who formed a typical labour force on an early medieval demesne, overseen by the reeve.

The reeve was no anonymous figure for he was 'a man of the manor', who 'ruled with a rod of iron', and whose local knowledge contributed much to the efficient working of the manor (Plucknett 1954, 6; Bennett 1926, 360). Indeed, it was not unusual for a reeve to hold office for several years. Competence must have been a factor combined with being in a position to operate in the black economy and to draw an income 'much higher than…accounts record' (Plucknett 1954, 360; Miller and Hatcher 1978, 193; Farmer 1996, 225). This is illustrated by the two well-known examples from Cuxham, where Robert Beneyt served as reeve from 1288 to 1311 and his successor, Robert Oldman from 1311 to 1349 (Harvey 1965, 65). The reeve's duties were manifold and included organising the tilling of the demesne, seeing that the grain was effectively threshed and properly stored, supervising the care of livestock and the maintenance of buildings, and at the end of the year handing over the profits of the manor (Page 1996, xviii).

At Itchington by the early fourteenth century a tradition of long service had been well established. In 1298 one of the cottages at Itchington was occupied by Agnes the daughter of Richard the reeve. He can be identified as Richard in le Hale (*i.e.* in the Hall, the lord's hall) whose half-virgate holding listed in the 1279 Hundred Rolls was eventually taken over by his son, Adam in le Hale. Most interestingly, Adam in le Hale, a half-virgater, shared his duties as reeve at Itchington with Roger the reeve (by-name unknown), a full virgater. From Michaelmas to 9 December 1306 and from 24 June to Michaelmas 1307 Adam served as reeve, and Roger in the intervening period. In 1310 Roger acted as reeve at the beginning of the accounting year, to be relieved by Adam on 25 January 1311. This enabled one man to be responsible for the winter sowing and the other for the spring sowing. The annual account was the work of both men and their debt to the lord was calculated *pro rata*. For example, of the outstanding sum of £65 2s 6¾d in 1307, a total of £51 15s 8¾d was deemed to be owed by Adam, and the remainder by Roger.

There is a puzzling curiosity in the account rolls concerning reeves. Although Adam and Roger at Itchington and William the reeve (by-name unknown) at Chadshunt were responsible for the annual accounts, there are regular references to *prepositus de Berkswich* at Itchington and *prepositus de Haywood* (both episcopal manors in Staffs.) at Gaydon. For example, according to the works accounts the former held a virgate at Itchington and the latter a virgate at Gaydon. In the 1307 account roll for Itchington the reeve of Itchington was quit of all autumn and summer works. But so too was the unnamed reeve of Berkswich. Likewise the reeve of Haywood was quit of commutation, carting firewood and all other customary works at Gaydon. Neither of the 'foreign' reeves held any apparent administrative responsibilities so how do we explain their tenure in these manors?

There is a further tantalising connection between Itchington and Berkswich. In 1313 and 1314 the reeve at Berkswich was William Bussell. In 1322 a few months after the death of the lord of the manor, Bishop Langton, a William Busshell was one of twelve jurors from Tachbrook, Itchington, Chadshunt and Gaydon who assisted in the compilation of an extent of the bishop's temporalities in Warwickshire. William Bussell is further listed as a taxpayer in the Itchington lay subsidy of 1327 (Bickley 1899–1902, 10). There is no record of either Berkswich or the by-name Bussell in the Staffordshire Hundred Rolls or the lay subsidy (Wrottesley 1884; 1889). Indeed, although there was a productive demesne and a large tract of waste at Berkswich, in 1298 the villeins lived in an adjacent hamlet.

All the reeves at Itchington and Chadshunt were quit of all the customary works performed by their unfree neighbours including customary week-works, love-boon reaping, and carting firewood. Interestingly the total benefit of this commutation at Chadshunt was *4s 6d* which was the annual stipend paid to the full-time *famuli*.

Stipendiary ploughmen (*akermanni*) were 'mostly selected among the customary holders, and enjoy[ed] an immunity from ordinary work as long as they perform[ed] their special duty'. In Postan's words they were given a 'labour option', holding their land either for rent or labour dues (Vinogradoff 1892, 147; Postan 1954, 24). It was not uncommon for ploughmen to be divided into two groups so that, as in the case of some Glastonbury Abbey manors, all the plough-drivers (*fugatores*) were stipendiary and paid in wages and grain, and all the plough-holders (*tenatores*) were service *famuli*' (Farmer 1996, 219).

At Tachbrook in 1298 there were three cottar *akermanni*: the first two were paired together in their duties and described as holding ten acres each, whereas the third had no partner and held 20 acres, half of which at one time must have been held by a fourth ploughman. All three were to benefit from the 'Saturday plough', whereby their own holdings were cultivated by the lord's plough-team on Saturdays. The ten-acre cottars probably had few if any beasts of their own; therefore the use of the lord's team would have been a great benefit (Postan 1954, 21; Homans 1960, 247).

The situation at Itchington was more complex. There were ten half-virgater *akermanni* in 1298 which matches the number of demesne ploughs (five). Five of the *akermanni* were women, including three widows. As women were never engaged in ploughing, their duties were presumably performed by a son or servant (Fox 1996, 551). Instead of being given the incentive of the 'Saturday plough', the Itchington *akermanni* were given the 'choice' between ploughing the lord's demesne or paying a commutation of 2s. In addition, they paid a rent in kind of three hens and a cock each at Martinmas. For example, in 1307 the reeve received 44 poultry in render, namely four apiece from the ten *akermanni* and four from the smith. The remuneration of only five ploughmen is recorded in the account rolls. They were paid in wages and grain and were probably *fugatores*. In 1321 the ten acremen must still have been employed as ploughmen for at Martinmas that year they rendered 40 hens between them and paid no commutation. During the long episcopal vacancy from 1358 to 1360 when the demesne was left uncultivated, they rendered 2s each in commutation as well as the 40 poultry.

At Chadshunt in 1307 there were six plough-teams and that year six ploughmen (probably *fugatores*) were remunerated in cash and in grain but there is no reference to the other six (probably *tenatores*). There is no evidence in the Hundred Rolls or the 1298 extent of any tenant holding land in return for ploughing services. Evidence for the remuneration of the six *tenatores* remains elusive.

Two carters were employed at both Itchington and Chadshunt. Most of their trips were made to the bishop's residences in Lichfield and London.

The *fugatores* and carters were each paid 4s 6d a year and allowed 4 quarters 2½ bushels of grain, as well as potage, which was a typical *famuli* allowance (Postan 1954, 22). One of the carters at Itchington – the 'master' carter – was given solely wheat, whereas the others were given a mixture of wheat, peas and maslin (a mixture of wheat and rye). For the other carter and five of the ploughmen at Itchington in 1307 the grain allowance was made up of wheat (42%), maslin (35%) and peas (23%); and in the same year at Chadshunt the ratio was 33%, 38% and 29% respectively. Much of the grain came from the tenants' contribution to multure, taken by the miller in return for grinding (Holt 1988, 48–9). Manorial officials preferred to distribute multure as mixed grain liveries to the *famuli* (Langdon 2004, 180). Indeed, it was very unusual for lords to sell more than a proportion of multure. It was used as a matter of course to feed the *famuli*. As the multure came from maslin that the peasants of the manor had had ground, it was possibly of a low quality and from the lord's point of view ideal for issuing to his servants (Holt 1988, 77).

As the price of grain soared in the opening two decades of the fourteenth century, payment in grain meant a very real increase. By contrast payment in cash represented a decrease. This was particularly the case where the *famuli* received the same payment, not just for years but for decades (Raftis 1957, 204). To counter rapidly rising grain prices, the composition of liveries was sometimes amended. By 1311 at Itchington there were two fewer *famuli* to feed, as there was one less ploughman and no shepherd. Nevertheless, the ration of wheat was drastically cut to only 16% and that of maslin more than doubled to 73%. About a quarter of the maslin had been purchased at 6*s* per quarter for feeding the *famuli* but the remainder came from multure and was doubtless of poorer quality. Since 1307 the price of wheat sold from the manor had risen from 2*s* 8*d* to 6*s* per quarter.

The smith supplied metal parts for the plough and repaired cartwheels, and received in return small cash payments and a customary bushel of malt each year. As noted above he was also exempted from nearly all customary works and paid an annual rent of four poultry.

At the bottom of the manorial heap of servants lay the *garciones*, for the most part undetectable. As demonstrated conclusively by Harold Fox, they were usually landless and not necessarily young, as a *garcio* 'so long as he never obtained land, remained one for the rest of his life' (Fox 1996, 521). There are small glimpses of their activities at Itchington and Chadshunt. For example, in 1307 one *garcio* was sent to Cannock (Staffs.), a round trip of about 110 miles, to fetch sheep, while two *garciones* were despatched to Lichfield, some 45 miles away, also to fetch sheep.

Whenever appropriate, casual labourers paid by the day were hired to perform a multitude of tasks, many of them specialist. At Chadshunt in 1307 a roofer was employed to work on the kiln, the stable, the cattle shed and even the *garderobe*, all of which took just over a week and for which he was paid 1½*d* a day. Two women were paid ½*d* a day each to be of service to him. The roofer hired to work on the grange at Itchington that year was paid more generously at 2*d* a day. In 1310 at Itchington repair work was carried out on the kiln, the stable, the hall and the grange but only a few days were devoted to this, giving the impression that it was patch-up work done prior to an episcopal visit. Occasionally casual labourers were hired to assist with the harvest. For example, in 1310 at Itchington thirty-five acres of corn (barely 16% of sown acreage) were reaped and gathered at a cost of 5½*d* per acre. This compares with the remaining 186½ acres reaped by customary labour at a works value of between 2¼*d* and 4½*d* per acre. Thirty quarters of wheat were threshed by hired hands at a cost of 2*d* per quarter. Two pitchers were hired for a fortnight to turn and stack corn and were paid a total of 5*s* 8*d*. In 1311 sixty acres of corn at Itchington (27% of sown acreage) were reaped by hired hands at a cost of 5*d* per acre. The remainder of the corn (164 acres) was reaped by customary labour totalling 572 works at a rate of 3½ works or 5¼*d* per acre. Again, hired hands threshed thirty-six quarters of wheat (*2d* per quarter) and forty-two quarters of dredge (1½*d* per quarter) at a total cost of 11*s* 3*d* and winnowed forty quarters of wheat, four quarters of peas, forty-two quarters of dredge and eight quarters of oats at a total cost of 1*s* 5*d*. The remainder of the threshing was done by customary labour and amounted to twenty-five quarters three bushels of wheat (worth four works or *2d* per quarter), eight quarters of oats (worth two works or 1*d* per quarter) and twelve quarters of dredge (worth four works or *2d* per quarter), amounting to 147 works worth 6*s* 1½*d*. Two pitchers and a stacker were employed for seventeen days at a cost of *2d* each per day.

Conclusion

At the beginning of the fourteenth century the Warwickshire manors of the bishop of Coventry and Lichfield produced grain mostly sent to Lichfield or kept for local use. Cultivation of the demesne was undertaken by customary tenants and a stipendiary labour force. Casual labourers were engaged as need arose and performed a range of specialist tasks. By 1360 a series of disasters led to the demise of direct cultivation. Most significant may have been the refusal of the diminished number of customary tenants to perform their customary dues. Although reality had caught up with the bishop by 1364, by which time the demesne at Chadshunt (and probably at Itchington and Tachbrook) had been leased out, ossified items continued to be copied *verbatim* in the account rolls for nearly two hundred more years. For example, references to the commutation of customary ploughings and autumn works at Itchington appear as late as 1450, namely:

> 6*s* 10½*d* from thirty-three ploughings due from two molmen and nine customary tenants of which each does three
> 5*s* 6*d* from thirty-three boons in autumn from the said two molmen and nine customary tenants of which they do three each at *2d* per boon
> 3*s* 8*d* from eleven cottars for twenty-two autumn works of which each cottar does two at *2d* each.

These three entries appear in identical form in the 1298 extent. They sound like the final lingering echoes of a long-forgotten past of villein servitude.

Bibliography

Primary Sources

Birmingham Central Library
432654, m. 10r, court held 22 April, 24 May 1361, m. 11r, court held 16 February 1362.

Lichfield Record Office
B/A/21/124079, Account roll of bishopric of Coventry and Lichfield, 1450.
D 30/11/102, Account roll Chadshunt, 1307.
D 30/11/101, Account roll Itchington, 1307.
D 30/11/99, Account roll Itchington, 1310.

D 30/11/100, Account roll Itchington, 1311.
D 30/11/81, Account roll Berkswich, 1313.
D 30/11/83, Account roll Berkswich, 1314.

Shakespeare Centre and Library, Stratford-upon-Avon
DR 10/2593, court held 17 October 1360.
DR 10/2594, court held 4 March, 1 April 1361.
DR 10/2597, court held 19 June 1364.

Staffordshire Record Office
D(W) 1734/J2268, Extent of bishopric of Coventry and Lichfield, 1298.

The National Archives: Public Record Office
E 136/12/17, Extent of the temporalities of the bishopric of Coventry and Lichfield, 1359.
E 143/9/1, Inventory of Walter Langton's property, 1322.
E 143/9/4, Extent of the temporalities of the bishopric of Coventry and Lichfield, 1360.
E 368/132, Extent of the temporalities of the bishopric of Coventry and Lichfield, 1360.
SC 6/1132/5, Extent of the temporalities of the bishopric of Coventry and Lichfield, 1322.

References

Bennett, H. S. (1926) The reeve and the manor in the fourteenth century. *English Historical Review* 41, 358–65.
Bickley, W. B. (ed.) (1899–1902) *The Lay Subsidy Roll, Warwickshire, 1327*. Supplements to the Transactions of the Midland Record Society 3–6.
Campbell, B. M. S. (2000) *English Seigniorial Agriculture, 1250–1450*. Cambridge: Cambridge University Press.
Cheney, C. R. (1961) Rules for the observance of feast-days in medieval England. *Bulletin of the Institute of Historical Research* 34, 117–47.
Dyer, C. (2000a) Compton Verney: landscape and people in the middle ages, in R. Bearman (ed.) *Compton Verney. A History of the House and its Owners*, 49–94. Stratford-upon-Avon: Shakespeare Birthplace Trust.
Dyer, C. (2000b) Work ethics in the fourteenth century, in J. Bothwell, P. J. P. Goldberg and W. M. Ormrod (eds) *The Problem of Labour in Fourteenth-Century England*, 21–41. York: York Medieval Press.
Farmer, D. L. (1996) The *famuli* in the later middle ages, in R. Britnell and J. Hatcher (eds) *Progress and Problems in Medieval England. Essays in Honour of Edward Miller*, 207–36. Cambridge, Cambridge University Press.
Fox, H. S. A. (1981) Approaches to the adoption of the midland system, in T. Rowley (ed.) *The Origins of Open-Field Agriculture*, 64–111. London: Croom Helm.
Fox, H. S. A. (1996) Exploitation of the landless by lords and tenants in early medieval England, in Z. Razi and R. M. Smith (eds) *Medieval Society and the Manor Court*, 518–68. Oxford: Clarendon Press.
Harvey, P. D. A. (1965) *A Medieval Oxfordshire Village: Cuxham 1240–1400*. Oxford: Oxford University Press.
Hilton, R. H. (1950) *Social Structure of Rural Warwickshire in the Middle Ages*. Oxford: Dugdale Society.

Hilton, R. H. (1967) *A Medieval Society: the West Midlands at the End of the Thirteenth Century*. London: Weidenfeld and Nicolson.

Holt, R. (1988) *The Mills of Medieval England*. Oxford: Basil Blackwell.

Homans, G. C. (1960) *English Villagers of the Thirteenth Century*. New York: Russell and Russell.

John, T. (ed.) (1992) *The Warwickshire Hundred Rolls of 1279–80. Stoneleigh and Kineton Hundreds*. Oxford: Oxford University Press.

Kosminsky, E. A. (1956) *Studies in the Agrarian History of England in the Thirteenth Century*. Oxford: Blackwell.

Langdon, J. (2004) *Mills in the Medieval Economy: England 1300–1540*. Oxford: Oxford University Press.

Miller, E. and Hatcher, J. (1978) *Medieval England. Rural Society and Economic Change 1086–1348*. London: Longman.

Neilson, N. (1910) *Customary Rents*. Oxford: Clarendon Press.

Page, M. (ed.) (1996) *The Pipe Roll of the Bishopric of Winchester 1301–2*. Winchester: Hampshire County Council.

Plucknett, T. F. T. (1954) *The Mediaeval Bailiff*. London: Athlone Press

Postan, M. M. (1954) *The Famulus: the Estate Labourer in the XIIth and XIIIth Centuries*, Economic History Review Supplement 2. Cambridge: Cambridge University Press.

Postles, D. (1984) Customary carrying services. *Journal of Transport History* (3rd series) 5.2, 1–15.

Raftis, J. A. (1957) *The Estates of Ramsey Abbey. A Study in Economic Growth and Organisation*. Toronto: Pontifical Institute of Medieval Studies.

Stone, D. (1997) The productivity of hired and customary labour: evidence from Wisbech Barton in the fourteenth century. *Economic History Review* 50, 640–56.

Upton, P. J. G. (2002) *Change and Decay: the Warwickshire Manors of the Bishop of Coventry and Lichfield from the Late Thirteenth to the Late Sixteenth Centuries*. Unpublished PhD thesis, University of Leicester.

Vinogradoff, P. (1892) *Villainage in England. Essays in English Mediaeval History*. Oxford: Clarendon Press.

Wrottesley, G. (ed.) (1884) *Collections for a History of Staffordshire: Vol. 5, part 1*. London: Harrison and Sons.

Wrottesley, G. (ed.) (1889) *Collections for a History of Staffordshire: Vol. 10, part 1*. London: Harrison and Sons.

CHAPTER SEVENTEEN

Thinking Through the Manorial Affix: People and Place in Medieval England

Richard Jones

For those interested in the English landscape, double-barrelled place-names such as Staunton Harold in Leicestershire (in the context of this volume we must surely begin here), Chaldon Herring (Dors.), Charlton Mackrell (Som.) and Burton Salmon (Yorks.) catch the eye. For they seem to represent a quintessentially English form of rurality. Such place-names have become the mainstay of fiction: few writers who seek to evoke that bucolic sense of a countryside untouched by modernity miss the opportunity to set their stories in landscapes which abound with these kinds of names. One might think of St Mary Mead – arguably the most well-known English place-name around the world; or the geography of Midsomer Murders where we find Midsomer Deverell, Midsomer Marsh, Midsomer Mallow, Midsomer Wellow, Midsomer Parva and Midsomer Worthy, Morton Fendel, Aspern Tallow, Martyr Warren, Newton Magna and Badger's Drift. Indeed, so synonymous are these names with a 'lost' or fondly remembered English idyll that they have become part of the nation's mythology and are key components in the building of its identity. More cynically, of course, they have become tools for those who seek to market England's tradition-rich and heritage-steeped image in a quest to capture the tourist dollar. On these grounds alone, there is a clear justification for the close study of these names, for it would seem that few other places hold such an important place in the English collective psyche.

Of the place-names that take this form by far the largest group are those that carry the name of an individual and more commonly a family that can be historically associated with the place through tenure – either as tenants or as lords of the manor. These are places that early editors of the county surveys of place-names described as carrying a feudal element, a category of name which extended to forms such as Grafton Regis (Northants.), Upton Archiepiscopi (Notts.), Toller Monachorum (Dors.), Cerne Abbas (Dors.) or equivalent anglicised forms such as King's Norton (West Midlands), Bishopsthorpe (Yorks.), Monks Risborough (Bucks.) and Canons Ashby (Northants.). The focus here will not be on these kinds of names but rather on those place-names that carry the names of seigneurial families, that is names with manorial affixes.

Normally the familial attestation appears as a suffix to the core name, such as Houghton Conquest (Beds.), Huish Champflower (Som.) or Stoke D'Abernon (Surr.). Less commonly the manorial element appears as a prefix as in Meynell Langley (Derbs.) and Glanvilles Wootton (Dors.), or might even be combined with the root name as found at Paulespury (Northants.), Perlethorpe (Notts.) and Westonbirt (Gloucs.).

The manorial affix has received remarkably little attention from place-name scholars. In part this is probably because their meanings are so transparent: onomasts like nothing better than a puzzle, a difficult or obscure etymology with which to wrestle. Consequently, affixes have tended to be noted and economically dealt with: Shipton Moyne (Gloucs.), 'The manor was held by the family of *Moygne* from the 13th century' (Smith 1964, 108). In part it may be explained by the apparent thoroughness of Tait's (1924) early treatment of the subject. This remains the most wide-ranging study of the manorial affix and its usage. Despite his concluding remarks, that such names represent an 'interesting and rather neglected class of place-names', no one has subsequently built on the foundation he provided (Tait 1924, 130). Reaney (1960) followed Tait closely but provided some useful additional examples. Only a very brief chapter, dedicated to affixes of all kinds, was provided by Cameron (1982, 100–9) in his general survey of English place-names. And the matter was entirely ignored by Gelling in *Signposts to the Past* (1988). Thorn's (1997) enquiry into the use of manorial affixes in Domesday Book only serves, in fact, to highlight the absence of the name types which are under review here. He identified not a single case of the name of a holder, either in the time of King Edward or King William, being separately affixed to a Domesday place-name, although he notes rare occurrences such as *Nederefroma Hamonis*, later Halmonds Frome (Heref.), which appear in later copies of the survey dated to the 1160s (Thorn 1997, 351).

In what follows a case will be built to suggest that place-names with manorial affixes deserve more attention than they have previously had. Since they combine both a settlement and human element in their name forms, they seem to offer a way of directly addressing the central theme of all landscape history and archaeology, the relationship that developed between people and place in the past. This is a vast subject and the analysis that is presented here is very far from complete. All that can be hoped for at present, therefore, is that by offering some early conclusions, and signalling lines of enquiry to be followed later, the future potential of an exhaustive study of the communities associated with these place-names will be made apparent.

Numbers and Distribution

The lack of historiography is all the more extraordinary given the sheer numbers of place-names involved. The *Cambridge Dictionary of English Place-Names* (*CDEPN*) contains over 550 occurrences (Watts 2004) and has been used here as the basis for the density distribution map in Figure 17.1. This reveals an uneven spread. Affixes are thick on the ground in the south-western counties

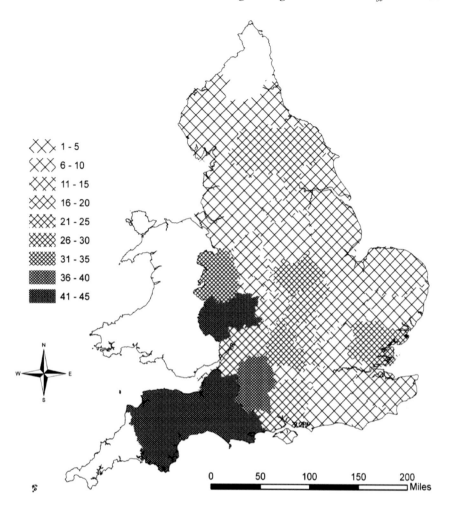

FIGURE 17.1. Density of manorial affixes reconstructed from entries found in Watts 2004

of Devon, Dorset and Somerset. There are relatively high densities in Wiltshire, Herefordshire, Worcestershire, Shropshire, Essex and Midland counties such as Oxfordshire. Elsewhere they are less numerous but nevertheless present in most counties. Indeed, Cornwall and Northumberland are exceptions to the more general rule that place-names of this kind can be found anywhere. *CDEPN* is, however, selective. It includes only those names that appear in the *Ordnance Survey Road Atlas of Great Britain* published in 1983 (Watts 2004, viii). Consequently, not all small settlements find an entry – important in the present context since manorial affixes often attach to these types of site – nor does it deal with lost settlements. Tait's comparable trawl, using the 1808 *Topographical Dictionary of England* produced a total falling just below 800 (Tait 1924, 126). Where a comparison can be drawn, it is possible to see that the 800 early nineteenth-century occurrences tend to flatten the pattern produced by a study of the 550 modern examples since there is some variation across counties in the level of the rise. The combined total for Buckinghamshire, Oxfordshire, Leicestershire and Northamptonshire, for instance, rises some 63 per cent, in

Berkshire and Hampshire the rise is 150 per cent, whilst in Wiltshire it is only 36 per cent (Table 17.1). Nevertheless the pattern remains recognizable.

Manorial affixes are notoriously unstable place-name forms, prone to loss or replacement. Tait noted that his group contained records of names that had fallen out of use, so direct comparison with Watts' figures (for surviving settlements only) is complicated. But what both are recording is a rump of a much larger earlier corpus of names. Thus, to the twenty-one surviving Northamptonshire examples can be added a further twelve instances where medieval manorial affixes have become redundant: Ashby St Ledger was recorded as Ashby Cranford in 1242; Greens Norton was referred to as Norton Davy between 1329 and 1369; Plumpton was Plumpton Saint John (after William de Seynt John rather than the church dedication) in 1341; Weedon Lois was otherwise Weedon Pinkney between 1282 and 1301; Hinton-in-the-Hedges was briefly recorded as Hinton Helye in the late twelfth century; Coton appears as Cotes Goldinton in 1220; Wicken was divided into two parts, Wick Hamon and Wick Dyve (see below); Castle Ashby was temporarily Ashby David; Milton carried the affix Malsores at the end of the fourteenth century; and Addington Waterville was an alias for Little Addington in 1287 (Gover *et al.* 1975). A similar pattern emerges in Nottinghamshire. To the surviving group of names here can be added Caunton (Nicholas d'Aivill, 1194–*c*.1260), Keyworth (Hynges, 1335), Low Marnham (Chaworth 1257–1446), Thorpe-in-the-Glebe (Bossard, 1242–1353), Tuxford (Alan son of Jordan, 1167), Upper Broughton (Sulney, 1242–1325), Watnall (Chauworth, 1319–1392) and the lost Sutton Passays (Gover *et al.* 1979).

The addition of these lost manorial affixes has a profound effect on the local geography of usage. A rather sparse distribution in Leicestershire, for example, is fleshed out by the inclusion of the twenty lost affixes revealing interesting concentrations in the east of the county around Melton Mowbray and in the north-west around Ashby de la Zouche (Fig. 17.2). What also emerges is the lack of these kinds of names within the immediate hinterland of Leicester (Cox 1971). Manorial affixes have a strong showing, too, in the surviving nomenclature of places in Ongar hundred in Essex: thus Norton Mandeville, Beauchamp Roding, Stanford Rivers, Stapleford Tawney, Stondon Massey, Theydon Bois Theydon Garnon and North Weald Bassett (Fig. 17.3). To these can be added Abbess Roding and Stapleford Abbots. However, at various times, particularly in the thirteenth and fourteenth centuries, the seigneurial signature in the place-names was even more obvious. Fyfield was Fyfield Beauchamp between 1306 and 1594; High Laver was variously linked with Eustace, Count of Boulogne (1167), William Fitz Aucher (1181), and the families of Gilbert de Breaute (1235), William de Bosco (1256) and John de Mucegros (1268); Little Laver was named after Ralph de Rovecestre (1200–1212) and Magdalen Laver

County	Tait	CDEPN
Berks. and Hants.	50	20
Bucks., Oxon., Leics., Northants.	162	99
Dev.	57	44
Dor.	66	44
Ess.	43	30
Som.	78	41
Wilts.	53	39
Yorks.	50	37

TABLE 17.1. Numbers of manorial affixes by region recorded by Tait using early nineteenth-century material and Watt using Ordnance Survey evidence from the 1980s

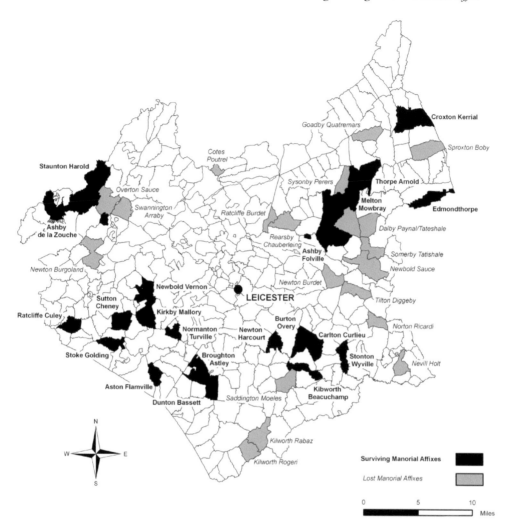

FIGURE 17.2. The geography of manorial affixes in Leicestershire

from the Trichet family (1212–1272); Loughton was Loughton Snarryng between 1239 to 1338; and Navestock was Navestock Glouernye for a short period in the middle of the thirteenth century (Reaney 1969, 52–87).

Why some manorial affixes stuck whilst others fell into disuse is clearly a question of some interest. It almost certainly relates to the register of the name and how it was used. Was the manorial affix assigned to places by a distant bureaucracy, for instance, or were these name-forms that were adopted by local communities themselves before being written down? Were these names which circulated simply in official written records or were they a part of daily speech? We will return to these ideas later, but for the moment it is sufficient simply to note that at various periods during the Middle Ages the manorial affix was a widely used device in English place-naming, which leads us to consider chronology.

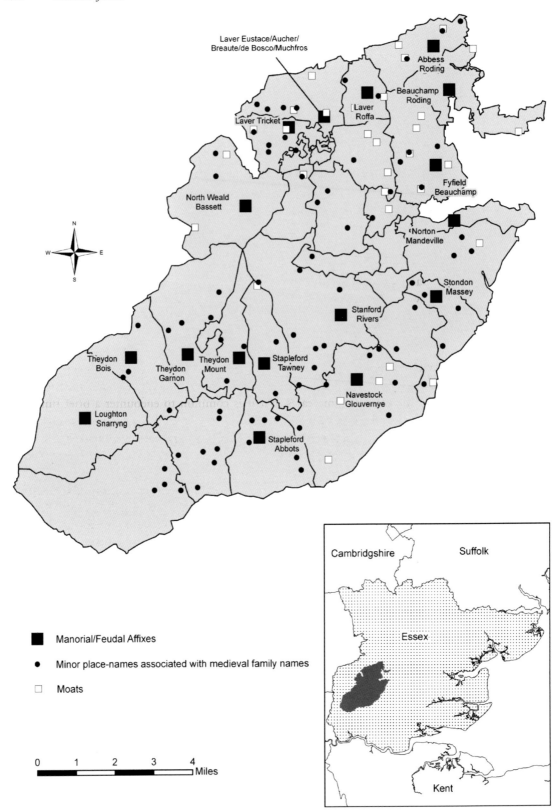

Laver Eustace/Aucher/
Breaute/de Bosco/Muchfros

Abbess
Roding

Beauchamp
Roding

Laver
Roffa

Laver Tricket

Fyfield
Beauchamp

North Weald
Bassett

Norton
Mandeville

Stondon
Massey

Stanford
Rivers

Theydon
Bois

Theydon
Garnon

Theydon
Mount

Stapleford
Tawney

Navestock
Glouvernye

Loughton
Snarryng

Stapleford
Abbots

■   Manorial/Feudal Affixes

●   Minor place-names associated with medieval family names

☐   Moats

Cambridgeshire   Suffolk

Essex

Kent

0   1   2   3   4
                    Miles

Chronology

Establishing when place-names were first used is fraught with difficulty. Dates of first record only provide a *terminus ante quem* for the name form, but it is rare to be able to make any assessment of just how long the name had circulated before being written down. Thus the first written attestations only offer an approximate date for the introduction of these name forms. A cautionary example is that of Weston Bampfylde (Som.), first noted as late as 1811, yet a tenant of this name can be placed here in 1316 (Watts 2004, 666). Did the name circulate latently for nearly five hundred years? Likewise, Herbert de Pinu held the manor of Washford (Dev.) in 1219, but the place-name Pyne, originally attached to a farm and later migrating to the main settlement, was first recorded only in 1650 (Gover *et al.* 1973, 397). Stoke Rochford (Leics.) was held by the family in 1303, yet the manorial affix only appears in 1545 (Watts 2004, 579). An intriguing subgroup are those later recorded place-names that seem to memorialize the manorial holders at the time of Domesday Book: thus we find Barrow Gurney (Avon; 1283), Bolton Percy (Yorks.; 1509), Drayton Parslow (Bucks.; 1268), Dunham Massey (Ches.; *c.*1280: Dodgson 1970, 19), Hartley Mauditt (Hants.; late thirteenth century: Coates 1989, 87), Heanton Punchardon (Dev.; 1297), Holme Lacy (Heref.; 1221), Horsted Keynes (Suss.; 1221), Hurstpierpoint (Suss.; 1279), Kingston Bagpuize (Oxon.; 1284), Mansell Lacy (Heref.; 1243), Sampford Arundel (Som.; 1240) and Willingale Spain (Ess.; 1254: Reaney 1969, 500).

These are extreme cases, but it is common to encounter a brief time lapse between when families or individuals can be placed in certain locations and the adoption of place-names which reflect this personal attachment. Thus Waters Upton (Salop) is first recorded as a name in 1346, but a Waters connection with the place can be traced back to 1242 (Watts 2004, 638–9). Seventy-five years separate the first Harcourt recorded as owner of Stanton (Oxon.) in 1193 and the name Stanton Harcourt noted in 1268–1281 (Gelling 1971, 282). And Lydiard Tregoose (Wilts.) is first mentioned in 1268, presumably named after Robert Traigoz who held the manor in 1242 less than a generation earlier (Gover *et al.* 1939, 35–6). There is no hard and fast rule about the speed with which family names might attach themselves to place-names. At times it seems to have followed after a very short association with a particular seigneurial family. Elsewhere it is clear that some late recorded names may well have had very long unrecorded histories.

It is clearly unwise, therefore, to apply an arbitrary cut-off point of, say, 1500 or 1550 as a date of first record indicative of their medieval usage existence, and why it is better to treat them as a complete group irrespective of when they first appear in the written sources. As Figure 17.4 shows, the great majority (65 per cent +) of manorial affixes that can still be found in modern place-names were first recorded in the thirteenth and first half of the fourteenth centuries. Local analysis of the patterns of naming associated with now lost manorial affixes indicates that they too were often being first coined in exactly the same period (see above).

FIGURE 17.3. The branding of a seigneurial landscape: the manorial affixes of Ongar Hundred, Essex

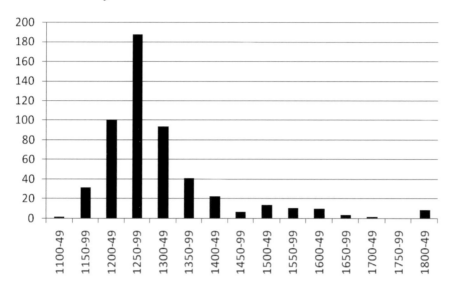

FIGURE 17.4. Date of the first record of the use of manorial affixes in surviving names from Watts 2004

Despite the objections that can be raised regarding what this histogram actually purports to show, it might be argued that there are good grounds for having confidence in the chronology of naming which it suggests. The lack of comparable names in Domesday Book, whose compilers favoured the use of simply *alius/alter* 'other' in the majority of cases, or more rarely *magna, major,* and *parva,* points to this being a post-Conquest phenomenon (Thorn 1997). Examples from the first half of the twelfth century are also rare. Only two cases can be found in the *Northamptonshire Survey* and none at all in the *Leicestershire Survey* (Round 1902; Stenton 1907). From the second half of the twelfth century, numbers begin to rise slowly, place-names almost invariably incorporating the names of particular individuals. Thus we find Hammon (Dors.) as *Ham Galfridi de Moiun* in 1194 and Tedstone Wafre (Heref.) as *Tedestorna R[oberti] Walfr'* in 1160x1170. This was a trend that continued into the early part of the 1220s where examples such as Orton Longueville (Cambs.; *Overton Henrici de Longa Villa,* 1220) and Meysey Hampton (Gloucs.; *Hamtone Rogeri de M(o)eisi,* 1221) might be cited.

From the 1230s, however, it was far more common for manorial affixes to refer to the family name than to particular individuals, as in the cases of Woodham Ferrers (Ess.; 1230), Ashby Folville (Leics.; 1232), Aston Cantlow (Warws.; 1232); Stoke Lacy (Heref; 1234x1239), Newbold Pacey (Warws.; 1235), Chaldon Herring (Dors.; 1235x1239, Weston Coleville (Cambs.; 1236), Norton Hawkfield (Avon; 1238) and Stondon Massey (Ess.; 1238). That the later form might commonly develop from the earlier is demonstrated by Coombe Bissett (Wilts.) which was *Cumba Maness' Biset* in 1167 but had simplified to *Coombe Byset* by 1288, and Coombe Keynes (Dors.), *Cumbe Willelmi de Cahaignes* in 1199 and Coombe Keynes by the thirteenth century (Watts 2004, 156). Thus it is entirely possible that the histogram lags behind the formation of the name but only perhaps by a few decades at the outside. There really was a place-name revolution in the thirteenth and fourteenth centuries which fundamentally altered the named landscape of England irrevocably.

Function and Purpose

Although nothing like a systematic nationwide examination has yet been undertaken on the source types in which first references to manorial affixes are found, it is clear that many make their initial appearance in the records of central government. In Leicestershire alone, twenty-three affixes are first encountered in the *Knights' Fees* of 1242–1243 (Table 17.2). As a survey of landholding, it is not surprising that administrators sought to differentiate manors by association with their lords, particularly where lordship in one place was divided (*e.g.* Kirby Bellars). More generally, it is difficult to ignore the fact that the peak in the recording of manorial affixes coincides exactly with the expansion of record keeping that was so symptomatic of the centralization of government in the thirteenth century. Consequently, the idea that many manorial affixes were initially coined by non-resident bureaucrats and that they were simply applied for administrative convenience is an attractive one. Such a suggestion may find support in the fact that many subsequently fell out of use, perhaps indicating that the manorial affix was not used by the community itself.

Ruthless government, particularly administrations that sought to raise taxes efficiently, needed to be able to differentiate between places sharing the same root name. It was important to know which Yardley or Drayton had paid or evaded a tax levy, particularly where more than one of these places was found within the same hundred or shire. The idea that one purpose, perhaps the principal purpose, of the manorial affix was to aid central government to exact revenues or to establish landholding patterns is certainly persuasive, given the apparent timing of the introduction of these name forms and the kinds of source in which they are first found. And it finds further support when the core names to which manorial affixes attached are considered. Rarely are they found combined with unusual or unique settlement names. Rather they are found attached to common cores: thus the three Gloucestershire Shiptons, Shipton Oliffe (1371), Shipton Solers (sixteenth century), and Shipton Moyne (1285–1375), together with Shipton Bellinger (Hants.; 1296) and Shipton Gorge (Dors.; 1594); or Sampford Courtenay, Sampford Peverell and Sampford Spinney (all Dev.; 1262, 1339, and 1281) with Sampford Arundel and Sampford Brett (both Som.; 1240 and 1306). Family names attached to Newtons across the country include Newton Burgoland (Leics.; 1242), Blossomville (Bucks.; 1202), Ferrers (Dev.; 1306), Harcourt (Leics.;

TABLE 17.2. Leicestershire manorial affixes first recorded in the Books of Fees

Modern Name	Manorial Affix	Date
Aston Flamville	Aston Flamville	1243
Cold Newton	Newton Burdett	1242
Coleorton	Overton Sauce	1242
East Norton	Norton Ricardi	1242
Edmondthorpe	Thorpe Chauars	1242
Edmondthorpe	Thorpe Tybetoft	1242
Goadby Marwood	Coutebi Quatremars	1243
Kibworth Harcourt	Kibworth Harcourt	1242
Kirby Bellars	Kirby de Fouker	1242
Kirby Bellars	Kirby de Sancto Amante	1242
Kirby Bellars	Kirby de Auvill'	1242
Kirby Bellars	Kirby de Wasteneys	1242
Little Dalby	Dalby Paynal	1242
Little Dalby	Dalby Tateshale	1242
Newton Burgoland	Newton Botiler	1242
Ratcliffe-on-the-Wreake	Ratcliffe Burdet	1242
Rearsby	Rearsby Chauberleing	1242
Somerby	Somerby Tatishale	1242
Somerby	Somerby Quatremars	1242
Sproxton	Sproxton Boby	1242
Swannington	Swannington Arraby	1242
Sysonby Lodge	Sysonby Perer	1242
Tilton	Tilton Diggeby	1242

1275), Kyme (Yorks.; 1275), Purcell (Oxon.; 1285–1474), Reigny (Cumb.; 1275x1276–1332), Solney (Derbs.; c.1300), Stacey (Hants.; fourteenth century), Tony (Wilts.; 1338), Tracy (Dev.; 1402) and Valence (Hants.; 1346). Other name groups where five or more manorial affixes have survived to the present day include the Actons, Astons, Broughtons, Burtons, Carltons, Combes, Comptons, Huttons, Marstons, Miltons, Moretons, Nortons, Prestons, Stokes, Suttons, Thorps, Uptons, Westons, Winterbournes and Woottons.

The desire to differentiate between separate vills and manors must certainly explain many instances of the use of manorial affixes, and such a prosaic explanation for their adoption may well account for the lack of interest shown in the further study of their application. But there are several objections that might be raised against this being a universal solution for the naming phenomenon. It might be noted, for instance, that many places sharing the same name remained undifferentiated, even where they lay within the same county, such as the four Brocktons in Shropshire or the three Skeltons in the Yorkshire North Riding. No manorial affixes survive attached to common place-name groups such as the Butterwicks, Chestertons, Deans, Dentons, Donningtons, Fords, Fyfields, Groves, Haltons, Hattons and Hiltons. Likewise they are not found with the Moultons, Southwicks, Staintons, Stapletons, Swintons, Tunstalls or Walcots.

Secondly, it should be recognized that the options available to those who sought differentiation were vast. The use of settlement (and presumably population) size in Domesday Book has already been remarked upon, hence the couplings of Great and Little. Widely used alternatives in the thirteenth and fourteenth centuries included relative position (Over, Middle, Nether) and points of the compass (North, South, East, West). Very common are the *juxta* names which distinguish one place from another through reference to a larger neighbouring settlement. All three of these, it might be noted, were dependent upon some level of local knowledge and, as naming conventions, were surely more likely to have been coined on site rather than in the offices of the Chancery or Exchequer. Likewise names such as Cold Higham (Northants.) or Cleycoton (Northants.), the latter referring to the nature of the soil, resonate with the daily experience of the resident community. In this context it is interesting to note examples such as Cold Newton (Leics.) where for a time the local appellative was used in parallel with Newton's various manorial affixes – Burdet and Marmion – and would eventually win out when memories of the seigneurial associations began to fade. Dominant craft industries might become the marker of place: the establishment of a major pottery manufactory in East Perry (Northants.) around the middle of the thirteenth century led to its renaming, Potterspury, by the late 1280s. Places might be named from their church, either from its appearance or from its dedication.

Something of the range available to place-namers can be gained from looking at the Rodings in Essex where we find Abbess Roding (tenure), Aythorpe Roding and Beauchamp Roding (manorial affixes), High Roding (position), Leaden Roding (from the lead roof of the church), Margaret Roding (church dedication) and White Roding (from the whiteness of the church walls?). The Rodings also show how different naming conventions might change over time. Beauchamp Roding was at various times known as Roding St Botulph from the church dedication; Aythorpe Roding was *Roynges Grimbaldi*, predecessor of *Aeitrop* in 1141–1163 and *Roynges St Mary* from the dedication in 1235; High Roding was *Roinges Doun' Bard'* in 1194, recorded as an individual who granted land in Roding to Dunmow Priory and *Roinges comitis (de) Warenn(i)e* in 1224 from William earl of Surrey who held the manor in 1088; and White Roding was *Magna Roynges* in 1235 (Reaney 1969).

What should be made, then, of the overall allocation of the qualifying terms found in place-names of the thirteenth and fourteenth centuries, and their tendency for shift or interchange? One conclusion might be that affixes compound with their core names on a haphazard basis and that it was simply a matter of chance as to whether they survived or disappeared, or whether they survived in one form or were replaced by another. An alternative view, however, would be to suggest that there was nothing random in their allocation or survival: that there were reasons why, for example, in places where the manorial descent was rather complicated particular families became memorialized in the place-name and not others, and reasons to explain why seigneurial families became so closely associated with some places and not others. To explore these ideas further we need to turn to some detailed case-studies.

Case Studies

Lillingstone Lovell (Bucks. but formerly Oxon.) and Lillingstone Dayrell (Bucks.) must have begun life as a single, one-hide, pre-Conquest Lillingstone estate. By 1086, this had been divided into two five-hide units, both named in the survey *Lelinchestane* (Mawer and Stenton 1925, 44; Morris 1978, 14.27). When the Dayrell family became resident lords of the later Dayrell manor is not precisely known, but they were certainly in possession in 1166–1167 when the place-name appears in the Pipe Rolls as *Litlingestan Daireli* (Page 1927, 188). The name, however, only became firmly fixed from the mid-fourteenth century, the first reference to the name found in the Forest Eyre of 1348 (Mark Page: pers. comm.; TNA: PRO, E 32/114, m. 2). At various times in the twelfth and thirteenth century Dayrell was commonly referred to as Lillingstone Parva as a means of differentiating it from Lillingstone Lovell, otherwise Magna Lillingstone. The Hundred Rolls inquiry of 1279 implies a total population of 190 people in Lovell and perhaps 150 people in Dayrell, in line with these assessments made on size (Jones and Page 2006, 131; Page and Jones 2007, 147)

The long tenure of the Dayrell family almost certainly explains the addition of the manorial affix. The 1166–1167 usage is precocious but does not appear to have been conventionally followed thereafter. By the early fourteenth century, however, the impact of Dayrell lordship was clearly visible elsewhere in the

FIGURE 17.5. Lillingstone Dayrell church (Photos: Richard Jones)

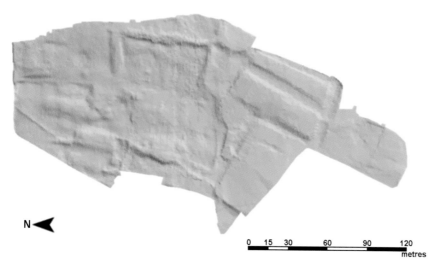

N◄

0   15   30   60   90   120
                                          metres

FIGURE 17.6. GPS survey of the manorial earthworks south of Lillingstone Lovell church

settlement. The village had grown perhaps three-fold in terms of population since 1086, an additional street being laid out south of the original one at some point in the late thirteenth century (Jones and Page 2007, 159–60). The church (Fig. 17.5), standing at the eastern end of the village, had also been enlarged, seeing its west tower and chancel rebuilt in the early to mid-thirteenth century, gaining its south aisle in the later part of the same century and a new arcade opening onto a possibly newly constructed north aisle in the early fourteenth century (Barnwell 2006, 6–7; Barnwell 2008). It might be tentatively suggested, therefore, that the manorial affix was favoured over Parva because seigneurial authority was so clearly visible in the physical fabric of the place.

FIGURE 17.7. Evidence of seigneurial investment in Wick Hamon. The thirteenth-century dovecot (left), first mentioned in 1248 and bakehouse (right) (Photo: Richard Jones)

Lillingstone Lovell (Bucks.) belongs to that group of place-names whose affixes show a degree of instability. From the middle of the fourteenth century, Lovell was known as Lillingstone Dansy, from the family of Margaret, wife of Peter Dansey on whom Lillingstone was settled in 1260 and who were almost certainly resident in the village in 1279 (Page 1927, 192; Page and Jones 2007, 147). It was during their tenure early in the fourteenth century that the manor was split into two parts, Overend and Netherend, the new moiety going to William Lovel through his marriage to Margery Hereward. William was still lord in 1346 when he received a grant of free warren in Lillingstone and it would descend with the family before the unification of the two parts in the late fourteenth century (Page 1927, 193). Why the Lovell name should win out in this context of divided lordship is therefore of some interest. Again it may relate to the scale of seigneurial investment in the village.

Archaeological survey has revealed that at some point in the late thirteenth century, and perhaps related to the division of the manor in the last decades of that century, the major part of the earlier village lying immediately south of the church was cleared to make way for a large manorial complex (Fig. 17.6; Jones and Page 2006, 160–3; Page and Jones 2007, 147). This radical replanning necessitated the diversion of the original village street, the removal of peasant properties and the creation of a new row of tofts and crofts for their use, laid out over former arable land. Given the timing of this reorganisation, this manorial intrusion is more likely to have been made on the initiative of the Lovells than the Danseys. Investment in the church followed a similar chronology. Little was altered during the thirteenth century although the south aisle and chapel may have been added between 1250 and 1275 (initial Dansey investment?). In the first part of the fourteenth century, however, the chancel was greatly enlarged, an elaborate piscina and sedilia were added, the northern nave arcade was replaced and a new north chapel was constructed (Barnwell 2006, 9; Barnwell 2008). By the late fourteenth century, then, the village would have presented every sign of powerful local lordship: a fashionable church and large manor house set in its own curia at its heart, neat rows of peasant properties at its edge. This was very much the village of the Lovells, with the Dansey's seigneurial signature far less prominent to inhabitant and visitor alike. The place-name memorialization from the late fourteenth century of the Lovell contribution to the physical fabric of the place tallies well with this sequence of events.

Neighbouring Lillingstone Lovell, but on the other side of the county boundary in Northamptonshire, is the village and parish of Wicken. Wicken began as two manors, both recorded in Domesday Book in undifferentiated *Wychale* forms (Thorn and Thorn 1979, 28.1; 54.2). From these, two later parishes developed. The single parish only took its final form in 1587, a process that had begun over one hundred years earlier by the unification of two manors, known as Wick Dive and Wick Hamon, under the lordship of Richard Woodville of Grafton in 1449 (Page and Jones 2007,150). For a time at least, then, both the Wicken manors carried manorial affixes (Riden 2002, 413). They are recorded in these forms from the second half of the thirteenth century; Hamon was first used in 1275 and Dive in 1293 (Gover *et al.* 1975, 107–8). Echoes of these family associations would survive into the seventeenth century but would eventually be lost.

In the twelfth-century *Northamptonshire Survey* Wick Hamon was named as *Wyca Mainfein* after Mainfelin who held the manor in 1166–7 (Round 1902, 374; Wick Mainfein is one of only two manorial affixes which appear in the *Survey*, the other being *Bateshasel Malesou(re)s*. This holding passed to his son Hamon and by 1185 his grandson also called Hamon, although it was held briefly by the Crown that year. His son, William, held the manor for the greater part of the first half of the thirteenth century. It passed to his brother Alan on his death in 1248 and on his death the same year to William's son John, being held in dower by Hawise, William Hamon's widow. John was holding the manor in chief in 1276. On his death the manor was held in dower by his widow Isabel, before eventually passing to his son John and by 1290 to his grandson also called John (Riden 2002, 422). The Hamon lordship extended over only two manors, Wick and Wolverton (Bucks.); they thus belonged to one of the lowest rungs of the medieval seigneurie. Nevertheless, their impact on the settlement layout and wider landscape of their Northamptonshire manor was massive. Under the lordship of William, the village almost certainly saw the building of a capital messuage, a demesne farm complex (Fig. 17.7), the church first mentioned in 1218, the emparkment of about a third of the wider estate (said to have been re-emparked in 1290), and the reordering of peasant tofts and crofts (Page and Jones 2007, 151). The use of the manorial affix from the mid-1270s, therefore, follows swiftly after these wholesale changes in much the same fashion as seen at Lillingstone Lovell. Archaeological survey in Wick Dive, revealing manorial earthworks at the centre of the village over and on top of earlier settlement zones, indicates that similar processes may have been in play here too. These examples point, then, towards the idea that places that took manorial affixes were places which experienced large-scale seigneurial intervention in the period immediately preceding the name change. This opens up the possibility that other place-names taking this form found their origins in the same kinds of local developments elsewhere.

Conclusions

This briefest of surveys of the use of manorial affixes reveals that the landscape of English place-names experienced revolutionary change during the thirteenth and fourteenth centuries. It has been possible to show the role that distant administrators, who required greater naming precision to carry out their duties efficiently, may have potentially played in this change. Equally it has been suggested that the nature of local lordship, particularly the scales of investment made by some manorial holders, may account for why some families became memorialised in place-names rather than others. One lesson to be taken from this, of course, is that the coining of names might have very different origins.

This does not obscure, however, a more fundamental observation, that the growing use of manorial affixes in the thirteenth and early fourteenth centuries represents a dramatic shift in the relationship between people and place at this period. Where once families took their names from places – toponymics – places were now taking their name from their owners. This even extended to the naming of individual properties outside village and hamlet cores, as the example of Ongar Hundred shows, or indeed to individual properties within the main settlements themselves. It is surely interesting to register, for example, that the surviving tenement names Burdons, Greneheys, and Waldriches in Cuxham (Oxon.) take their name from families of tenants who lived here in the fourteenth century (Harvey 1965, 27). Why this shift should have taken place certainly merits further attention. It must surely be bound up with broader social and economic changes of the period, more efficient record keeping and intensifying practices of social display. It might also perhaps be associated with the greater attachment lordly families felt to their English holdings in the aftermath of the loss of Normandy in 1204 and their continental estates.

What has not been considered here are the families whose names become attached to certain places. It has long been noted, for instance, that many great medieval family names – such as the Nevills and the Mowbrays – are poorly represented, whilst *arrivistes* such as the Bassets are much more prominent (Tait 1924, 127–128). This again has been summarily explained by the fact that the places which took these names tended to be small, and if part of a larger barony, would naturally adopt the names of their under-tenants rather than their overlord. But as the Lovells at Lillingstone (a cadet branch of the Lovells of Minster Lovell (Oxon.) and Hamons in Wicken prove, lords of the lowest rank were doing interesting things with their estates in this period. What they were doing and what motivated their actions are crucial questions to address in the broader exploration of the relationship between people and place as it developed during the course of the Middle Ages. These are issues which are likely to be most profitably addressed through detailed prosopographical study of those families found in manorial affixes, allied with further archaeological exploration of the places where such name forms are found, even if the association between settlement and family was brief and has now been lost. The potential of the manorial affix has therefore only just begun to be tapped.

Bibliography

Barnwell, P. (2006) *The Whittlewood Project: Notes on Medieval Churches*. Unpublished English Heritage Report. http://ads.ahds.ac.uk/catalogue/archive/whittlewood_ ahrb_2006/downloads_theme.cfm (December 2009).

Barnwell, P. (2008) The medieval churches of Whittlewood Forest. *Ecclesiology Today* 41, 3–27.

Cameron, K. (1982) *English Place-Names*. London: Batsford.

Coates, R. (1989) *The Place-Names of Hampshire*. London: Batsford.

Cox, B. (1971) *Place-Names of Leicestershire and Rutland*. Unpublished PhD thesis, University of Leicester.

Dodgson, J. McN. (1970) *The Place-Names of Cheshire, Part 2*. English Place-Name Society 45.

Gelling, M. (1971) *The Place-Names of Oxfordshire, Part 2*. English Place-Name Society 24.

Gelling, M. (1988) *Signposts to the Past*. Chichester: Phillimore.

Gover, J. E. B, Mawer, A. and Stenton, F. M. (1939) *The Place-Names of Wiltshire*. English Place-Name Society 16.

Gover, J. E. B, Mawer, A. and Stenton, F. M. (1973) *The Place-Names of Devon, Vol. 2*. English Place-Name Society 9.

Gover, J. E. B, Mawer, A. and Stenton, F. M. (1975) *The Place-Names of Northamptonshire*. English Place-Name Society 10.

Gover, J. E. B, Mawer, A. and Stenton, F. M. (1979) *The Place-Names of Nottinghamshire*. English Place-Name Society 17.

Harvey, P. D. A. (1965) *A Medieval Oxfordshire Village. Cuxham 1240–1400*. Oxford: Oxford University Press.

Jones R. and Page, M. (2006) *Medieval Villages in an English Landscape: Beginnings and Ends*. Oxford: Windgather Press.

Mawer, A. and Stenton, F. M. (1925) *The Place-Names of Buckinghamshire*. English Place-Name Society 2.

Morris, J. (ed.) (1978) *Domesday Book: Buckinghamshire*. Chichester: Phillimore.

Page, M. and Jones, R. (2007) Stability and instability in medieval village plans: case studies in Whittlewood, in M. Gardiner and S. Rippon (eds) *Medieval Landscapes*. Oxford: Windgather Press, 139–52.

Page, W. (ed.) (1927) *Victoria History of the County of Buckinghamshire, Vol. 4*. London: Archibald and Constable.

Reaney, P. H. (1960) *The Origins of English Place-Names*. London: Routledge.

Reaney, P. H. (1969) *The Place-Names of Essex*. English Place-Name Society 12.

Riden, P. (ed.) (2002) *Victoria History of the County of Northampton, Vol. 5*. London: Institute of Historical Research.

Round, J. H. (1902) The Northamptonshire Survey, in W. Ryland, D. Adkins and R. Serjeantson (eds) *Victoria History of the County of Northampton, Vol. 1*. London: Archibald and Constable, 357–392.

Smith, A. H. (1964) *The Place-Names of Gloucestershire, Part 1*. English Place-Name Society 38.

Stenton, F. M. (1907) Leicestershire Survey, in W. Page (ed.) *Victoria History of the County of Leicestershire, Vol.* 1. London: Archibald and Constable, 339–354.

Tait, J. (1924) The feudal element, in A. Mawer and F. M. Stenton (eds) *Introduction to the Survey of English Place-Names*. English Place-Name Society 1.1, 115–132

Thorn, F. and Thorn, C. (eds) (1979) *Domesday Book: Northamptonshire*. Chichester: Phillimore.

Thorn, F. R. (1997) 'Another Seaborough', 'The other Dinnaton': some manorial affixes in Domesday Book, in A. R. Rumble and A. D. Mills (eds) *Names, Places and People. An Onomastic Miscellany in Memory of John McNeal Dodgson*. Stamford: Paul Watkins, 345–378.

Watts, V. (2004) *The Cambridge Dictionary of English Place-Names*. Cambridge: Cambridge University Press.

H. S. A. Fox:
Published Works

Compiled by Graham Jones

1970
The boundary of Uplyme. *Transactions Devonshire Association* 102, 35–48.
Going to town in thirteenth-century England. *Geographical Magazine* 42, 658–67.
Reprinted in A. H. Baker and J. B. Harley (eds) (1973) *Man Made the Land: essays in English historical geography*, 69–78. Newton Abbot: David and Charles.

1971
Subdivided fields in south and east Devon. *Transactions and Proceedings of the Torquay Natural History Society*, 16 (a note).

1972
Field systems of east and south Devon. Pt. 1, east Devon. *Transactions Devonshire Association* 104, 81–135.
The study of field systems. *Devon Historian* 4, 3–11.

1973
Outfield cultivation in Devon and Cornwall: a re-interpretation, in M. Havinden (ed.) *Husbandry and Marketing in the South-West, 1500–1800*, 19–38. Exeter: University of Exeter.

1975
The chronology of enclosure and economic development in medieval Devon. *Economic History Review*, 2nd series, 28.2, 181–202.
(With D. R. Stoddart) The original *Geographical Magazines*, 1790 and 1874. *Geographical Magazine* 47, 482–7.

1976
Register of Research in Historical Geography. Belfast: Institute of British Geographers.

1977
The functioning of bocage landscapes in Devon and Cornwall between 1500 and 1800, in M. J. Missonnier (ed.) *Les Bocages: Histoire, ecologie, economie*, 55–61. Rennes: Institut National de la Recherche Agronomique.

1978
The origins of the two- and three-field system in England: past conjectures and future research, in M. Kielczewska-Zaleska (ed.) *Rural Landscape and Settlement Evolution in Europe*, 109–18. Warsaw: Polish Academy of Sciences.

1979

(Co-editor with R. A. Butlin) *Change in the Countryside: essays on rural England, 1500–1900*. Oxford and London: Basil Blackwell and Institute of British Geographers.

Local farmers' associations and the circulation of agricultural information in nineteenth-century England, in H. S. A. Fox and R. A. Butlin (eds), 43–63.

Bocage landscapes in Devon and Cornwall: practices and preferences, 1500–1850, in P. Flatrès (ed.) *Paysages Ruraux Européens* 297–313. Rennes: Universitée de Haut Bretagne.

1981

Approaches to the adoption of the Midland system, in T. Rowley (ed.) *The Origins of Open-field Agriculture*, 64–111. London: Croom Helm.

1982

Local History through Maps: an exhibition of maps and photographs. Leicester: University of Leicester.

1983

Contraction: desertion and dwindling of dispersed settlement in a Devon parish. *Medieval Village Research Group Annual Report* 31, 40–42.

1984

Some ecological dimensions of medieval field systems, in K. Biddick (ed.) *Archaeological Approaches to Medieval Europe*, 119–58. Kalamazoo, Michigan: Western Michigan University.

1986

The alleged transformation from two-field to three-field systems in medieval England, *Economic History Review*, 2nd series, 39.4, 526–48.

Exeter, Devonshire, *circa* 1420, in R. A. Skelton and P. D. A. Harvey (eds) *Local Maps and Plans from Medieval England*, 163–69. Oxford: Clarendon Press.

Exeter, Devonshire, 1499, in R. A. Skelton and P. D. A. Harvey (eds) *Local Maps and Plans from Medieval England*, 329–36. Oxford: Clarendon Press.

Southwestern borderlands: the land; Prehistory and early history; Rural settlements; Farming landscapes; Industries and towns; Coastal settlements, in *The Domesday Project*. London: BBC Publications.

1988

Social relations and ecological relationships in agrarian change: an example from medieval and early modern England, *Geografiska Annaler* 70.1, 105–15. Reprinted in U. Sporrong (ed.) *(1990) The Transformation of Rural Society, Economy and Landscape*, 125–35. Stockholm: Kulturgeografiska Institutionen.

1989

Peasant farmers, patterns of settlement and *pays*: transformations in the landscapes of Devon and Cornwall during the later middle ages, in R. Higham (ed.) *Landscape and Townscape in the South-West*, 41–74. Exeter: University of Exeter.

The people of the wolds in English settlement history, in M. Aston, D. Austin and C. Dyer (eds) *The Rural Settlements of Medieval England: studies dedicated to Maurice Beresford and John Hurst*, 77–101. Oxford: Basil Blackwell.

1991

The occupation of the land: Devon and Cornwall, in E. Miller (ed.) *The Agrarian History of England and Wales III: 1348–1500*, 152–74. Cambridge: Cambridge University Press.

Farming practice and techniques: Devon and Cornwall, in E. Miller (ed.) *The Agrarian History of England and Wales*, 303–23. Cambridge: Cambridge University Press.

Tenant farming and tenant farmers: Devon and Cornwall, in E. Miller (ed.) *The Agrarian History of England and Wales*, 722–43. Cambridge: Cambridge University Press.

Land, labour and people, 1042–1350. *Journal of Historical Geography* 17, 457–64.

1992

(Ed.) *The Origins of the Midland Village. Papers prepared for a discussion session at the Economic History Society's annual conference, Leicester, 1992*. Leicester.

The agrarian context, in H. S. A. Fox (ed.) *The Origins of the Midland Village*, 36–72. Leicester.

1994

Medieval Dartmoor as seen through its account rolls, in D.Griffiths (ed.) *The Archaeology of Dartmoor: perspectives from the 1990s. Proceedings Devon Archaeological. Society* 52, 149–71.

The millstone makers of medieval Dartmoor. *Devon and Cornwall Notes Queries* 7, 153–57.

1995

Servants, cottagers and tied cottages during the later middle ages: towards a regional dimension. *Rural History: Economy, Society, Culture* 6, 125–54.

1996

Exploitation of the landless by lords and tenants in early medieval England, in Z. Razi and R. M. Smith (eds) *Medieval Society and the Manor Court*, 518–68. Oxford: Clarendon Press.

(Ed.) *Seasonal Settlement*. Leicester: University of Leicester.

Introduction: transhumance and seasonal settlement, in H. S. A. Fox (ed.) 1–23.

Cellar settlements along the South Devon coastline, in H. S. A. Fox (ed.) 61–9.

Fishing in Cockington documents, in T. Gray (ed.) *Devon Documents in Honour of Mrs Margery Rowe*, 76–82. Exeter: *Devon and Cornwall Notes and Queries*.

Landscape history: the countryside, in D. Hey (ed.) *The Oxford Companion to Local and Family History*, 266–73. Oxford: Oxford University Press.

Director's foreword, in L. McCann (ed.), *Introduction to the Arundell Archive*. Truro: Cornwall County Council.

1997

From seasonal to permanent settlement: fishing sites along the South Devon coast from the fourteenth century to the sixteenth, in P. Holm and O. U. Janzen (eds) *Northern Seas Yearbook 1997*, 7–19. Esbjerg, Denmark: Fiskeri-og Søfartsmuseet.

1998

The people of Woodbury in the fifteenth century. *Devon Historian* 56, 3–8.

Co-operation between rural communities in medieval England, in P. Sereno and M. L. Sturani (eds) *Rural Landscape between State and Local Communities in Europe. Past and Present*, 31–48. Allesandria: Edizioni dell'Orso.

Agriculture and field systems, in P. E. Szarmach, M. T. Tarvomina and J. T. Rosenthal (eds) *Medieval England: an encyclopedia*, 11–12. Hamden, Connecticut: Garland Publishing.

Foreword, in J. Brooker and S. Flood (eds) *Hertfordshire Subsidy Rolls, 1307 and 1334*, vii–viii. Hertford: Hertfordshire Record Society.

The 'Leicester School' in the South West. *Medieval Settlement Research Group Annual Report* 13, 17–19.

1999

Medieval farming and rural settlement, in R. J. P. Kain and W. L. D. Ravenhill (eds) *An Historical Atlas of South-West England*, 297–304. Exeter: University of Exeter Press.

Medieval rural industry, in R. J. P. Kain and W. L. D. Ravenhill (eds) *An Historical Atlas of South-West England*, 322–29. Exeter: University of Exeter Press.

Medieval urban development, in R. J. P. Kain and W. L. D. Ravenhill (eds) *An Historical Atlas of South-West England*, 424–31. Exeter: University of Exeter Press.

Foreword: woodland history, in B. Schumer, *Wychwood: the Evolution of a Wooded Landscape*, vi–xi. Charlbury: Wychwood Press.

2000

The Wolds before about 1500, in J. Thirsk (ed.) *The English Rural Landscape*, 50–61. Oxford: Oxford University Press.

(Co-editor with O. J. Padel) *The Cornish Lands of the Arundells of Lanherne, Fourteenth to Sixteenth Centuries*. Exeter: Devon and Cornwall Record Society.

The Cornish landscape in the sixteenth century and later, in H. S. A. Fox and O. J. Padel (eds) *The Cornish Lands of the Arundells of Lanherne, Fourteenth to Sixteenth Centuries*, lxviii–c. Exeter: Devon and Cornwall Record Society.

Conventionary tenements and tenant farmers at the close of the middle ages, in H. S. A. Fox and O. J. Padel (eds) *The Cornish Lands of the Arundells of Lanherne, Fourteenth to Sixteenth Centuries*, ci–cxx. Exeter: Devon and Cornwall Record Society.

2001

The Evolution of the Fishing Village: landscape and society along the South Devon coast, 1086–1550, Oxford: Leopard's Head Press.

Coastal settlement. *Medieval Settlement Research Group Annual Report* 16, 5.

2002

(With H. Kitsikopoulos) Campbell on late-medieval English agriculture: two views. *Journal of Economic History* 62.1, 213–16.

2003

Richard McKinley: an appreciation, in D. Hooke and D. Postles (eds) *Names, Time and Place: Essays in memory of Richard McKinley*, xvi–xx. Oxford: Leopard's Head Press.

Farmworkers' accommodation in later medieval England: three case studies from Devon, in D. Hooke and D. Postles (eds) *Names, Time and Place: Essays in memory of Richard McKinley*, 129–64. Oxford: Leopard's Head Press.

2004

Vancouver, Charles (1756–*circa* 1815), in *New Dictionary of National Biography*. Oxford: Oxford University Press.

2005

Taxation and settlement in Medieval Devon, in M. Prestwich, R. Britnell and R. Frame (eds) *Thirteenth Century England X: Proceedings of the Durham Conference 2003*, 167–85. Woodbridge: Boydell Press.

2006

Fragmented manors and the customs of the Anglo-Saxons, in S. Keynes and A. P. Smyth (eds) *Anglo-Saxons: studies presented to Cyril Roy Hart*, 78–97. Dublin: Four Courts Press.

Foreword, in S. Turner (ed.) *Medieval Devon and Cornwall: shaping an ancient countryside*, xi–xvi. Oxford: Windgather Press.

2007

Two Devon estuaries in the Middle Ages: fisheries, ports, fortifications and places of worship. *Landscapes* 8.1, 39–68.

2008

Butter place-names and transhumance, in O. J. Padel and D. N. Parsons (eds) *A Commodity of Good Names. Essays in honour of Margaret Gelling*, 352–64. Donington: Shaun Tyas.

2009

The petitions of mariners and fishermen, in M. Rubin (ed.) *Medieval Christianity in Practice*, 76–80. Princeton: Princeton University Press.

2010

Lords and wastes, in R. Goddard, J. Langdon and M. Müller (eds) *Survival and Discord in Medieval Society. Papers in Honour of Christopher Dyer*, 29–48. Turnhout: Brepols.

Acknowledgement

A version of this bibliography appeared in *Landscape History* (Jones, G. (2007) Harold Fox: an appreciation, *Landscape History* 29, 5–15). We are grateful to the Society for Landscape Studies for permission to use it here.

Index

Numbers in italic refer to Figures.